A century

This century has witnessed an explosive growth in psychology that has changed irrevocably our conception of what it means to be human. Psychology has developed applications in almost every occupation involving people, from pathology to policing, education to engineering, sport to space exploration. It is one of the most widely read subjects in higher education and many of its concepts have become assimilated into popular culture.

A Century of Psychology takes a critical look at the achievements, disappointments, divisions and breakthroughs that a hundred years of activity in the discipline have produced. As we reach the end of this first century of psychology, it also takes a look at what mankind might expect from psychology in the future. Written by a team of internationally recognized experts, it begins with a critical review of methodology and its limitations. It continues with discussion of gender, educational psychology, learning, intellectual disability, clinical psychology and the emergence of psychotherapy. Community psychology, preventive psychology and organizational psychology are appraised. State-of-the-art presentations of research on reasoning, goal striving, neuropsychology and emotion are included.

A critical review with a broad perspective of major applications and research areas, *A Century of Psychology* will provide a stimulating summary for novices and old hands alike.

Ray Fuller is a senior lecturer and fellow of Trinity College, Dublin. His previous publications include *Seven Pioneers of Psychology* (1995).
Patricia Noonan Walsh is a lecturer and director of the Centre for the Study of Developmental Disabilities at University College, Dublin, and
Patrick McGinley is director of the Brothers of Charity Services for children and adults with learning disabilities in the west of Ireland.

A century of psychology

Progress, paradigms and prospects for the new millennium

Edited by
Ray Fuller, Patricia Noonan Walsh and
Patrick McGinley

In association with the European Federation of Professional
Psychologists' Associations and the Psychological Society of
Ireland

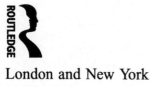

London and New York

First published 1997
by Routledge
11 New Fetter Lane, London EC4P 4EE

Simultaneously published in the USA and Canada
by Routledge
29 West 35th Street, New York, NY 10001

© 1997 Selection and editorial matter,
Ray Fuller, Patricia Noonan Walsh and Patrick McGinley;
individual chapters © the contributors

Typeset in Times by LaserScript, Mitcham, Surrey
Printed and bound in Great Britain by TJ International Ltd, Padstow, Cornwall

British Library Cataloguing in Publication Data
A catalogue record for this book is available from the British Library

Library of Congress Cataloging in Publication Data
A century of psychology: progress, paradigms, and prospects for the new millennium/
edited by Ray Fuller, Patricia Noonan Walsh, and Patrick McGinley.
    p.   cm.
  Papers originally presented at the 5th European Congress of Psychology held in
Dublin, in July 1997.
  Includes bibliographical reference and index.
    1. Psychology–History–20th century–Congresses.   I. Fuller, Ray, 1943–
II. Walsh, Patrician Noonan, 1944–   III. McGinley, Patrick.
BF105.C44   1997
150'.9–dc21   97-3892

ISBN 0–415–16219–X (hbk)
ISBN 0–415–16220–3 (pbk)

Know Thyself

Know then thyself, presume not God to scan;
The proper study of mankind is Man.
Placed on this isthmus of a middle state,
A being darkly wise and rudely great:
With too much knowledge for the Sceptic side,
With too much weakness for the Stoic's pride,
He hangs between; in doubt to act or rest,
In doubt to deem himself a God or Beast,
In doubt his mind or body to prefer;
Born but to die, and reasoning but to err;
Alike in ignorance, his reason such
Whether he thinks too little or too much:
Chaos of thought and passion, all confused;
Still by himself abused, or disabused;
Created half to rise and half to fall;
Great lord of all things, yet a prey to all;
Sole judge of truth, in endless error hurled:
The glory, jest, and riddle of the world!

Alexander Pope (1688–1744)

Contents

Figures and tables

FIGURES

TABLES

Contributors

Amparo Belloch is Professor of Psychopathology in the Department of Personality, Assessment and Psychological Treatments, Faculty of Psychology, University of Valencia, Spain. In 1982 she was appointed Reader in the University of Valencia and to the Chair of Psychopathology in 1987. Her training in clinical psychology focused on work with anxious and depressed patients, first in private practice and later in the psychological clinic of the Department of Personality at Valencia, which she co-founded. She is Head of the Masters Programme in Clinical Psychology at the University of Valencia. She has been nominated by the Ministry of Education to the National Committee of Clinical Psychology, charged with developing the Spanish government's training programme for clinical psychologists based on an internship system. Since 1995 she has been the President of the *Asociacion Espanola de Psicologia Clinica y Psicopatologia*, and is Editor-in-Chief of *Revista de Psicopatologia y Psicologia Clinica*.

Ruth M.J. Byrne is a lecturer in the Psychology Department at Trinity College, Dublin. She worked previously in the Medical Research Council's Applied Psychology Unit in Cambridge, the Psychology Department at the University of Wales College of Cardiff and the Computer Science Department at University College Dublin. She was awarded a BA in psychology from University College, Dublin in 1983, and a PhD in cognitive psychology from Trinity College, Dublin in 1987. She is a Fellow of Trinity College, and of the Psychological Society of Ireland. She is co-author of a number of books on the cognitive science of deductive reasoning, and her recent journal articles report experimental and computational tests of alternative theories of deduction. Her current research extends the mental model theory of deductive reasoning to account for imaginary counterfactual thinking.

Adrian Furnham was educated at the London School of Economics where he obtained a distinction in an MSc Econ and at Oxford University where he completed a DPhil in 1981. He has subsequently earned the degrees of DSc (1991) and DLitt (1995). Previously a lecturer in Psychology at Pembroke College, Oxford, he is now Professor of Psychology at University College,

London. He has held scholarships and visiting professorships at, amongst others, the University of New South Wales, the University of the West Indies and the University of Hong Kong. He has written over 400 scientific papers and twenty-five books and is ranked the second most productive psychologist in the world since 1980. He is a Fellow of the British Psychological Society. He is on the editorial board of a number of international journals, as well as the board of directors of the International Society for the Study of Individual Differences. He is also a founder-director of Applied Behavioural Research Associates, a psychological consultancy.

Peter M. Gollwitzer holds the Social Psychology and Motivation Chair at the University of Konstanz in Germany (since 1993). He studied psychology and educational sciences at the University of Regensburg (BA 1973), and social psychology at the Ruhr-University Bochum (MA 1977). In 1981, he received a PhD from the University of Texas at Austin, and in 1988 the habilitation from the University of Munich. His research interests cover a broad range of issues in social and motivation psychology. He has written and edited books on various aspects of goal setting and goal attainment. He is on the editorial board of a number of German and international journals and since 1996 has been a member of the Academia Europaea. In 1990, he received the Max Planck Research Award.

Sheila Greene is a graduate of the University of Dublin, Trinity College and of the University of London Institute of Psychiatry where she trained as a clinical psychologist. From 1971 to 1973 she was Head Psychologist of the Maternal and Infant Health Study, the Boston branch of the NIH Collaborative Perinatal Study. In 1973 she took up a lecturing post in Trinity College, Dublin. In 1991 she was elected to fellowship of the Psychological Society of Ireland and in 1992 to fellowship of Trinity College, Dublin. In the same year she was elected as Dean of Arts (Humanities) and has only recently returned to the normal academic life of teaching and research. She is Co-director of the Dublin Child Development Study, which started in 1985 and is ongoing. She is co-founder of the Trinity College Children's Centre, which conducts research and develops policy and practices relevant to children and adolescents. Her doctoral research was on depression and hopelessness but for the last ten years most of her publications have been in the area of child development.

Peter W. Halligan is a Research Fellow at the Neuropsychology Unit, University Department of Clinical Neurology and Rivermead Rehabilitation Centre. He is a Chartered Psychologist and Fellow of the British and Irish Psychological Societies. Professional memberships also include the British Neuropsychological Society, the European Brain and Behaviour Society, the Society for Research in Rehabilitation, the Association of British Neurologists, the British Neuropsychiatry Society and the Brain Research Association. In 1993 he received the British Psychological Society Spearman Medal, awarded for outstanding contribution in a psychologist's first ten years since graduate membership. He is currently Editor of the new journal *Cognitive Neuropsychiatry* and Associate Editor of *Neuropsychological Rehabilitation* and *Applied Neuropsychology.*

Ingrid Lunt has psychology degrees from the universities of Oxford, Oslo and London. She worked as a clinical psychologist and an educational psychologist before moving to the London University Institute of Education where she has responsibility for the postgraduate training of educational psychologists. She is currently President of the European Federation of Professional Psychologists' Associations (EFPPA) and President Elect of the British Psychological Society. She has carried out research in the fields of special educational needs provision, school organization and pupil deviance, psychological assessment and professional aspects of psychology, and has published widely in these fields.

Roy McConkey is Professor of Learning Disabilities at the University of Ulster, Northern Ireland. He previously held posts with the Brothers of Charity Services in Scotland, St Michael's House, Dublin and at the Hester Adrian Research Centre, University of Manchester. He is a consultant to UNESCO, the British Council, the Cheshire Foundation International and Save the Children Fund (UK) and has undertaken assignments in Africa, India, Sri Lanka, the Asia-Pacific Region and Guyana, South America. He was a member of the Review Group into Mental Handicap Services set up by the Irish Minister for Health, and a member of the Learning Disability Committee of the Mental Health Foundation, London. He is a Fellow and Past President of the Psychological Society of Ireland.

Marina Manthouli is a clinical psychologist, group analyst and family therapist. She received her BA degree in education from Montclair University, New Jersey. She was Assistant Professor at the Higher Technical Institution, Athens for fifteen years. In 1981 she received an MA in Counselling Psychology, and in 1982 started training and personal therapy in a five-year programme at the Institute of Group Analysis, Athens. At the same time, she trained at the Institute of Psychological Evaluation and later at the Institute of Family Therapy. She is a member of the Association of Greek Psychologists, the Institute of Group Analysis, Athens, the Group Analytic Society, Athens, the Group Analytic Society, London, the Institute of Psychological Evaluation and the Institute of Family Therapy. She was President of the Association of Greek Psychologists from 1993 to 1995 and at present is Special Secretary of the Association and represents it in EFPPA and all international groups. She had the honour of being President of the IVth European Congress held in Athens in 1995.

John C. Marshall is the Director of the MRC Neuropsychology Unit, University Department of Clinical Neurology and a member of the MRC External Scientific Staff. He specializes in the assessment, investigation and treatment of language and visual-spatial disorders. He is currently Editor of the *Journal of Neurolinguistics* and on the editorial boards of twelve other leading neuropsychological or linguistic journals.

J.R. Newbrough is Professor of Psychology, Human Development and Special Education and a John F. Kennedy Scholar at Peabody College of Vanderbilt University. He received his doctoral degree from the University of Utah in 1959. He completed a post-doctoral fellowship in community mental health at the Department of Psychiatry, Massachusetts General Hospital-Harvard Medical School in 1960. He entered the US Public Health Service Commissioned Corps that year to serve his military obligation and was assigned to the Mental Health Study Center, National Institute of Mental Health, Adelphi, Maryland. In 1966, he joined the faculty of the Department of Psychology, George Peabody College for Teachers, Nashville, Tennessee where he directs the Community Psychology programme, and he directed the Center for Community Studies, John F. Kennedy Center for Research on Education and Human Development until 1980. He was Editor of the *Journal of Community Psychology* from 1975 to 1990 and continues as Editor Emeritus responsible for special issues.

Arne Öhman received his PhD from the University of Uppsala in 1971. He has held visiting appointments at the Institute of Psychiatry in London and the University of Wisconsin-Madison, USA. He was Professor of Somatic Psychology at the University of Bergen, Norway from 1976 to 1982, and Professor of Clinical Psychology at the University of Uppsala from 1982 to 1992. In 1993 he became Professor of Psychology at the Department of Clinical Neuroscience, Karolinska Institute, Sweden. He is a past-president of the Society for Psychophysiological Research, a member of *Academia Europeia* and the Finnish Academy of Science and Letters. He has served as a member of the Swedish Research Council for Humanities and Social Sciences and the Standing Committee for Social Science at the European Science Foundation. He currently chairs the Committee for Psychology at the Royal Swedish Academy of Science, the Scientific Council of the Swedish Psychological Association and the Scientific Programme Committee for the XXVII International Congress of Psychology. His research interests range from psychological factors and interventions in coronary heart disease to psychophysiological indicators of vulnerability to schizophrenia and to the psychology of emotion, with special reference to fear and anxiety.

Ype H. Poortinga studied psychology at the Free University in Amsterdam where he obtained his Master's degree in 1965 and his PhD in 1971. From 1965 to 1972 he worked at the National Institute for Personnel Research in Johannesburg and since then at Tilburg University in the Netherlands. He has held a part-time professorship at the University of Leuven in Belgium since 1993. He has been Secretary-General of the International Association for Cross-Cultural Psychology (IACCP) and President of the International Test Commission (ITC), the IACCP, the Dutch Psychological Association (NIP) and the European Federation of Professional Psychologists' Associations (EFPPA). His most consistent interest has been in the conditions under which psychological data obtained in different cultural populations can be meaningfully compared.

Marc Richelle is Professor Emeritus of the University of Liège (Belgium) where he taught experimental psychology from 1962 to 1995. He received his higher education at Liège, Geneva and Harvard. Early in his career, he did some cross-cultural and anthropological field work in North and Central Africa and in Israel. In 1960, at the University of Liège he founded the psychological laboratory, where operant techniques were first used on the European Continent. He was President of the Belgian Psychological Society and of the Association de Psychologie Scientifique de Langue Française. He has been and still is very active in promoting European projects: from the very first stage of ERASMUS, he initiated a rapidly developing ICP-network in psychology, and he is currently chair of the Compostela Group, a large university network. He was awarded the prestigious Quinquennial John-Ernest Solvay Prize delivered by the Belgian Science Foundation. He is Doctor *honoris causa* of the universities of Lille 3-Charles-de-Gaulle, of Geneva and of Coïmbra.

Edmund T. Rolls is Professor of Experimental Psychology at the University of Oxford. He performs research on the neurophysiology of vision; the neurophysiology of taste, olfaction and feeding; neural mechanisms of memory and emotion; and the operation of real neuronal networks in the brain. He is Associate Director of the Medical Research Council Interdisciplinary Research Centre for Cognitive Neuroscience at Oxford University.

Salli Saari obtained her Master's degree from the University of Helsinki in 1968 and a PhD from the University of Turku in 1981. Since 1985 she has held the post of Associate Professor at the University of Helsinki. She was President of the Finnish Union of Psychologists from 1981 to 1993, of the Federation of Psychologists' Associations from 1992, and of the Organizing Committee of the Third European Congress of Psychology in Tampere, Finland in 1993. She has been a member of the Executive Council of the European Federation of Professional Psychologists' Associations (EFPPA) since 1995 and a delegate to the EFPPA General Assemblies since 1988. She is a member and former Chair of the National Specialists Board of Psychologists (1993 to 1994). She was the architect of the 1994 Finnish legislation concerning psychologists and in the same year was awarded Psychologist of the Year for her work in the field of crisis and catastrophe psychology. Since 1993 she has been Leader of the National Catastrophe Psychology Group.

Rhoda K. Unger is Professor of Psychology at Montclair State University in New Jersey and a Visiting Professor of Psychology and Women's Studies at Brandeis University. She has also been a Visiting Professor at the University of Haifa. She did her undergraduate work at Brooklyn College and received her PhD in experimental psychology from Harvard University. She has been President of Division 35 (Psychology of Women) of the American Psychological Association and twice a member of the executive committee of Division 9 of APA (Psychological Study of Social Issues). She is a Fellow of APA and received the first Carolyn Wood Sherif Award from Division 35. She has also received two distinguished publication awards and a recent distinguished career award from the Association for Women in Psychology and a distinguished leadership award from the Committee for Women in Psychology of APA. She is the author/editor of seven books.

Bernhard Wilpert was born in Breslau, Silesia and studied Psychology, Sociology and Anthropology in Tübingen and Bonn in Germany and, with a Fulbright award, in Eugene, Oregon, USA. He gained his doctorate from the University of Tübingen, supported through a grant from the Volkswagen Foundation. He was a Research Fellow at the Science Centre in Berlin where he undertook international comparative studies of management, participation and the introduction of new technologies. Since 1978 he has been Professor of Work and Organisational Psychology in Berlin. In 1989, the University of Ghent, Belgium conferred on him the degree of Doctor *honoris causa* for international comparative organizational research. He is currently President of the International Association of Applied Psychology (1994 to 1998). His current research interests include safety and reliability in complex sociotechnical systems with high hazard potential.

Géry d'Ydewalle is a Félicien Cattier Fellow of the Francqui Foundation and CRB Fellow of the Belgian American Educational Foundation. He was awarded a PhD in psychology at the University of Leuven, Belgium in 1975. He was guest research Professor at the Rockefeller University in New York in 1978. He has held the position of Professor at the University of Leuven since the early 1980s and is the Director of the Laboratory of Experimental Psychology. He has been an invited professor at Birkbeck College, London, at the London School of Economics and at the University of Liège. He is a member of the Belgian Royal Academy of Science and current President of the International Union of Psychological Science. He was Vice-President of the International Social Sciences Council, a member of the General Committee of the International Council of Scientific Unions, and Past-President of the Belgian Psychological Society. In 1992 he received the highest scientific award of Belgium, the Francqui Prize. Former Editor of the *International Journal of Psychology* and current member of a number of editorial boards, he has authored and co-authored numerous publications on perception and memory.

Preface

This century has witnessed an explosive growth in psychology which has changed irrevocably our conception of what it means to be human. The number of individuals engaged in the profession has grown from a select few researchers and practitioners in 1900 to a body of several hundred thousand worldwide today. Psychology has developed applications in just about every human occupation involving people, from pathology to policing, education to engineering, sport to space exploration. It is now one of the most widely read subjects in second and third level education and many of its concepts have become assimilated into popular culture.

The impending approach of the new millennium provides a convenient juncture at which to stand back and appraise this growth, to review the strengths and achievements, the weaknesses and failures of the last 100 years of scientific and professional psychology. It is also a vantage point from which to peer into the next century, anticipating new directions for the discipline.

This opportunity was grasped by the organizers of the Fifth European Congress of Psychology held in Dublin in July 1997. Eighteen mainly European experts, representing the rich diversity of contemporary basic and applied psychology, accepted an invitation to review their respective fields and present a keynote address to the congress. They were also invited to develop their ideas more fully for publication and this book is the result.

The chosen theme of the congress was '*dancing on the edge*', capturing a sense of celebration at the boundary of the century but also providing a metaphor for scientific progress, arising from the tension between on the one hand the hard edge of systematic observation and on the other the dance-like exploration of ideas that enables theoretical advance. The authors have taken up this theme from the perspectives of their own research and professional interests in a variety of ways.

Ype Poortinga sets the scene with a critical review of *methodology* in psychology, arguing that the study of complex behaviour probably has not shown as much progress as psychologists like to believe. In part because of limitations in the accuracy of measurement and the essential unpredictability of behaviour due to its dynamic nature, he concludes the danger of overgeneralization is likely to remain the Achilles heel of psychological measurement. Rhoda Unger suggests that probably the most important recent contribution of feminist theory to psychology is the concept of *gender* as a social construct and that feminist theory has been unique in focusing on similarities in the way societies construct marginality for groups with low power within them. Sheila Greene integrates both themes in her review of the course of *developmental psychology* over the century, identifying the need to confront the complexity of behaviour and to recognize the socially constructed, value-laden concepts of the child and of so-called normality in development. Marc Richelle describes the main break-throughs which have shaped the psychology of *learning* over the past fifty years and laments the relative lack of integration with other fields of psychological enquiry and deficiencies in putting scientific knowledge on learning to work effectively.

Roy McConkey argues that there can never be a psychology of *intellectual disability per se* and yet for the past 100 years psychologists have acted as though there was one. Psychology has contributed assessment, interventions and research. Testing brought shame to psychology but its reputation has been salvaged by psychological interventions aimed at overcoming disabilities. Amparo Belloch reviews the history of *clinical psychology*, concluding that it is now consolidated as a scientific discipline. However, there is a real need to bridge research and practice – to use the influence of our scientific activity to benefit society. Marina Manthouli documents the emergence of *psychotherapy* during the twentieth century and criticizes the social view of illness as being defined by medical, therapeutic and diagnostic technology, instead of conceiving the person as an integrated system with inherent potentials. Psychotherapists must take responsibility for shaping therapeutic settings with specific structure, context and content which are acceptable to the patient, respect the patient's needs and allow personal growth. She predicts that psychotherapy in the future will be practised in the richer social environment of the group. Ingrid Lunt claims that *educational psychology* is the earliest application of psychology. She describes how it has been caught between the separate disciplines of education and psychology and is drawn in opposite directions by their different epistemologies and methodologies. She concludes that the challenge has never been more urgent to understand teaching and learning, classroom and school organization and the factors which affect pupils' development and progress.

In reviewing the history of *community psychology*, John Newbrough argues that the approach of human science is more appropriate than logical positivism to the development and application of community psychology. Indeed he forecasts that the tension between these two paradigms will lead eventually to a split into two psychologies. Salli Saari takes on the issue of *preventive psychology*, focusing on the role of social and environmental factors in the development of personality and emotional disorders. She indicates that the thrust of the third mental health revolution lies in the quest for prevention of emotional disorders through social and community interventions aimed at their social determinants. Finally in the area of health, Adrian Furnham discusses *alternative treatment* through the intriguing question of why the 'strange, varied, contradictory and bizarre collection of alternative/complementary/non-allopathic treatments should mesmerize sophisticated Western populations who have the technological sophistication of modern medicine available to them?' Are we witnessing here a flight from science?

Bernhard Wilpert argues that any *organizational* output – whether a product, quality, safety, job satisfaction, or good decision making – typically results from a complex interaction of the social, organizational and technical components of a given subsystem. As a consequence, individual work can only be appraised when it is embedded within its organizational context. He suggests that there is a growing contradiction between the reduction in the demand for active, human work and the continued high subjective importance of working. Resolution of this contradiction will require revolutionary concepts.

Ruth Byrne reviews the current state-of-the-art in research on the *psychology of reasoning* and argues that if we are to understand any aspect of individuals – their personalities, emotional problems, everyday likes and dislikes – we need to understand their mental life. She characterizes alternative theories of deduction which provide different perspectives on the nature of human reasoning and on the issues of rationality, errors in reasoning, and the influence of content and context. Will a single coherent theoretical framework eventually emerge? Peter Gollwitzer explores the concepts of *'goals'* and *'goal striving'* which represent volitional, self-regulatory behaviour. He finds that how people frame their goals affects how successfully they will behave in an achievement situation. Future research should explore how people integrate self-regulatory strategies of goal pursuit with self-defensive strategies aimed at the protection of self-esteem. Géry d'Ydewalle illustrates how the information-processing paradigm has the potential to enrich considerably research on *perception* and provides several examples from the Louvain Laboratory of Experimental Psychology. Arne Öhman describes the process of *attention* in terms of a beam moving across perceptual fields. What research clearly tells us is that this process is not random but is governed by representations in memory about the non-attended terrain, a substantial part of which may be evolutionarily primed. Peter Halligan and John Marshall define *cognitive neuropsychology* as being primarily concerned with characterizing how normal cognitive processes may be impaired after acquired brain damage. The approach conceptualizes complex mental processes in terms of information-processing systems comprised of separate but interconnected subsystems. They argue that the main contribution of the cognitive neuropsychological approach lies in the theoretical framework it offers for informing the study and understanding of breakdown in cognitive functioning. Finally, Edmund Rolls presents a modern theory of *emotion* and shows how at least some of its processes can be seen to be implemented in the information processing performed by certain brain regions. He concludes that cognitive neuroscience is bringing much new insight to the problem of consciousness.

Though wide-ranging in its exploration, this book does not pretend to provide comprehensive coverage of contemporary psychology – such a mission would be impossible given the constraints of space and availability of authors. What we hope to have provided is a collection of stimulating, personal essays which, in Yeats' phrase, 'sing...of what is past, or passing, or to come'. Whatever the strengths and weaknesses of psychology, we have been changed utterly by it. This has not been *a* century of psychology but *the* century of psychology. The edge of the new millennium is a time to celebrate this, a time to dance. It is a pleasure to invite you, the reader, to come join this dance!

It is with grateful thanks that we record the administrative assistance of Thérèse Brady and Teresa Walsh and the technical wizardry of Lisa Cullen and John Conboy.

Ray Fuller, Patricia Noonan Walsh and Patrick McGinley
Dublin and Galway, 1997

Abbreviations

APA	American Psychological Association
BPS	British Psychological Society
EARLI	European Association for Research on Learning and Instruction
EAWOP	European Association of Work and Organizational Psychology
EFPP	European Federation of Psychoanalytic Psychotherapists
EFPPA	European Federation of Professional Psychologists' Associations
EGATIN	European Group of Analytic Training Network
ENOP	European Network of Organizational and Work Psychologists
IAAP	International Association of Applied Psychology
IACCP	International Association for Cross-Cultural Psychology
ISPA	International School Psychologists' Association
ITC	International Text Commission
SPSSI	Society for the Psychological Study of Social Issues

1 Brown, Heisenberg and Lorenz

Predecessors of twenty-first-century psychology?

Ype H. Poortinga[*]

The main theme of this chapter is reflected in the title. Brown, Heisenberg and Lorenz have contributed in an important way to the understanding of physical phenomena by showing that there are essential limitations to the accuracy of measurement and the predictability of physical events. The chapter has two parts. In the first part an account is given of the achievements and limitations of a century of psychological measurement and research, with an emphasis on the tendency of psychologists to over-generalize results. This is followed by an interlude in which the ideas of the three above-mentioned scientists are summarized. The brief second part indicates a possible way in which psychological measurement theory can be extended to approach the uncertainty and unpredictability that appear to be inherent in behaviour.

PART I

The century of psychology

The most eminent forefather of Dutch psychology, Gerard Heymans, delivered in 1909 an address in which he stated that all technical innovations of the previous century had not made mankind much happier. In his view happiness requires wisdom. We need to know ourselves and others. Heymans predicted that this knowledge would come from psychology: 'A time will come when psychology will be past its formative years, leave the school to enter life; that moment will be one of the most important in the history of humanity' (Heymans 1909, quoted in Soudijn 1988: 217).

This optimism about the happiness of humanity and the role of psychology has largely dissipated. More recent statements originate from a gloomier world view, but are not necessarily more modest about the future role of psychology.

---

[*] The invitation for this chapter contained the following brief: 'What we would like you to present and write is a personal view of the strengths and weaknesses, the achievements and the failures, of the last 100 years of psychology in the area of 'Measurement: theory and practice' and include your estimation and recommendations for where psychology might go in the next century.' What appeared to be asked for was an interpretative account that by its very nature is somewhat foreign to the notion of measurement. Let us hope that measurement will not suffer.

The Japanese psychologist Toda (1971) has speculated that psychology will make as much progress in the next century as physics has made in the past century. With a bit of irony, he attributes to psychology the position of the master science, for the simple reason that social systems will break down in modern societies where the traditional concern for food and other essentials does not continue to absorb most of the energy of people.

As an antidote to these grandiose views I can mention that in the opinion of Mehryar (1984), any view from the western establishment on psychology is beside the point. For the Third World, to which the majority of the world's inhabitants belongs, he recommends that psychologists cannot do better than remind the peoples in these countries of the need for political struggle to relieve them from their position of poverty.

The century of measurement

There seems to be no other science where methodological and measurement issues are receiving attention to the same extent in introductory texts as in psychology (Dehue 1996). Unassailable progress has been made with respect to the mathematical and formal statistical aspects of measurement. At mid-century, Stevens (1951) had formulated four different types of measurement scale. By that time factor analysis had already become established, followed later by other developments of which especially the analysis of covariance structures deserves to be mentioned. In the 1960s, consensus had been reached on the concept of validity, at least temporarily, and generalizability theory was around as well as the first models for what is now commonly known as item response theory.

In the 1970s there were authoritative texts on measurement (Krantz *et al.* 1971) and psychometrics (Lord and Novick 1968) that will undoubtedly be extended and refined, but it seems unlikely that they will be overturned. There are journals for psychometric theory as well as journals of applied measurement. Of great practical importance to professionals are numerous textbooks on methodology and statistical analysis and on psychological testing from which future psychologists learn about psychological measurement. In the last fifteen years a new phenomenon has gained prominence that has had a major impact on technical sophistication in data analysis, namely the computer package for statistical analysis. More than anything else the large-scale availability of powerful computers has made multivariate models of scaling and analysis popular. LISREL and EQS have become household words in many journals outside the measurement literature, even though one may doubt whether authors and readers appreciate sufficiently the pitfalls and limitations of these models.

Measurement has had great relevance for experimental psychology, the main paradigm of twentieth-century psychology. Methodological sophistication of designs for data collection and of procedures for the analysis of data is closely related to issues of measurement. Principles of sampling, the testing of the null-hypothesis as well as analysis of variance and linear regression analysis have become common knowledge among psychologists.

The impact of measurement is even more evident in what Cronbach (1975) has named 'correlational', as distinct from 'experimental' psychology. It is just about a century ago that Binet and Simon constructed the first intelligence test. This formed the beginning of what has become the most extensive enterprise based on psychological measurement, namely the prediction of future performance of school and employment criteria of testees, on the basis of the assessment of current cognitive abilities and personality traits.

There remain many problematic aspects at a technical level, but these fall outside the scope of this chapter. Here the focus is on measurement as it relates to the advancement of psychology as a science and a profession. I discern two or perhaps three major problems with the applied aspects of psychological measurement. The first concerns the testing of the null-hypothesis and the interpretation of significant results. The second problem is an undue optimism about the quality of representation in measurements of psychological attributes. Together they contribute to the third, more general, issue, that psychologists appear to be inclined to over-generalize their results.

Undoubtedly the Neyman–Pearson framework for testing the null-hypothesis can be counted as an achievement. However, over time it has become almost a ritual and the outcome is often misinterpreted. Knowledgeable prophets have warned against this form of idolatry for a long time. One of them is Cohen who in a recent review formulated a core objection as follows:

> All psychologists know that *statistically significant* does not mean plain-English significant, but if one reads the literature, one often discovers that a finding reported in the Results section studded with asterisks implicitly becomes in the Discussion section highly significant or very highly significant, important, big.

> (Cohen 1994: 1001)

In part the solution to the problem is obvious; next to statistical significance the proportion of variance explained should be reported. However, this still happens relatively rarely. Moreover, an orientation towards differences has the danger of overlooking similarities. For example, in cross-cultural psychology, where the effects of all kinds of unwanted variables or cultural bias lead to a high a priori probability of finding differences between samples of subjects, the testing of the null-hypothesis in the long run may well contribute to an overemphasis of the impact of cultural variation on behaviour (cf. Malpass and Poortinga 1986).

The problem of representation is widely seen as a critical and difficult issue. In correlational psychology the concept of validity holds a central position and there is strong emphasis on the empirical analysis of validity of psychometric instruments. However, levels of validity coefficients considered acceptable are typically low. This means that the relationship between the measurement device and the psychological attribute that it supposedly represents is diffuse and leaves scope for alternative interpretation. The use of more advanced psychometric techniques helps, but is not always a remedy. At the time when a psychologist still delivered data on punch cards at computer centres, it was a practical joke to carry out a requested factor analysis on a random rather than the real data set; the allegation was that the psychologist would make sense of the outcome regardless. Models for the analysis of covariance structures have undoubtedly improved this situation, but the legendary 'flexibility' of a program like LISREL (Jöreskog and Sörbom 1993) unfortunately does not only apply to input, but also to the search processs for some kind of structure.

The over-interpretation of the outcome of null-hypothesis tests and low validity coefficients can be said to have a common origin. Psychologists appear to be convinced too easily that their results have the meaning they are supposed to have. In the next section this point will be elaborated in a brief and obviously selective review of the achievements of psychology.

A century of experiments

Many points of view are possible, but I would guess that the most outstanding and lasting academic achievement is the formulation of principles of learning by Pavlov and Skinner. It is rather unimaginable that at some future time there will be university curricula of psychology in which the student is not exposed to the notions of conditioning and reinforcement. There are other achievements of experimental psychology that will presumably withstand the test of time. At the very least, psychological research has contributed to important insights in the areas of sensation, perception and motor skills, and in the functioning of the human brain and nervous system.

The topics mentioned are characterized by an accumulation of knowledge. At times progress may be difficult to detect because researchers explore erroneous directions, but an increase in knowledge can be detected over longer periods. One sophisticated expression of this orientation to science is the evolutionary epistemology of Campbell, who notes:

> What is characteristic of science is that the selective system, which weeds out among the variety of conjectures, involves deliberate contact with the environment through experimentation and quantified prediction, designed so that outcomes quite independent of the investigator are possible.
>
> (Campbell 1988: 416)

Some of the experimental knowledge has found its way into application. For example, in the fields of human engineering or human–machine interaction there are studies ranging from research on the discriminability of coins to the steering of large tankers with a delayed reaction to the rudder (Wagenaar *et al.* 1978). However, the extension of experimental psychology to behaviour in everyday situations more often has not been very successful.

This is shown sharply in the so-successful domain of learning. The generalization of reinforcement principles by Skinner in his (in)famous *Walden Two* (Skinner 1948) is a clear case of over-generalization, but also more modest expectations for the explanatory power of learning theory for complex behaviour turned out not to be realistic. The sometimes ingenious reinforcement schedules that were invented in the 1950s are already hardly remembered. It took a long time to recognize the limited transfer of learning that in turn imposed severe limits on applicability. It is probably not too far-fetched to argue that strict adherence to standard experimental procedures, especially null-hypothesis testing, has played a role.

Learning theory was succeeded by cognitive psychology. From a theoretical perspective it meant that unobservable mental events once more acquired the central position that had been denied by the mechanistic S–R paradigm. The cognitive revolution has not inspired much new development in psychological measurement. Indirectly, it has probably paved the way for qualitative traditions that will be discussed below.

In 1966, Garcia and Koelling were the first to report that there are predispositions to favour certain stimulus–response associations over others and that as a consequence a stimulus cannot be linked with equal ease to virtually any response, as assumed by learning theorists. Since then there has been a growing challenge to the one-sided emphasis on the influence of the social environment and on the plasticity of human behaviour that characterized learning theory and, to a lesser extent, cognitive theory. A new biologically oriented psychology has been constructed that extends beyond neurological and physiological variables, incorporating ethological and sociobiological thinking and encompassing complex patterns of developmental and social behaviour.

There can be no doubt that interesting findings have already emerged from human ethology and evolutionary psychology, demonstrating, for example, the universal presence of 'motherese' – the tone of voice in which adults speak to young babies (Papousek and Bornstein 1992) – and cross-cultural similarities in preferences for selection of marriage partners, including systematic differences between the male and female sexes in these preferences (Buss 1989). However, from the outsider's perspective, perhaps the most striking aspect of the sociobiologically inspired literature of authors like Eibl-Eibesfeldt (1989) or Tooby and Cosmides (1992) is the almost ideological character of the evolutionary paradigm; an evolutionary explanation is invoked even for proximate variables that are readily defined in historical (for cultural populations) or even situational terms (for individuals). In a study like that of Buss, the amount of variance that fits an explanation in terms of 'nature' but cannot be accounted for by 'culture' is small.

Lack of success for the experimental paradigm is perhaps most evident in the largest field of psychological practice, namely clinical diagnosis and therapy. At the same time, it is not an area which excels in the modesty of its theories and applications. The range of variation in the theories that have been constructed is large with respect to aetiology as well as treatment. The mere mention of names like Freud, associated with early childhood years as the origin of later mental pathologies, Rogers, with the role of the therapist in the treatment situation, and Wolpe, with the learning history of the individual, should be sufficient to demonstrate this variation, which in many instances reflects mutual inconsistencies if not actual incompatibilities. Discord with unsatisfactory research outcomes has led many clinicians to denounce the scientific basis of their professional activities, although at the same time those activities derive their professional status largely from their systematic study within psychology (Dawes 1994; Schönpflug 1993). Recent reviews (Lipsey and Wilson 1993; Seligman 1995) suggest that psychotherapy is more effective than nontreatment, but elaborate meta-analysis was needed to substantiate this. For the individual client there remains a considerable margin of uncertainty about the success that can be expected from intervention. There also remains a lack of clarity about the relative rate of success of various types of psychological intervention. As a consequence, there are few standard treatments in the area of mental health, unlike in somatic medicine. Of course it can be argued that the range of variation and uncertainty psychologists have to deal with is of a different order (a point to which I shall return below), but this does not close the major gap that continues to exist between findings from controlled studies and the experience-based convictions of many practitioners.

In view of the limited generalizability of experimental research to everyday behaviour, it is not surprising that the epistemological principles of the mid-century nomological approach, in which the experiment is considered to be the royal road of scientific progress, have been challenged. The alternative perspective of postmodernism and constructivism, in which the law-like character of psychological functioning is largely rejected, has become most visible in social psychology. In various theoretical formulations there is an emphasis on the understanding of the unique behaviour event, its contextuality (Shweder 1991), its intentionality (Eckensberger and Meacham 1984) and its historicity (Gergen 1973). The rejection of the possible merits of earlier approaches tends to be strong. For example, Billig (1987), who goes back to classical studies of rhetoric, finds more there for his analysis of thinking and arguing than in the modern literature of experimental social psychology. The criticisms of Harré, Shotter and Gergen on the achievements embedded in this literature are if anything even harsher.

A century of tests and questionnaires

Binet and Simon were successful where more theory-driven attempts at capturing the psychological processes underlying intelligence, like those of Galton who equated intelligence with mental speed, had not been successful. In fact, it is fair to state that to this very day psychologists do not have a good conceptual grasp of intelligence, the variable that they have more than any other been assessing with tests. There is a range of theories, models and metaphors to represent intelligence (Sternberg 1990). For all major theories of intelligence and cognitive development, including those of Stern, Spearman, Thurstone, Guilford and Piaget, substantial empirical validity was mustered. However, it is difficult to imagine how these can all be complementary and simultaneously valid perspectives.

A similar argument pertains to the numerous traits of personality theory. Eventually some traits may lose their appeal (usually when they are no longer supported by their inventor), but they are not abandoned because they have been falsified. It is informative to think about how personality traits, and for that matter cognitive abilities, are derived. According to Carr and Kingsbury (1938, mentioned in Fiske 1971: 32), we first describe behaviour with adverbs (he acted intelligently), then we use adjectives (he is intelligent) and later refer to nouns (he has a lot of intelligence). In this way qualities of behaviour become attached to the person. The limited validity of personality constructs has led to alternative conceptions in which situational determinants are more prominent (for example, trait by situation interactions), but the recent popularity of the so-called 'big five' dimensions shows that the structural approach based on linear additive models is alive and well, although the amount of variance in practically relevant variables that can be explained in this way remains limited.

With some exaggeration it can be claimed that psychological tests have been successful only inasmuch as they form inventories of domains of overt behaviour. This explains the success of the route Binet and Simon have taken and that has been followed later in personality theory. The more an instrument captures a representative sample of the behaviour of interest, the more successfully it can be used for prediction. When test scores are taken as a sign or index of some underlying hypothetical construct that is less well defined in terms of its behaviour manifestations, the predictive power of psychological measurement dwindles. By and large, personality traits are far more diffuse in terms of the behaviours that they supposedly cover than cognitive abilities; the relative lack of success of personality testing is commensurate.

The questionable status of cognitive abilities, as more than descriptive labels of fairly narrow domains, becomes evident if one tries to extend the use of instruments to cultural populations with a behaviour repertoire that deviates from that in the industrialized Western nations, with their largely uniform formal educational curriculum. Theories postulating essential differences in abstract thinking between literates and illiterates still exist, but the empirical evidence indicates that abilities like syllogistic reasoning do not so much reflect new mental functions induced by historico-cultural developments (suggested by Luria and Vygotsky), but specific algorithmic conventions (Segall *et al.* 1990). Cole and his sociocultural school (Scribner and Cole 1981) have been especially successful in demonstrating that cognitive performances can be accounted for in terms of particular features of the cultural context.

Of three major fields of application of psychological measurement, namely educational assessment, selection, and clinical diagnosis and evaluation, the latter is the most problematic. In view of the state of theory development mentioned earlier, this is not surprising. On the one hand one finds a continuing commitment to objective measurement, on the other hand there are many practitioners and even researchers who have given up the use of psychometric methods. Among those who still favour tests, more than a few have turned to projective techniques like the Rorschach. This method was initially used not only to gain insight into the deeper layers of psychological functioning of testees with mental health problems, but also as a basis for prediction in other applied settings. In the 1950s and 1960s it became clear from validation studies that the Rorschach had no empirical validity as a predictor of any practical criterion and that there was also little support for its construct validity in clinical settings. Renewed efforts have been made to strengthen the psychometric basis, but a few years ago the Dutch Committee on Tests rated the Rorschach as insufficient (the lowest rating) on theoretical rationale as well as reliability and validity (Evers *et al.* 1992).

Even when clinical assessment procedures have non-zero validity, the values of validity coefficients will be low. This raises the question of the quality of decisions based on the scores of clients. From the famous tables by Taylor and Russell (1939) on the predictive value of selection, it is known that, when a diagnostic category has a low rate of occurrence in a population, the probability of a false positive or a false negative can be higher than the probability of a true positive. In The Netherlands the recent dismissal, in a court case concerning incest, of evidence based on anatomically correct dolls has been a painful reminder to the profession of the danger of too much reliance on psychometrically weak findings.

Qualitative analysis as an alternative?

A strong rejection of traditional measurement is found in part of the literature on qualitative analysis. There are objections to the rigid harness of the standardized test and experimental procedures, as well as to the epistemological principles of objectivity in measurement and the status of scientific knowledge as a representation of external reality (Guba and Lincoln 1994).

At the more mundane level of actual data analysis, the term 'qualitative' is often used when there are no measurement procedures that result in a scale for which relations between scale points can be specified in quantitative terms (interval and ratio type scales), and when measurement is only feasible on ordinal or nominal scales (cf. Asendorpf and Valsiner 1992). From a measurement viewpoint there does not seem to be much difference of opinion about this. In the past, psychologists have often been too optimistic about the scale level they could assume; the choice of a scale level should be dependent on the scaling properties that are allowed by the data.

More important are methodological debates that are reminiscent of the traditional nomothetic–idiographic contrast. The controversies include a variety

of issues about admissible data, the scientific status of the unique eve
constellation of events, and the status of the researcher in the process of
collection and interpretation. It is sometimes thought that opinions of sub
about their own internal state would not be admissible in psychometric research
traditions rooted in (post)positivism. This appears to be a misconception;
philosophers of science like Popper allow such data. More problematic is the
scientific status of unique events. For example, Lincoln and Guba (1985) argue
for the 'transparency' of a description as a criterion for acceptability. For the
psychometrically inclined psychologist, transparency is not a sufficient criterion;
when doubt arises about an interpretation there has to be a possibility of
replication or some other form of extension of evidence. Related to the status of
the unique event is the role of the person. Traditional research procedures try to
minimize the influence on the process of data collection and interpretation of the
researcher as a person. Laboratory experiments meet this condition best;
incidental observations meet this condition hardly at all.

Perhaps the contrast between quantitative and qualitative analysis is
emphasized too strongly. In an eloquent essay, Reichardt and Rallis (1994)
point to numerous similar concerns underlying both forms of enquiry for
evaluation research. From a more psychometric tradition, Messick (1995) argues
for an integrated approach to validity in which values are seen as an intrinsic part
of testing. Nor is the potential of qualitative analysis questioned here. When a
distinction is made between discovery and justification in the scientific process
(paraphrasing Reichenbach 1938), much of the process of exploration and the
generation of hypotheses (or diagnoses for individual clients) has qualitative
features. However, researchers of a constructivist or postmodern inclination,
who advocate qualitative analysis, tend to incorporate also the phase of
justification. Breaking away from the limitations of methods that are meant to
safeguard independence of data from the researcher, they extend the realm of
science. This has potentially far-reaching consequences. There are many things
which we believe and which have never been tested. Our world is primarily the
world of everyday experienced reality, where we perhaps believe that the earth is
flat. As long as the belief is shared by everyone, there is little reason for
experimentation and testing. Science begins only when there is uncertainty and a
competing alternative to established wisdom. Scientists cannot measure
everything, but they tend to have an opinion about everything. They always
did, but while opinions that could not be validated with independent methods
were traditionally frowned upon in psychology, they are now given credibility,
thus increasing the danger of over-generalization that was described as a central
problem earlier in this chapter.

The arguments in this part mainly refer to presumed, and in part undoubtedly
real, achievements. Little reference has been made to realms of measurement
which are even more problematic, especially the measurement of change and
growth. Such an extension would merely underline, but not alter, the suggestion
that emerges from the arguments presented. A critical overview seems to suggest

that current traditions in psychological measurement and research somehow offer a less than satisfactory representation of the organization of behaviour.

INTERMEZZO

Early in the nineteenth century the botanist Robert Brown was the first to observe through a microscope the apparently random movements of colloid particles in a solution. This Brownian movement is caused by molecules that collide with the particles. The movements of the particles follow the laws of Newtonian mechanics. However, the number of molecules in the solution makes the direction of movement of any particle at any moment in time essentially random and the prediction of such an event utterly impossible.

Heisenberg is well known for the formulation of the uncertainty principle in quantum mechanics. In popular terms it states that the location and the speed of an electron cannot be measured simultaneously. Another formulation with direct parallels in psychological measurement is that the measurement procedure interacts with what is being measured.

The meteorologist Edward Lorenz discovered that very slight variations in the initial value of a parameter could lead to rapidly diverging outcomes of computer simulations of atmospheric disturbances. He ventured the opinion that the fluttering of the wings of a butterfly in the rain forest of Brazil could result in a hurricane in North America several days later. This was the beginning of chaos theory. Another formulation to model sudden changes is the catastrophe theory developed by Thom (1975). Such models of non-linear dynamics have in common that they make essentially unpredictable changes understandable. It should be noted that chaos and catastrophe are constrained within boundaries; the weather in a week's time may be beyond prediction, but there is never a hurricane in winter. One poorly understood aspect of complex systems is the self-organizing capacity that emerges from internal feedback loops and sensitivities. Sometimes disorganized systems crystallize into a high degree of order.

The three theorists mentioned deal with events from physics, a discipline traditionally associated with deterministic relations between antecedents and consequents and with the precise predictability of concrete events.

PART II

The difficulties described in Part I point to the need for other perspectives on psychological measurement. In the Intermezzo some aspects of physical measurement were mentioned that were taken to reflect a basic indetermination of physical phenomena that goes beyond measurement error as defined in traditional psychological measurement models.

It is likely that there is also an essential unpredictability due to the dynamic nature of behaviour. Perhaps this indicates a possible direction for a future framework for psychological measurement. I would like to make the following suggestions based on some earlier analyses of the relationship between behaviour and cultural context (Poortinga 1992, 1997).

Behaviour between constraints and affordances

In most situations there is a large number of possible courses of action. The range of behaviours that is actually observed is usually limited. Apparently, one might say, there are constraints that curtail the set of alternatives open to a person. This set can be imagined as a multidimensional space demarcated by limiting constraints or boundaries. Constraints can be internal to the organism (as with a phobia), due to either biological or experiential inheritance; they can also be external due to context. Moreover, they can be defined at various levels. At the biological and physiological level, genetic transmission leads to universal propensities of the species, and to individual variations in these propensities. The ecological and socio-historical context imposes limits on many behaviour patterns, in an absolute sense (for example, (non-)availability of books) or in a relative sense (for example, what is considered proper in a community). Other important constraints for the individual derive from the earlier life course. The most immediate level of constraints is that of the here-and-now situation in which the range of choices of the person is limited by factors at each of the levels mentioned, as well as by situational demands.

Constraints limit the range of behaviours available to a person, but within these boundaries there usually remains a range of behaviour alternatives (i.e. affordances or opportunities). Within this range the choice of a specific action is not predictable or explainable in a lawful manner, i.e. the prediction of a specific event cannot have a higher value than the a priori probability that this event will take place. Inasmuch as there are differences between groups of people or between individuals that show regularity in patterns of occurrence, there should be scope for (quasi-)experimental analysis of boundary conditions and predictive measurement. Inasmuch as there is freedom from constraints the search for systematic antecedent–consequent relationships will be fruitless; within the range of choice, description and *post hoc* reconstruction of events are the appropriate form of analysis. If behaviour is considered from this perspective, it has an aspect of essential unpredictability.

The space of alternatives is only defined reasonably well in restricted situations with clearly stipulated behaviour alternatives, like the laboratory experiment or the multiple-choice test. In such an instance there is only limited instability, reflected in measurement error. Measurement in the traditional sense presupposes a strict ordering of observed behaviour alternatives. In chaos theory, not the actual choices but the boundary conditions (i.e. the range of choices that is available to a person) are the focal point of attention. In most real life situations, behaviour is unstable within fairly wide boundaries, and there is little measurable order within this space of opportunities. From this perspective there is an aspect to behaviour that is reminiscent of chaos.

Admittedly, the boundaries between constraints and affordances are much more diffuse and less well definable in the realm of behaviour than in weather systems. Nevertheless, non-linear dynamics represent a way of thinking that is rapidly gaining attention in psychology. A brief consultation of *PsychLit* or other reference systems shows that most empirical studies with this approach have been conducted in physiological psychology and related areas. But there are also numerous publications in which the assets of non-linear dynamic models are examined for other areas of psychology such as social and clinical psychology. Particularly fascinating is the idea that stage transitions, and the emergence of higher stages of organization over time in ontogenetic development, can be described in terms of non-linear dynamics (Thelen 1995; Van Geert 1994). So far most studies are descriptive, or at best analytic. There are few empirical studies, mainly because large data sets are needed to achieve a sufficient accuracy of estimation of parameters in these models.

Professional interventions interact with the space of opportunity. With a superficial assessment procedure, the effect may be insignificant. However, any exploration in depth, in which the multifaceted space of the behaviour opportunities of a person is mapped out in detail, for example, in psychotherapy, is in itself likely to affect that space in more than a minor way. In passing it may be noted that in a broader context psychologists have markedly influenced the behaviour patterns of people in societies in which they are strongly present.

Chaos and catastrophe theories have another implication with potentially far-reaching consequences for professional practice. They can make clear that there are many questions which cannot be solved unambiguously on the basis of any knowledge. Diagnosis and intervention then have to be based on knowledge about boundary conditions. The psychologist can provide information about unlikely or unpromising courses of events, rather than about the most likely course of events. Even trying to find the best solution may be a wrong strategy. Starting from boundary conditions it is usually possible to reject at least some suggested solutions to a problem on the basis of available evidence. For some other alternatives it can be indicated that they are unlikely to yield positive results. In respect of the remaining alternatives there will be no advice to offer; after all it has to be recognized that there is essential uncertainty.

It may be noted that chaos and catastrophe theories are nomological; the uncertainty of events is within defined boundaries. At the same time they should appeal to those who want to give a place in psychology to unpredictable and only retrospectively understandable events.

CONCLUSION

Progress in science presumes an accumulating body of knowledge. By this standard the study of complex behaviour has probably not shown as much progress as psychologists would like to believe. Nomothetic approaches have shortcomings because many manifestations of behaviour cannot be captured in prediction formulas. Idiographic orientations are lacking in explicit procedures for ruling out alternative interpretations. For the future this makes it necessary that the scope of psychology as a science and profession is better defined than it has been in this century. One step towards this goal may be the further development of non-additive and non-linear measurement models that acknowledge indeterminacy of behaviour beyond measurement error. Unfortunately, models of chaos and catastrophe have even more degrees of freedom than traditional models; no less than the older models they lend themselves to over-optimistic interpretation. Thus, the danger of over-generalization is likely to remain the Achilles heel of psychological measurement and in this sense the new century is likely to inherit some of the infirmities of the old.

REFERENCES

Asendorpf, J.B. and Valsiner, J. (eds) (1992) *Stability and Change in Development: A Study of Methodological Reasoning*, Newbury Park, CA: Sage.

Billig, M. (1987) *Arguing and Thinking: A Rhetorical Approach to Social Psychology*, Cambridge: Cambridge University Press.

Buss, D.M. (1989) 'Sex differences in human mate preferences: evolutionary hypotheses tested in 37 cultures', *Behavioral and Brain Sciences* 12: 1–49.

Campbell, D.T. (1988) 'Evolutionary epistemology', in E.S. Overman (ed.) *Methodology and Epistomology for Social Science: Selected Papers of Donald T. Campbell* (pp. 393–434), Chicago: University of Chicago Press.

Cohen, J. (1994) 'The earth is round (p<.05)', *American Psychologist* 49: 997–1003.

Cronbach, L.J. (1975) 'Beyond the two disciplines of scientific psychology', *American Psychologist* 30: 116–127.

Dawes, R.M. (1994) *House of Cards: Psychology and Psychotherapy Built on Myth*, New York: The Free Press.

Dehue, T. (1996) 'De beproefde procedures', *De Psycholoog* 31: 273–279.

Eckensberger, L.H. and Meacham, J. A. (1984) 'Essentials of action theory: a framework for discussion', *Human Development* 27: 166–172.

Eibl-Eibesfeldt, I. (1989) *Human Ethology*, New York: Aldine de Gruyter.

Evers, A., Van Vliet-Mulder, J.C. and Ter Laak, J. (1992) *Documentatie van Tests and Test Research in Nederland* [Documentation of Tests and Test Research in the Netherlands], Amsterdam: NIP.

Fiske, D.W. (1971) *Measuring the Concepts of Personality*, Chicago: Aldine.

Garcia, J. and Koelling, R.A. (1966) 'Relation of cue to consequence in avoidance learning', *Psychonomic Science* 4: 123–124.

Gergen, K.J. (1973) 'Social psychology as history', *Journal of Personality and Social Psychology* 26: 309–320.

Guba, E.G. and Lincoln, Y.S. (1994) 'Competing paradigms in qualitative research', in N.K. Denzin and Y. Lincoln (eds) *Handbook of Qualitative Research* (pp. 105–117), Thousand Oaks, CA: Sage.

Jöreskog, K.G. and Sörbom, D. (1993) *LISREL 8*, Chicago: Scientific Software International.

Krantz, D.H., Luce, R.D., Suppes, P. and Tversky, A. (1971) *Foundations of Measurement* (Vol. 1), New York: Academic Press.

Lincoln, Y.S. and Guba, E.G. (1985) *Naturalistic Inquiry*, Beverly Hills, CA: Sage.

Lipsey, M.W. and Wilson, D.B. (1993) 'The efficacy of psychological, educational, and behavioral treatment', *American Psychologist* 48: 1181–1209.

Lord, F.M. and Novick, M.R. (1968) *Statistical Theories of Mental Test Scores*, Reading, MA: Addison-Wesley.

Malpass, R.S. and Poortinga, Y.H. (1986) 'Strategies for design and analysis', in W.J. Lonner and J.W. Berry (eds) *Field Methods in Cross-cultural Research*, (pp. 47–84), Beverly Hills, CA: Sage.

Mehryar, A. (1984) 'The role of psychology in national development: wishful thinking and reality', *International Journal of Psychology* 19: 159–167.

Messick, S. (1995) 'Validity of psychological assessment', *American Psychologist* 50: 741–749.

Papousek, H. and Bornstein, M.H. (1992) 'Didactic interactions: intuitive parental support of vocal and verbal development in human infants', in H. Papousek, U. Jürgens and M. Papousek (eds) *Non-verbal Communication: Comparative and Developmental Approaches* (pp. 209–229), Cambridge: Cambridge University Press.

Poortinga, Y.H. (1992) 'Towards a conceptualization of culture for psychology', in S. Iwawaki, Y. Kashima and K. Leung (eds) *Innovations in Cross-cultural Psychology* (pp. 3–17), Amsterdam: Swets and Zeitlinger.

—— (1997) 'Towards convergence?', in J.W. Berry, J. Pandey and Y.H. Poortinga (eds) *Handbook of Cross-cultural Psychology (2nd edn, Vol. 1, Theory and Method)* (pp. 347–387), Boston: Allyn & Bacon.

Reichardt, C.S. and Rallis, S.F. (1994) 'Qualitative and quantitative inquiries are not incompatible: a call for a new partnership', in C.S. Reichardt and S.F. Rallis (eds) *The Qualitative-Quantitative Debate: New Perspectives* (pp. 85–91), San Francisco: Jossey Bass.

Reichenbach, H. (1938) *Experience and Prediction*, Chicago: University of Chicago Press.

Schönpflug, W. (1993) 'Applied psychology: newcomer with a long tradition', *Applied Psychology: An International Review* 42: 5–66.

Scribner, S. and Cole, M. (1981) *The Psychology of Literacy*, Cambridge, MA: Harvard University Press.

Segall, M.H., Dasen, P.R., Berry, J.W. and Poortinga, Y.H. (1990) *Human Behavior in Global Perspective*, New York: Pergamon / Boston: Allyn & Bacon.

Seligman, M.E.P. (1995) 'The effectiveness of psychotherapy: the Consumer Reports study', *American Psychologist* 50: 965–974.

Shweder, R.A. (1991) *Thinking Through Cultures: Expeditions in Cultural Psychology*, Cambridge, MA: Harvard University Press.

Skinner, B.F. (1948) *Walden Two*, New York: McMillan.

Soudijn, K.A. (1988) 'De toekomst van de psychologie', in W. Goddijn, J.L. Goedegebuure, K.A. Soudijn and H.J.A. Verdaasdonk (eds) *Aftellen tot 200*, Tilburg: Tilburg University Press.

Sternberg, R.J. (1990) *Metaphors of Mind: Conceptions of the Nature of Intelligence*, Cambridge: Cambridge University Press.

Stevens, S.S. (1951) 'Mathematics, measurement and psychophysics', in S.S. Stevens (ed.) *Handbook of Experimental Psychology*, New York: John Wiley.

Taylor, H.C. and Russell, J.T. (1939) 'The relationships of validity coefficients to the practical effectiveness of tests in selection: discussion and tables', *Journal of Applied Psychology* 23: 565–578.

Thelen, E. (1995) 'Motor development: a new synthesis', *American Psychologist* 50: 79–95.

Thom, R. (1975) *Structural Stability and Morphogenesis*, Reading, MA: Benjamin.

Toda, M. (1971) 'Possible roles of psychology in the very distant future', in *Proceedings of the XIX International Congress of Psychology*, London: British Psychological Association.

Tooby, J. and Cosmides, L. (1992) 'The psychological foundations of culture', in J. Barkow, L. Cosmides and J. Tooby (eds) *The Adapted Mind: Evolutionary Psychology and the Generation of Culture*, New York: Oxford University Press.

Van Geert, P. (1994) *Dynamic Systems of Development: Change between Complexity and Chaos*, New York: Harvester Wheatsheaf.

Wagenaar, W.A., Vroon, P.A. and Janssen, W.H. (eds) (1978) *Proeven op de Som*, Deventer: Van Loghum Slaterus.

2 The three-sided mirror

Feminists looking at psychologists looking at women

Rhoda K. Unger

The purpose of this chapter is to look at the development of the psychology of women over time in terms of three separate (albeit overlapping) questions represented by the three-sided mirror in its title:

- Did an increasing number of women contributing research to psychology influence it in terms of theory and content?
- What was the effect upon psychological paradigms when women and/or gender became the object of scrutiny?
- How can feminism influence the theory and practice of psychology?

These three questions may help us to determine the importance for future paradigm change of women, gender and feminism, ingredients which appear to be inextricably intertwined as the title of this chapter indicates. But how are they connected? First, I will examine content areas considered important to the psychology of women in the United States to determine whether researchers' sex determined the questions they asked. Next, I will examine whether changes in the kinds of subject populations studied have had important consequences for revision of method and theory. I will then explore the way ideology affects the lenses used and the problems examined. Finally, I will predict some future directions of a feminist psychology of women and gender.

RESEARCHER SEX AND THE CONTENT OF SCHOLARSHIP IN THE PSYCHOLOGY OF WOMEN

Prejudice and discrimination against women

The study of the psychology of women developed within a particular political-historical context. It emerged during the second wave of feminist activism in the United States as women within academia became outraged at the continuing inequality between the sexes in a variety of social as well as political and economic domains. It is not surprising, therefore, that attempts to demonstrate the extent of discrimination against women were among the earliest studies in the field.

Many of these studies used traditional psychological methodology either to look at sexism within psychology and academia in general or to examine the processes of sex discrimination at an interpersonal level. Although such studies could be viewed as manifestations of personal concern or self-interest by those who were likely to be the targets of such discrimination, some of this early research was actually done by men.

Philip Goldberg (1968), for example, conducted one of the earliest studies in the area. He found that women were more likely to evaluate essays purportedly written by women more poorly than identical essays purportedly written by men. Other early researchers (Rosenkrantz *et al.* 1968; Broverman *et al.* 1970) found that both male and female college students held similar stereotypes about the traits traditionally ascribed to women and men. They also found that traditional women's traits were seen as less socially desirable. The principal researcher was male in one of these studies and men were involved as integral parts of the research team for these and subsequent studies.

These studies did not represent any kind of major shift of methodology. They employed the traditional methodology of experimental social psychology. Researchers manipulated the sex of target individuals and attempted to demonstrate that prejudice and discrimination existed based solely on external criteria such as sex. Such studies did, however, indicate a shift in theoretical framework. The bases for negative judgements were seen as external to the target individual and not, therefore, 'his or her fault'. This kind of conceptualization was part of a move away from the study of sex differences (based on assumptions about intrapsychic causality) towards the study of sex as a social variable (Unger 1979b). It was similar to the paradigm shift from studies in race differences to studies of prejudice found among social psychologists following the Second World War (Samelson 1978).

Once they had demonstrated that prejudice and discrimination against women were pervasive, researchers began to ask more subtle questions. For example, feminist psychologists of both sexes have been interested in the way self–other attributions influence attitudes about discrimination. Faye Crosby (1982, 1984) pioneered work on the ways women use selective awareness to deny personal discrimination. She has consistently found that women and members of other groups which suffer economic and societal disadvantage tend to report that they, personally, are doing well although they recognize discrimination against other members of their own social category.

Crosby's work helped to elucidate some of the mechanisms by which people internalize negative views about people like themselves. People possess more information about their own than about others' behaviours. Thus, they see themselves as exceptions to any kind of group categories. They do not appear to be aware, however, of the inconsistencies between what they say about themselves and what they say about others although from an observer's perspective, they appear to be in identical circumstances.

Awareness of discrimination appears to be a key to change in this area. For example, if victims of discrimination are made aware that their judges are biased against members of their group, they have been found to be more able to resist the devastating psychological impact of negative judgements (Dion 1975; Dion *et al.* 1978).

Another major area of research involves the kind of cues that trigger negative stereotypes. Several prominent social psychologists have indicated that physical appearance appears to be the most important cue in differentiating between females and males (Deaux and Lewis 1984; Spence and Sawin 1985). But research on physical appearance by social psychologists has often been quite different from that of researchers who focused on the psychology of women. Social psychologists have tended to concentrate on questions about how trait attributions are influenced by the individual's level of physical attractiveness (Hatfield and Sprecher 1986). They have also been concerned with the kind of potentially universal physical characteristics that underlie physical appearance judgements (Zebrowitz, in press).

In contrast, feminist researchers have been more concerned with examining the impact of sociopolitical context on judgements involving physical appearance. Philip Goldberg, for example, was the first investigator to demonstrate prejudice against feminists (Goldberg *et al.* 1975). He found that less attractive women were more likely to be perceived as feminists than attractive women even though, in actuality, feminists did not differ from non-feminists in their physical appearance. This study received much attention. In a later replication we found that feminists were not 'unique'. Assumptions of unattractiveness were associated with many forms of sociopolitical deviance (Unger *et al.* 1982). We also found that, under some conditions, these assumptions apply to male as well as female targets.

The role of power

Despite the fact that feminism is almost synonymous with changes in power dynamics, many of the psychologists who became interested in gender issues in the early 1970s managed to ignore the central role of power. This neglect is less surprising when one realizes that power has been a problematic area for psychology in general. The study of power and related concepts such as status, influence and control has waxed and waned throughout the twentieth century (cf. Griscom 1992).

Important social psychologists such as Dorwin Cartwright (1959) and Carolyn Sherif (1982) did call for renewed attention to power in their presidential addresses to the Society for the Study of Social Issues (SPSSI) and Division 35 of APA respectively. Nevertheless, power continued to be ignored, especially by US psychologists. Some links between researcher characteristics and content area may be found, however. Researchers from groups with a marginal position within society appear to be more likely to study social power in preference to processes that are more popular with mainstream psychology such as social influence and locus of control (Unger 1986). The latter two terms are, of course, more decontextualized and easier to manipulate within the laboratory than social power. They also lend themselves more readily to theories involving individual intrapsychic causality rather than the impact of socio-historical forces.

As one might expect, early research in the psychology of women was concerned with issues of status and power. As is the case for the study of prejudice and discrimination, this research did not differ methodologically from more traditional social psychological research except for its use of a wider range of subject populations and social contexts. It did, however, differ in terms of its concern for the sociopolitical implications of its findings.

The pioneering work on the relationship of power to interpersonal behaviour between the sexes was done by Nancy Henley (1973). She demonstrated that sex, race and class differences in 'touch privilege' exist. She argued that sex and power are highly confounded so that we tend to confuse power differences with sex differences. Later work (Mayo and Henley 1981) focused on how sex-related differences in nonverbal behaviours reflect and maintain power differentials. In contrast, more traditional social psychologists focused on findings showing that women are better at identifying nonverbal cues than are men (Hall 1985).

A number of early empirical studies looked at the social mechanisms that control gender differentiated behaviours. These found, for example, that women who used forms of 'male' power were penalized. Women who used male forms of power were seen as colder and more aggressive than comparable males, but they were not seen as more competent (Johnson 1976). Both women and men were found to be more likely to exclude a competent woman from their group than a competent man, whereas they were more likely to include an incompetent woman than an incompetent man (Hagen and Kahn 1975). The men appeared to like competent women only when they did not have to interact with them. Only feminist women preferred a 'masculine' competent woman to a 'feminine' one (Spence *et al.* 1975).

Similar findings can be found in current social psychological journals. For example, Linda Carli (1990) demonstrated recently that groups of men were more likely to be persuaded by an unassertive woman whereas assertiveness had no impact upon the effectiveness of men.

Since so few psychologists in the United States have done empirical work on power, it is difficult to determine whether the sex of investigators has influenced their choice of questions in this area. There is some reason to believe, however, that it is social activism rather than researcher sex which determines whether one will do work on power and status (Unger 1986). Both Hagen and Kahn are male and Johnson's work derived from a PhD dissertation under the supervision of Bert Raven, who did classic theoretical work on the social bases of power (French and Raven 1959). Other important work on gender and power in groups has been conducted by Kenneth Dion (1985). All these individuals have been actively involved in SPSSI – APA's division concerned with the study of social issues. Their sociopolitical values and theoretical framework – as evidenced by their professional identification – appear to play a larger role than their sex in defining their research questions.

Personal epistemology and research questions

Many scholars in the psychology of women early recognized the connection between ideology and scholarship (cf. Sherif 1979; Unger 1982, 1983; Riger 1992). Much of this work has been theoretical in nature. There has been relatively little empirical work in this area partly because of the difficulty in validating the relationship between philosophical constructs and behaviour.

I have, however, been conducting research for over ten years that suggests that it is researchers' epistemological stance rather than their sex that better explains what kinds of research questions they ask. We have found, for example, that both males and females who identify themselves as feminist have similar constructionist epistemologies (Unger *et al.* 1986). Leaders in Division 35 and SPSSI also share constructionist views about how the world works (Unger 1984–1985). Constructionist views include belief in the relative nature of truths, concern for subjectivity, focus on the individual as a source of authenticity and authority, and acknowledgement of the role played by chance as well as historical forces in the determination of events. Constructionist individuals also appear to prefer environmental explanations over biological ones and to be sympathetic towards efforts to create social change (Unger *et al.* 1986).

We have found that a number of additional ideological markers predict attitudes in students better than demographic variables such as sex or race (Unger *et al.* 1986; Unger and Jones 1988). Religiosity appears to be an excellent predictor of epistemology independent of the particular form of Judeo/ Christian/Moslem religion practised (Unger and Safir 1990). Religious individuals had a more positivist epistemology in Israel as well as in the United States. This epistemology was associated with both political and scientific conservatism.

Differences in religiosity appear to be more important in predicting world view than are sex differences. In Israel, for example, religious Jewish women were found to have epistemological beliefs much more similar to those of religious men than to those of secular women (Unger 1992).

Ideological labels – whether religious or secular – can be confounded with demographic markers. Women are, of course, more likely to be feminists than men. However, it is the label 'feminist' that appears to predict what kinds of research questions an individual finds inspiring. People who accept this label appear to identify women as a constructed social grouping rather than a biological category (cf. Unger 1984–1985; Ricketts 1989). One does not have to be a woman, however, to have this kind of viewpoint.

WHAT IS FEMINIST PSYCHOLOGY?

Since I am arguing that ideological stance is related to research priorities, it seems important to offer some ways to distinguish between a feminist approach to sex and gender and other ways of looking at this content area. This is a difficult and somewhat dangerous undertaking. The shift from a psychology of women to feminist psychology has been a gradual one and the paradigm shift is not yet complete. Nevertheless, context and advocacy rather than methodology appear to be the key for understanding changes in the character of the field.

The personal is political

Many early feminist studies were explicitly political in nature. Many early researchers had an activist agenda. For example, Linda Fidell (1970) provided a dramatic example of discrimination against women in psychology with a study that could not easily be replicated in today's more suspicious times. She sent department 'chairmen' (used advisedly in terms of the time period) a collection of *curricula vitae* of junior faculty with the justification that she was trying to find out what criteria determined whether or not they would be hired and the rank and salary that would be offered to them. The chairs received different versions of the same *curricula vitae* with male or female names attached. She found that men were more likely to be hired than women with the same qualifications and offered higher ranks with fewer qualifications. Her study was considered important enough to be published in the *American Psychologist*, the journal of record of the American Psychological Association.

This study was an empirical verification of what those of us in the job market during this period already knew. It was, however, the kind of evidence that psychologists were more willing to listen to and accept than our personal stories. It provides an early example of feminist research – an empirical study used not just to test a hypothesis, but as a justification for social and political action such as changes in APA's criteria for the accreditation of programmes.

In another such study I looked at biases in the teacher evaluation process. I examined 'real' faculty evaluations at my home university and found that sex discrimination was more subtle than simple reactions to whether the instructor was female or male would suggest. Although average overall teaching evaluations were the same for male and female faculty members, women faculty were penalized by students of both sexes for having demanding standards, although such standards had no impact on the evaluations of men (Unger 1979a). The instrument and the circumstances were apparently identical, but they did not allow for the sexism of students who seemed to punish women faculty for their presumed lack of nurturant qualities. These studies indicated that one could not assume that the social environments for women and men were the same even when they appeared to occupy equivalent roles and social positions.

I conducted this research because student evaluations had been used against me during a tenure evaluation. Feminist psychologists are often more explicit than traditional psychologists about the personal history that provokes their professional questions. This kind of reflexivity demonstrates how the personal becomes professional. The researcher attempts to deal with an issue that has become salient in her own life or one that her experience has taught her does not work the way formal methodology and theory say it should. I have suggested elsewhere (Unger 1993) that it was no accident that Naomi Weisstein, who had suffered a great deal of sexist discrimination during her early career (cf. Weisstein 1977) studied constructivist processes in both her studies of gender and her research on the neurology of perception. Nancy Datan (1986) was explicitly self-reflective about such processes when she discussed how her own life stage influenced the kinds of questions she asked about women's mid-life transitions.

While feminist questions may differ, feminist methods do not appear to diverge much from mainstream psychology. A number of researchers have concluded that research in the psychology of women does not differ in methodology from that found in more traditional journals (Fine 1985; Lykes and Stewart 1986). Some have suggested, in fact, that there is no such thing as a feminist methodology (Peplau and Conrad 1989).

I would suggest that differences between feminist and mainstream psychology are more likely to be found in the discussion rather than the methods or results sections of research papers. Traditional researchers are both more individualistic and apolitical in their focus. For example, even though they would agree that stereotyping is a normative process, they would not be likely to make statements such as those found in this early paper from Philip Goldberg:

> sexism approaches being a culturally fixed and almost universal attitude . . . it would seem that final explanations of the phenomenon are not profitably to be looked for at the level of individual psychology. Indeed, neither explanation nor solution is likely located there, although the price of sexism is paid for person by person.
>
> (Goldberg 1974: 62)

I do not know what aspects of Philip Goldberg's life made him such an explicit early feminist. Relatively few men have been such strong political advocates of women within US psychology. However, in-group advocacy is certainly not limited to the psychology of women.

As more formerly neglected groups move from '*margin to center*' (hooks 1984), issues of researcher objectivity continue to become more salient (cf. Morawski 1994). If there is an intimate relationship between the personal and political in all scholarship, then every research question reflects the concerns of one or another group. Psychology could not recognize this relationship, however, until a substantial number of researchers from various ethnic/cultural backgrounds became active in the field.

Intrapsychic, interpersonal and institutional power

Traditional social psychologists have played an important role in elucidating the mechanisms through which gendered behaviours are developed and manifested. They have done particularly excellent work on the perceptual and behavioural processes underlying the self-fulfilling prophecy (Geis 1993). However, the cognitive social view of sex and gender also has flaws (Sampson 1981; Unger 1989). The most important flaw is its apparent inability to recognize the systemic and pervasive nature of oppression in various societies. The behavioural mechanisms of prejudice and discrimination may be expressed by individuals, but the targets do not appear to be a matter of individual choice. Moreover, the kind of laboratory research engaged in by most social psychologists does not lend itself well to a consideration of their own covert assumptions about the world and the meaning of their own methodology.

The cognitive 'revolution' has, moreover, moved social psychology away from the societal context and back towards intrapsychic levels of analysis. In the United States, at least, psychology appears to retain an intrapsychic bias (Kahn and Yoder 1989). Many psychologists appear to have been socialized to believe that we are not doing psychological research unless we can 'explain' what is going on within people's heads. The need for this kind of explanation has led to a view of prejudice as simply another form of normal information processing.

This turn to the study of perceptions and cognitions has come at some cost to activist research. Thus, although behaviour can be changed by rules and laws, perceptual change requires much more long-term solutions such as changes in familial socialization, educational strategies and/or cultural norms. Internal explanations for social inequalities are, however, very popular with society as a whole as well as within the discipline (Mednick 1989). They have been characterized as problematic by more activist feminists in the field. As Martha Mednick has pointed out: 'the focus on personal change diverts scholarship and action away from questions that could be directed toward an understanding of the social foundations of power alignments and inequity' (p. 1122).

However, once psychologists involve themselves in situations where 'real' power differences exist, they seem to find that their definitions of power also change. The label a researcher uses to define 'power' seems to determine how he or she looks at it. Thus, looking at sources of power (such as interpersonal control) within the self can mask the extent and violence by which many women are oppressed (Kitzinger 1991; Koss 1990; Reid 1993).

A few feminist psychologists such as Brinton Lykes and her colleagues (Lykes *et al.* 1993) have studied the plight of women under conditions of state-supported violence. They argue that 'normal' psychological evaluations do not apply under such conditions. Others, such as Michelle Fine (Fine and Zane 1988), have looked at the behavioural consequences for African American and

Latina adolescents educated in schools that practise both racial and gender oppression. Unlike subjects investigated within the laboratory, these groups of women have few opportunities to exercise social influence or demonstrate their need for control (cf. Fine 1983–1984).

These individuals may not even be aware of their need for control. In an important theoretical paper in this area, Erika Apfelbaum (1979) pointed out that once systems of inequality are internalized, the overt use of coercive techniques for social control is no longer necessary. Marginalized individuals will accept their own inferiority.

Ignoring the importance of power differentials in women's and men's lives can result in a psychology of gender that stresses 'sex differences' (Unger 1979b; Mednick 1989). This theoretical position is very comfortable for those who prefer a conservative *status quo*. Studies documenting differences between women and men (for example, fear of success, women's ways of knowing, and more recently, conversational misunderstanding) have received great attention from the media. Interactive and systemic theories of power have, in contrast, received little attention and are often seen as polemics rather than respectable scientific research.

Even more problematic for feminist psychology, the confounding of power differences with sex differences continues to be ignored by some researchers who study women and gender. Of course, power is confounded with racial/ethnic differences as well. In fact, it may be impossible to ask meaningful questions about sex differences once we take race/ethnicity, sexual orientation, class and age (as well as other forms of social categorization) into account. The diversification of research populations is, however, in its infancy in feminist as well as more mainstream psychological research.

The asking of questions about sex differences that ignore power issues does not appear to be related to a researcher's sex. Some female researchers such as Carol Gilligan and Deborah Tannen are extremely popular with the media and their books are widely read by the general public. Repeated critiques from the scholarly community (cf. Crawford 1995; Torres 1992) arguing that their work ignores the fact that males remain the more powerful sex in virtually every behavioural transaction have gone unheard.

Neither Gilligan nor Tannen have attempted to control systematically for the effect of power and status despite the fact that repeated laboratory studies have shown that power differences are more predictive of behaviour than are gender differences (cf. Unger and Crawford 1996). Furthermore, conversational dynamics are not neutral with respect to power. In a recent study, for example, Marianne LaFrance (1992) found that when a lower status person interrupted a higher status partner, he or she was seen as more disrespectful than when status differentials were maintained. Women who interrupted men were also seen as more disrespectful than men who interrupted women. These women received more opprobrium because they used a social privilege that they were not acknowledged to possess.

Social construction as a research framework

Increasingly, feminist psychologists recognize the interactive nature of the person and her social context. They also understand that profound aspects of the social context such as dominance cannot be easily reproduced in the laboratory. Although the laboratory experiment has been attacked by feminist psychologists for many years, only recently have feminist researchers begun to offer some viable alternatives.

Probably the most important recent contribution of feminist theory to psychology is the concept of gender as a social construct. Social construction is not simply an argument for the environmental origin of gendered traits. Rather, constructionists argue that gender is not a trait of individuals at all, but simply a construct that identifies particular behaviours that are understood to be appropriate to only one sex (Bohan 1993). Interpersonal transactions both construct and maintain gender and may be independent of the individual's actual biological sex. In this sense, one could argue that gender is a 'verb' rather than a 'noun' (Unger 1988).

It is of interest that empirical research by traditional social psychologists provides the foundation for this view of gender as a social construction. It draws, for example, upon a number of laboratory studies that demonstrate the impact of the sex composition of the other people in one's environment (cf. Dion 1985) and the potent effect on people's behaviour of other's people's perceptions of their gender (cf. Deaux and LaFrance, in press). Under some circumstances, individuals of either sex can be made to behave in a 'gendered' manner if expectations about them can be manipulated effectively (Skrypnek and Snyder 1982). Most such manipulations must, of course, be carried out when people are not face-to-face with each other since a person's sex is probably the single most salient characteristic he or she possesses and cannot easily be ignored (cf. Unger and Crawford 1996).

The unique contribution of feminist theory is its focus upon similarities in the way societies construct marginality for groups with low power within them. Researchers are, for example, beginning to examine the politics of skin colour (Russell *et al.* 1992). They have found that like the cue of femaleness, skin colour can predict occupational success, salary and social desirability within, as well as outside of, the African-American community. These studies show that oppressive beliefs can be internalized and shared by the marginalized as well as dominant groups.

Examination of constructionist processes can help to avoid the 'politics of identity' in which various groups' oppressions are measured against each other to determine relative need. This is because the social context rather than the individual's experience becomes the focus of scrutiny. But social construction can also produce conceptual problems if researchers do not recognize that every group (including those with power) is socially constructed. Fortunately, a scholarly literature has begun to develop that looks at the social construction of 'whiteness' as well as of various markers of marginality (cf. Fine *et al.*, 1997; Frankenberg 1993; Roman 1993).

The contextualization of meaning

Recognition of the subtle impact of institutionalized oppression means that psychologists cannot assume that even apparently equal environments will produce either identical experiences or equitable outcomes. For example, Abigail Stewart's longitudinal studies of women who had attended Radcliffe in the early 1960s (Stewart and Ostrove 1993) found that working-class women had felt more alienated there than their middle- and upper-class peers. The impact of social class persisted for many years after graduation. These women regarded the marital role with more suspicion than their more privileged classmates and reported that the women's movement had confirmed and supported their sceptical views of middle-class gender norms.

Comparison between historical cohorts appears to be a particularly useful way to look at situated shifts in meaning (cf. Stewart and Healy 1989). Cohorts reflect changes in critical circumstances so that apparently similar experiences generate differing meanings at different times.

One example of such effects can be found in a recent study by Erika Apfelbaum (1993) on women political leaders. Although all Western European democracies may 'look alike', Apfelbaum found that women leaders in Norway and France differed greatly in their views of themselves and their accomplishments. French women leaders tended to see themselves as more illegitimate, more alienated from their male companions, and less representative of the feminist movement than did their Norwegian counterparts. Apfelbaum attributed part of this effect to culturally bound ideology about sexual relationships. She noted, however, that attitudes among the French women have begun to change in the Norwegian direction among the younger cohort of leaders. Such differences in the meaning of similar experiences cannot be explored without taking into account these women's historical and situational context.

Current studies of the impact of single-sex and single-race education also support the idea that legal equality does not always produce social equality. Sadker and Sadker (1994) have amply documented the ways in which teachers in the United States treat boys and girls differently. Recent fine-grained analyses indicate that African-American girls, in particular, must negate their cultural differences from the Anglo norm in order to be successful in school (Fordham 1993). Unwillingness to divest themselves of their cultural identity appears to contribute to the dropping out of secondary school of intellectually able African-American girls (Fine and Zane 1988).

CURRENT CONTROVERSIES

Feminist psychology today is certainly not monolithic. A number of areas of controversy have developed among those whom one would clearly identify as feminist psychologists. Differences have emerged because feminist psychologists now study many different groups of women. The needs of these differing populations have led to disagreements about what are the most effective research strategies. Covert agendas involving the value of various forms of political advocacy and how they relate to research also underlie these conflicts. I will discuss a few exemplary areas of controversy in order to demonstrate that these dilemmas are both complex and, perhaps, unresolvable.

How important are sex differences?

Difference is not a neutral concept in our society. Disagreements between various feminist psychologists cannot be dismissed as merely methodological quibbles (cf. Hare-Mustin and Marecek 1990). Important methodological questions do, however, exist in this area. These include how big a gender-related difference has to be before we consider it a difference and how generally it has to be found. Ideological differences may underlie differing views about whether sex differences are worthy of study. The critical question may be more a matter of judgement than a matter for empirical tests. When one tries to answer the question of 'How big is big?', one is actually asking how meaningful is a given sex difference and what are the criteria by which we determine its importance.

There was a time when feminists believed that questions about sex differences would disappear as researchers demonstrated that such differences were relatively small, inconsistent and contextual in nature. However, questions about sex-related differences have re-emerged. One of the factors responsible for renewed interest in the area is the development of meta-analysis as a tool to examine findings in a large number of independent studies. However, feminist psychologists can also differ about the meaning of the same effect size (Eagly 1995; Hyde 1994).

Differences among feminist scholars in this area appear to be related to the definition of feminism which they endorse. This definition, in turn, determines what they see as the most viable option for creating equality between women and men. Whether or not a given sex difference exists has important implications for social policy. Recently, for example, the APA provided expert witnesses for a case in the US Supreme Court in support of a woman manager's charge of sex discrimination against her corporation (Fiske *et al.* 1991). The APA and the social psychologists who served as experts assumed that the sexes do not differ in any meaningful way. They might have taken a different position if they believed that women managers performed less well than comparable men.

Has the level of discrimination against women decreased?

While it is clear that obvious forms of discrimination against women have declined, more subtle forms of discrimination can still be documented (Caplan 1993). Forms of sexism that went unexamined in the 1970s have also been noticed. Feminist researchers, for example, have documented a high incidence of acquaintance rape as well as other forms of violence against women (Koss 1990). These studies often focus on women's stories of their experiences and its aftermath.

On the other hand, social psychologists sometimes cite studies indicating a reduction of discrimination against women (cf. Aries 1996). Who is correct? This answer may be found in methodological differences between the two groups of researchers which influence interpretations of their results. Social psychologists, for example, often use standardized and objective questionnaires that may minimize the level of societal sexism found. But women do not always name forced sexual contact as rape. Changing norms about what is acceptable coercion may have contributed to the perception that the rate of sexual assault has increased in recent years.

Alternatively, social psychologists may exaggerate perceptions of women's agency and efficacy because their usual subjects – white, middle-class college students – are largely unaware of the various forms of oppression in society and appear to be functioning well. Since social psychologists rarely use qualitative or phenomenological methodology, their research is unlikely to delve into the private or unconscious aspects of women's lives. Thus, social psychological studies may minimize both the extent and the personal costs of sexism.

Where does power reside?

The link between gender and power presents a double bind for feminists. To assume, for example, that direct and coercive forms of power are almost exclusively the property of males denies women both their agency and their complicity in maintaining unequal power relationships between groups. A view of gender that neglects the individual as an agent of change risks classifying women as passive victims. But ignoring evidence of the overwhelming nature of gender, race and class oppression can lead to unrealistic expectations about the power of individual women to achieve.

Researchers are presented with this kind of dilemma whenever they focus too exclusively on either personal or structural power. Yoder and Kahn phrased this dilemma very well in their introduction to their special issue on gender and power:

> It seems myopic to discuss individual empowerment when the root of much gender-based oppression is societal. Similarly, it seems overwhelming to concentrate exclusively on societal oppressions when the building blocks of social change are committed individuals.
>
> (Yoder and Kahn 1992: 385–386)

The relationship between group identity and personal responsibility is a key area of controversy among feminists today as well as among others committed to social change. This relationship may be particularly problematic for individuals who have been personally successful in our society while the group with which they identify remains culturally marginalized and financially impoverished (cf. LaFromboise *et al.* 1995; McCombs 1986).

FUTURE QUESTIONS

Can a psychology of women continue to exist?

Feminism has been heavily influenced by postmodernist theory which proposes that neither a stable self nor collective identity exist, but are continually constructed as a function of social forces. This theory would seem to say that there is no such thing as stable personality or individuality. If this view is correct, psychologists cannot generalize – either about any one woman or about groups of women. We are left with the individual's life experiences and the meaning she extracts from them. But these meanings, too, are transient. They are subject to constant reconstruction by the individual as her circumstances change.

Postmodernist theory is also problematic in terms of social activism. Just as there is no evidence to support the idea that personal insight produces personal change, there is no evidence that cultural knowledge empowers the drive for social change. Postmodernism also rejects the idea of reality in favour of an array of equivalent culturally distinct voices. This theoretical framework can induce paralysis in the feminist empiricist (Unger 1996).

Can the psychology of women transcend current feminist theory? I wish I could end with this question rather than try to resolve it – even partially. I think its resolution lies in the recognition that we must explore gender at a societal as well as at an interpersonal or intrapsychic level. Women (and men) must be viewed in terms of a collective identity similar to Brinton Lykes' (1985) concept of '*social individuality*'. In her concept, there is no separation between self, other selves and society. They constitute each other in an inextricable whole. Although not stated explicitly, this was an ideal of second-wave feminism. The '*personal was political*' in the sense that what happened to each woman happened to all women and that change would empower all. But researchers have had to broaden their perspective because they now recognize that all women are not alike and that sex is not always the most important definitional label.

One solution is to look at how manifestations of gender at the societal level affect individuals from different groups. Michelle Fine and her colleagues at the University of Pennsylvania Law School, for example, have examined what happens to women and people of colour as a result of exposure to the high-status institutions of a competitive, individualistic society (Fine and Addelston 1996; Guinier *et al.*, in press). They found that women enter elite law schools with equivalent qualifications to men, but with a greater interest in social welfare than their male peers. They found that both white women and people of colour described themselves as alienated during their first year of law school. By the second year, complaints about harassment and the dehumanizing environment had disappeared. So, too, had the women's interest in working for social justice. They had become more like the men, but at a cost. Despite equal credentials, these women did not perform as well as men during their law school years.

Fine and Addelston argue that sexist and racist institutional policies create and enable a sense of entitlement in the white men for whom they are designed. Women and people of colour who are 'let into' elite institutions 'pay' for their partial sense of entitlement by abandoning their group identities and their concern for social change. The price of becoming 'honorary men' appears to be a loss of a sense of agency as well as problems with emotional health.

How can we usefully multiply our categories?

Feminist psychology has become more complex as increasing numbers of women (and men) from previously marginalized groups have begun to enter the field. They have continued to expand psychology's epistemology. Their input has helped feminist psychology to go beyond models that simply add sex and gender to existing psychological studies. It is this indirect effect of newer groups' experiences and epistemology that will influence the field as we enter the second millennium. They will influence us both to multiply categories and to acknowledge contradiction.

Categorization processes affect everyone – not just members of marginalized groups. Although every individual belongs to at least one sexual, racial and social class category simultaneously, such categories do not have an equal cultural meaning. While individuals of one group are disadvantaged by a social label, others are privileged by not being subject to that label. And it is society rather than the individual that decides whether or not a particular label will be imposed. This aspect of the categorization process tends to be ignored by social psychologists who work only within a laboratory context.

Psychologists must begin to distinguish between social labels and situated identities. This is good mental health practice as well as good research practice. Thus psychologists can assist individuals who suffer stress from conflicting views of the self by helping them to view identities as situated rather than essential parts of themselves. From this viewpoint, individuals are free to choose which aspect of themselves is most salient at the time without feeling that they have to abandon other aspects of their identity. This insight may be helpful to women of colour who are frequently put in the difficult position of either reacting to the racism of white society or reacting to the sexism of white society and the men of their own group. They often feel that they must choose which form of oppression is more meaningful to them.

Can we learn to acknowledge contradictions?

Definitions of normal and healthy behaviour will be expanded as psychologists recognize that a number of different definitions may be equally valid under some circumstances. The labels applied to an individual or his or her group are sometimes contradictory. Marginalized populations appear to be more susceptible to double binds than other groups. Double binds are situations in which the individual is confronted with two contradictory definitions of appropriate behaviour. The individual may not be aware of these culturally based definitions and, in any case, has little power to change them without some form of collective action.

Some white women and men and women of colour have little power to define themselves or to challenge contradictions in others' definitions. They may, moreover, be subject to competing definitions both from the dominant society and the ideology of their own ethnic group. Assertiveness, for example, may be particularly problematic for women from groups that value feminine modesty and/or submissiveness even more than the dominant culture does. For them, assertiveness may be perceived not only as unfeminine, but also as an abandonment of traditional cultural values (Unger 1995).

Integrating other forms of identity such as race/ethnicity into gender studies will not be easy (cf. Landrine 1995). There is little history to draw upon here. First of all, we will have to study many more groups of women. But the real challenge to the field in the year 2000 and beyond will be how to decide when and why any particular group of women (or men) is relevant for answering a particular research question. Of course, these decisions will also influence which within-sex or between-sex comparisons are seen as valid.

Such questions involve the use of political and moral as well as scientific criteria (Unger 1995). They also require innovative theories and methods. Psychology may have to recognize that some dilemmas are not absolutely resolvable and that 'solutions' need to be constantly redefined. This is not the Achilles heel of psychology – it is our virtue. Certainty is possible only in a homogeneous and unchanging world.

REFERENCES

Apfelbaum, E. (1979) 'Relations of dominance and movements for liberation: an analysis of power between groups', in W.G. Austin and S. Worchel (eds) *The Social Psychology of Intergroup Relations* (pp. 188–204), Monterey: Brooks/Cole).
—— (1993) 'Norwegian and French women in high leadership positions: the importance of cultural contexts upon gendered relations', *Psychology of Women Quarterly* 17: 409–429.
Aries, E. (1996) *Men and Women in Interaction: Reconsidering the Differences*, New York: Oxford University Press.
Bohan, J.S. (1993) 'Regarding gender: essentialism, constructionism, and feminist psychology', *Psychology of Women Quarterly* 17: 5–21.

Broverman, I.K., Broverman, D.M., Clarkson, F.E., Rosenkrantz, P.S. and Vogel, S.R. (1970) 'Sex-role stereotypes and clinical judgments of mental health', *Journal of Consulting and Clinical Psychology* 34: 1–7.

Caplan, P.J. (1993) *Lifting a Ton of Feathers*, Toronto: University of Toronto Press.

Carli, L.L. (1990) 'Gender, language, and influence', *Journal of Personality and Social Psychology* 59: 941–951.

Cartwright, D. (1959) 'Power: a neglected variable in social psychology', in D. Cartwright (ed.) *Studies in Social Psychology* (pp. 1–14), Ann Arbor, MI: University of Michigan Press.

Crawford, A. (1995) *Talking Difference: On Gender and Language*, London: Sage.

Crosby, F. (1982) *Relative Deprivation and Working Women*, New York: Oxford University Press.

—— (1984) 'The denial of personal discrimination', *American Behavioral Scientist* 27: 371–386.

Datan, N. (1986) 'Corpses, lepers, and menstruating women: tradition, transition, and the sociology of knowledge', *Sex Roles* 14: 693–703.

Deaux, K. and LaFrance, M. (in press) 'Gender', in D. Gilbert, S. Fiske and G. Lindzey (eds) *The Handbook of Social Psychology*, 4th edn.

Deaux, K. and Lewis, L. L. (1984) 'The structure of gender stereotypes: interrelationships among components and gender labels', *Journal of Personality and Social Psychology* 46: 991–1004.

Dion, K.L. (1975) 'Women's reaction to discrimination from members of the same or opposite sex', *Journal of Research in Personality* 9: 292–306.

—— (1985) 'Sex, gender, and groups', in V.E. O'Leary, R.K. Unger and B.S. Wallston (eds) *Women, Gender, and Social Psychology*, Hillsdale, NJ: Erlbaum.

Dion, K.L., Earn, B.M. and Yee, P.H.N. (1978) 'The experience of being a victim of prejudice: an experimental approach', *International Journal of Psychology* 13: 197–214.

Eagly, A.H. (1995) 'The science and politics of comparing women and men', *American Psychologist* 50: 145–158.

Fidell, L.S. (1970) 'Verification of sex discrimination in hiring practices in psychology', *American Psychologist* 25: 1094–1098.

Fine, M. (1983–1984) 'Coping with rape: critical perspectives on consciousness', *Imagination, Cognition, and Personality* 3: 249–267.

—— (1985) 'Reflections on a feminist psychology of women', *Psychology of Women Quarterly* 9: 167–183.

Fine, M. and Addelston, J. (1996) 'Questions of gender and power: the discursive limits of sameness and difference', in S. Wilkinson (ed.) *Feminist Social Psychologies; Contemporary International Perspectives*, Milton Keynes: Open University Press.

Fine, M. and Zane, N. (1988) 'Bein' wrapped too tight: when low income women drop out of high school', in L. Weis (ed.) *Dropouts in Schools: Issues, Dilemmas, Solutions*, Albany: SUNY Press.

Fine, M., Powell, L., Weis, L. and Wong, M. (1997) *Off White: Essays on Race, Culture and Society*, New York: Routledge.

Fiske, S.T., Bersoff, D.N., Borgida, E., Deaux, K. and Heilman, M.E. (1991) 'Social science research on trial: use of sex stereotyping research in Price Waterhouse v. Hopkins', *American Psychologist* 46: 1049–1060.

Fordham, S. (1993) 'Those loud black girls: (black) women, silence, and gender "passing" in the academy', *Anthropology and Education Quarterly* 24: 3–32.

Frankenberg, R. (1993), *White Women, Race Matters: The Social Construction of Whiteness*, Minneapolis: University of Minnesota Press.

French, J.R.P. and Raven, B. (1959) 'The bases of social power', in D. Cartwright (ed.) *Studies in Social Psychology* (pp. 150–167), Ann Arbor, MI: University of Michigan Press.

Geis, F.L. (1993) 'Self-fulfilling prophecies: a social psychological view of gender', in A.E. Beall and R.J. Sternberg (eds) *The Psychology of Gender* (pp. 9–54), New York: Guilford Press.

Goldberg, P.A. (1968) 'Are women prejudiced against women?', *Transaction* 2: 28–30.

—— (1974) 'Prejudice toward women: some personality correlates', *International Journal of Group Tensions* 4: 53–63.

Goldberg, P.A., Gottesdiener, M. and Abramson, P.R. (1975) 'Another put-down of women? Perceived attractiveness as a function of support for the feminist movement', *Journal of Personality and Social Psychology* 32: 113–115.

Griscom, J.L. (1992) 'Women and power: definition, dualism, and difference', *Psychology of Women Quarterly* 16: 389–414.

Guinier, L., Fine, M. and Balin, J. (in press) *Becoming Gentlemen: The Education of Women at the University of Pennsylvania Law School*, Boston: Beacon Press.

Hagen, R.I. and Kahn, A.S. (1975) 'Discrimination against competent women', *Journal of Applied Social Psychology* 5: 362–376.

Hall, J.A. (1985) *Nonverbal Sex Differences: Communication Accuracy and Expressive Style*, Baltimore: Johns Hopkins University Press.

Hare-Mustin, R.T. and Marecek, J. (eds) (1990) *Making a Difference: Psychology and the Construction of Gender*, New Haven, CT: Yale University Press.

Hatfield, E. and Sprecher, S. (1986) *Mirror, Mirror: The Importance of Looks in Everyday Life*, Albany, NY: State University of New York Press.

Henley, N.M. (1973) 'Status and sex: some touching observations', *Bulletin of the Psychonomic Society* 3: 91–93.

hooks, b. (1984) *Feminist Theory: From Margin to Center*, Boston, MA: South End.

Hyde, J.S. (1994) 'Can meta-analysis make feminist transformations in psychology?', *Psychology of Women Quarterly* 18: 451–462.

Johnson, P. (1976) 'Women and power: toward a theory of effectiveness', *Journal of Social Issues* 32: 99–110.

Kahn, A.S. and Yoder, J.D. (1989) 'The psychology of women and conservatism: rediscovering social change', *Psychology of Women Quarterly* 13: 417–432.

—— (eds) (1992) 'Women and power', *Psychology of Women Quarterly* 16: 4 (whole).

Kitzinger, C. (1991) 'Feminism, psychology, and the paradox of power', *Feminism and Psychology* 1: 111–129.

Koss, M.P. (1990) 'The women's mental health research agenda: violence against women', *American Psychologist* 45: 374–380.

LaFrance, M. (1992) 'Gender and interruptions: individual infraction or violation of the social order?', *Psychology of Women Quarterly* 16: 497–512.

LaFromboise, T., Bennett, S., Running Wolf, P. and James, A. (1995) 'American Indian women and psychology', in H. Landrine (ed.) *Bringing Cultural Diversity to Feminist Psychology: Theory, Research, and Practice* (pp. 197–239), Washington, DC: American Psychological Association.

Landrine, H. (ed.) (1995) *Bringing Cultural Diversity to Feminist Psychology: Theory, Research, and Practice*, Washington, DC: American Psychological Association.

Lykes, M.B. (1985) 'Gender and individualistic vs. collectivist bases for notions about the self', *Journal of Personality* 53: 356–383.

Lykes, M.B. and Stewart, A.S. (1986) 'Evaluating the feminist challenge to research in personality and social psychology: 1963–1983', *Psychology of Women Quarterly* 10: 393–412.

Lykes, M.B., Brabeck, M.M., Ferns, T. and Radan, A. (1993) 'Human rights and mental health among Latin American women in situations of state-sponsored violence: bibliographic resources', *Psychology of Women Quarterly* 17: 525–544.

McCombs, H.G. (1986) 'The application of an individual/collective model to the psychology of black women', in D. Howard (ed.) *The Dynamics of Feminist Therapy* (pp. 67–80), New York: Haworth Press.

Mayo, C. and Henley, N.M. (eds) (1981) *Gender and Nonverbal Behavior*, New York: Springer-Verlag.

Mednick, M.T.S. (1989) 'On the politics of psychological constructs: stop the bandwagon, I want to get off', *American Psychologist* 44: 1118–1123.

Morawski, J.G. (1994) *Practicing Feminisms, Reconstructing Psychology: Notes on a Liminal Science*, Ann Arbor, MI: University of Michigan Press.

Peplau, L.A. and Conrad, E. (1989) 'Beyond nonsexist research: the perils of feminist methods in psychology', *Psychology of Women Quarterly* 13: 379–400.

Reid, P.T. (1993) 'Poor women in psychological research: shut up and shut out', *Psychology of Women Quarterly* 17: 133–150.

Ricketts, M. (1989) 'Epistemological values of feminists in psychology', *Psychology of Women Quarterly* 13: 401–415.

Riger, S. (1992) 'Epistemological debates, feminist voices: science, social values, and the study of women', *American Psychologist* 47: 730–740.

Roman, L.G. (1993) 'White is a color! White defensiveness, postmodernist, and anti-racist pedagogy', in C. McCarthy and W. Crichlow (eds) *Race Identity and Representation in Education* (pp. 71–88), New York: Routledge.

Rosenkrantz, P.S., Vogel, S.R., Bee, H., Broverman, I.K. and Broverman, D.M. (1968) 'Sex-role stereotypes and self-concepts in college students', *Journal of Consulting and Clinical Psychology* 32: 287–295.

Russell, K., Wilson, M. and Hall, R. (1992) *The Color Complex: The Politics of Skin Color among African Americans*, New York: Harcourt Brace Jovanovich.

Sadker, M. and Sadker, D. (1994) *Failing at Fairness: How America's Schools Cheat Girls*, New York: Scribner.

Samelson, F. (1978) 'From "race psychology" to "studies in prejudice": some observations on the thematic reversals in social psychology', *Journal of the History of the Behavioral Sciences* 14: 265–278.

Sampson, E.E. (1981) 'Cognitive psychology as ideology', *American Psychologist* 36: 730–743.

Sherif, C.W. (1979) 'Bias in psychology', in J.A. Sherman and E.T. Beck (eds) *The Prism of Sex: Essays in the Sociology of Knowledge* (pp. 93–133), Madison: University of Wisconsin Press.

—— (1982) 'Needed studies in the concept of gender identity', *Psychology of Women Quarterly* 6: 375–398.

Skrypnek, B.J. and Snyder, M. (1982) 'On the self-perpetuating nature of stereotypes about women and men', *Journal of Experimental Social Psychology* 18: 277–291.

Spence, J.T. and Sawin, L.L. (1985) 'Images of masculinity and femininity', in V.E. O'Leary, R.K. Unger and B.S. Wallston (eds) *Women, Gender and Social Psychology* (pp. 35–66), Hillsdale, NJ: Erlbaum.

Spence, J.T., Helmreich, R. and Stapp, J. (1975) 'Likability, sex-role congruence of interest, and competence: it all depends upon how you ask', *Journal of Applied Social Psychology* 5: 93–109.

Stewart, A.J. and Healy, J.M. Jr (1989) 'Linking individual development and social changes', *American Psychologist* 44: 30–42.

Stewart, A.J. and Ostrove, J.M. (1993) 'Social class, social change, and gender: working-class women at Radcliffe and after', *Psychology of Women Quarterly* 17: 475–497.

Torres, L. (1992) 'Women and language: from sex differences to power dynamics', in C. Kramarae and D. Spender (eds) *The Knowledge Explosion: Generations of Feminist Scholarship* (pp. 281–290), New York: Teachers College Press.

Unger, R.K. (1979a) 'Sexism in teacher evaluation: the comparability of real life and laboratory analogs', *Academic Psychology Bulletin* 1: 163–170.

—— (1979b) 'Toward a redefinition of sex and gender', *American Psychologist* 34: 1085–1094.

—— (1982) 'Advocacy versus scholarship revisited: issues in the psychology of women', *Psychology of Women Quarterly* 7: 5–17.

—— (1983) 'Through the looking glass: no Wonderland yet! (The reciprocal relationship between methodology and models of reality)', *Psychology of Women Quarterly* 8: 9–32.

—— (1984–1985) 'Explorations in feminist ideology: surprising consistencies and unexamined conflicts', *Imagination, Cognition, and Personality* 4: 395–403.

—— (1986) 'Looking toward the future by looking at the past: social activism and social history', *Journal of Social Issues* 42, 1: 215–227.

—— (1988) 'Psychological, feminist, and personal epistemology', in M.M. Gergen (ed.) *Feminist Thought and the Structure of Knowledge* (pp. 124–141), New York: New York University Press.

—— (1989) 'Sex, gender, and epistemology', in M. Crawford and M. Gentry (eds) *Gender and Thought*, New York: Springer-Verlag, (pp. 17–35).

—— (1992) 'Will the real sex difference please stand up?', *Feminism and Psychology* 2: 231–238.

—— (1993) 'The personal is paradoxical: feminists construct psychology', *Feminism and Psychology* 3: 211–218.

—— (1995) 'Cultural diversity and the future of feminist psychology', in H. Landrine (ed.) *Bringing Cultural Diversity to Feminist Psychology: Theory, Research, Practice* (pp. 413–431), Washington DC: American Psychological Association.

—— (1996) 'Using the master's tools: epistemology and empiricism', in S. Wilkinson (ed.) *Feminist Social Psychologies: International Perspectives*, Milton Keynes: Open University Press.

Unger, R.K. and Crawford, M. (1996) *Women and Gender: A Feminist Psychology* (2nd edn), New York: McGraw Hill.

Unger, R.K. and Jones, J. (1988) *Personal Epistemology and its Correlates: The Subjective Nature of Sex and Race*, Meadowlands, NJ: International Society of Political Psychology.

Unger, R.K. and Safir, M. (1990) 'Cross cultural aspects of the Attitudes about Reality Scale', paper presented at the annual meeting of the American Psychological Association, Boston, MA.

Unger, R.K., Draper, R.D. and Pendergrass, M.L. (1986) 'Personal epistemology and personal experience', *Journal of Social Issues* 42: 67–79.

Unger, R.K., Hilderbrand, M. and Madar, T. (1982) 'Physical attractiveness and assumptions about social deviance: some sex by sex comparisons', *Personality and Social Psychology Bulletin* 8: 293 -301.

Weisstein, N. (1977) '"How can a little girl like you teach a great big class of men?", the chairman said, and other adventures of a woman in science', in S. Ruddick and P. Daniels (eds) *Working it Out* (pp. 241–250), New York: Pantheon.

Yoder, J. and Kahn, A. (1992) 'Toward a feminist understanding of women and power', *Psychology of Women Quarterly* 16: 381–388.

Zebrowitz, L. (in press) *Reading Faces: Window to the Soul?* Boulder, CO: Westview Press.

3 Child development

Old themes and new directions

Sheila Greene

Developmentalists have a ready metaphor to hand to describe the history of their own discipline. Thus one might be tempted to pinpoint the date when developmental psychology was born, to view developmental psychology at the turn of the century as being in its infancy and to ask whether or not it has now, after travelling on through its childhood and youth, arrived at its maturity or whether it is still suffering from the '*sturm und drang*' of adolescence. I have resisted this temptation. Using the metaphor of steady, progressive development through predictable stages may always have been glib, but from the standpoint of the 1990s to write in this way would be to invite embarrassment. We have reached a different vantage point in terms of our general understanding of science and in particular of our understanding of the history of child psychology.

It could be argued, and indeed has been argued most persuasively by Kessen (1990), that for most of this century, developmental psychologists shared the Western conviction that the march of science and civilization was leading us onwards and upwards. As a discipline, developmental psychology may well have been more prone than other branches of psychology to this belief in progress, since it is intrinsic to the concept of development itself. In reality, some of the more hopeful recent developments are rediscoveries of insights which were lost or are variations on very old themes.

The notion of science as a linear, unified enterprise advancing towards the truth or truths which could be expressed in universal laws or quantified in theorems was challenged fundamentally by Kuhn's book, *The Structure of Scientific Revolutions* (1962), which argued that the history of science could be seen as the struggle for ascendancy between competing scientific paradigms. Kuhn was but one of many theorists who attacked fondly held nineteenth- and early twentieth-century beliefs in absolutist notions such as progress and universal truth. The cherished idols of the modern era have been subject to the sceptical analysis of those writers who have been influenced by the postmodern shift in consciousness.

Inevitably this postmodern sensibility has become evident in the work of developmental psychologists. Its influence can be detected in a number of changes in contemporary preoccupations and practice. A self-critical stance has been brought to histories of the discipline (e.g. Bronfenbrenner *et al.* 1986; Bradley 1989). There is a new willingness to unpick the previous self-congratulatory discourse, to deconstruct and reinterpret. In this process a tangled story has emerged, or rather numerous tangled stories have emerged. Just as literary history, when re-examined through a feminist lens, permits the rediscovery of buried women writers, the new histories of developmental psychology have disinterred psychologists whose place in the history of the discipline deserves reappraisal. Accordingly, the work of early writers like Baldwin and Dewey has been reread and re-evaluated (Cairns 1992; Cahan 1992). What is of particular interest now is that the work of these rediscovered writers, given its quality and undoubted resonance for psychologists of our time, was relatively neglected in its own time and certainly did not become part of the received history of the discipline. Despite the fact that this century has seen very distinctive phases in terms of the dominant perspectives on child development in Europe and North America, some underlying assumptions about the nature of development and the nature of childhood have been constant, as have underlying assumptions about the appropriate methodology for the discipline. The mood of scepticism and doubt which is emblematic of our time – though not necessarily common to all – has led in recent years to a radical re-examination of the foundational assumptions of the discipline.

WHAT IS DEVELOPMENT?

One mark of the new critical reflectiveness is the attack on 'developmentalism', which could be defined as the imposition of an unwarranted uniformity of structure and directionality on to the changes associated with the ageing process. For most of this century the notion of uni-directional and natural progression lurked at the heart of the word 'development' and at the heart of developmental psychology.

Morss (1990) traces the naturalistic assumptions behind the traditional developmental paradigm back to the romantic notions of social progress and human perfectibility which emerged in the nineteenth century. Theories about evolution proliferated at this time and the views which were taken up by influential figures like Herbert Spencer and G. Stanley Hall were in many ways pre-Darwinian. Early developmentalists were certainly more concerned with notions to do with recapitulation and evolutionary hierarchies than with natural selection. As Morss notes,

> Perhaps the most fundamental assumption concerning an overall picture of individual development is that of *progress*. Derived from, or at least legitimated by biological sources, the notion that the individual gets better and better as time passes has been central to most developmental thinking.
>
> (Morss 1990: 173)

The most obvious consequence of this commitment to ontogenetic progression can be seen in the proliferation of stage theories of development, Freud, Piaget, Erikson and Kohlberg being examples of the most well-known stage theories in relation to child development. They all see development as moving towards what Labouvie-Vief and Chandler (1978) have called an idealistic end-point, different in each case. Erikson (1965) encapsulates the biological thinking and the prescriptiveness behind these stage theories when he says, 'the healthy child, if halfway properly guided, merely obeys and on the whole can be trusted to obey inner laws of development' (p. 61).

To the extent to which psychologists adhere to an unexamined and outdated form of biological thinking, there is undoubtedly a place for the critique offered by radical critics like Morss (1990, 1996), Bradley (1989) and Burman (1994). However, they are not alone in their dissatisfaction with the conceptualizations of development which have dominated this century to date and there are definite signs of change. Some contemporary definitions of developmental psychology do not emphasize progression alone, they also emphasize regression. For example, Magnusson states 'Development of living organisms refers to progressive or regressive changes in size, shape and function during the lifetime' (Magnusson 1995: 20) and Baltes similarly refers to development as characterized by gains and losses (Baltes 1987). This shift begs the question whether the terms development or developmental are appropriate defining terms for this discipline, since their emerging usage in psychology does not correspond to any dictionary definition.

Despite the fact that adherence to a nineteenth-century form of biological thinking can be seen to have produced a developmental psychology which was unduly prescriptive and universalistic, it is essential that the study of child development comes to terms with the nature of the biological contribution to psychological development and change. In relation to child psychology it is inescapably the case that many psychological changes are prompted by, or associated with, changes brought about by the growth and maturation of the body. Flavell (1970) goes further and claims that 'it is the underlying presence of a biological growth process that lends to childhood changes their inevitability, magnitude, directionality, within-species uniformity and irreversibility' (p. 248).

No one would wish to deny the importance of physical maturation to childhood. However, what is questionable is the commitment on the part of child psychologists this century to the view that psychological change has the same characteristics and dynamic as physical change. Thus, just as the development of dentition occurs in a predictable, universal sequence in all healthy children, so, it has been assumed, does cognition, or attachment, or the self-concept, or moral reasoning. What such a perspective leaves out of account is the fact that, although many of the psychological phenomena of interest are subject to change, the nature of that change may not be identical to or even comparable with genetically prompted physiological changes. Some psychological 'developments' result from a process which can only be understood by reference to the active, constructive role of the person or the meaning-infused interactions of that person with others. Psychological phenomena are to a greater extent socially and historically contingent and many of the important changes that occur in childhood are – to contradict Flavell – not inevitable, uni-directional and uniform.

As doors were opened to awareness of the complex nature of biological influences, the central role of social and cultural influences, the active role of the person in shaping her or his own development, it became clear that human psychological change across time defies neat characterizations and that the old meaning of development has proven inadequate. The restricted developmental paradigm has operated like a strait-jacket in this century and it is time for it to be discarded.

In recent decades, the study of child development has been strongly influenced by advances in another discipline, so close as to be at times indistinguishable from it: that of life-span developmental psychology. Of course, life-span psychology can be seen to subsume child psychology but for a long time developmental psychology was confined to the study of children and adolescents. Examining psychological development from the life-span perspective casts a very different light on childhood. Much of the challenge to long-lived assumptions about development in childhood arrived with the extension of theory and research into adulthood. Thus the tendency to see childhood as a world apart psychologically has diminished and the inadequacies of reductive accounts of psychological development have become strikingly evident when they are applied to adults, to ourselves. Issues to do with continuity and discontinuity, constancy and change are highlighted by a life-span perspective in which recognition of the relative open-endedness and unpredictability of developmental processes has become unavoidable. The life-span developmental approach has helped to highlight the multiple mechanisms invoved in the process of developmental change and to indicate the way in which childhood experiences may or may not be carried forward into adulthood (Baltes 1987; Rutter 1989).

At this point in time most developmental researchers would see themselves as only just beginning to understand the causes of development. The starting point for early developmentalists was to decide on *where* to look for the explanation – the biology of the organism or the environment.

NATURE AND NURTURE

Most child development textbooks start off with a history of the struggle between the empiricists – neatly epitomized by Locke and his *tabula rasa* – and the nativists, championed by Rousseau and his 'noble savage'. The resolution of the conflict, which was seen to continue in child development with the opposing views of the behaviourists like Watson and the maturationists like Gesell, was the civilized compromise of interactionism. Anastasi's paper 'Heredity, environment and the question, "How?"' (Anastasi 1958) marked a new way forward and supposedly put an end to the question, '*How much*?' As we have seen in recent years, with publications such as *The Bell Curve*, this question has still not gone away (Hernstein and Murray 1994). In their rational moments the vast majority of child psychologists would reject extreme environmentalism and extreme hereditarian views. However, when it comes to the crunch most developmental psychologists seem to lean in one direction or the other and the old dichotomy can be seen in the emphasis on either genetic determinants or environmental/social determinants. The persistence of this split could be seen recently in the dispute that took place in the pages of *Child Development* between Scarr and Baumrind (Scarr 1992; Baumrind 1993). Baumrind took exception to Scarr's view that 'genotypes drive experiences' and argued that 'the details of socialization patterns are crucial to an understanding of normal and deviant development'. Although the vocabulary and the data are different the essentials of the old debate remain.

In relation to the origins of individual differences, the way forward might be seen in the work of those behavioural geneticists, such as Plomin, who do not diminish the role of environment but assert quite convincingly that the data which provide evidence of the strength of hereditary influence on individual development 'provide the best available evidence for the importance of environmental influence' (Plomin 1989: 105). On the other side, environmentalists find it increasingly difficult to disregard findings on the contribution of genetic factors to individual differences in ability or temperament or on the role of biological preparedness in determining the character of children's activities and experiences. Bronfenbrenner, for example, has taken the biological into fuller account in recent modifications of his ecological systems theory (Bronfenbrenner and Ceci 1994). Plomin considers that 'modern theory and research in both nature and nurture are converging on the interface between them' (Plomin 1994: 20). New concepts, such as niche-picking, active, passive and evocative genotype–environment effects and proximal processes are emerging as researchers struggle more assiduously to answer the question, '*How*?' by identifying the mechanisms involved in the interplay between genes and environment (Scarr and McCartney 1983; Bronfenbrenner and Ceci 1994).

At a species level, the importance of biologically based propensities and competencies cannot be denied, although the resurgence of interest among developmentalists in evolutionary theory as a grand explanatory framework (e.g. Belsky 1995) is surprising, given its inability to account for complex psychological phenomena and its reliance on circular reasoning.

WHAT DEVELOPS?

For most of this century, the focus of interest in relation to the psychological development of the child has been very restricted. Even the so-called 'grand theories' which have dominated child psychology in this century can be seen as focusing on an aspect of children and their psychology rather than the full picture. Thus we have 'the child as conditionable organism' of the behaviourists, 'the instinctual child' of Freud, 'the child as logical thinker' of Piaget. More recently we have the child as information processor and the social child.

There are interesting signs of attempts to break down the long-standing barriers between the realms of cognition, emotion and social development, which can be seen, for example, in recent work on social cognition (for example, work on the theory of mind and person perception) and on the social-regulatory function of emotions (for example, work on emotional self-regulation and social referencing). A consequence of the adoption of the supposed natural science method by mainstream child psychology has been the fragmentation of 'the child'. As Magnusson (1995) notes, we have concentrated on variables rather than on individuals. In recent years there has been a welcome renewal of discussion of the need for a holistic model of development and models have been offered by a number of theorists such as Magnusson himself (1995) and Bronfenbrenner (1995).

Adopting a particular perspective on what it is that develops can all too readily lead to a very narrow vision. There are undoubtedly many examples of this kind of narrowed perspective and its consequences from the early days of the discipline onwards, but I will take just one example from the study of infancy.

According to Piaget, the development of the concept of object permanence is an essential step on the road to rationality. Piaget observed that if a toy is hidden underneath a cloth in front of the infant's eyes the infant will fail to search for the toy. Others have replicated his observations. Piaget claims that the infant has not yet understood that objects are permanent and that they cannot disappear in this manner. The achievement of object permanence occurs with the development of the child's capacity to represent the world mentally, thus freeing her or him from the here and now intelligence which is the hallmark of the sensori-motor period. Although critics of Piaget abound, his interpretation of his observations and the conclusions he drew about the crucial importance of the child's arrival at an understanding of the permanence of objects have been uncontested.

In a recent article, Greenberg (1996) points out that an alternative light can be cast on the child's understanding of the existence of objects. He says, 'Piaget and his intellectual heirs have forgotten that the "permanent" object is in principle and a priori impermanent and incapable of existing forever' (p. 118). Greenberg takes, as an example of Piaget's bias, the pre-operational child's failure to understand the conservation of matter. He re-examines one of Piaget's examples to do with the children's responses to the dissolving of a sugar cube. Piaget states,

> the conservation of matter does not seem necessary to the child three to six years old in cases of changes of state or even changes of form. Sugar melting in water is believed to be returning to the void. . . . Just as the baby begins by believing that objects return to the void when they are no longer perceived

and emerge from it when they re-enter the perceptual field, so also the six year old child still thinks that a substance which dissolves completely is annihilated.

(Piaget 1954: 417–418)

As Greenberg points out, children are correct in thinking that the cube has been destroyed *qua* cube, although they have failed to understand that the matter which constituted the cube is still present in a different form.

Piaget's dismissive approach to the child's understanding of the impermanence of objects, arguably as important to their understanding of the world as an understanding of the possibility of conservation or of the relative permanence of some objects, is seen as a consequence of his emphasis on scientific, logico-mathematical thought. Rationality is thus equated with thinking of objects as permanent, invulnerable and infinite and irrationality with the failure to treat objects as though they had these properties. In fact, the infant must develop a rational understanding of the extent to which objects, including people, can be impermanent. Greenberg's article can be seen as representative of the current, deconstructive approach. It is notable that decades of criticism of Piaget have left untouched Piaget's assumptions about the nature of human rationality and its origins since these particular assumptions were cherished, one assumes, as much by his critics as by Piaget himself. Greenberg can also be seen as representative of the current interest in breaking down barriers between theoretical accounts of the child's cognitive, social and emotional experiences. His dissatisfaction with the received interpretation originated in his interest in 'that other form of reason that concerns itself with those impermanent objects of desire that are the focus of love and hate, hunger and revulsion, attachment and loss'(1996: 130).

WHO IS THE CHILD?

Putting the child back together again is not enough; we also have to recognize the richness and plurality that exists in the lives of children, the sources of their heterogeneous experiences and the resultant constraints on the production of universalistic accounts of developmental processes.

The object of knowledge for mainstream child psychologists of the twentieth century has been 'the child'. This objectification of children has been the inevitable consequence of the emulation of the natural sciences and the associated quest for universal laws. Clearly there has had to be some recognition of individual differences, but the need to describe 'the development of the child', and the underlying assumption that much of what develops represents an unfolding of natural propensities, leads to a process that has been labelled the normalization of child development (Walkerdine 1984). In the history of child development, normalization can be seen to go hand in hand with the biological view of development. The discipline has created norms against which all children's (and parents') behaviour has been judged. Normalization constrains all children since it determines people's expectations of them and their own expectations of themselves. Children who do not conform to the natural developmental path are liable to be seen as deviant. In a circular process, children from the culture, class or gender that is excluded from the definition of what is developmentally the norm are fated to be categorized as deviant, and therefore problematic.

In the latter part of this century, the Civil Rights Movement and other social changes have led to a greater awareness of the extent of exclusion and of the role of science in perpetuating a middle-class, Western and male-centred view of the universe. The picture of ideal or 'normal' development promoted by child psychologists was also permeated with these kinds of bias, although the delusion that science was a value-free enterprise kept people from a recognition of their own embeddedness in ideology.

Since, for most of this century, mainstream child psychology conceptualized the child in much the same way as a chemist conceptualizes an interesting compound, it made absolute sense for the psychologist to take the child into a laboratory for closer inspection and testing. To use Kessen's term, the child was seen as 'isolable' (Kessen 1979). Bronfenbrenner's accusation that much of mainstream developmental psychology could be summarized as 'the science of the strange behaviour of children in strange situations with strange adults for the briefest possible periods of time' (Bronfenbrenner 1979: 19) heralded a welcome awakening of concern for the ecological validity of child development research. The recognition of the problem of lack of ecological validity was part of a movement within developmental psychology to reconceptualize the nature and significance of the child's social context. This reconceptualization has had a perceptible impact on the focus of research, with an increased interest on the part of psychologists in observing children in their home, play or school settings and in understanding how they negotiate and understand their social world. With the recognition of context and a renewed appreciation of the importance of culture comes a recognition of the plurality of children's experiences and an acknowledgement of the narrow cultural focus of much of the child development work carried out this century.

The questioning of traditional assumptions underpinning norms and prescribed sequences has led to an increased recognition and understanding of the heterogeneity that exists in children's lives and experiences. It is only comparatively recently that developmental psychologists have taken on board a view of culture as intrinsic to the child's psychology and not just an add-on which could be pared away to reveal the true child underneath. Contemporary child development is thus more about children in their cultures than about the child in isolation.

A further basic dichotomy which has been played out in this century is between the view of the child as passively responding to the forces operating upon him or her versus the view of the child as an active agent in his or her own development. This is a struggle which has reached a resolution. The view of the child as active would appear now to be dominant – which is not to say that the child's behaviours and experiences are not constrained, since inevitably they are – but that children play an active role in shaping their own environments and in making sense of them.

REINSTATING MEANING

It could be argued that, in child psychology, as in other branches of psychology, a great deal has been lost by the neglect of the role of personal meaning in human life. Again, one can see evidence of a forgetting of earlier insights. For example Dewey (1899) saw psychology as centrally involved with understanding issues concerned with meaning and issues concerned with values. He said, 'Psychology, after all, simply states the mechanisms through which conscious value and meaning are introduced into human experience' (Dewey 1899: 150).

Piaget had a great interest in the child's understanding of the world but he saw that world primarily in physical terms. Vygotsky has reminded psychologists of the extent to which the child's understanding of the world, whether it be the world of objects or of people, is socially mediated. As Bruner points out in his recent book *Acts of Meaning*, 'the child does not enter the life of his or her group as a private and autistic sport of primary processes, but rather as a participant in a larger public process in which public meanings are negotiated' (1990: 13). The larger public process is culture which is permeated with meaning.

Bruner (1990) argues that 'psychology stop trying to be "meaning free" in its system of explanation. The very people and cultures that are its subject are governed by shared meanings and values' (p. 20). He is not alone in his appeal. It is somewhat reassuring to hear a similar view being expressed most forcibly by Sperry, one of the major figures in neuropsychology and a winner of the Nobel Prize, who sees a sea-change not only in psychology but in science, on the horizon. He sees a time approaching when 'The former stark, strictly physical, value-empty, and mindless cosmos previously upheld by science becomes infused with cognitive and subjective values and rich emergent macrophenomena of all kinds' (Sperry 1995: 506).

THE CHILD'S PERSPECTIVE

In line with their outdated natural science model of their relationship to their subject matter, for too long psychologists have seen as objects the people who were the focus of their observations or experiments – although in a strange inversion of meaning they have referred to them as 'subjects'. In child development, as in other areas of psychology, there is a new appreciation of the necessity to take 'the subject's' perspective into account. There are increasing numbers of studies which involve the observation and recording of meaningful chunks of children's behaviour and in which children's own, naturally occurring activities and narratives are given pride of place. There are many examples. One is Furth and Kane's recording and analysis of the spontaneous, pretend play three 4–5-year-old girls who are planning and enacting a 'royal ball' (Furth Kane 1992) and another is Dunn's account of the social interactions of young children in their home settings in which she 'observed the children within the drama and excitement of family life' (Dunn 1988: vii).

Qualitative methodologies, which had been part of the psychologist's armamentarium earlier this century, but had been all but forgotten in the misguided insistence on quantification and nothing else, have been rediscovered and elaborated. An example of the insights to be gained from the application of qualitative methods can be found in the research of Gilligan and her colleagues with adolescent girls. In *Meeting at the Crossroads*, Brown and Gilligan (1992) describe the development of a method of recording, listening to and attempting to understand girls' voices. They were concerned to find an approach which would let the girls speak to them in their own words. They call their method the 'Listener's Guide' and through it they have obtained new insights into the girls' experiences as they travel from late childhood into adolescence. It is interesting to recall that Bühler as far back as 1927 collected and analysed information from the diaries of teenage girls but that this kind of qualitative work fell into disfavour in mainstream developmental psychology for the following half century (Bühler 1927 cited by Cairns 1983).

Bruner (1990) and others have called for an approach to children's psychology which is interpretive and hermeneutic. Such an approach, which recognizes the importance of meaning in human psychology and of the need to address the existence of subjectivities and inter-subjectivities, may permit a scholarly understanding which is more consonant with the dynamic of children's lives as they are experienced and constructed. An interpretive approach does not mean the abandonment of objectivity, it simply takes account of and respects the role of meaning and subjectivity. It can complement other approaches and methodologies, it does not necessarily supplant them. To use Kagan's terminology, there is a need for both the objective and the subjective frames in developmental psychology (Kagan 1984). The discipline is impoverished if it fails to find a way for them to co-exist.

APPLYING THE SCIENCE

Despite early concerns on the part of some child psychologists about 'the perils of popularization', histories of the discipline show that the work of developmental psychologists has never stayed in the laboratory, nor was it insulated from the political concerns and ideological commitments of the time, despite its pretensions to being value-free. As Schlossman (1985) and Smuts (1985) point out, from a very early stage the pressure to apply new theories and supposedly 'pure' research was strong and some psychologists were themselves strong advocates of the view that the redemption of society lay in the proper management of children and that psychology had a major role to play in that process. Schlossman refers to the 'gospel of child development' in the United States and similarly the Newsons in the United Kingdom refer to 'the cult of child development' (Schlossman 1985: 65; Newson and Newson 1974).

Through their interventions in advising parents and teachers and policy makers, psychologists have had an impact on the upbringing, education and management of generations of children and also played their part in shaping society's notions about the nature of the child, thus playing a central role in 'the social construction of childhood'.

Child psychology has been involved in a circular process by which it is both directing and directed by the prevalent political and historical circumstances. The way in which child psychology can lend itself to prop up the *status quo*, or the status which is politically desired, is well illustrated by Riley's analysis of the role of child psychology in the glorification of motherhood in post-Second World War Britain (Riley 1983). At the end of the war, state-funded nurseries, previously needed to enable mothers to join the work-force and support the war effort, were closed overnight and mothers became isolated in their homes. Thus the jobs were left to the returning soldiers and mothers were free to concentrate on producing and raising the next well-adjusted generation who, Bowlby's early work assured them, required their constant presence and devotion.

Advice to parents, or, more often than not, to mothers, on child-rearing provides a salutary reminder of the faddishness of child psychology and the problems involved in applying developmental research. Advice to mothers from experts has had a much longer history than that of the formal discipline of child development but the early experts were also in the habit of leaning on access to specialized knowledge or 'science' for the justification of their views.

Hardyment starts her history of three centuries of advice on child care by quoting the words of a British physician:

> It is with great Pleasure I see the preservation of Children become the Care of Men of Sense. In my opinion this Business has been too long fatally left to the management of Women, who cannot be supposed to have a proper knowledge to fit them for the Task.
>
> (William Cadogan (1748) cited in Hardyment 1983: 10)

Nearly two hundred years later the view of 'Men of Sense' was still that mothers are not capable of rearing children properly and that science will provide the answers. Although Watson (1928) considered that 'the world would be considerably better off if we were to stop having children for twenty years (except for experimental purposes) and were then to start again with enough facts to do the job with some degree of skill and accuracy' (p. 16), he swallowed his principles and gave mothers the benefit of his advice and his science.

In magazine articles and in his best-selling book *Psychological Care of Infant and Child*, Watson promoted a new and scientific approach to child-rearing based on behaviourism (Watson 1928). Watson's pronouncements on child-rearing, in which parents were admonished for hugging and kissing their children and in which the main aim seemed to be to produce little self-contained automatons who bothered their parents as little as possible, seem bizarre and unacceptable from our vantage point today.

The influence of Freud, Bowlby and Piaget on child-rearing manuals can also be traced. Hardyment (1984) gives an example of the Freudian, Buxbaum, author of *Your Child Makes Sense: a Guidebook for Parents* (1951), who advised parents that 'from birth onwards children feel the pressures of urgent bodily needs and powerful instinctive urges (such as hunger, sex and aggression) which clamour for satisfaction' (p. vii).

Toilet training created particular difficulties in the household devoted to rearing children the Freudian way. According to Fraiberg (1959), the child who produces a bowel movement 'comes to regard this act in the same way that an older child regards a loved person' and to flush it down the toilet was 'a strange way to accept an offering of such value' (p. 93).

The favoured theories changed in due course. By the 1960s and 1970s the influence of Piaget is more apparent. Leach, the psychologist author of the very popular child care manual *Baby and Child* (1977), shows her Piagetian leanings when she tells her readers,

> If you provide the space, equipment and time for your child's play, she will see to the development of her thinking for herself. She is the scientist and inventor: your job is merely to provide the laboratories, the facilities and a research assistant – you – when she needs one.
>
> (Leach 1977: 351)

Twenty years later, this view of the young child as independent scientist does not chime with the current Vygotskian emphasis on socially supported learning.

In the last few decades, child developmentalists, fed on cognitive developmental and attachment theories, tell the modern mother that she should always be alert to her child's needs, ready to interact, to provide the right kind of stimulation combined with plenty of warmth and sensitivity. She is expected to be well informed and actively involved. As Urwin points out, the current emphasis on the need for quality maternal involvement has led to 'the idea that the normal mother can function as a tutor or pedagogue' (p. 184) and that children need lots of 'one-to-one attention' (p. 182) (Urwin 1985). This expectation creates a burden of obligation which, Urwin's study suggests, many mothers feel guilty about since they invariably fail to give sensitive, loving stimulation and attention at all times. It is not hard to imagine the feelings of harassed mothers as they read: 'housework can seem like pleasant play all over the house if you are prepared to take the baby with you and bounce her on the bed you are making, play peep-bo around the furniture and give her a duster to wave' (Leach 1977: 270).

A review of the numerous ways in which the findings of developmental psychology have been applied is well beyond the scope of this chapter. Some of the hailed contributions of the discipline to the welfare of children can be seen, with hindsight, to have been less than helpful. For example, the IQ test has often been used oppressively as a way of labelling and excluding rather than a way of understanding and assisting children. Binet himself opposed the view of intelligence as a fixed attribute and said, 'We must protest and react against this brutal pessimism. With practice, enthusiasm and especially with method one can succeed in increasing one's attention, memory and judgment and in becoming literally more intelligent than one was before' (Binet 1909: 126). He would probably have been horrified at what happened to his invention. There are plenty of cautionary tales but there is also considerable evidence of success.

Some developmental psychologists today argue that the need for careful analysis, well-informed advice and tried-and-tested interventions has never been greater. From different sides of the Atlantic, leading developmentalists have expressed their concerns about the circumstances in which young people are growing up. Rutter comments on 'the substantial body of literature indicating that . . . there has been a considerable rise in the level of psychosocial disturbances in young people over the last half century' (Rutter *et al.* 1995: 62). Bronfenbrenner also sounds a pessimistic note, warning of 'a progressive decline in American society of conditions that research increasingly indicates may be critical for developing and sustaining human competence throughout the life course' (Bronfenbrenner 1995: 643).

It is clearly necessary to be cautious about such pronouncements and the criteria for judging whether things are getting better or worse must be subject to the closest scrutiny. Even if there is little change, there are far too many children leading lives which are less happy and less fulfilled than they could be. As Erikson said in 1950, 'human childhood provides the most fundamental basis for human exploitation'. At best, this exploitation consists of children being used as the repository of the desires and expectations of their parents and their society. At worst, children are neglected and abused or trapped in distressing situations not of their own making. Many children are caught up in the wars and conflicts created by the adults around them and there are, sadly, few signs of change in that direction. Psychologists have a role to play in understanding and helping these children. As Scarr noted in 1979,

> Unlike some academic fields of psychology where swings away from application have been pronounced, child psychology has not strayed too far into abstraction. There have always been real children whose welfare could be served by new knowledge and new applications.
>
> (Scarr 1979: 810)

It is clear that if the psychologist is to act in the service of children he or she does so from a particular value base and that it is incumbent on us to at least make our values clear, open to challenge and revision. Sarason calls for applied psychologists to be 'advocates of social change' rather than 'willing agents of social policy' (Sarason 1981: 176). Whatever the standpoint one takes, intervening in the lives of children is a political act and should be recognized as such.

ALTERNATIVE VISIONS OF THE FUTURE

Predicting the future is always a risky occupation. If I had to make a prediction about the major theoretical thrust in the immediate future I would say that it would be in the elaboration of the social and cultural perspective on child development and in the exploration of the child's own phenomenal and subjective world. Lerner and Dixon note the beginning of this shift, commenting that 'the growing interest in contextualism during the 1970s and 1980s was associated with the recession of the other major models to the backburner of theoretical and empirical activity' (Dixon and Lerner 1992: 36). As Morss (1996) points out, the reincorporation of the social into the developmental perspective of the child takes a number of different forms, ranging from the examination of the child *plus* his or her social influences to radical social constructionism to the Marxist critical psychology of development espoused by Morss himself. Once again it must be recognized that an appreciation of the extent to which the child's psychology is socially constructed is not new. A hundred years ago, James Mark Baldwin said, 'The development of the child's personality could not go on at all without the modification of his sense of himself by suggestions from others. So he himself, at every stage, is really in part someone else, even in his own thought of himself' (Baldwin 1897: 30).

Other people's predictions will be quite different. I was interested to see in the recent textbook by the British psychologists Butterworth and Harris (1994) that, in a section called 'Developmental psychology in the twenty-first century', their first prediction is 'an ever closer link between developmental psychology and developmental biology. . . . Advances in evolutionary theory, in genetics and in the biology of the developing nervous system are beginning to give evidence that converges with the behavioural and cognitive measures typical of developmental psychology.' Their second prediction concerns closer links between developmental psychology and new theoretical models in biology such as 'selectionism' or 'neural Darwinism' (Butterworth and Harris 1994: 229). This would not be the future as I see it or, perhaps more to the point, as I would like to see it, since it places an emphasis on biological explanations to the detriment of the other sources of explanation. But these eminent British psychologists are probably correct. The future will be built on many different, sometimes compatible and sometimes incompatible visions.

In his examination of the future of developmental psychology, Kessen concludes: 'whatever style of reasoning we adopt, the evidence of past decades, from different cultures and from different groups in the United States, supports a strong case against the Grand Simplicities of theory or of method' (Kessen 1990: 29). His view applies equally to Europe. Whatever the future holds it will not be neat and simple. If it is, we can be sure that we have gone seriously awry. Our examination of the past should tell us that in human psychology the simple formulation is usually an inadequate formulation. The time of grand theories in psychology has gone, notwithstanding the claims of evolutionary psychology. Child development has had more than its share of these grand theories, and despite their importance in the history of the discipline, each has toppled in its turn. But the need for grand thinkers has not gone. It would seem from the data-driven and, at best, micro-theoretical nature of much of the research into child development – the kind of work which can be methodologically meticulous but terminally uninteresting – that large-scale theorizing is to be avoided. Thankfully, there are many developmentalists who, despite impeccable credentials as empiricists, are also interested in the big issues. I have in mind people like Bronfenbrenner, Rutter, Baltes, Kagan and Bruner.These writers synthesize and systematize and generate fresh hypotheses. To a greater or lesser extent, they are also willing to stand back and ask what it all means and whether it could be done any better. People with the capacity to act and think in this way are always going to be essential in a discipline like developmental psychology, where a self-critical stance may help to guard against answers which may not only be wrong, but also dangerous.

CONCLUSION

In this century we have explored a multiplicity of methodologies and tried out a multiplicity of theories. The history of the discipline is the history of the assembly and dismantling of theoretical frameworks. The overturning of old ways of viewing the child and the search for the best way to conceptualize his or her development continues, but the interest in examining the basic assumptions of the discipline is currently particularly intense as befits this era of scepticism and deconstruction.

As we approach the closing years of the twentieth century, there are many recent signs of an increased willingness to confront the complexities involved in understanding children's development and also of willingness to construct conceptual frameworks and methods which will enable the study of these complexities. It is to be hoped that we can use this changed consciousness and the experience accumulated over the past decades to advance to an understanding of children which does better justice to their complex, changing and multiple ways of being in and with their worlds.

REFERENCES

Anastasi, A. (1958) 'Heredity, environment and the question 'How?', *Psychological Review* 65: 197–208.

Baldwin, J.M. (1897) *Social and Ethical Interpretation in Mental Development: A Study in Social Psychology*, New York: Macmillan.

Baltes, P.B. (1987) 'Theoretical propositions of life-span developmental psychology: on the dynamics between growth and decline', *Developmental Psychology* 23: 611–626.

Baumrind, D. (1993) 'The average expectable environment is not enough: a response to Scarr', *Child Development* 64: 1299–1317.

Belsky, J. (1995) 'Expanding the ecology of human development: an evolutionary perspective', in P. Moen, G.H. Elder and K. Luscher (eds) *Examining Lives in Context: Perspectives on the Ecology of Human Development*, Washington, DC: American Psychological Association.

Binet, A. (1909) *Les Idées Modernes sur les Enfants*, Paris: Ernest Flammarion.

Bradley, B.S. (1989) *Visions of Infancy: A Critical Introduction to Child Psychology*, Cambridge: Polity Press.

Bronfenbrenner, U. (1979) *The Ecology of Human Development: Experiments by Nature and Design*, Cambridge, MA: Harvard University Press.

—— (1995) 'Developmental ecology through space and time: a future perspective', in P. Moen, G.H. Elder and K. Luscher (eds) *Examining Lives in Context: Perspectives on the Ecology of Human Development*, Washington, DC: American Psychological Association.

Bronfenbrenner, U. and Ceci, S.J. (1994) 'Nature–nurture reconceptualized in developmental perspective: a bioecological model', *Psychological Review* 101: 568–586.

Bronfenbrenner, U., Kessel, F., Kessen, W. and White, S. (1986) 'Toward a critical social history of developmental psychology: a propaedeutic discussion', *American Psychologist* 41: 1218–1230.

Brown, L.M. and Gilligan, C. (1992) *Meeting at the Crossroads: Women's Psychology and Girls' Development*, Cambridge, MA: Harvard University Press.

Bruner, J. (1990) *Acts of Meaning*, Cambridge, MA: Harvard University Press.

Bühler, C. (1927) 'Die ersten sozialen Verhaltungsweisen der Kindes', in C. Bühler, H. Hetzer and B. Tudor-Hart (eds) *Soziologische und Psychologische: Studien uber das Erste Lebensjahr*, Jena: Fischer.

Burman, E. (1994) *Deconstructing Developmental Psychology*, London: Routledge.

Butterworth, G. and Harris, P.L. (1994) *Principles of Developmental Psychology*, Hove: Lawrence Erlbaum.

Buxbaum, E. (1951) *Your Child Makes Sense: A Guidebook for Parents*, London: Allen & Unwin.

Cadogan, W. (1748) *Essay on the Nursing and Management of Children*, London: John Knapton.

Cahan, E.D. (1992) 'John Dewey and human development', *Developmental Psychology* 28: 205–214.

Cairns, R.B. (1983) 'The emergence of developmental psychology', in P.H. Mussen (ed.) *Handbook of Child Psychology. Volume 1: History, Theory and Methods*, New York: John Wiley & Sons.

—— (1992) 'The making of a developmental science: the contributions and intellectual heritage of James Mark Baldwin', *Developmental Psychology* 28: 17–24.

Dewey, J. (1899) 'Psychology and social practice', in J.A. Boydston (ed.) *The Middle Works of John Dewey*, Carbondale, IL: Southern Illinois University Press.

Dixon, R.A. and Lerner, R.M. (1992) ' History of systems in developmental psychology', in M.H. Bornstein and M.E. Lamb (eds) *Developmental Psychology: An Advanced Textbook*, Hove: Lawrence Erlbaum.

Dunn, J. (1988) *The Beginnings of Social Understanding*, Oxford: Blackwell.

Erikson, E. (1965) *Childhood and Society*, Harmondsworth: Penguin.

Flavell, J. H. (1970) 'Cognitive changes in adulthood', in L.R. Goulet and P. Baltes (eds) *Life-span Developmental Psychology: Research and Theory*, London: Academic Press.

Fraiberg, S. (1959) *The Magic Years: Understanding and Handling the Problems of Early Childhood*, New York: Scribner.

Furth, H.G. and Kane, S.R. (1992) 'Children constructing society: a new perspective on children at play', in H. McGurk (ed.) *Childhood Social Development: Contemporary Perspectives*, Hove: Lawrence Erlbaum.

Greenberg, D.E. (1996) 'The object permanence fallacy', *Human Development* 39: 117–131.

Hardyment, C. (1983) *Dream Babies: Three Centuries of Good Advice on Child Care*, New York: Harper & Row.

Hernstein, R.J. and Murray, C.M. (1994) *The Bell Curve: Intelligence, Class and Structure in American Life*, New York: Free Press.

Kagan, J. (1984) *The Nature of the Child*, New York: Basic Books.

Kessen, W. (1979) 'The American child and other cultural inventions', *American Psychologist* 34: 815–820.

—— (1990) *The Rise and Fall of Development*, Worcester, MA: Clark University Press.

Kuhn, T.S. (1962) *The Structure of Scientific Revolutions*, London: University of Chicago Press.

Labouvie-Vief, G. and Chandler, M. (1978) 'Cognitive development and life-span developmental theories: idealistic versus contextual perspectives', in P. Baltes (ed.) *Life-span Development and Behaviour. Vol. 1*, New York: Academic Press.

Leach, P. (1977) *Baby and Child*, London: Michael Joseph.

Magnusson, D. (1995) 'Individual development: a holistic integrated model', in P. Moen, G.H. Elder and K. Luscher (eds) *Examining Lives in Context: Perspectives on the Ecology of Human Development*, Washington, DC: American Psychological Association.

Morss, J.R. (1990) *The Biologising of Childhood: Developmental Psychology and the Darwinian Myth*, Hove: Lawrence Erlbaum.

—— (1996) *Growing Critical: Alternatives to Developmental Psychology*, London: Routledge.

Newson J. and Newson, E. (1974) 'Cultural aspects of childrearing in the English speaking world', in M. Richards (ed.) *The Integration of the Child into a Social World*, Cambridge: Cambridge University Press.

Piaget, J. (1954) *The Construction of Reality in the Child*, New York: Ballantine Books.

Plomin, R. (1989) 'Environment and genes: determinants of behaviour', *American Psychologist* 44: 105–111.

—— (1994) *Genes and Experience: The Interplay Between Nature and Nurture*, London: Sage.

Riley, D. (1983) *War in the Nursery: Theories of the Child and Mother*, London: Virago.

Rutter, M. (1989) 'Pathways from childhood to adult life', *Journal of Child Psychology and Psychiatry* 30: 23–51.

Rutter, M., Champion, L., Quinton, D., Maughan, B. and Pickles, A. (1995) 'Understanding individual differences in environmental-risk exposure', in P. Moen, G.H. Elder and K. Luscher (eds) *Examining Lives in Context: Perspectives on the Ecology of Human Development*, Washington, DC: APA.

Sarason, S.B. (1981) *Psychology Misdirected*, New York: The Free Press.

Scarr, S. (1979) 'Psychology and children: current research and practice', *American Psychologist* 34: 809–811.

—— (1992) 'Developmental theories for the 1990s: development and individual differences', *Child Development* 63: 631–649.

Scarr, S. and McCartney, K. (1983) 'How people make their own environments: a theory of genotype–environment effects', *Child Development* 54: 424–435.

Schlossman, S. (1985) 'Perils of popularisation: the founding of *Parents'* Magazine', in A.B. Smuts and J.W. Hagen (eds) *History and Research in Child Development*, Monographs of the Society for Research in Child Development 50: 65–77.

Sperry, R.S. (1995) 'The future of psychology', *American Psychologist* 50: 505–506.

Urwin, C. (1985) 'Constructing motherhood: the persuasion of normal development', in C. Steedman, C. Urwin and V. Walkerdine (eds) *Language, Gender and Childhood*, London: Routledge & Kegan Paul.

Walkerdine, V. (1984) 'Developmental psychology and the child-centred pedagogy', in J. Henriques, W. Hollway, C. Urwin, C. Venn and V. Walkerdine (eds) *Changing the Subject: Psychology, Social Regulation and Subjectivity*, London: Methuen.
Watson, J. B. (1928) *Psychological Care of Infant and Child*, New York: Norton.

4 The psychology of learning

Retrospect and prospect

Marc Richelle[*]

With the admittedly important exception of Pavlov – on whom we shall comment briefly in a moment – the psychology of learning has not been a product of the European scientific tradition. It has been linked in the first half of the twentieth century with the behaviourist school of thought, and therefore it has been developed mainly in the United States. Chapters on learning in European textbooks, when they occurred, reviewed material from American laboratories. Experts in the field were very few on the Continent, and usually their contribution consisted in importing some experimental or theoretical aspect(s) of the behaviourist production. Interestingly enough, they did not establish a research group that would significantly extend and perpetuate their own work. Maybe they did not succeed in – or they simply did not really want to achieve – that goal. In any event, European psychology of learning remained essentially in the hands of individuals. There has been no school to be compared with the Hullian or Skinnerian groups, and it has remained so until today. The situation is somewhat different in the UK, where a number of individuals and groups were active in the last thirty years or so, not only contributing important empirical studies, but major theoretical work (e.g. Mackintosh 1974).

Neither did the psychology of learning ever appear, in Europe, as the core of a general theory of psychology, while in its home country, the USA, major figures in the field regarded their own endeavours not so much as contributions to the study of learning but rather as the basis for a general theory of behaviour. Prominent books were entitled *Principles of Behavior, An Introduction to Behavior Theory* (Hull 1943), *The Behavior of Organisms* (Skinner 1938), and *Purposive Behavior in Animals and Men* (Tolman 1932). They were not about learning, they were about behaviour; that is, the very subject matter of psychology.

---

[*] As the editors of this book offered the authors more freedom of style than is usually given in scientific publications, I have occasionally used the pronoun *I* to signal a personal view or account of which I am aware, rather than resorting to rhetoric formulae of the type 'In the present author's view'. This is not to say that paragraphs not marked in that way are claimed by the author himself to be unquestionably objective. Whatever our efforts to reach objectivity, we all know we have been shaped by our individual intellectual history, with all its irrational ingredients.

Although conditioning, as first described and analysed by Pavlov, was eventually integrated in the empirical findings providing the material for theories of learning, Pavlov himself never defined his own work as a study of learning. He gave it a much wider scope; he viewed it as a functional study of the higher nervous system, and called himself a physiologist, not a psychologist, let alone a psychologist of learning.

This is why a young psychologist educated in Western Europe in the middle of the twentieth century did not know much about learning, and was not likely to meet among his teachers, however prestigious, any specialist in learning. This was exactly my case. It is no wonder then that, when I was offered a chance to have direct contact with USA psychology, the psychology of learning, and the generalized theories of behaviour derived from it, they would appear new and attractive to me.

The European psychological tradition had, of course, its own tenets. Some particular fields or approaches were given preference as the basis of general theories. Development was one of them, structuralism (mainly rooted in the study of perception) was another, respectively illustrated by Piagetian constructivism and by the Gestalt school. We shall return to some aspects of the European tradition when we venture into some (wishful) prospects for the future.

FIFTY YEARS OF PROGRESS IN THE FIELD OF LEARNING

Compared with what it was fifty years ago, the field of learning, as many other fields of psychology, has been exploding in many directions. It has lost, however, its prominent position as the basis for general psychological theory, leaving the place to other more favoured areas or conceptual frames, such as information processing.

Let us try to capture the main breakthroughs which have shaped the psychology of learning from the end of the Second World War up to the present. I shall do so with my own European background, and my own intellectual history, including the critical encounter with the psychology of learning in the mid-1950s. I do not claim to provide an objective picture, but there is, after all, no such thing as an objective picture in these matters.

Five major lines of progress must be pinpointed, in my view. The first is the expansion of operant conditioning; the second is the successful exploration of the neurobiology of learning processes; the third is the integration in learning theory of variables emphasized by ethology; the fourth is the development of the cognitive theory of associative learning, and the fifth is the elaboration of mathematical formalization. Each of these five lines deserves a few words of comment.

Operant conditioning

Although some new schools of thought have belittled Skinner's contributions, and have occasionally built their own success upon the alleged ruins of radical behaviourism, I still think that operant conditioning, both as a laboratory method and as a conceptual tool for a theory of adaptive behaviour, has been a major breakthrough. Its real significance has been widely overlooked or has been overshadowed by opponent theoretical positions. I am pretty confident that history will put these things right again, and that 'natural selection' in scientific hypotheses will eventually retain a number of features of operant analysis currently discarded. In truth, operant conditioning appeared earlier than the mid-twentieth century, but it was only in the 1950s that it was propagated and elaborated to become the laboratory procedure we know today and to serve as the core of a general theory of behaviour, which has since fallen into disgrace.

Let me point to some of the characteristics of operant conditioning as a method, which were quite novel in their context. Ingenious laboratory technology, soon to be tremendously improved by computer on-line controls, provided for an unprecedented degree of automatized control, offering in its turn new possibilities for long-term longitudinal studies on individual subjects. This constituted a dramatic change, and radical progress, compared with the group approach in maze studies and the resulting illusion of the mean. It opened the door to an experimental approach to individuals in applied settings, such as the teaching and therapeutic environments. Operant techniques were also put to work to deal with problems heretofore inaccessible or accessible only in humans: for example, animal psychophysics. Such techniques are now widely used in most advanced researches in behavioural pharmacology, in perceptual neurobiology, in the study of animal cognition, to mention only a few of their numerous applications, and they have their place in the empirical work that founds the information processing/cognitivist learning theories.

If we agree that techniques are no less important than theoretical intuitions in the making of a science, that both bring each other reciprocal support, we shall recognize that operant conditioning was, indeed, a significant step in the empirical study of learning, or more generally of behaviour.

We shall probably not reach the same sort of agreement as to the value of operant conditioning as a conceptual tool towards a general theory – be it of learning or of behaviour. This is because cognitive theories have relegated to the back of the stage the role of reinforcement, which is central in the notion of selection-by-consequences derived from the operant model. Maybe when the polemical tone of the debate has calmed down, the relevance of Skinner's theory will be recognized in the framework of contemporary theories sharing an evolutionary model.

Neurobiology of learning

By the middle of the twentieth century, psychologists did not have to argue much to make legitimate the independence of their science with respect to physiology: it sufficed to point to those important domains in which behavioural enquiry was far more advanced than its neurophysiological counterpart. Learning was one of those fields, rich in data from the psychological laboratory, while neurophysiological studies were rather disappointing. Lashley's quest for the engram was the prototype of the inconclusive character of the most patient and expert research of brain mechanisms involved in learning. From Pavlov to Hebb, general hypotheses had been formulated, but with few empirical findings to support them. Notwithstanding, they have turned out to be seminal for work carried out in the second part of the twentieth century. For example, the old view that learning involves a consolidation of previously existing connections, rephrased by Hebb in 1949, has known an impressive revival with connectionist networks.

These so-called neuromimetic models are only one aspect of the progress made in the last forty years or so, using all the resources of modern neurobiology, at the neurophysiological, neurochemical, neuropharmacological levels, using increasingly refined methods of lesions, stimulation, self-stimulation, systemic or localized drug administration, and more recently cerebral imagery. From the decoding of neural mechanisms of habituation and conditioning in invertebrate simple models, such as *Aplysia*, to identification of structures and pathways involved in instrumental conditioning or in the learning of highly specific behaviour such as birds' song, the neurobiology of learning today is much more than an attempt to describe the neural correlates of learning, in a sort of parallel search matched to the behavioural analysis. It provides crucial information to check hypotheses drawn from purely psychological studies, and it is, in that sense, part of an integrated research strategy which hopefully will become the rule in the future.

For obvious methodological and ethical reasons, studies in the neurobiology of learning are carried out mainly with animal subjects. Let us note finally that they traditionally merge the concepts of learning and memory, a 'detail' to be retained for later discussion.

Integrating comparative psychology

One of the most significant events in the field of learning has been the encounter with ethology. It was originally somewhat conflictual, as exemplified by Lorenz (1965), but it eventually led learning psychologists to recognize the species-specific constraints on learning, and ethologists to accept the importance of learning mechanisms in a general account of behaviour, whatever the species being considered (the change in Lorenz's thinking in this respect can be measured by comparing his view in the above mentioned book and later works such as Lorenz 1981; for an example of the integration between both fields, see Staddon 1983).

This encounter made psychologists aware of the limitations of their approach to learning, using a few selected species and selected laboratory situations. They had to admit that taking into account all the varieties of behaviour exhibited in natural environments (most of which are hardly amenable to laboratory investigation) results in a far more complex picture than the one they had until then. They had to enlarge their view of learned behaviour to put it in the broader frame of the mechanisms set during biological evolution which make for the tuning between species and the ecological niche in which they evolved and now live. This made them more modest in their ambition to build general psychological theories on the basis of learning processes, as they had not hesitated to do in the past.

Cognitive theories of associative learning

The cognitive approach to learning processes has contributed in an important way to theory and to correlative empirical studies in the last thirty years. It had been prepared by interpretations proposed earlier for some findings in maze learning, especially by Tolman's analysis of latent learning in terms of cognitive maps. It shifted emphasis from response-centred theory to event-processing models. These apply mainly to Pavlovian situations and to spatial learning problems, but extensions to instrumental/operant learning have been attempted.

This is not the place to debate whether this is *the* paradigm for learning, as Dickson implicitly claimed (Dickson 1980). If it offers a dominant paradigm, it has not gained consensus: it has a number of more or less divergent variants. It does not really account for the tremendous complexity of learned behaviour. Emphasis on event processing leaves out the problem of action: organisms presumably do not process information for its own sake, but as part of their activities. Resorting to the concept of representations can be useful at some points, but it brings with it all the semantic difficulties of one of the most elusive concepts of contemporary psychology. And so on.

In spite of these and other restrictions, cognitive theories (the plural is more appropriate) of learning represent a major step in the field. They have enriched the body of empirical data, whatever the place they will be given in future theorizing, and they have refined the level of analysis and interpretation. If cleared of the theoretical assertiveness often associated with them, they appear to complement rather than replace alternative views. Their use of a common language and their sharing of a common frame of reference with other subfields of cognitive psychology has undoubtedly favoured integration.

Mathematical formalization

Mathematical formalization is taken as a sign of maturity of a science. Sometimes, in fields of knowledge still far from maturity, it so occurs that attempts at 'pseudo-formalization' are made to gain scientific dignity. Psychologists in the field of learning have occasionally indulged in such exercises. Hull is the most famous case. His equations were not really helpful heuristically, because they could not be implemented in empirical work, could not be checked with facts, nor lead to revised hypotheses after being matched to data. The field of learning was in that respect far behind other fields of experimental psychology, such as psychophysics.

The scene has now changed. Mathematical models have invaded some parts of the field, providing for the expected fruitful interaction between models and data. The major example is of course *the matching law*. Its various versions have provided not only powerful tools in data analysis but openings to more general theoretical concepts of adaptive behaviour and to interdisciplinary confrontation with other fields where similar models are used, such as ethology and econometrics. It is not the least by-product of these highly abstract models that they shed light on issues such as choice and self-control, issues which had not been viewed as especially amenable to formal approaches.

NEGLECTED ISSUES

The progress summarized above has not achieved all that one might have expected. We shall now turn to some neglected issues, questions and approaches which, for some reason, did not receive the attention they deserved, and which, hopefully, they will be given in the future.

Integration with related fields of psychology

For observers from outside, the compartmentalization of knowledge in modern psychology must appear as a surprising feature. I always shared the same feeling. Is it not astonishing that the psychology of learning has developed along its own tracks, with little interest in integration with other fields, such as intelligence or developmental psychology?

I shall emphasize the latter, because it is probably the most striking case of reciprocal neglect, and the one that has had the most damaging consequences in the applications of modern psychology, especially in the field of education. Further, because the developmental approach has been so central in the European psychological tradition, and because I was trained myself in one of the most famous schools in this very respect. The Geneva School, since it was founded, took a developmental orientation; but a number of other places or schools of thought in Europe had or would soon have their own brand of developmentalism: Paris with Henri Wallon, Vienna with Bühler, ethology with Lorenz, not to speak of the earlier Freudian constructs. Common to these otherwise highly diverse approaches is the concept of development as an explanatory device, not as a mere descriptive tool. Contrary to Skinner's view, Piaget's endeavour was not just using age as another independent variable. It was providing an ontogenetic account of how behaviour and thought are constructed. The same applies to other great developmentalist theories.

Given that an organism's growth – especially a human organism – is the period of life in which so many things are learned, one would expect that those who are interested in development would spontaneously look at contributions of specialists in learning processes, and try to integrate those processes in a general account. One would no less obviously expect that psychologists working on learning would show some curiosity in development. There are amazingly few developmental studies on animal learning, and learning psychologists, when they have been working on children, typically focus on the demonstration of the learning processes in young organisms rather than on the analysis of interactions between genuinely developmental variables and learning. Until today, to my knowledge, no one has seriously attempted to build a synthetic theory of development *and* learning, based on cross-fertilization of both fields. In practice, this results in the perpetuation of the fragmented presentation of these two major chapters of psychology to those who engage in educational professions: in most cases they are offered some developmental piece, let us say Piaget, and some learning dish, maybe Skinner, and they are left with the challenge of reconciling these separate models by themselves.

The same dissociation can also easily be described between learning and intelligence, which, when it has not been approached developmentally, has been studied in a structural perspective, with no attention to the general adaptive value of learning processes, from the elementary levels upward. Most learning psychologists, on their side, have disregarded the continuities from basic learning mechanisms to problem solving and thought. That state of affairs has had the same consequences in the teaching of educational psychology. Hopefully, the twenty-first century will see the merging of these three areas of psychology in one integrated synthesis.

Integration between subfields of learning

Perhaps we should not be over-optimistic if we consider how difficult it is to reach integration within the field of learning itself. Astonishingly enough, learning psychology, in the traditional sense, is still kept separate from the neighbouring field of memory, and vice versa, while both fields would appear to any sound mind to deal with the same subject matter, simply attacked from different angles. Most textbooks present the relevant material in different chapters, accepting without comment the completely different theoretical frameworks and making no attempt to recognize, let alone solve, the paradox (admittedly, there are, fortunately, exceptions: see among others Catania 1992). In fact, the merging of both has been realized almost exclusively by psychobiologists, as noted above. Besides that, there has been little effort to build a common language or to cross-refer equivalent phenomena from one field to the other (a case in point is contextual and state-dependent learning, thoroughly documented both in animal conditioning studies and in human memory). That separation can be explained by the distinct historical origins (memory studies grew from Ebbinghaus's pioneering work, while learning was the privileged territory of behaviourists), the distinct experimental procedures used, and the target species: memory is mostly studied in humans, learning in animals. The latter difference has contributed to further increase separation in the last decades because of the disrepute into which animal studies have fallen in modern cognitive psychology; it has been shown that most textbooks fail to mention animal studies as the source of a number of statements, especially in the field of learning and memory (see Domjan and Purdy 1995).

Another area of learning in the broad sense that has developed in isolation relative to the psychology of learning is the study of acquired motor skills. It has remained the territory of specialists of complex movements, mostly in humans, such as writing, or refined motor activities in sport. Again, a satisfying general theory of learning should encompass those processes as well. Why there has been no *rapprochement* is, once again, a matter of historical tradition, and of differences in emphasis which did not make for cross-fertilization. (Interestingly enough, the chapter on 'Human movement control' in *Stevens' Handbook of Experimental Psychology* is under the heading *Cognition*, not *Learning*, between a chapter on psycholinguistics and a chapter on 'Representation in memory' (Pew and Rosenbaum 1988).)

The study of memory has been mainly carried out using verbal or perceptual material, which have made it especially open to an information-processing approach. The study of learning on the other hand has focused on motor responses. Two experimental strategies have been favoured by experimenters in the last decades. One is inherited from maze studies popular in the neobehaviourist period; it addresses complex locomotor responses involved in orientation in space; it has taken over the cognitive map metaphor and explored both the cognitive representational and the neurophysiological aspects; it turns out to be one of those well-defined areas of research in which cognitivist concepts have been shown to be especially fruitful and where an integrated psychobiological approach has been worked out (see O'Keefe and Nadel 1978). The other strategy is operant conditioning, with its exceptional efficiency in dealing with a number of new and old issues. However, the choice of rate of responses as the main measure of behaviour has resulted in almost complete neglect of structured motor responses (of what Skinner called the *topography* of responses). The limitations of such a one-sided approach have been discussed with reference to ethology, which gives priority to motor patterns, but it has not been discussed with reference to the study of motor skills. The latter field has largely built upon another concept, i.e. *motor programme*, drawn – as the cognitive map – from the insightful theorizing of another behaviourist widely recognized as a precursor of cognitivism, Karl Lashley.

Research on motor skills is an especially significant example of a cognitivist approach integrating the neurophysiological aspects of its subject matter, and in addition, preserving the importance of action as the *raison d'être* of information processing, an obvious point which, to my view, has been overlooked in some extreme forms of cognitivism.

Differential approach to learning

Since its beginnings, scientific psychology has been in search of human nature and general laws, and in that quest it has discarded inter- and intra-individual differences as obstacles to be neutralized if they could not be eliminated. The ideal prescribed by Quételet (1835) in his famous *Essay on Social Physics* has been the psychologists' credo. Variations were treated as deviations (a word loaded with theoretical connotations) from the mean or whatever central value was supposed to capture universals of human nature. They were not to be accounted for, and still less were they thought to have any function in human nature, or any explanatory value. As a subject of scientific enquiry they were relegated to the domain of applied psychology, where admittedly they had to be taken into account for all practical purposes, when pupils had to be advised which curriculum they should engage in, employees had to be selected, or patients were to receive psychological help. But they did not have their place in a general psychological theory.

The psychology of learning shared the common stand and disregarded variations as irrelevant to learning theories. Insofar as this view was – and still is – tightly linked with methodological habits or necessities, it was strengthened by the wide use of group designs in experimental work. Classical maze studies, as well as recent investigations on event processing, comply with the tradition.

However, there had been some hints from prominent scientists in the field to look at differences and variations. Pavlov was not much concerned with group studies; he studied individual dogs, certainly with the aim of drawing general laws from his experiments, but also with attention to inter-individual differences, which led him to develop a typology (a very partial solution to the problem of differences, but evidence that at least the problem has been identified). More important was Skinner's decisive rupture with group studies in the behaviourist laboratories, to focus on individual behaviour analysed over long periods of time. Skinner stigmatized the illusory learning curves drawn from groups of rats in mazes, and suggested turning to refined observation of what happens in individual organisms. The technique of operant conditioning was precisely appropriate to that aim. It allowed a description of both inter-individual and intra-individual variations, and opened the way to accounting for them in a general theory of learning, and eventually to endow them with a completely different status compared with the traditional treatment they were given. Skinner himself devoted most of his theoretical works in the last twenty-five years of his career to elaborate his selectionist theory, applying a key concept of evolutionary biology; that is, the selective action of the environment over the variations of the living matter, to individual behaviour and to culture.

Surprisingly enough, in spite of Skinner's obvious central concern with variation as an essential element of his theory, neither he nor the majority of specialists of operant techniques undertook experimental work to study behavioural variations. Explanations for that state of affairs plausibly include the attraction of more direct outcomes of highly automatized technology put to work in the study of schedules of reinforcement and steady states, with an emphasis on stability. Experimenters in the Skinnerian tradition seem to have shared the common belief and missed the importance of variations looked at in their own right. They stuck to the 'demonstration of stability' rather than turn to the 'exploration of variability', after the formula forged by Gigerenzer *et al.* (1989). Exceptions have been few, in spite of the fact that available experimental procedures and data-processing methods now provide rigorous control for testing hypotheses on the nature, sources and functions of variability.

The systematic study of variations in the learning process would not only fulfil the requirement for giving empirical foundation to what appears to me to be the more important part of Skinner's theory; it would establish bridges between learning theory and important trends in other sciences on the one hand, and within psychology on the other (Richelle 1991, 1995).

The selectionist model has gained renewed interest in the recent past, especially in neurobiology, with Edelman's *neural Darwinism* and Changeux's *generalized Darwinism* (Edelman 1987; Changeux 1983; Changeux and Dehaene 1989). Both propose that the same process is at work at the phylogenic level to account for the emergence of new forms in the living world and at the ontogenic level to account for neural development and, quite importantly, both provide empirical evidence to support their view. Both neuroscientists unhesitatingly suggest extending the model to the psychological level. This strengthens the hypothesis, as formulated by Skinner, that a similar mechanism might be at work in individual learning, and would encourage the search for empirical evidence at the behavioural level also. It is worth noting that earlier uses of the selectionist model in other fields, such as Popper's use in the history of science (Popper 1972), find new support in the current context.

Looking at the learning individual organism as a *generator of diversity*, producing the material upon which the selective process will operate, is also conducive to bridging the gap between learning processes and higher adaptive behaviour as studied under the label of problem solving or creativity. Intra-individual variations are no longer seen as deviations from the central value providing an estimate of the subject's constancy or stability through time (the mirror image of the reliability of tests or whatever measuring instrument is used). They are expressions of a basic property of the subject, which is the very condition for the building of larger repertoires. They are not simple accidents in performance, but the very core of an ever-changing competence. The selectionist model is, at the moment, the best candidate for a unifying theory of adaptive processes at the individual level, from elementary associative connections to the highest products of the human mind.

Inter-individual differences also have their place in the model, reflecting the same principle at the level of the species. Differential psychology, long relegated to the applied fields of psychology, with little impact on general theory, has moved in the last two decades or so to a totally different perspective, at least in some schools of thought (most representative in this respect is the work of Reuchlin and his co-workers (Reuchlin and Bacher 1989; Reuchlin *et al.* 1990; Lautrey 1995)). Confronted with the extraordinary richness of human behaviour, it has abandoned the idea that all the variations observed are simply deviations from typical human nature. They are, on the contrary, human nature itself, viewed from a population rather than a normative perspective. The sphere of learning is likely to exhibit more inter-individual variations than any other psychological function, providing for the exceptional learning capacities of a given species as a whole, and this would apply to the human species more than to any other. It would seem advisable for learning psychologists to pay attention to them at last.

Applied issues

Insofar as applications of psychology are dealing in one way or another with changing the state of human affairs, they all involve learning processes. Learning psychology would therefore appear to be a major source of know-how in any professional practice, be it in work situations, individual treatment, or more conspicuously in education. No doubt the background of many professionals includes some training in the psychology of learning, but in most cases as part of their basic courses in general and experimental psychology, with little relevance to their future practice, except perhaps for those engaged in applied activities explicitly rooted in learning psychology, such as behaviour modification and behavioural therapy. In some European countries, it is still the case that even the training for educational professions includes almost nothing in the field of learning.

That state of affairs is partly due to the fact, already alluded to, that a large part of the psychology of learning has been established through animal studies, which many see as irrelevant to human issues, and the more so since animal subjects have fallen into disrepute as a valid source of psychological knowledge. But this is not the whole story. Specialists in learning should blame themselves for not having succeeded in selling their knowledge to those who should most normally use it. As pointed out above, they have been working in reciprocal isolation with respect to other fields of psychology, including applied settings, such as developmental and differential psychology. Consequently, practitioners have often made their choice of one of these fields as their major source of inspiration at the expense of learning psychology, a choice possibly based on some reasonable cost–benefit balance, but more likely influenced by contextual factors. For example, in French-speaking Europe, for better or for worse, the developmental tradition is given much more room in educational psychology than the psychology of learning.

Perhaps the main reason for the poor impact of learning psychology is to be found in its historical links with behaviourism. The rejection of behaviourism by some influential cognitivist schools of thought has discarded, after a classical baby-and-bath confusion, the accumulation of essential findings of learning studies. These findings, however, are still good material for professionals, especially in the absence of any consistent alternative theory of learning in humans: sophisticated cognitive theories elaborated to account for animal data do not really have their counterpart for humans; cognitive psychology has emphasized (verbal) memory, which does not cover the whole field of learning; the information-processing centred approach has overlooked the role of action in educational situations. By leaving out of consideration a number of contributions of learning psychology, with the justification that they do not pertain to the modern stream of thought, psychologists have deprived themselves of relevant concepts and practical tools.

This is but one aspect of a typical attitude of psychologists as compared with most other applied scientists. In all sciences, knowledge evolves and changes through time; no theory is definitive; but even drastic changes, as observed when one paradigm, in the Kuhnian sense, replaces a preceding one, do not annihilate all previously acquired practical, applied know-how. Scientific applications, even more so than developments in basic science, are seen as cumulative, not as earthquake changes. There is still a lot of classical mechanics in the art of building a car or a bicycle; rules of hygiene in hospitals have not been thrown out by the discovery of antibiotics. Why should we expect that new psychological theories – often less new than is claimed – would radically supplant earlier ones, even in their applications? What psychologists need is a more serene view of their own field, as undergoing permanent evolution, not as a chain of revolutions. And a modest sense of the cumulative character of their stock of tools for practice.

CONCLUSIONS

Science is a selective process, the future of which is little, if at all, influenced by individuals' wishes or dreams. My view of the present and the past is idiosyncratic, and assuming it has some relevance, it is not likely to influence much of the future. Let us play the millenarist game, however, and venture a few suggestions, which I would tend to implement if invited to decide the priorities for the coming years. Some have to do with learning psychology proper, others are more general, along the lines of the preceding reflections on the integration of learning psychology in the wider scope of psychology at large.

Although I would certainly not discourage the pursuit of research, currently quite successful, on cognitive, event-processing interpretations of associative learning or on formal modelling of relations such as *the matching law*, I would favour well-established investigations, especially aimed at testing the hypothesis of the role of behavioural variations in the learning processes.

Perhaps going against the current, I would still promote animal research as the essential condition for disentangling what is specific to our species and what is common to us and to more or less remote biological beings. Those who have continued to explore animal capacities, using learning situations, have kept producing unexpected new findings on cognitive performances in non-humans – equivalence relations, transitive relations, refined timing, etc. – which throw light on or raise questions as to the interpretations of related competencies in humans.

Some reference to animal learning is a prerequisite for conclusive studies on the role of symbolic and verbal behaviour in human learning, another area of investigation worth promoting. Experimenters have already taken advantage of selected situations, such as training of athletes, or training of complex professional skills, to describe with increasing precision the benefits, and also possible counterproductive effects, of verbal instructions, verbal anticipation or verbal accompaniment of action. This vein is one of the more promising towards a general theory of learning, and certainly one of the most relevant to educational applications of all sorts.

Developmental studies, linking rather than juxtaposing developmental concepts and concepts from the field of learning, should be given more attention, both for their theoretical significance and because of their importance in education.

At a more general level, what we need, at the turn of the century, is a linguistic cleaning in depth. Psychology is plagued, more so than half a century ago, by semantic inconsistencies. Words are used in technical contexts in an unbelievably loose manner, with little concern for their polysemic properties: *representation* and *image*, to mention just two examples, have multiple meanings, which authors do not always take care to specify. Different words are used by different authors with no awareness that they refer to the same things: Hunt (1984) points to the equivalence between 'internal representation' and 'discriminative stimulus' as well as between other dyads from information-processing vocabulary and the Skinnerian lexicon. Effort towards linguistic clarity and simplicity is not only an obvious improvement in scientific communication; in the case of psychology, including the psychology of learning, it leads to demystification of theories, which often claim originality while they bring little more than verbal novelty applied to old concepts. A large part of the discourse on expert versus novices sounds pretty trivial and looks like rediscovering the psychology of learning.

At the level of theories, my expectations for the near future would be that psychologists in the field of learning would turn more problem centred than theory focused. Issues in learning in animals and humans cannot be reduced to a *manichaean* conflict between behaviourism and cognitivism or between cognitivism and connectionism: they refer to empirical reality, be it in the laboratory or in real life. You do not get rid of them by eliminating the '-ism' historically linked with them. Whatever your feelings towards radical behaviourism, you do not fully dispose of the problem of reinforcement by resorting to the abstraction of regularities through event processing. It does not matter much that the former has been central in Skinnerian theory and the latter in cognitive models; what is important is that both are aspects of learning processes which must be considered in any acceptable account of learning.

Finally, it is my hope that scientific knowledge on learning will be put to work in practice during the twenty-first century more efficiently than has been the case to date. As pointed out above, messages from psychologists to people in education and other real-life contexts have been excessively loaded with theoretical preferences, fluctuating as the paradigms in favour changed, bringing about in the professionals' mind confusion or, eventually, distrust and rejection of any psychological contribution to practical affairs. I think that the psychology of learning has a lot to contribute to practical issues, but it has, by and large, failed to do it because of the persistence of a quasi-ideological style of psychologists in stating their views. Modern society, confronted as it is with so many changes, deserves a more pragmatic approach to its problems. Let us hope that psychologists will be able to meet that challenge.

REFERENCES

Catania, A.C. (1992) *Learning*, (3rd edn), London: Prentice-Hall.

Changeux, J.-P. (1983) *L'Homme Neuronal*, Paris: Fayard.

Changeux, J.-P. and Dehaene, S. (1989) 'Neuronal models of cognitive functions', *Cognition* 33: 63–109.

Dickson, A. (1980) *Contemporary Animal Learning Theory*, Cambridge: Cambridge University Press.

Domjan, M. and Purdy, J.E. (1995) 'Animal research in psychology: more than meets the eye of the general psychology student', *American Psychologist* 50: 496–503.

Edelman, G.M. (1987) *Neural Darwinism: The Theory of Neuronal Group Selection*, New York: Basic Books.

Gigerenzer, G., Swijtink, Z., Porter, T., Dasto, L., Beatty, J. and Krüger, L. (1989) *The Empire of Chance*, Cambridge: Cambridge University Press.

Hull, C.L. (1943) *Principles of Behavior, An Introducton to Behavior Theory*, New York: Appleton Century Crofts.

Hunt, E. (1984) 'A case study of how a paper containing good ideas, presented by a distinguished scientist, to an appropriate audience, had almost no influence at all', *Behavioral and Brain Sciences* 7: 597–598.

Lautrey, J. (ed.) (1995) *Universel et Différentiel en Psychologie*, Paris: Presses Universitaires de France.

Lorenz, K. (1965) *Evolution and Modification of Behavior*, Chicago: University of Chicago Press.

—— (1981) *Fundamentals of Ethology*, New York: Springer.

Mackintosh, N.J. (1974) *The Psychology of Animal Learning*, New York: Academic Press.

O'Keefe, J. and Nadel, L. (1978) *The Hippocampus as a Cognitive Map*, Oxford: Oxford University Press.

Pew, R.W. and Rosenbaum, D.A. (1988) 'Human movement control: computation, representation and implementation', in R.C. Atkinson, R.J. Herrnstein, G. Lindzey and R.D. Luce (eds) *Stevens' Handbook of Experimental Psychology* Vol. 2 (473–509), New York: John Wiley & Sons.

Popper, K.R. (1972) *Objective Knowledge: An Evolutionary Approach*, Oxford: Oxford University Press.

Quételet, L.A.J. (1835) *Sur l'Homme et le Développement de ses Facultés, ou Essai de Physique Sociale*, Paris: Bachelier.

Reuchlin, M. and Bacher, F. (eds) (1989) *Les Différences Individuelles dans le Développement Cognitif de l'Enfant*, Paris: Presses Universitaires de France.

Reuchlin, M., Lautrey, J., Marendaz, C. and Ohlmann, T. (eds) (1990) *Cognition: l'Individuel et l'Universel*, Paris: Presses Universitaires de France.

Richelle, M. (1991) 'Reconciling views on intelligence?', in A.H. Helga Rowe (ed.) *Intelligence, Reconceptualization and Measurement* (19–33), Hillsdale, NJ: Lawrence Erlbaum Associates-ACER.

—— (1993) *B.F. Skinner, A Reappraisal*, London: Lawrence Erlbaum Associates.

—— (1995) 'Eloge des variations', in J. Lautrey (ed.) *Universel et Différentiel en Psychologie* (35–50), Paris: Presses Universitaire de France.

Skinner, B.F. (1938) *The Behavior of Organisms*, New York: Appleton Century Crofts.

Staddon, J.E. (1983) *Adaptive Behavior and Learning*, Cambridge: Cambridge University Press.

Tolman, E.C. (1932) *Purposive Behavior in Animals and Men*, New York: Appleton Century Crofts.

5 Intellectual disability

A psychological assessment

Roy McConkey

People with intellectual disability have danced on the edge of human society for centuries. This chapter critically reviews how the embryonic psychological science of mental testing reinforced their exclusion from communities, a state of affairs which began to be rectified only in the second half of the twentieth century. Subsequently, psychological interventions and research stimulated their habilitation and prompted major shifts in service systems for these people and their families.

None the less, the history of separation has cast long shadows. To this day, intellectual disability is still viewed by many as an entity of study within the wider discipline of clinical psychology. Perpetuation of this myth severely blunts the impact which other branches of psychology can make to the betterment of people's lives while protecting mainstream psychologists from facing up to searching questions regarding the relevance of their research, the value-base to which they are working and their responsibilities for moulding social and cultural perceptions of atypical people.

A WORLD OF DIFFERENCE

> Disabled people, whatever the origin, nature and seriousness of their handicaps and disabilities, have the same fundamental rights as their fellow citizens of the same age, which implies, first and foremost, the right to enjoy a decent life, as normal and as full as possible.
>
> (United Nations 1975)

Intellectual disability is the most prevalent handicapping condition throughout the world. But whatever name is used, and over the past century there have been many – mental handicap, mental retardation, severe learning difficulties – the impression is given of a unitary disability which is akin to visual impairment or hearing loss. This is patently not so. We now realize that the term is best thought of as an umbrella label for a range of disabling conditions of diverse origins. Genetic factors are thought to account for around 60 per cent of people called 'intellectually disabled', of which Down's

Syndrome is the largest single group. Environmental causes have been implicated in the remaining 40 per cent, including maternal infection during pregnancy, diet and substance abuse, extreme prematurity and childhood infections (Mental Health Foundation 1993).

Obviously such diverse causes produce different consequences on the biology of the young children resulting in marked variations in their development, but even the same cause, such as an extra twenty-first chromosome as in Down's Syndrome, impacts very differently on developing humans. For example, a longitudinal study of over 200 babies in Manchester, England found that by the age of 2, one-sixth of infants with this syndrome were developing on a par with their peers, with few signs of being disabled, whereas for another one-sixth, they had barely mastered the skills of a six-month old. As the years pass, the gap becomes even wider (Cunningham 1982).

A third source of variation within this population is in terms of their life experiences. Family interactions, environmental circumstances, opportunities to socialize, schooling or the lack of it, are all known influences on children's development and are likely to interact in unknown ways with a child's biology.

In sum then, there never can be a psychology of intellectual disability *per se*. Yet for the past 100 years and more, psychologists have either constructed such a discipline or acted as though there was one. For them, a lack of intelligence was the unifying concept among all the human diversity which was so obviously apparent even to the untutored eye. The Intelligence Quotient (IQ), the undisputed creation of psychology in the early 1900s, became a tool for selection and exclusion and unwittingly reinforced some of the worst myths which human culture has spawned about people who were deemed to be 'mentally defective'.

Many decades were to pass before psychologists responded to the needs of the intellectually disabled, by exploring the nature of their disabilities and designing ways of overcoming their handicaps. In so doing, many valuable lessons have been learned but none more so than that a common humanity – and psychology – unites us all. Yet to this day, in most English-speaking countries, intellectual disability is still seen as a specialism within clinical psychology; the consequence being that other branches of the discipline have little to contribute to, or learn from people who bear the label of 'intellectually disabled'.

In this chapter, I shall review the broader view taken by society towards people with intellectual disabilities, examine the contribution made by psychologists in terms of assessment, intervention and research and, finally, try to predict the future trends which will enable these people to obtain their rights that are so often proclaimed but which have proved so elusive to obtain.

CULTURAL DISPOSITIONS

Mental retardation is more than a failure to behave appropriately; certainly it is more than an individual's psychology. Mental retardation is rooted in our culture and in our biology.

(Baumeister 1987: 800)

Intellectual disability is as old as humanity. Throughout recorded history, these people have been recognized as different from others in the tribe. In Pre-Christian Ireland, for example, the fifth-century Brehon Laws identified the following distinct categories: 'idiots, fools and dotards; persons without sense and madmen'. These groups were exempt from certain punishments and protected from exploitation.

In England, mention is made in a fourteenth-century statute of a distinction between the 'born fool' and the 'lunatic'. In the case of the latter, the Crown could take possession of his property during an illness but with 'born fools' it reverted permanently to the King, subject only to an obligation to provide for the individual's personal needs (Clarke and Clarke 1996).

In Continental Europe, churchmen pronounced on the probable causes of idiocy. For St Augustine they were a punishment from God for the evils of mankind, whereas Martin Luther believed they resulted from the sins of individual parents. Common folk invoked fairies and demons who stole the human child, leaving a changeling in its place (Ryan and Thomas 1980).

However, it was not until the nineteenth century that formal provision began to be made for the education and care of 'idiots'. Seguin (1846) wrote 'while waiting for medicine to cure idiots, I have undertaken to see that they participate in the benefit of education'. His methods, based around sensory and muscular development, were to have an enduring influence on later educationalists such as Montessori.

In Scotland, the achievements of the Earlswood Asylum were noted in the Edinburgh Review (1865): 'the solitary and useless are made social and industrious, while relieved of the blight of their deplorable condition, they become conscious of their humanity, as well as in a measure independent, happy and confident, instead of helpless, sad and distrustful' (cited in Ryan and Thomas 1980: 97).

However, by the end of the century in most of the industrialized countries of Europe, this benign treatment had given way to much harsher regimes. Various reasons have been invoked. First, the enormous social changes and the rapid growth of cities led to increases in both the size and types of public institutions; for the old, orphans and lunatics as well as for 'idiots'. Second, Darwin's theories led to fears that the national genotype would become contaminated if people of low intelligence were allowed to breed unhindered. Incarceration in single-sex establishments was an expeditious solution and in Britain, the building of large institutions for about 2,000 patients in isolated country areas became a definite policy of the authorities (Felce 1996); a policy shared with Continental Europe and the new world, and one which spread quickly to the countries of the British Empire.

Throughout the first half of the twentieth century, the numbers of people admitted to 'mental handicap' hospitals steadily increased in Britain, reaching a peak of some 100,000 patients in the 1950s. Fortunately, the second half of the twentieth century was to tell a different story. As families resisted admitting their sons or daughters to institutional care, so the number of day care centres for children and occupational centres for adults increased. Alternative forms of residential provision began to be promoted, stimulated by the 'normalization' movement in Scandinavia. For example, the Mental Retardation Act (1959) in Denmark aimed to create an existence for the mentally retarded as close to normal living conditions as possible (Bank-Mikkelson 1980).

However, a generation was to pass before de-institutionalization became an accepted policy in most industrialized societies. Even so, great variations still exist among the countries of Europe, with Iceland, Norway and Sweden reporting the largest drop in numbers living in residences for more than fifty people. While the numbers remain largely unchanged in Ireland, Poland and Bulgaria, in The Netherlands they show a slight increase (Hatton *et al.* 1995).

In the 1990s, all British children with intellectual disabilities now live with their natural or adoptive parents or foster families, a high proportion attend ordinary pre-school facilities and a growing number are enrolled in mainstream schools for at least part of their primary education. Most older teenagers have the option of taking educational or vocational courses at colleges of further education, following which they can take part in a range of leisure, social educational and work options available through local day centres. An increasing number also manage to obtain some paid employment. On leaving the family home, they are likely to live in 'group homes', that is, ordinary houses for up to six people with paid staff supporting the residents. Similar scenarios are found in the more affluent countries of Europe.

THE CONTRIBUTION OF PSYCHOLOGY

> Mental retardation workers have a special responsibility not only to conduct research but to advocate for better lives for retarded persons.
>
> (Zigler *et al.* 1990)

Given the broad canvas painted above of social policy towards people with intellectual disabilities, what have been the particular contributions – for better and worse – made by psychologists to the treatments which these people have received both individually and collectively and how has the involvement of psychologists with people who have an intellectual disability evolved over the past century?

Psychological assessment

For most of the twentieth century in Europe, people with an intellectual disability were treated as 'mental' patients; cared for in hospitals run by medical directors, who were invariably psychiatrists, and staffed by nurses and 'care assistants'. Ironically the advent of intelligence testing in the early 1900s helped to buttress and consolidate this model of care.

The original intention of Alfred Binet, the father of mental testing, was to identify Parisian children who were failing in schools primarily for environmental reasons rather than because they were congenitally retarded. Apparently, Binet was well aware that his measures could describe a child's functioning only at the time of test and would have no necessary bearing upon prognosis. Moreover, he explicitly rejected the notion of intellectual constancy (Clarke and Clarke 1996).

By the 1920s though, IQ testing had taken firm root as it offered an apparently objective measure of identifying those who were considered to be 'mentally defective'. Any doubts which Binet may have had about predictive validity or possible variations in scores over time were soon forgotten by his successors. Indeed, the self-fulfilling prophecy inherent in the removal of these people from society went unquestioned and nowhere more blatantly than in the exclusion of children with IQ scores of under 50 from the formal education system, because they were deemed 'ineducable'. Indeed, so strong was the belief in the constancy of the IQ scores that when children were seen to improve on intelligence tests, the concept of 'pseudo feeble-mindedness' was invoked, the implication being that the original test result was wrong!

Despite the psychometric inadequacies of the tests and the gross imprecision of the concept they attempted to measure, IQ scores have influenced for the worse the lives of hundreds of thousands of people with disabilities over some two generations, much to the shame of latter-day psychologists. In Britain, for example, it was the 1970s before children with measured IQs of less than 50 were given the right to education, a right still denied in some other European countries.

Of course, greater pressures than those wielded by psychologists sustained these abuses but what is inexcusable is the failure of psychology to acknowledge three truisms that, with hindsight, were readily apparent.

First, IQ as traditionally measured is not a predictor of a person's capacity to learn the skills needed for everyday living (Baumeister 1987; Howe 1988). Although this fact has been confirmed by numerous research findings from the 1960s onwards, it was well known to families and carers long before then. In recent years, an increased interest has developed in 'dynamic' assessment methods which actively examine children's capacity to learn within test situations. However, the main stimulus for this development appeared to come from the disproportionate numbers of children from immigrant and ethnic minorities who were being classed as 'mentally retarded' (Rutland and Campbell 1996).

Another influence has been a rediscovery of the theories of Russian psychologists such as Vygotsky (1978), who eschewed the structural notions of intelligence so favoured by Western theorists and proposed instead a model which emphasized the social influences on children's growth of competence.

Second, intelligence tests focused on a narrow range of cognitive skills to the neglect of other more salient forms of 'intelligence', in particular what has been termed 'practical' and 'social' intelligence (Greenspan and Granfield 1992). The former includes the activities of daily living, often referred to as adaptive behaviours such as self-care, home living, health and safety, while the latter refers to a person's social competence, for instance in negotiating relationships, in reciprocal communication and in role-taking. Had earlier tests attended to these dimensions of intelligence, the link between assessment and remediation would have been more evident.

The third criticism of intelligence tests, indeed of testing generally, is that it presumes the 'problem' resides solely within the individual and by omission does not explore the impact of social, cultural and environmental factors. For example, the link between the effects of poverty and the presence of significant developmental disabilities has been strongly documented through decades of research (Bruininks 1991). Yet by 'blaming' the victims for their low IQs and poor social adaptation, attention was taken away from social policies which would ameliorate poverty and deprivation.

Gold (1975) reflected this line of thought in his redefinition of mental retardation as 'people whose level of functioning requires from society significantly above average training procedures and superior assets in adaptive behaviour manifested throughout life' (p. 1). In sum, the problem is better conceived as ours rather than theirs.

Latter-day psychologists have taken many of these lessons to heart. This is best exemplified by the definition and classification of mental retardation proposed recently by the American Association on Mental Retardation (Luckasson *et al.* 1992). This envisages assessment occurring along three dimensions: (1) the person's capabilities in both intellectual and adaptive skills; (2) the impact which environments such as home, work/school and community have on the person's functioning, and (3) the supports needed to improve the person's functional capabilities.

Such a comprehensive assessment can take many hours to complete; it must be done in partnership with the people who know the person intimately; it will use a variety of 'assessment' tools including naturalistic observations and rating scales as well as normative tests; it will integrate the insights and opinions of various clinicians, and crucially the conclusions will lead to a specific plan of action for the individual, often referred to as an individual educational or habilitation plan. How well current clinical practice meets these standards is unknown – psychologists have a poor record at assessing themselves – but at least clear standards are now agreed.

None the less, a number of criticisms remain. Assessments rarely embrace the transactional perspective which dominates much current psychological thinking in children's growth of competence. Second, repeat assessments are rarely undertaken, hence variability in the person's performance is often missed. Third, temperamental and motivational factors are often ignored and yet they may impact significantly on the person's development (Wishart 1996).

Psychological interventions

If testing brought shame to psychology, then psychological interventions aimed at overcoming disabilities salvaged its reputation. Admittedly the origins of intervention can be traced to individuals such as Itard and Seguin in the mid-1850s, but a century was to elapse before it became widely accepted that people considered to have severe mental handicap could develop new competencies and that the strategies for doing this were relatively easy to implement. However, some decades passed before interventions became widely used with families and within services and even today it would be foolhardy to suggest that they are applied systematically and consistently within our service systems.

Psychological interventions broadly took two forms: first, instituting new types of services, and second, devising teaching and management programmes tailored to individual needs. An early example of the former was Jack Tizard's 'Brooklands' experiment in which children were moved from a hospital ward to a smaller, more homely setting, where they had their own clothes and toys. This was staffed by houseparents and run on educational principles (Tizard and Grad 1961). These and other 'demonstration' projects were to fuel a reappraisal of accepted residential child care practices in British hospitals.

Interventions with individual clients were pioneered mainly by psychologists. These were based on behavioural technologies and initially drew heavily on Skinnerian theories. Early successes were training in employment skills for moderately handicapped young adults (Clarke and Hermelin 1955) and teaching programmes for self-care skills (such as toilet training) with severely and profoundly handicapped youngsters (Berkson and Landesman-Dwyer 1977). Successful attempts were also made to modify undesirable behaviours through behavioural techniques, of which aggression to others and self-injury tended to be the most common. Behaviour modification soon proved a viable alternative to the two popular approaches of the day: sedation through drugs and constraint coupled with isolation.

In the 1960s, particular attention came to be paid to early intervention programmes for use with infants who were at risk of developmental delay, the so-called 'Head Start' programmes in the United States. Although these met with mixed success, they spawned an interest in extending these ideas to biologically damaged infants.

During the 1970s and early 1980s a plethora of curriculum guides for use in early intervention programmes was published and despite the protestations of their creators none has been proven to be significantly better than any other

(Farran 1990). In retrospect this is not surprising, as the guides often shared significant features, namely promoting mobility, self-care and fine-motor competencies through setting explicit learning targets; breaking tasks down into small steps, and repeated teaching activities. The successes are probably attributable to the teaching strategy rather than the details of the curriculum activities.

Equally, the curriculum guides share common failures. In particular, the impact on the child's language acquisition, symbolic thinking and socializing skills has been disappointing. The wisdom of hindsight coupled with advances in developmental theorizing provide a convincing explanation, namely that such skills cannot be taught through one-to-one structured teaching. Rather they are acquired by children through social interactions in naturally occurring contexts (Tizard and Hughes 1984). Hence the emphasis in intervention programmes of the 1990s has shifted to optimizing the child's transactions with his or her usual carers in familiar environments. Joint engagement in household routines and mutually enjoyable play activities offers scope for promoting child initiations and parental responsiveness, both of which are more likely to facilitate language and symbolic growth (Harris *et al.* 1996).

In this approach parents and carers become the primary 'therapists' for their child; a strategy which necessitated psychologists developing new skills in working with parents. This in turn brought a greater appreciation of the impact that a child with disability can have on family functioning and the range of supports which families may require (Mittler and Mittler 1994). By the mid-1980s, Dunst (1985) was to conceive of early intervention as, 'the aggregation of the many different types of aid, assistance, and resources that individuals and groups provide to families of young children'. This would include the emotional and practical support offered by family and neighbours as well as the range of inputs from professional workers and services.

The focus of intervention has broadened from the individual to embrace the social and cultural contexts in which the child lives. Indeed, this trend now extends to interventions with people of all ages. For example, young adults with an intellectual disability have experienced great difficulty in obtaining paid employment despite having attended training centres for many years. A new style of intervention known as 'supported employment' trains people on the job and provides a network of supports for them, either informally through co-workers or by employing 'job coaches'. Such approaches have resulted in severely handicapped people holding down a paid job (Walsh *et al.* 1994).

The 1970s onwards saw an expansion in the number of professional workers from various disciplines, such as therapists and special educators, working in services for people with intellectual disabilities. It is a tribute to psychology that many modelled their approaches on methods pioneered by psychologists. Indeed, so successful has been the 'take-over' that the role of psychologists in services has tended to become retrenched to co-ordinating multidisciplinary assessments and tackling the more intractable behaviour problems of individuals.

In common with the spirit of the 1980s, the term 'challenging behaviours' was coined to encourage the view that problem behaviours such as physical aggression, self-injurious behaviours, destruction of property and sexual assaults are ones which 'challenge' service systems to respond more effectively to the particular needs of certain people. However, debates rage on the definitions and numbers of people who exhibit serious challenging behaviours and the models of service they require.

The issue has become especially contentious in countries where institutional care is contracting. The kernel of the debate is whether specialist centres need to be provided for these people or whether their needs can be met by developing the competence and expertise of community services. In the latter model, peripatetic specialist teams provide practical assistance and advice to local personnel. To date, evidence for the efficacy of this approach is sparse but we do have a better understanding of the conditions under which community-based services can be successful (Emerson *et al.* 1994). Personally, I am persuaded that we have no alternative but to go down this road, otherwise we risk re-creating institutions. Moreover, clinical experience suggests that such behaviours can be moderated through constructive strategies based around interpersonal approaches and environmental contingencies.

What then are the broader lessons we can learn from psychological interventions with people who have intellectual disabilities? First, the most significant impact of interventions may not be in changed behaviours but in altered attitudes. Gallagher (1992) posited that the real value of early intervention programmes lay 'in a new spirit of optimism and encouragement within the family of the affected child'. Such a conclusion could equally well apply to the pioneering work of Tizard as well as to the latter-day successful amelioration of antisocial behaviours. We have much to learn though about the factors which influence the feelings of families, front-line staff and even psychologists!

Second, as I have attempted to show above, interventions have increasingly adopted a transactional perspective with a strong emphasis on creating supportive social contexts in naturalistic settings. This stands in marked contrast to traditional therapies which aimed to remediate deficits in the child or adult. However, this new approach challenges us to find new methods for assessing and changing the interactions of parents and staff, and for creating better social contexts to promote development.

Third, psychologists have been preoccupied with discovering and proving the 'main effect' of their interventions, namely that it holds for groups of people. Yet the lesson from all sorts of interventions is that their effects vary for different people and across different circumstances. For instance, many early interventionists now agree with the conclusions of Sameroff and Fiese (1990), who wrote that 'cost-effectiveness will not be found in the universality of a treatment but in the individuation of programmes that are targeted for specific children, in a specific family and in a specific social context'.

Finally, interventions strive for a common goal, namely to provide a better life for the person with disability. However, this apparently obvious statement raises moral and ethical dilemmas for practitioners, of which the most common are: how to ensure an equitable distribution of scarce resources; whose needs are you employed to meet – those of the service system or the client; and how do you reconcile conflicting demands among groupings of clients in which a common 'treatment' may prove beneficial to one person but detrimental to others, for example, sustaining a person with severely challenging behaviour in a community house with three other residents?

It is an illusion to think that psychological interventions are 'value-free' and the dilemmas they pose demand to be debated openly in much the same way that issues around medical interventions have now entered the public arena. The consolation is that these are the fruits of success.

Psychological research

The third contribution of psychology has been in the field of psychological enquiry, although this is barely a generation old. Initially, researchers were preoccupied with comparisons with non-disabled groups. These took two forms: comparisons with age peers, and with people of comparable mental ages. These designs reflected two contrasting views of intellectual disability: was their development comparable to that of non-disabled people but at a slower rate, or did they have specific intellectual defects? The latter would be detected if the groups were matched on their mental development, or so it was argued.

This research design, derived from the biological sciences, was – and still is – deceptively appealing for investigators. However, it soon became apparent that it is fraught with many pitfalls, which if not attended to can make the results virtually uninterpretable (Heal 1970).

The most serious problem arises when the matching is done on only one variable, leaving other significant variables uncontrolled. For instance, in contrasting the language competence of pre-schoolers with and without Down's Syndrome, any differences can only be attributed to the syndrome when all other explanatory variables have been controlled or randomized – such as hearing loss, the family's socioeconomic status and the mother's use of language with the child, to name but three. As it is clearly impossible to do this except with large samples using multivariate analyses, comparative designs are best avoided.

Indeed, sampling presents the biggest difficulty to researchers in this field. Given the biological heterogeneity of this group and variety of life experiences which they may have encountered, it is impossible to obtain any form of representative sample of 'people who have an intellectual disability'. At best, such samples could be obtained for people with particular syndromes, although this can be extremely difficult to do with syndromes of low frequency. Alternatively, samples could be obtained which are representative of individuals living within designated geographical areas even though this poses major logistical problems. In the event, psychologists have usually opted for neither, using instead 'convenience' samples containing unknown and unacknowledged biases. Consequently much of the published literature contains conflicting results and unreplicated conclusions.

A second weakness has been a propensity to use cross-sectional designs based on measures taken at one point in time. While this has yielded some useful descriptive information, the findings do not enable causal relationships to be established, although this has not stopped such interpretations from being made.

A third problem, in common with psychological research in other fields, is that little attention has been paid to the unreliability inherent in many of the measures used in investigations, for example in rating scales and performance measures. Moreover, there is increasing evidence that inconsistency of responses may be a feature of many people with intellectual disabilities (Wishart 1996). In these circumstances, it is vital that 'chance' variability is not mistaken for actual differences.

Finally, as Skidmore (1996) has pointed out, a great deal of research has been dominated by a psycho-medical paradigm which conceptualizes the disability as 'arising from deficits in the neurological or psychological make-up of the child, analogous to an illness or medical condition'. Latterly, two other paradigms have come to the fore, which he terms 'sociological' and 'organizational'. The former tends to focus on the effects of labelling, exclusion and power relationships; whereas the latter emphasizes deficiencies in systems, such as schools, and how they can be remedied. A common limitation in all three paradigms, he argues, is their tendency to reductionism, namely 'to explain an irreducibly complex phenomenon in terms of a single unidirectional model of causation'.

That said, however, psychological research has challenged many common assumptions and brought important issues to the fore. In my experience the following research strategies have tended to have the greatest impact. First, the measures used were simple and straightforward, based on factual information or frequency counts of observed behaviours in natural settings with correspondingly little recourse to statistics to substantiate interpretation of the data. Second, longitudinal designs usually yield much more interesting data and have the advantage of identifying possible causal relationships. In this respect, single case studies can be most influential, as are 'follow-up' studies of groups of clients who received particular services. Third, the increasing acceptability of qualitative data has brought a much richer and more humane account of people's lives and experiences than can be conveyed through numbers. It has also given voice to the people most affected by the disability, notably parents and the people themselves.

Fourth, the research needs to blend the paradigms noted above by attending to significant social and organizational factors as well as to the characteristics of the person with the disability. Hence an evaluation of intervention programmes needs to examine the impact on families and their social supports as well as the developmental gains made by the child. Finally, but most crucially, the research addresses a salient issue on which decisions have to be made. Very often this is not derived from psychological theory but rather, as in Masters' (1984) definition of decision-driven research, *[it] comprises the conversion of a socially important question into a research endeavour.*

Ironically, some of the earliest research in the field of intellectual disability meets these standards better than much of the published work in today's journals. Why should this be? An appealing explanation for me is that the most effective researchers tended to be those working in services and who were committed to providing a better life for these people and their families. Once individuals with a disability became 'subjects' of study by professional researchers based in universities, inevitably the priorities shifted away from research as a means to an end to becoming an end in itself.

FUTURE PROSPECTS

The trends of inclusion, participation, integration and personal empowerment are part of an important movement that possesses the potential of creating a better future for citizens with mental retardation.

(Bruininks 1991: 248)

Following Naisbitt's (1982) dictum that 'trends like horses are easier to ride in the direction they are already going', in this section I shall attempt to summarize the implications for psychology of three trends which are set to take us into the new millennium. They are offered with more hope than confidence, as I am conscious that pendulums swing backwards as well as forwards!

From therapy to relationships

A recurring theme in this review has been the importance of social influences in developing the competencies of people with intellectual disabilities. As psychologists, we have much to learn about how we can assess and nurture relationships. An obvious example is in the field of enhancing communication with people who have limited verbal expression and understanding. Despite this being the most obvious and pernicious of handicaps resulting from this disability, surprisingly little attention has been paid to its amelioration. Likewise, the insight emerging from recent research in social psychology on the formation and sustaining of relationships has had little impact on the style of interventions promoted with children and adults who have intellectual impairments (Conville 1992).

On a more pragmatic and personal level, the switch away from traditional therapy has major implications for the formal and informal roles which psychologists play in services. Two resolutions are possible: first, psychologists become adept at working with and through the people who have established relationships with their clients. No longer do psychologists carry out assessments and write programmes, rather this becomes the responsibility of parents and front-line staff. Instead, psychologists will develop and train them to fulfil these functions. Or the traditional role of psychologists changes so that they can forge a close relationship with the people they are employed to help. In this instance, it is likely that in service systems they will fulfil particular service functions and have other job titles. In this respect psychological insights from organizational psychology may prove particularly useful (Handy 1988). Both scenarios have significant implications for how psychologists are trained to work in this field.

From buildings to community

Over the past decades, the medical emphasis that once dominated disability has faded as educational and social needs received recognition and attention. But Zigler's (1990) comments on early intervention are a salutary reminder that 'no amount of counselling, early childhood curricula, or home visits will take the place of jobs that provide decent incomes, affordable housing, appropriate health care, optimal family configurations' (p. xiii).

Wider issues of social policy often impinge more on family circumstances and people's well-being than does the specific help offered to families through multidisciplinary teams of disability professionals. The need for multisectorial co-operation and co-ordination is all the greater but the unresolved issue is how to achieve this without building yet more bureaucracies that remove professionals from direct contact with families (Myers 1990).

Here I suspect we could usefully learn from the experiences of our colleagues in developing countries (O'Toole and McConkey 1995). First, their lack of social service infrastructures means that a key strategy is the empowering of people within communities to help themselves. Services that are locally autonomous are more likely to respond quickly and effectively than are larger, regional services.

Second, service staff often have to fulfil a much wider range of support functions, including health promotion, marital guidance and income generation, to name but three. The trend towards 'key workers' and 'named persons' for families is a welcome development which will only come fully to fruition as the job holders forgo their original specialism and actively expand their talents to meet a wider range of child and family needs.

Third is the willingness to enlist and train people from the local community as 'supporters' although they may have no previous experience of disability. Family-based respite care schemes and supported employment options are excellent examples of innovations which can come about through the active involvement of local people. The requisites for this to happen are for professionals to share their knowledge and insights, to build trusted relationships within their communities and to show a willingness to share responsibility and decision making. Will the psychologists of the future be able to meet this challenge?

From paternalism to rights

And so we come back to where we started: the rights of people with intellectual disabilities. Throughout the twentieth century their rights were often suppressed and ignored, but if those days are gone, how can tomorrow's psychologists demonstrate a respect for their rights?

If we take for granted that this respect will be apparent in all their personal interactions with clients and families – which sadly is not a safe presumption at present – then the key issue to my mind will revolve around accountability. The onus is on us to account to them as to how we fulfil the role for which we are employed. This means actively reviewing with them and their advocates the quality of the service on offer from psychologists and working with them to improve it. Similar evaluations and reviews will need to be done for all services and I can foresee psychologists making a major contribution to this endeavour (McConkey 1996).

Ultimately though, it is the personal values of individuals rather than their expertise and experience which determine the respect they give to people's rights. Some will argue that the values which now dominate in technologically advanced societies – self-sufficiency, competition, monetary gain – militate against respect for the rights of disadvantaged groups. Others will contend that it is precisely through taking a rights perspective that we will keep alive a feeling of community that is becoming more elusive in such societies. Either stance is a reminder to all workers in disability services that their work is invariably influenced – for better or worse – by wider social values. In this regard psychologists have a particular responsibility to actively mould and develop these values, so that the children of the new millennium, as yet unborn, will not be left 'dancing on the edge' as were their forebears of a century ago.

REFERENCES

Bank-Mikkelson, N.E. (1980) 'Denmark', in R.J. Flynn and K.E. Nitsch (eds) *Normalisation, Social Integration and Community Services*, Baltimore: University Park Press.

Baumeister, A.A. (1987) 'Mental retardation: some concepts and dilemmas', *American Psychologist* 42: 796–800.

Berkson, G. and Landesman-Dwyer, S. (1977) 'Behavioral research on severe and profound mental retardation (1955–1974)', *American Journal of Mental Deficiency* 81: 428–454.

Bruininks, R.H. (1991) 'Mental retardation: new realities, new challenges', *Mental Retardation* 29: 239–258.

Clarke, A.D.B. and Clarke, A.M. (1996) 'The historical context', in B. Stratford and P. Gunn (eds) *New Approaches to Down's Syndrome*, London: Cassell.

Clarke, A.D.B. and Hermelin, B. (1955) 'Adult imbeciles: their abilities and trainability', *Lancet* 2: 337–339.

Conville, R.L. (1992) *Relational Transitions: The Evolution of Personal Relationships*, New York: Praeger.

Cunningham, C.C. (1982) *Down's Syndrome: An Introduction for Parents*, London: Souvenir Press.

Dunst, C.J. (1985) 'Rethinking early intervention', *Analysis and Intervention in Developmental Disabilities* 5: 165–201.

Emerson, E., McGill, P. and Mansell, J. (1994) *Severe Learning Disabilities and Challenging Behaviours: Designing High Quality Services*, London: Chapman & Hall.

Farran, D.C. (1990) 'Effects of intervention with disadvantaged and disabled children: a decade review', in S.J. Meisels and J.P. Shonkoff (eds) *Handbook of Early Childhood Intervention*, Cambridge: Cambridge University Press.

Felce, D. (1996) 'Changing residential services: from institutions to ordinary living', in P. Mittler and V. Sinason (eds) *Changing Policy and Practice for People with Learning Disabilities*, London: Cassell.

Gallagher, J.J. (1992) 'Longitudinal interventions: virtues and limitations', in T. Thompson and S.C. Hupp (eds) *Saving Children at Risk: Poverty and Disabilities*, Newbury Park, CA: Sage Publications.

Gold, M. (1975) 'A new definition of mental retardation', unpublished paper, University of Illinois, USA.

Greenspan, S. and Granfield, J.M. (1992) 'Reconsidering the construct of mental retardation: implications of a model of social competence', *American Journal on Mental Retardation* 96: 442–453.

Handy, C. (1988) *Understanding Voluntary Organizations*, Harmondsworth: Penguin.

Harris, S., Kasari, C. and Sigman, M. (1996) 'Joint attention and language gains in children with Down's Syndrome', *American Journal on Mental Retardation* 100: 608–619.

Hatton, C., Emerson, E. and Kiernan, C. (1995) 'People in institutions in Europe', *Mental Retardation* 33: 132.

Heal, L.W. (1970) 'Research strategies and research goals in the scientific study of the mentally subnormal', *American Journal of Mental Deficiency* 75: 10–15.

Howe, M.J.A. (1988) 'Intelligence as an explanation', *British Journal of Psychology* 79: 349–360.

Luckasson, R., Coulter, D.L., Polloway, E.A., Reiss, S., Schalock, R.L., Snell, M.E., Spitalnik, D.M. and Stark, J.A. (1992) *Mental Retardation: Definition, Classification and Systems of Support*, Washington, DC: American Association on Mental Retardation.

McConkey, R. (ed.) (1996) *Innovations in Evaluating Services for People with Intellectual Disabilities*, Chorley, England: Lisieux Hall Publications.

Masters, J.C. (1984) 'Psychology, research and social policy', *American Psychologist* 39: 851–882.

Mental Health Foundation (1993) *Learning Disabilities: The Fundamental Facts*, London: Mental Health Foundation.

Mittler, P. and Mittler, H. (eds) (1994) *Innovations in Family Support for People with Learning Disabilities*, Chorley, England: Lisieux Hall Publications.

Myers, R.G. (1990) *Toward a Fair Start for Children*, Paris: UNESCO.

Naisbitt, J. (1982) *Megatrends: Ten New Directions for Transforming our Lives*, New York: Warner Books.

O'Toole, B. and McConkey, R. (eds) (1995) *Innovations in Developing Countries for People with Disabilities*, Chorley, England: Lisieux Hall Publications.

Rutland, A.F. and Campbell, R.N. (1996) 'The relevance of Vygotsky's theory of the "zone of proximal development" to the assessment of children with disabilities', *Journal of Intellectual Disability Research* 40: 151–158.

Ryan, J. and Thomas, F. (1980) *The Politics of Mental Handicap*, Harmondsworth: Penguin.

Sameroff, A.R. and Fiese, B.H. (1990) 'Transactional regulation and early intervention', in S.J. Meisels and J.P. Shonkoff (eds) *Handbook of Early Childhood Intervention*, Cambridge: Cambridge University Press.

Seguin, E. (1846) *Traitement moral, hygiene, et education des idiots, et autres enfants arriéres*, Paris: Balliere Tindall.

Skidmore, D. (1996) 'Towards an integrated theoretical framework for research into special educational needs', *European Journal of Special Needs Education* 11: 33–47.

Tizard, B. and Hughes, M. (1984) *Young Children Learning: Talking and Thinking at Home and School*, London: Fontana.

Tizard, J. and Grad, J.C. (1961) *The Mentally Handicapped and their Families*, London: Oxford University Press.

United Nations (1975) *Declaration on the Rights of Disabled Persons*, New York: United Nations.

Vygotsky, L. (1978) *Mind in Society: The Development of Higher Mental Functioning*, Cambridge, MA: Harvard University Press.

Walsh, P.N., Lynch, C. and de Lacey, E. (1994) 'Supported employment for Irish adults with intellectual disability', *International Journal of Rehabilitation Research* 17: 15–24.

Wishart, J.G. (1996) 'Avoidant learning styles and the cognitive development in young children', in B. Stratford and P. Gunn (eds) *New Approaches to Down's Syndrome*, London: Cassell.

Zigler, E. (1990) 'Foreword', in S.J. Meisels and J.P. Shonkoff (eds) *Handbook of Early Childhood Intervention*, Cambridge: Cambridge University Press.

Zigler, E., Hodapp, R.M. and Edison, M.R. (1990) 'From theory to practice in the care and education of mentally retarded individuals', *American Journal on Mental Retardation* 95: 1–12.

6 One hundred years of clinical psychology

Roots, doubts and hopes

*Amparo Belloch**

Lightner Witmer, founder of the first psychological clinic at the University of Pennsylvania, is associated with the birth of clinical psychology. The date, 1896, is undisputed and it is agreed that Witmer deserves to be named as the founder (Garfield 1974). Without questioning this fact, this chapter investigates why the birth of clinical psychology was made possible. This journey in time is important, not only because it might help us to better understand the way clinical psychology has developed, but also to understand where it is now. My purpose, however, is not to relate *the history* of clinical psychology, but rather to examine some of the conceptual changes that have taken place in the field, especially since the end of the First World War and up to the present time. Before doing so, I would like to examine briefly the roots of these changes.

ROOTS

When we examine the origins of a science, it is easy to be so taken up with the present that we hinder our ability to capture the spirit of a particular era (Stocking 1965). A century ago, Witmer conceived the excellent idea of founding the first psychological clinic leading to the birth of a new profession, clinical psychology, related to the new science of psychology.

Psychology developed throughout Europe during the last quarter of the nineteenth century. An atmosphere of change resulted from the effects of industrialization on prevailing social norms (Reisman 1976). New social values which had inspired the French Revolution one hundred years earlier – respect for others, individual freedom, equality and solidarity – penetrated deeply, spreading like wildfire over the continent: 'the movement was for an amelioration of social conditions on the basis of the dignity and rights of the individual' (Reisman 1976: 16). In this atmosphere, science also experienced remarkable changes that can be summarized by two aspects. First, natural observation (like that of Hippocrates) and reflexive thought (like philosophical

* The author wishes to express her gratitude to Professor V. Pelechano as well as to Dr R. Banos and Dr C. Perpina for their valuable comments and assistance with this chapter.

enquiry) gave way to controlled observation and the need to predict the course of events. Scepticism, relativism and mechanics were characteristic of the 'new science' (Pinillos 1980, 1993; Reisman 1976). The possibility of *experimenting* with reality, of actively intervening in it, not only observing it, distinguished true scientific activity from philosophic thought. Second, scientists became aware that they could influence social change: Pinel, Tuke, Todd, Itard and Dix are examples. Indeed, this atmosphere facilitated the emergence of new sciences. Psychology developed with Wundt in Germany; anthropology with Evans-Pritchard in England, and sociology with Comte in France.

Many great thinkers contributed to psychology as a field of philosophical thought – Avicenna and Maimonides, Vives, Huarte de San Juan, Feijoo, Descartes, Spinoza, and even Leibniz and Kant. Wundt, however, had received a medical as well as a philosophical education. His interest was in studying the conscious content of the human mind, selecting sensations as the elements of immediate experience. Several English philosophers – J. S. Mill or A. Bain among others – were also interested in the study of sensations. Nevertheless, their focus, associationism, did not convince Wundt. His medical training obliged him to investigate other areas. He 'discovered' Berlin's early physiologists, such as Muller and Helmholtz. It is no coincidence that his first book, considered to be the first text of scientific or experimental psychology, was *Grundzuge der Physiologische Psychologie*. Six editions between 1873 and 1911 marked its success in disseminating the new psychological science. An experimental orientation distinguished it from its traditional philosophical roots.

However, Wundt's name is not the only one we should refer to in order to reconstruct the history of psychology, particularly if we wish to trace the origins of clinical psychology. Brentano, Galton, Cattell and the extensive group in the psychodynamic tradition were certainly much more important. Brentano published *Psychologie vom Empirischen Standpunkt* in 1874, when Wundt published *Grundzuge*. Brentano believed that mental acts could be differentiated from physical phenomena in terms of their object: 'every mental phenomenon is characterized by what . . . we might call reference to a content, direction toward an object or imminent objectivity' (Brentano 1874, quoted in Berrios 1992: 305). Physical objects were susceptible to experimentation. However, psychological objects had *intentionality* and Brentano believed only intuition could approach these.

With his hypothesis on the 'intentionality of acts of experience', Brentano sought to place the 'psychological subject' in the centre of psychological theorization. It is not surprising that he inspired some of the most influential models of European clinical psychology. Gestalt psychology provided the foundation for several types of psychotherapy and was the predecessor of some of the current postulates of the cognitive model. Husserl led the phenomenological movement with which Karl Jaspers, founder of psychopathology, became associated. Jaspers suggested a basic character for this discipline which contrasted with the applied nature of psychiatry. He described its fundamental mission as bridging clinical activity and psychological theorization and experimentation.

Galton's approaches were much closer to practical, applied scientific activity and their repercussions in clinical psychology were to be associated with this perspective. Interested in measuring physical and mental characteristics, Galton helped to develop diagnostic techniques in the measurement of mental abilities, the first activity of clinical psychologists. He was fascinated by the ideas of his cousin, Charles Darwin, especially the variation of individual characteristics and the related process of natural selection (Bernstein and Nietzel 1980).

Cattell, an American psychologist, who in 1886 took his doctorate in psychology under Wundt in Leipzig, was mainly interested in the application of experimental psychological methods to the study of individual differences. His interest increased after meeting Galton at Cambridge University. When Cattell returned to the United States, he founded a laboratory devoted to the measurement of individual differences and coined the term 'mental test' (1890). Perhaps his major contribution to clinical psychology was his emphasis on 'practical applications of tests in the selection of people for training and as indicators of disease' (Reisman 1976: 29).

Finally, the psychodynamic model, initiated in France by Mesmer and developed much later by Braid in England and by Leibault, Bernheim and Charcot in France, emphasized the power which unconscious experiences have in human development. This model offered clinical psychology not only a new conception of mental illness which might be psychological in part, but also a new treatment based firmly on the power of speech and the engagement of the individual who now assumed a degree of moral responsibility in the illness and healing processes. The emphasis on 'the psychological' was especially related to an irrational model of the human mind. Emotions are the elements which guide thought and behaviour. The new model opened the door for the development of psychological, as opposed to organic treatment programmes.

The roots of clinical psychology are well known, explaining its birth and marking its later development. Elsewhere, we shall analyse the doubts and debates which have taken place and which in some cases persist. These include different theoretical models to explain mental disorders – those based on the scientific-experimental tradition of Wundt as opposed to those derived from Brentano's research; the diverse roles of the clinical psychologist – testing, psychotherapy, research and others; and debates about a scientific-experimental orientation compared with a professional or applied orientation. We shall return to these points.

While all the foregoing events happened in nineteenth-century Europe, the birth of clinical psychology officially took place in the United States. The reasons behind this geographic shift are many, but all are related to a characteristic aspect of the North American culture: its eminently practical and applied conception of culture and scientific activities, namely the need to put science at the service of society. As Korchin said, the functionalist and pragmatic themes in American psychology provided a particularly receptive soil for clinical and other applied psychologies. Americans had little patience for either a psychology that dissects into minute detail the structures of the mind . . . or for a psychology that speculates grandly about the ultimate nature of the human mind.

(Korchin 1983: 5)

In 1896, Witmer, an American who had studied with Cattell and followed him to Wundt's laboratory in Leipzig, proposed to the American Psychological Association clinical psychology as an applied discipline:

Clinical Psychology is derived from the results of an examination of many human beings, one at a time, and the analytic method of discriminating mental abilities and defects develops an ordered classification of observed behavior, by means of postanalytic generalizations . . . the psychological clinic is an institution for social and public service, for original research, and for the instruction of students.

(Collins, quoted in Brotemarkle 1947: 65)

Witmer is credited with creating our profession, its name and some of its distinctive characteristics. However, as Bernstein and Nietzel stated (1980: 44), 'Witmer got clinical psychology rolling, but had little to do with steering it.' He was scarcely relevant in the development and consolidation of clinical psychology; for some merely a historical anecdote (Watson 1953). First, he paid little or no attention to the developments which were taking place in psychology, especially in the areas of diagnosis – for example, the Binet-Simon scale – and therapy, particularly in psychoanalysis (Bernstein and Nietzel 1980; Reisman 1976). Second, perhaps Witmer's colleagues were not yet prepared to accept a professionalization of psychology, then perceived as being more like 'pure' scientific activity (Reisman 1976). Third, Witmer's clinic was centred almost exclusively on childhood problems, while the thrust of clinical psychology was driven by the assessment of adults (Bernstein and Nietzel 1980). Finally, it is difficult to admit that a single individual had created a profession or science. History shows us that truly exceptional individuals may do so. Witmer was by no means such a person. Consequently a whole set of related events, some of which are mentioned here, and not a single event, is what can most likely help us to understand the rise of clinical psychology, its evolution and later development.

GROWTH AND DEVELOPMENT

By the end of the First World War, few doubted that psychology was both an independent scientific activity and a new profession (Reisman 1976):

Largely because of the way in which it responded to the practical demands and the opportunities of the military emergency, psychology today occupies a place among the natural sciences which is newly achieved, eminently desirable, and highly gratifying to the profession.

(Yerkes 1919, quoted in Reisman 1976:135)

The most influential factor in the expansion of the practice of clinical psychology was the assessment and measurement of mental abilities, especially intelligence (Pintner 1931). Crucially, use of the Binet-Simon scale spread in Europe and the United States. In contrast to Witmer's tests, the Binet-Simon assessed higher human functions and considered individual differences. While it sprang from educational psychology and aimed primarily at classification, the scale opened a new world to the new profession. Psychological clinics devoted to the evaluation and diagnosis of mental abilities, first in children and later in adults, proliferated, largely in the United States. The impact of the First World War on the large-scale use of tests is also well known. Test content expanded beyond assessing intelligence, defining the role of the clinical psychologist as an expert in the use and interpretation of tests with children, non-hospitalized adults and even mental patients (Bernstein and Nietzel 1980).

Clinical psychologists began to develop instruments to measure personality, interests and emotions. Many were developed and based on the European psychoanalytic approach which had made a deep impression on North American clinical psychology. This movement reached the United States through the work of a psychologist, G. Stanley Hall, who had invited Freud, Jung and Ferenczi to give a series of addresses marking the twentieth anniversary of Clark University in Massachusetts. The Freudian approaches turned out to be very attractive to North American clinical psychologists largely because they were the only ones which gave some explanation of the relationship between individual and environment. Clinical psychology needed these explanations and they were not provided by the elementalist and structuralist proposals of Wundt and his followers.

In the absence of uniform regulations, problems related to training of clinical psychologists arose for the first time. These new professionals became much in demand, yet were ignored by the only professional organization of the time, the American Psychological Association (APA). Anyone could use the title 'clinical psychologist'. To establish order, the independent American Association of Clinical Psychologists was formed in 1917. Although it did not last long (it became part of the APA two years later), the first of several disputes related to the role and training of clinical psychologists took place.

The evolution of clinical psychology from the end of the First World War has been well documented elsewhere (Bernstein and Nietzel 1980; Garfield 1974; Kelly 1961; Korchin 1976, 1983; Reisman 1976; Skakow 1978; Watson 1953). I wish to highlight the conceptual changes which have taken place in the field and their influence on scientific and professional development. My comments are drawn from the results of a study which explored the conceptual evolution of clinical psychology by examining publications in the field (Belloch *et al.* 1983).

The study was based on work published by clinical psychologists which appeared in various categories in *Psychological Abstracts* between 1927, the first year in which it was published, and 1980. Despite the inherent limitations in studies based on just one bibliographic source of data, principally North American, the research provided some interesting conclusions.

First, variation in terminology is striking (see Table 6.1), and may be interpreted as a logical consequence of the development of a new scientific-professional activity seeking its own identity. Thus it reveals the existence of important changes in the conceptual orientation of the discipline as well as the interests of clinical psychologists themselves.

The time series analysis indicated six distinct phases which correspond more or less to changes in terminology. Table 6.2 illustrates these periods with their respective denominations. Most striking, perhaps, is the apparent correlation of these phases with some notable events in the history of clinical psychology.

1927 to 1939

The first phase corresponds to the period between the First and Second World Wars. It has two key characteristics: the consolidation of clinical psychology as an independent discipline, and the proliferation of diverse schools – Behaviourism, Gestalt, Psychoanalysis – with their ensuing rivalry. Perhaps for these reasons, Koch (1964) termed this the 'era of theory'. During these decades clinical psychology grew from infancy to adolescence, rather undernourished but quick and tempestuous (Watson 1953). Diverse areas of study acted as catalysts. Pavlov's work on experimental neuroses was collected by Lashley in *Brain Mechanisms and Intelligence* (1927). Constitutionalists such as Krestchmer and Sheldon, together with the work of Gestaltist Kurt Lewin on conflict, also contributed. The psychodynamic movement exerted a growing influence on all areas of clinical psychology, including childhood psychopathol-

Table 6.1 Topics used to group the publications on clinical psychology in *Psychological Abstracts* (1927–1980)

Years	Topics
1927–1936	Nervous and mental disorders
1937–1946	Functional disorders
1947–1960	Behaviour deviations
	Clinical psychology, guidance and counselling
1961–1965	Abnormal psychology
	Therapy and guidance
1966–1972	Clinical psychology
1973–1980	Clinical psychology
	Physical and psychological disorders
	Treatment and prevention

Table 6.2 Periods of clinical psychology according to the time series analysis on the publication in *Psychological Abstracts* (1927–1980)

Periods	Topics
I. 1927–1939	Nervous and mental disorders
	Functional disorders
II. 1940–1946	Functional disorders
III. 1947–1960	Behaviour deviations
	Clinical psychology, guidance and counselling
IV. 1961–1966	Abnormal psychology
	Therapy and guidance
V. 1967–1975	Clinical psychology
	Physical and psychological disorders
	Treatment and prevention
VI. 1976–1980	Clinical psychology
	Physical and psychological disorders
	Treatment and prevention

ogy. Melanie Klein published *The Psychoanalysis of Children* in 1932, and Leo Kanner, *Child Psychiatry* in 1935.

Why did so many models flourish? One answer seems especially important (Stone 1985). A major consequence of the First World War was the appearance of many cases of shell-shock which exposed the limitations of psychiatry, then rather biological in its orientation. This encouraged the search for other referential structures of which psychoanalysis was undoubtedly the best known and most important. Shell-shock was a disorder which affected well-nourished, previously healthy men, many of whom had volunteered to serve. They hardly resembled the multitude of mentally ill people who were treated in the asylums and who, for the most part, belonged to the *lumpenproletariat* (Pilgrim and Treacher 1992). Consequently, it was not only necessary to seek new models to explain satisfactorily the breakdown in the minds of these groups of 'normal' men, but serious doubt was cast on the usefulness of the available service resources for attending the patients adequately. It is not surprising that the corresponding topic describing such studies changed from a classical medical-psychiatric formula, 'Nervous and Mental Disorders' to 'Functional Disorders', a topic related to the functionalist tradition of North American psychology initiated by Williams James and conceptually closer to the dynamic approaches.

Together with the proliferation of models, psychologists dedicated to clinical psychology as well as their typical instruments, the tests, also flourished. It is notable that this cycle coincided with the publication of F.L. Wells' book, *Mental Tests in Clinical Practice*, in which he distinguished the psychologist from the tester. The phase concluded with two significant events: the death of Freud in 1939 and two particularly important publications – Anastasi's *Differential Psychology* (1937) and Murray's *Explorations in Personality* (1938).

Explorations was a book about research which also unfolded a profoundly important conception of personality. This conception was organismic when the rest of psychology was atomistic. It included a sophisticated view of human motivation when others were stuck with drives and instincts. It required holistic and imaginative methods of assessment when others were adding up scores on paper-and-pencil tests. And it led to the construction of a far-reaching ego psychology at a time when psychoanalysts had barely begun to think about ego psychology.

(White 1981: 3)

During this period, Beck introduced the Rorshach Test in the United States. Finally, applied psychologists in North America – clinical, educational, consulting, business and industrial – unhappy with the excessively academic focus of the APA, withdrew in order to form their own association, the American Association of Applied Psychology (AAAP).

1940 to 1946

The second, shorter phase may be characterized by the 'triumph of functionalism' which had previously been initiated. Functionalism was apparent in three aspects. First, mental disorders were described as functional. James' psychodynamic focus, until now virtually ignored by academic psychology in North America, was adopted. Second, psychodynamics dominated both clinical settings and the contents of publications. At the same time, the role of clinical psychologists diversified. No longer merely testers at the service of psychiatrists, psychologists now intervened actively in the direct treatment of patients. The inclusion of clinical psychology in psychotherapy was due mainly to the increase in the number of people with war-related mental problems and a shortage of psychiatrists. Other psychotherapeutic approaches, such as self-help, client-centred therapy (Rogers 1942) and counselling – categorized within clinical psychology – evolved. Third, by the end of the war, in Germany and in England, the psychodynamic model expanded into the area of non-mental disorders or psychosomatic medicine. Alexander, Funkestein and Masserman advanced the model in the United States. Finally, in 1945 a reconciliation was reached between the APA and the AAAP.

1947 to 1960

The third phase is probably one of the most important. Although their roots were complementary, the split between 'clinical psychology, guidance and counsel-ling' and 'behaviour deviations' (Table 6.2) revealed two distinct orientations – applied-professional and scientific-academic. The need for reconciliation between the APA and the AAAP in 1945 at the end of the second cycle mirrored the division. In 1949 the famous Boulder Conference established guidelines for the professional training of clinical psychologists, first in North America and later in other countries.

The introduction of the term 'behavioural deviation' deserves special attention. It was a time of significant conceptual changes charting a path for clinical psychology up to the present. The term 'disorder' (mental or functional as in earlier periods) was now not used, but 'deviated behaviour' was. Yet we must ask: deviated from what? The answer is clear: from 'normal behaviour', which is indeed the central focus of psychology. The behaviourist model of psychology, based on learning processes, was initiated by Watson in 1919 and was later developed by Thorndike, Tolman, Hull, Guthrie and Skinner, among many others. It was constituted within the conceptual and methodological referent of 'true' scientific psychology, restricting its field of theorization, at least in the beginning, to *observable behaviour*. From this point on, the qualification of normality depended on whether or not the observer decided that the behaviour in question was in line with the social norm. Therefore, the criterion of validation was external and social. The information that the patient provided about her or himself had little or no relevance.

The psychodynamic model had been present through the early stages of the development of clinical psychology, and until then it had been the most important alternative to biologically oriented psychiatry. It was practically eliminated from the official and academic psychological scene, being replaced by the behaviourist model for explaining psychopathologies. Similarly, the predominance of psychodynamics in the psychotherapeutic context was also replaced by the ever-growing acceptance of Rogers' psychotherapeutic orientation (1951a, 1951b) to which Ellis's 'rational-emotive therapy' would later be added.

If we dig a bit deeper into the reasons explaining this gradual replacement of the psychodynamic model with the behavioural one, we find the following causes among others. First, the dynamic orientation had *also* been accepted by psychiatrists, especially English and North American, as an alternative model of behaviour and particularly in the area of psychotherapy. As Pilgrim and Treacher pointed out, 'in 1954 the American Medical Association declared psychotherapy to be a medical procedure. The logic of this position was that psychologists practising psychotherapy were doing so illegally' (1992: 14). The 'war' between psychiatry and clinical psychology was underway and, for the moment, the psychiatrists had seemingly won the first battle. Second, psychology had begun to advance its own non-biological explanatory models. In some aspects these models were consistent with the programmes of Wundt, and they offered enough of a methodological guarantee to be catalogued as 'scientific'.

In summary, the models conformed to the prevailing positivist programme of science. The behaviourist model was undoubtedly the most coherent with this programme, and it was also easily transported to the clinical context. It allowed for the explanation, diagnosis and treatment of any mental disorder at any age, through individualized or group treatment depending on the nature of the problem and the aims of the treatment programme. Overall, it allowed for all of this from *within* the field of psychology. What is more, it produced a truly curious and even amusing fact: through this model, psychologists were 'allowed' to assail psychiatrists through an attack on the psychodynamic model that they upheld. It was attacked for being anti-scientific or possibly pseudo-scientific, inefficient compared to behaviourism, the model of modern clinical psychology.

In this context, the famous studies of Hans Jürgen Eysenck (1952, 1960, 1964) should be included as they helped to consolidate the position of clinical psychology primarily in Europe, or those of Astin (1961) and Yates (1958) in North America. Criticism of the effectiveness of psychotherapy-psychiatry also spread later on to diagnostic and classification models of mental illnesses, as opposed to those for which behaviourism offered its own alternative (functional analysis) and its own conceptual objective (abnormal behaviour).

All things considered, we can speak about a kind of 'pride in being a psychologist', not without a certain sense of triumph linked to the first 'truly psychological' models in the area of psychotherapy (Rogers, Kelly) and to the behaviourist model of psychology, which fulfilled the requirements of a positivist natural science. It might not be exaggerated to state that the experimental psychology (paradigm of scientific psychology) models and clinical psychology models had until then never been so similiar. This union produced many outcomes. New ways to diagnose and conceptualize mental disorders were developed. Treatment programmes for diverse disorders proliferated. Clinical psychology widened to encompass physical health and illness with a focus radically different from the psychodynamic. Behaviourism was the official, academic model of psychology, especially in North America. It was this option alone which emerged to validate the scientific credentials of clinical psychology.

1961 to 1966

The fourth phase consolidated and extended the preceding one. Abnormal behaviour was reaffirmed as the basic object of study in clinical psychology. Eysenck's *Handbook of Abnormal Psychology* (1960) was a paradigm of this stance. Abnormal psychology replaced the earlier 'behaviour deviations', forming the 'basic science' of clinical psychology, and serving as a bridge between clinical and general psychology. Therapy and guidance encompassed the applied aspects of clinical psychology and replaced the generic category of 'clinical psychology' present in the earlier phase. Behaviour modification appeared after 1960 in three different countries: North America, England and South Africa (Pelechano 1979). Although there were already many North American specialists in this field, behaviour modification became an organized and united movement in many places after this date (Bernstein and Nietzel 1980). Specialists seized upon events as diverse as Szasz's (1960, 1961) devastating criticism of the biomedical model of illness applied to mental disorders and Kuhn's famous text *The Structure of Scientific Revolutions* (1962) as complementary 'proofs' of their arguments. In this way, they obtained extraordinary validation outside psychology itself. A change in name marked the last year of this cycle. 'Clinical psychology' was again used as the Chicago Conference of 1965 took place, reaffirming the utility of the behaviourist model of clinical psychology much as the Boulder conference had done.

1967 to 1975

With the fifth phase, the generic category of clinical psychology reappeared. The reasons for this return are various, but I shall highlight only four. First, under the unitary denomination the two areas which define clinical psychology were outlined: the academic-oriented (physical and psychological disorders) and the professional-oriented (treatment and prevention). These areas are likewise the two essential requirements which clinical psychologists should carry out in their training. Second, research and clinical psychological activity were open to other important fields. Abnormal psychology began to deal with physical as well as mental disorders. Third, therapeutic intervention at a primary level was increasingly needed to prevent the onset or exacerbation of mental disorders. Programmes of this kind were devised at the University of Rochester (Cowen and Zax 1968; Zax and Cowen 1967). Psychiatric hospitals were gradually replaced by community-based centres which offered out-patient services and rehabilitation programmes. These changes opened the way for a community orientation towards mental *health*, rather than the treatment of mental *disorder*. Behaviour modification co-existed with diverse psychotherapies and set up new forms such as 'brief psychotherapy' (Bellak and Small 1965). Fourth, perhaps most importantly, many clinical psychologists who until then had defended behaviourism enthusiastically began to see limitations to the concept of abnormality and its behaviourist associations.

Reasons for this disenchantment were grounded in the reliance of behaviourism on two learning processes – classical conditioning and instrumental learning – to explain human behaviour. Paradoxically, it now distanced itself from what psychology as a whole was doing, whereas it had formerly drawn clinical psychology closer to psychology. Psychology had advanced greatly in understanding mental processes as diverse as learning, memory, thought, imagination and language. Disciplines such as social and personality psychology, dismissed by radical behaviourism (Lundin 1961) were undoubtedly useful for clinical psychology, providing advances which did not reduce methodological purity and rigor.

A new cognitive psychological model entered the scene after the 1950s through cybernetics, information theory and general systems theory. Logical positivism and operationalism, the epistemic bases of behaviourism, were in decline. Rationalism substituted for radical empiricism. The notion of *psychological fact* was being replaced with that of the *event*, namely with a dynamic conception of psychological reality marked by a strong component of intentionality which tremendously complicated the problem of objectivity in psychology. Sociocultural epistemology (Kuhn) favoured the criticism of the naturalist model of behaviourism (Pinillos 1980). Research indicated that it is possible to learn through simple observation without appealing to reinforcement or conditioning. Mischel's (1968, 1973) devastating criticism of theories which posited stable and highly consistent personality traits influencing the person's behaviours across different situations had an enormous impact on psychology. It questioned the capacity of traits, evaluated through highly reliable and valid tests, to predict behaviour without taking into account the context in which the behaviour occurred: 'What has been questioned is the utility of inferring broad dispositions from behavioral signs as the basis for trying to explain the phenomena of personality and for making useful statements about individual behaviour' (Mischel 1973: 262). Formerly enthusiastic behaviourists became perplexed in the light of events undermining their security. They contributed to a crisis within the body of behavioural theory at the heart of scientific psychology. Thus, psychology itself entered a critical period with clinical psychology, although since its foundation psychology has tended towards crisis – no sooner had Wundt started the discipline than Brentano proposed an alternative (Pinillos 1980).

1976 to 1980

The crisis became more evident in the sixth and final phase. The three general topics of the earlier cycle persisted (clinical psychology, physical and psychological disorders, and treatment and prevention), but subcategories were restructured and indicators of productivity changed. A significant example is the percentage of studies in the area of psychotherapy and counselling which was 26 per cent, while only 15 per cent corresponded to studies in behaviour therapy and behaviour modification. Almost 23 per cent covered the area of health care services.

The crisis spread beyond clinical psychology to affect other areas of health, particularly medicine. The first systematic criticism of the traditional biomedical model arose. It was described as excessively deterministic, mechanistic and reductionist, and unable to explain the complex processes involved in human illness. A radical change in focus was proposed to encompass biological, psychological and social aspects of illness in order to understand and treat it properly: the bio-psycho-social model (Engel 1977). The crisis enlarged to encompass nearly all scientific and professional domains in which human health and illness are treated. Its consequences for clinical psychology are difficult to analyse as we lack historical perspective. In the following sections I shall offer views, necessarily personal and not at all exhaustive, on what our actual situation is, where we have gone wrong, where our strength lies as well as what future perspectives await us.

THE LAST FIFTEEN YEARS: FAILURE, SUCCESS AND DOUBTS

Two significant events took place in 1980 which changed the orientation and status of clinical psychology and set up future challenges. First, the American Psychiatric Association published the third edition of the *Diagnostic and Statistical Manual of Mental Disorders*. Second, Matarazzo, first president of a new APA division, defined health psychology, a new applied discipline. Both of these events had very different repercussions as much on the conceptual level as on the professional, but they coincided in marking a considerable change in orientation of clinical psychology and its professional status. In the creation and development of these two events there were, in my opinion, successes and failures which set up a number of challenges for the future of clinical psychology.

Classification and diagnostic systems

DSM-III (APA 1980) represented a true revolution in the classification and psychiatric diagnosis of mental disorders. Not only was current symptomatology taken into account, but also the individual's background, level of adaptation, severity, pattern of personal characteristics and associated physical illnesses. The *Manual* reflected efforts to reach a consensus among professionals with little reference to theory. Its authors aimed at inter-professional communication, improved knowledge of mental disorders and rigorous investigation. Clinical psychology welcomed DSM-III, quickly restructuring its textbooks to reflect the new clinical criteria. Clinical psychology and psychiatry could at last speak the same language, it seemed, although the common language was and continued to be psychiatric (APA 1994).

Sharing the same language may help to understand complex problems such as mental disorders. However, it is questionable whether we are aware of the cost involved in using a borrowed language which is not useful in reaching our objective. I shall offer a few examples. First, we have re-adopted 'mental disorders', a term which disappeared from *Psychological Abstracts* in 1937, replacing it first with 'functional disorders' and then with 'behaviour deviations' and 'abnormal behaviour'. The paradox is that the authors of *DSM-IV* themselves are not satisfied with the term 'mental disorder' which they conceptualize as 'a clinically significant behavioral or psychological syndrome or pattern that occurs in an individual' (APA 1994: xxi). Second, where do we find in DSM what we now know about attention, perception, memory or imagination in the descriptions of disorders such as anxiety, depression, schizophrenia, paranoia, amnesia, and so on? If we review the diagnostic criteria of, for example, schizophrenia, the mere presence of hallucinations or delusions may be sufficient to meet criterion A, characteristic symptoms. The *Glossary of Technical Terms* defines 'delirium' as 'a false belief based on incorrect inference about external reality' (APA 1994: 765) and 'hallucination' as 'a sensory perception' (APA 1994: 767). These definitions bear no relation to current psychological research on thought and perception or psychopathological work on deliria and hallucinations. Third, the option for a polythetic categorization of mental disorders sets up innumerable theoretical and practical dilemmas. For example, co-morbidity across disorders may lead to arbitrary decisions when including the patients in one diagnostic category and not in another. Heterogeneity of clinical characteristics threatens diagnostic validity and reliability: many patients are habitually classified as NOS – Not Otherwise Specified. The distinction between Axis I, clinical disorders, and Axis II, personality disorders, is often arbitrary, for example schizophrenia or schizotypal personality disorder; social phobia or avoidant personality disorder; mood disorder or borderline personality disorder; substance use disorder or antisocial personality disorder? (Clark *et al.* 1995). Moreover, it may be neither useful nor valid to separate exclusively mood disorders from anxiety disorders in view of the dimensional characterization derived from current psychopathological research (Barlow 1988, 1992; Moras and Barlow 1992).

Current systems of psychiatric diagnosis are of doubtful practical use, at least in the area of clinical psychology. Do they help us to understand mental disorders from a psychological perspective, helping us to integrate basic psychological research and clinical practice? Knowing other ways of understanding reality is undoubtedly a healthy exercise. Perhaps it is not so healthy to adopt these other ways without criticism, especially if they only add to our confusion or if they convert the little or great knowledge we have painstakingly acquired throughout history into nothing more than a mirage. It seems to me that relying on the DSMs or any other system such as OMS (ICD–10) as *our only and best diagnostic* referent is a mistake which may be extraordinarily costly. We may be tempted to reduce psychopathology to operational criteria of biologically oriented characteristics (Widiger and Trull 1991). Further, the psychological diagnosis implies a dimensional consideration, a continuum between the normal and the pathological or abnormal, and this is basically a consideration which is incompatible with the exclusive categorial characterization, *a more botánica*, of mental disorders.

Psychiatric systems hold heuristic value for research and enable interprofessional communication. However, we should not be tempted to consider them as the perfect synthesis of two of the functions that clinical psychologists have been painstakingly adopting over the years: the diagnosis of mental disorders and the understanding and explanation of their nature, or rather, their psychopathology. Naturally, the third function, psychotherapy, would inevitably be affected if we denied a predominantly psychological foundation for the other two.

This psychological foundation has progressed considerably during the last fifteen years, due to a great extent (although not exclusively) to the adoption of the cognitive model in psychopathological research (Belloch *et al.* 1995; Brewin 1988; Dryden and Rentoul 1991; Fernández-Alvarez 1992; Reed 1988; Williams *et al.* 1988). Cognitive psychopathology has probably been one of the areas of psychological research and theorization that has most advanced in recent years, generating a number of important explanatory models of complex mental disorders, such as schizophrenia (Frith 1992; Hemsley 1987, 1988, 1995), depression (Beck 1967, 1987; Ingram 1990), anxiety (Barlow, 1988; Last and Hersen 1988; Mathews and MacLeod 1994; Öhman 1993; Sandin 1995), hypochondria (Barsky 1992; Kellner 1994; Warwick and Salkovskis 1990) or eating disorders (Garner and Bemis 1982; Treasure 1991), to name a few.

One of the most significant features of these models is their profound relationship with psychological research into complex mental processes (attention, perception, memory, thought, language, etc.) which, from my point of view, represent a guarantee for the viability of these models, in addition to the revival of the old Jasperian project on the necessity of establishing psychopathological theorization in psychology. In this sense, psychopathology is beginning to occupy its corresponding place: that of a discipline that can best carry out the functions of establishing an unwavering bridge between psychological research and clinical practice. This represents, in my opinion, an unquestionable success. However, it is yet to be explained if this cognitive psychopathology will also be able to integrate aspects as important for the clinical psychologist as the emotions and affects within the still excessively formalist and mechanistic framework of current cognitive psychology (Bem and Keijzer 1996). The clinical psychologist is interested in knowing not only how abnormal processes of knowledge work, but also which contents are processed and how these contents may regulate the functioning of the processes on which they rest. This is a challenge which is still pending for psychopathology today.

Health psychology

Clinical psychology has traditionally dealt with mental disorders, but it has also dealt with the so-called functional disorders and concomitant psychological disorders involved in the whole process of physical illness (Florin and Fiegenbaum 1991). The psychodynamic model was, in this sense, a pioneer in establishing the psychosomatic consideration for illnesses, but it hardly advanced comprehension of the mutual influences between psychological and somatic aspects of illness or the development of psychological techniques of intervention in order to strengthen these influences. This latter aspect was, however, developed by behaviour modification and biofeedback techniques. Both groups of procedures encouraged the creation of behavioural medicine (Brannon and Feist 1992) conceived as 'the interdisciplinary field concerned with the development and integration of behavioural and biomedical science, knowledge and techniques relevant to health and illness' (Schwartz and Weiss 1978: 250). A sub-speciality, behavioural health, developed at about the same time. Its objective was 'maintenance of health and prevention of illness and dysfunction in currently healthy persons' (Matarazzo 1980: 807). A new discipline, health psychology, subsumed these developments and established a new professional field: 'health psychologists are psychologists first and specialists in health second. Psychology is the noun that identifies the subject matter; health is the adjective that describes the client, problem or setting to which psychology is applied' (Brannon and Feist 1992:19).

We are at the point of consolidation of a field of activity for clinical psychologists, and even though it was always more or less present, it now seems to have reached a definitive status. This is, of course, a success. The doubt lies in the implications it may have for the consideration of clinical psychology as a unitary discipline. If the introductory chapters of the manuals of health psychology are read in detail (for example, those of Brannon and Feist 1992; Feuerstein *et al.* 1986; Stone *et al.* 1987; Taylor 1986, 1990), we see that coincidentally it was conceived as an 'inter-discipline', different as well as separate from clinical psychology, which is, in turn, considered in the best of cases, as one more of its psychological sources or roots, as is biopsychology, personality psychology and experimental psychology, among others.

The main reason used in arguments to differentiate between health psychology and clinical psychology is that the latter deals with illnesses while the former deals with health. In other studies, I have developed the questions that provoke arguments like the preceding ones (Belloch 1996; Belloch and Olabarría 1993) and they can be summarized as follows. First, rigid boundaries between health and illness do not seem sustainable. Health is not merely an absence of illness. Second, if clinical psychology deals with mental illnesses and health psychology with physical illnesses affecting the psychological state, we incline towards embracing mind–body dualism. A fateful consequence is the view that the causes of physical and mental illnesses differ radically, a view incompatible with adoption of the bio-psycho-social model on which health psychology is said to be based. Third, while health psychology has declared an emphasis on human health, an analysis of the contents of publications (Bishop 1994; Echeburua 1993; Pitts and Phillips 1991; Sarafino 1994) suggests, rather, a 'psychology of illness' (Echeburua 1993). Finally, all these questions lead us to think that the discipline lacks an epistemological rationale, along with a certain amnesia about the history of clinical psychology. It seems there is some confusion between the (probable) need for specific training of clinical psychologists who wish to specialize in the area of prevention and health education (which would perhaps be what characterizes health psychology) and the (improbable) existence of fundamental epistemological differences between health psychology and clinical psychology.

Diversity of models

The psychodynamic model dominated clinical psychology in its first years. It was replaced in the 1950s by the behaviourist model. Fierce criticism, personal as well as scientific, marked the transition. Today, various models co-exist more or less peacefully: psychodynamic, humanistic, existential, behavioural, cognitive, systemic, and so on. The very profusion of alternative and often incompatible models is a certain sign of a pre-paradigmatic or pre-scientific stage, in Kuhn's view. If so, history suggests that the crisis for psychology is chronic. Another explanation for diversity is that the search for truth is incompatible with scientific knowledge: 'the idea of reducing all scientific knowledge to a single way of thinking about reality represents the survival of a discursive line belonging to mechanistic theory' (Pelechano 1996: 175). We are confronted with an extraordinarily broad range of problems, contexts, causes and maintenance factors. No single model is likely by itself to emerge as the best, most effective one. It seems to me more a success than a failure to admit that diverse problems require diverse solutions. However, I do not wish to say that we should unquestionably adopt an 'everything goes' attitude, because 'not everything goes, and not everything that goes, goes for the same price; nor does it go in the same way' (Pelechano 1996: 174). On the contrary, I believe that clinical psychology will advance as long as it is able to practise the eclecticism that, in its original philosophic meaning, consisted in trying to reconcile those doctrines that seemed best or true, even if they came from different theoretical systems. But we should not forget that such practice demands much more complex training and richer knowledge. Moreover, as a scientific attitude, eclecticism should be accompanied by a systematic analysis of the accumulated results and evidence which will offer keys to which model or strategy is most effective for a specific problem.

Finally, the current debate among psychotherapists and clinical psychologists, or therapists with different training, confuses a profession, clinical psychology, with one of its activities, psychotherapy. Professional clinical psychologists require general preparation in many psychological disciplines, psychotherapy and others, followed by a period of specialization in group work, psychotherapy, education, research or the like. Adequate training in a particular type of psychotherapy should be available after qualification. In short, it seems that the debate is erroneous and poorly focused. To paraphrase Heinz Werner when speaking about the evolution of living organisms, a clinical psychologist is a living organism, continually growing and evolving. The process of evolution advances from slight differentiation to an increasingly specialized stage. But the living organism should be able to integrate these advances and specializations into a coherent whole. If not, it runs the risk of disintegrating.

HOPES

Witmer only managed a 'slight elevation of the eyebrows on the part of a few of the older members' (Brotemarkle 1947: 65) when he proposed clinical psychology to his colleagues of the APA. After all these years, our fellow psychologists have no doubt become accustomed to our presence and do a bit more than raise an eyebrow when we set out our problems and achievements. It is unquestioned that clinical psychology has now reached maturity.

The disoriented childhood, the malnourished and stormy adolescence that Watson (1953) attributed to clinical psychology, have given way to a mature state in which the profession has been consolidated as an independent entity within psychological science. Much research in psychology is clinical; many university students aspire to be clinical psychologists.

Doubts persist. What is the best preparation? What areas should be studied? What is the specific role of the clinical psychologist? The wide array of roles and clinical practice settings cause identity problems. However, we should not allow diversity of roles to become a constant questioning of our identity. It is urgent to design specific models of training matched to particular roles and settings to enable specialization to follow common, core training, so that future clinical psychologists may draw on the widest mix of resources.

This is a task which must be faced as soon as possible and not only for scientific or conceptual reasons. In 1991, the Directive 89/48/EEC under article 27 of the Treaty of Rome urged all Member States of the European Community (EC) to participate in an effort to harmonize the study programmes of diverse professional fields in order to allow for the free circulation of professionals within the EC. Future clinical psychologists should be in direct contact with reality, firmly within the national system of public health. Their programme should be comprehensive, up to date and coherent. It should integrate theory and practice, should be supervised by clinical psychologists and adopt a bio-psycho-social frame of reference which involves work on multidisciplinary teams.

We must try especially to bridge practice and research. The practical or applied clinical psychologist must be convinced that systematic research is not a luxury but a true necessity. The clinical psychologist who has chosen to do research must make the effort to know and understand the problems faced by the applied clinical psychologist in order to offer plausible and cost-effective solutions (Beutler *et al.* 1995). For instance, one of the typical problems that hinders the application of the results of clinical research is that it often refers to the average patient, a statistical abstraction that has little or nothing to do with the real 'case' (Maling and Howard 1994).

We must continue to search for better solutions to old problems by creating models which allow for the generation of specific intervention strategies. Clinical psychology must diversify its methods in order to be useful to an ever-growing number of problems, institutions and individuals (Korchin 1983). It must also respond as quickly and effectively as possible to new social problems that arise in our societies – clinical psychology is a social science. As an applied discipline, it should relieve individual suffering, enhance well-being and ensure the right to a balanced and healthy life.

In conclusion, I suggest that these are some of the most important challenges that we face. Important debates on which model of preparation to choose, or what conceptual structures are adequate, should not distract us from our objectives. Clinical psychology has been consolidated as a scientific discipline. Therefore, it seems to me that our task is to progress through perfecting our methods and analysing their effectiveness, continuing to bring our knowledge to all who need it. This means, quite simply, to use the influence of our scientific activity to benefit society just as Pinel, Tuke or Dix did in their own time. Unless this is our goal, then the conceptual and theoretical debate will remain an exercise in dilettantism.

REFERENCES

American Psychiatric Association (APA) (1980) *Diagnostic and Statistical Manual of Mental Disorders, 3rd edition*, Washington: APA.
—— (1994) *Diagnostic and Statistical Manual of Mental Disorders, 4th edition*, Washington: APA.
Astin, A.W. (1961) 'The functional autonomy of psychotherapy', *American Psychologist* 16: 75–78.
Barlow, D.H. (1988) *Anxiety and Its Disorders. The Nature and Treatment of Panic and Anxiety*, New York: Guilford Press.
—— (1992) 'Diagnosis, DSM-IV, and dimensional approaches', in A. Ehlers, W. Fiegenbaum, I. Florin and J. Margraf (eds) *Perspectives and Promises of Clinical Psychology* (pp. 13–22), New York: Plenum Press.
Barsky, A.J. (1992) 'Amplification, somatization, and the somatoform disorders', *Psychosomatics* 33: 28–34.
Beck, A.T. (1967) *Depression. Clinical, Experimental and Theoretical Aspects*, New York: Harper & Row.
—— (1987) 'Cognitive models of depression', *Journal of Cognitive Psychotherapy* 1: 5–37.
Bellak, L. and Small, L. (1965) *Emergency Psychotherapy and Brief Psychotherapy*, New York: Grune & Stratton.
Belloch, A. (1996) 'Mentes y cuerpos: amores, desamores y renuncias' ('The mind and the body: loves, coldnesses, and renunciations'), in V. Pelechano (ed.) *Psicologia Clinica y/o Psicologia de la Salud* (Clinical Psychology and/or Health Psychology) (pp. 71–105), Valencia: Promolibro.
Belloch, A. and Olabarría, B. (1993) 'El modelo bio-psico-social: un marco de referencia necesario para el psicologo clinico' ('The biopsychosocial model: a necessary framework for clinical psychologists'), *Clinica y Salud* 4: 181–190.
—— (1994) 'Clinical psychology: current status and future prospects', *Applied Psychology* 43: 193–211.
Belloch, A., Ibanez, E. and Tortosa, F. (1983) 'Desordenes mentales, psicologia anormal y psicologia clinica: un proceso unitario?' ('Mental disorders, abnormal psychology and clinical psychology: a unitary process?'), in H. Carpintero (ed.) *Historia y Teoria Psicologica* (History and Theory in Psychology) (pp. 107–136), Valencia: Alfaplus.
Belloch, A., Sandin, B. and Ramos, F. (eds) (1995) *Manual de Psicopatologia*, Madrid: McGraw-Hill.
Bem, S. and Keijzer, F. (1996) 'Recent changes in the concept of cognition', *Theory and Psychology* 6: 449–469.
Bernstein, D.A. and Nietzel, M.T. (1980) *Introduction to Clinical Psychology*, New York: McGraw-Hill.
Berrios, G.E. (1992) 'Phenomenology, psychopathology and Jaspers: a conceptual history', *History of Psychiatry* III: 303–327.
Beutler, L.E., Williams, R.E., Wakefield, P.J. and Entwistle, S.R. (1995) 'Bridging scientist and practitioner perspectives in clinical psychology', *American Psychologist* 50: 984–994.

Bishop, G. (1994) *Health Psychology: Integrating Mind and Body*, Boston: Allyn & Bacon.

Brannon, L. and Feist, I. (1992) *Health Psychology: An Introduction to Behaviour and Health, 2nd edition*, Belmont, CA: Wadsworth.

Brewin, C.R. (1988) *Cognitive foundations of Clinical Psychology*, Hove: LEA.

Brotemarkle, R.A. (1947) 'Fifty years of clinical psychology: 1896–1946', *Journal of Consulting Psychology* 11: 1–4.

Clark, L.A., Watson, D. and Reynolds, S. (1995) 'Diagnosis and classification of psychopathology: challenges to the current system and future directions', *Annual Review of Psychology* 46: 121–153.

Cowen, E.L. and Zax, M. (1968) 'Early detection and prevention of emotional disorders: conceptualization and programming', in J.W. Carter, Jr (ed.) *Research Contributions from Psychology to Community Mental Health* (pp. 46–59), New York: Behavioral Publications.

Dryden, W. and Rentoul, R. (eds) (1991) *Adult Clinical Problems. A Cognitive-Behaviour Approach*, London: Routledge.

Echeburua, E. (1993) 'La psicologia de la salud: un constructo mal enfocado', ('Health psychology: a lack of focus construct'), in V. Pelechano (ed.) *Psicologia, Mitopsicologia y Postpsicologia* (pp. 249–272), Valencia: Promolibro.

Ellis, A. (1958) 'Rational psychotherapy', *Journal of General Psychology* 59: 34–49.

Engel, G.L. (1977) 'The need for a new medical model: a challenge for biomedicine', *Science* 196: 130–136.

Eysenck, H.J. (1952) 'The effects of psychotherapy: an evaluation', *Journal of Consulting Psychology* 16: 319–324.

—— (1960) *Handbook of Abnormal Psychology*, London: Pitman.

—— (1964) 'The nature of behavior therapy', in H.J. Eysenck (ed.) *Experiments in Behaviour Therapy* (pp. 1–15), London: Pergamon Press.

Fernández-Alvarez, H. (1992) *Fundamentos de un modelo integrativo en Psicoterapia* (Basis for an integrative model in psychotherapy), Buenos Aires: Paidos.

Feuerstein, M., Labbe, E.E. and Kuczmierczyk, A.R. (1986) *Health Psychology: A Psychobiological Perspective*, New York: Plenum Press.

Florin, I. and Fiegenbaum, W. (1991) 'Clinical psychology: its successes and perspectives', in A. Ehlers, W. Fiegenbaum, I.Florin and Y. Margraf (eds) *Perspectives and Promises of Clinical Psychology* (pp. 3–10), New York: Plenum Press.

Frith, C.D. (1992) *The Cognitive Neuropsychology of Schizophrenia*, Hove, Sussex: Lawrence Erlbaum.

Garfield, S.L. (1965) 'Historical introduction', in B.B. Wolman (ed.) *Handbook of Clinical Psychology* (pp. 125–140), New York: McGraw-Hill.

—— (1966) 'Clinical psychology and the search for identity', *American Psychologist* 21: 353–362.

—— (1974) *Clinical Psychology: The Study of Personality and Behaviour*, New York: Aldine.

Garner, D.M. and Bemis, K. (1982) 'A cognitive-behavioural approach to anorexia nervosa', *Cognitive Therapy and Research* 6: 1–27.

Hemsley, D.R. (1987) 'An experimental psychological model for schizophrenia', in H. Hafner, W. F. Gattaz and W. Janzarik (eds) *Search for the Causes of Schizophrenia* (pp. 179–188), Heidelberg: Springer.

—— (1988) 'Psychological models of schizophrenia', in E. Miller and P. Cooper (eds) *Adult Abnormal Psychology* (pp. 101–127), London: Churchill Livingstone.

—— (1995) 'La esquizofrenia: modelos explicativos' ('Schizophrenia: explanatory models'), in A. Belloch, B. Sandin and F. Ramos (eds) *Manual de Psicopatologia* (pp. 503–533), Madrid: McGraw-Hill.

Ibañez, E. and Belloch, A. (1989) 'Psicologia academica y psicologia profesional en el campo de la clinica' ('Academic psychology and professional psychology in the clinical domain'), *Anuario de Psicologia* 41: 33–48.
Ingram, R.E. (ed.) (1990) *Contemporary Psychological Approaches to Depression*, New York: Plenum Press.
Jaspers, K. (1946) *Allgemeine Psychopatologie, 4th edition*, Berlin: Springer.
Kellner, R. (1994) 'Psychosomatic syndromes, somatization and somatoform disorders', *Psychotherapy and Psychosomatics* 61: 4–24.
Kelly, E.L. (1961) 'Clinical psychology –1960: report on survey findings', *American Psychological Association, Division of Clinical Psychology Newsletter* 14, 1: 1–11.
Koch, S. (1964) 'Psychology and emerging conceptions of knowledge as unitary', in T. W. Wann (ed.) *Behaviorism and Phenomenology: Contrasting Bases for Modern Psychology*, Chicago: The University of Chicago Press.
Korchin, S.I. (1976) *Modern Clinical Psychology*, New York: Basic Books.
—— (1983) 'The history of clinical psychology: a personal view', in M. Hersen, A. E. Kazdin and A.S. Bellack (eds) *The Clinical Psychology Handbook* (pp. 5–19), New York: Pergamon Press.
Kuhn, T.H. (1962) *The Structure of Scientific Revolutions*, Chicago: University of Chicago Press.
Last, C.G. and Hersen, M. (eds) (1988) *Handbook of Anxiety Disorders*, Oxford: Pergamon Press.
Lundin, R.W. (1961) *Personality: An Experimental Approach*, New York: Macmillan.
Maling, M.S. and Howard, K.I. (1994) 'From research to practice to research to . . .', in P.F. Talley, H.H. Strupp and S.F. Butler (eds) *Psychotherapy Research and Practice: Bridging the Gap*, New York: Basic Books.
Matarazzo, J. (1980) 'Behavioral health and behavioral medicine: frontiers for a new health psychology', *American Psychologist* 35: 807–817.
Mathews, A. and MacLeod, C. (1994) 'Cognitive approaches to emotion and emotional disorders', *Annual Review of Psychology* 45: 25–50.
Mischel, W. (1968) *Personality and Assessment*, New York: John Wiley & Sons.
—— (1973) 'Toward a cognitive social learning reconceptualization of personality', *Psychological Review* 80: 252–283.
Moras, K. and Barlow, D.H. (1992) 'Dimensional approaches to diagnosis and the problem of anxiety and depression', in A. Ehlers, W. Fiegenbaum, I. Florin and I. Margraf (eds) *Perspectives and Promises of Clinical Psychology* (pp. 23–37), New York: Plenum Press.
Öhman, A. (1993) 'Fear and anxiety as emotional phenomena: clinical phenomenology, evolutionary perspectives and information-processing mechanisms', in M. Lewis and I.M. Haviland (eds) *Handbook of Emotions* (pp. 511–536), New York: Guilford Press.
Pelechano, V. (1979) 'Terapia y modificacion de conducta', ('Behaviour therapy and behaviour modification'), *Boletin de la Fundacion Juan March* 78: 3–18.
—— (1996) 'Psicologia clinica, psicologia de la salud y la busqueda del santo grial' ('Clinical psychology, health psychology and the search for the Holy Grail'), in V. Pelechano (ed.) *Psicologia Clinica y/o Psicologia de la Salud* (pp. 163–204), Valencia: Promolibro.
Pilgrim, D. and Treacher, A. (1992) *Clinical Psychology Observed*, London: Routledge.
Pinillos, J.L. (1980) 'Observaciones sobre la Psicologia scientifica' ('Notes on scientific psychology'), *Analisis y Modificacion de Conducta* 13: 537–590.
—— (1993) 'La Psicologia en la encrucijada' ('Psychology at the crossroads'), in V. Pelechano (ed.) *Psicologia, Mitopsicologia y Postpsicologia* (pp. 27–42), Valencia: Promolibro.
Pintner, R. (1931) *Intelligence Testing*, New York: Henry Holt.

Pitts, M. and Phillips, K. (1991) *The Psychology of Health: An Introduction*, London: Routledge.

Reed, G.E. (1988) *The Psychology of Anomalous Experience*, Buffalo, NY: Prometheus Books.

Reisman, I.M. (1976) *A History of Clinical Psychology*, New York: Irvington Publishers.

Rogers, C.R. (1942) *Counseling and Psychotherapy*, Boston, MA: Houghton Mifflin.

—— (1951a) 'Studies in client-centered psychotherapy. III. The case of Mr. Oak: a research analysis', *Psychological Service Center Journal* 3: 47–165.

—— (1951b) *Client-centered Therapy*, Boston, MA: Houghton Mifflin.

Sandin, B. (1995) 'Teorias sobre los trastornos de ansiedad', ('Theories on anxiety disorders'), in A. Belloch, B. Sandin and F. Ramos (eds) *Manual de Psicopatologia* (pp. 113–169), Madrid: McGraw-Hill.

Sarafino, E.P. (1994) *Health Psychology: Biopsychosocial Interactions*, New York: John Wiley & Sons.

Schwartz, G.E. and Weiss, S.M. (1978) 'Behavioral medicine revisited: an amended definition', *Journal of Behavioral Medicine* 1: 249–251.

Skakow, D. (1978) 'Clinical psychology seen some 50 years later', *American Psychologist* 33: 148–158.

Stocking, G.W. (1965) 'On the limits of "presentism" and "historicism" in the historiography of the behavioral sciences', *Journal of the History of the Behavioral Sciences* 1: 211–217.

Stone, G.C., Weiss, S.M., Matarazzo, J.D., Miller, N.E., Rodin, I., Belar, C.D., Follick, M.J. and Singer, J.E. (eds) (1987) *Health Psychology: A Discipline and a Profession*, Chicago: University of Chicago Press.

Stone, M. (1985) 'Shellshock and the psychologists', in W.F. Bynum, R. Porter and M. Shepherd (eds) *The Anatomy of Madness*, London: Tavistock.

Szasz, T. (1960) 'The myth of mental illness', *American Psychologist* 15: 113–118.

—— (1961) *The Myth of Mental Illness: Foundations of a Theory of Personal Conduct*, New York: Hoeber-Harper.

Taylor, S.E. (1986) *Health Psychology*, New York: Random House.

—— (1990) *Health Psychology, 3rd edition*, New York: McGraw-Hill.

Treasure, J. (1991) 'Long-term management of eating disorders', *International Review of Psychiatry* 3: 43–58.

Warwick, H.M.C. and Salkovskis, P.M. (1990) 'Hypochondriasis', *Behavior Research and Therapy* 28: 105–117.

Watson, R.I. (1953) 'A brief history of clinical psychology', *Psychological Bulletin* 50: 321–346.

White, R.W. (1981) 'Exploring personality the long way: the study of lives', in A.I. Rabin, J. Aronoff, A.M. Barclay and R.A. Zucker (eds) *Further Explorations in Personality* (pp. 3–19), New York: John Wiley & Sons.

Widiger, T.A. and Trull, T.J. (1991) 'Diagnosis and clinical assessment', *Annual Review of Psychology* 42: 109–33.

Williams, J.M., Watts, F.N., MacLeod, C. and Mathews, A. (1988) *Cognitive Psychology and Emotional Disorders*, Chichester, Sussex: John Wiley & Sons.

Yates, A.J. (1958) 'The application of learning theory to the treatment of tics', *Journal of Abnormal and Social Psychology* 56: 175–182.

Zax, M. and Cowen, E.L. (1967) 'Early identification and prevention of emotional disturbance in a public school', in E.L. Cowen, F.A. Gardner and M. Zax (eds) *Emergent Approaches to Mental Health Problems* (pp. 331–351), New York: Appleton Century Crofts.

7 The influence of psychology on psychotherapy during the twentieth century

Marina Manthouli

INTRODUCTION

As we approach the threshold of the twenty-first century, interest in the future of psychology is reaching its peak. Although psychology is expected to play its most important role in the future, it has already borrowed from and has lent to other professions a great amount of knowledge, especially in the course of this century. Increasingly, it influences other fields such as education and economics. Above all, psychology contributes to the understanding, diagnosis and treatment of psychological problems as well as most models of psychotherapy. It is interesting to focus on the ancient roots of psychology, the very beginnings of the study of the psyche, which is traced as far as twenty-four centuries ago in Ancient Greece.

The psyche and psychic phenomena were investigated even earlier, in the Homeric years. In Homer's epics, we find many references to man as a living organism possessing a psyche dwelling in the stomach or the heart, or even in the head! Later, philosophy treated the psyche as the basis of logical life, linked to the organization of the city-state; in other words, to civilization. We find references to the collective as well as the individual psyche, through the descriptions of wars. On the other hand, Greek drama, which mainly brings forward the conflicts of heroes and their emotional breakdown, constitutes the pathway leading to the development of human nature (Romilly 1992). However, psychology as a science was founded by the philosophers. Heraclitus and other pre-Socratic philosophers recognized the difficulties and the extent of problems related to the human psyche. From the sixth to the fourth century BC, Greek philosophy reflects the progress of psychology.

The Pythagoreans accepted the existence of the psyche. They were the first to speak about its immortality and about reincarnation. In Athens in the fifth century BC, Socrates' discussions included ways of improving the life-style, of cultivating, liberating and improving the psyche. Socrates pretended ignorance and professed knowledge and virtue. The principle of 'know thyself', inscribed on the wall of Apollo's temple in Delphi, does not refer to psychological advice, but it demonstrates the significance attributed to an accomplished man. In Plato's dialogues, there are multiple investigations of the psyche and psychic phenomena. However, the first one who wrote systematically about psychology is Aristotle (Romilly 1992).

With Aristotle, psychology acquired a novel orientation which governed it for centuries and influenced the modern psychologists. His contribution to psychology is enormous, in particular the fact that he placed the psyche 'in the heart'. He was the one who wrote the first treatise in psychology, '*On the Psyche*', known by its Latin title, *De Anima*. Aristotle defined the psyche (*De Anima, II*: 412) as the first 'entelehia' (i.e. the cause and the origin acting and producing psychic and biological phenomena) of an organism having all the capacities required for life. It is obvious that for Aristotle the psyche is the source that gives life to the body, it is the strength mobilizing the functions that maintain life, the original source of biological and psychic functions, the 'nutritive', the 'sensitive', the 'imaginative' and the 'rational'. The manifestations of these functions are the 'motor' and the 'digestive' which is divided into wish and will. The most important of these psychic functions is the 'rational', which is a manifestation of the 'mind', the mental element of man, constituting the immortal part of human nature. In his writings, there are many observations on psychic phenomena. Aristotle was the first to observe and express the law of the psychological association of psychic images on the basis of their similarity, contrast and cohesion in time and space. His work *De Anima* refers to his predecessors and constructs an analytical psychology. Although it is considered as the first text treating this discipline, it is astonishing how modern his method is in elucidating all the elements concerning the different sensations on which he experimented.

Aristotle and Plato were great philosophers with different starting points. Aristotle observed and analysed a phenomenon. He placed it next to other phenomena, thus constructing a system (a method that Wundt and Titchener tried to use a thousand years later). Plato regarded things through the question 'What is the objective?' The first tended to be more theoretical, while the other was more interested in practical aspects. Plato's psychology is influenced by his own philosophy regarding the state and social ethics. Aristotle worked on a manual which treated all the mental processes, sensations, perceptions, emotions, following the course of his observations and experimentation (Roback 1992).

Hippocrates, the father of medicine, was the first to claim that all diseases are due to an organic dysfunction or to an adverse environmental effect. He described the main psychological disorders for the first time. The terms he used are still in use today – hysteria, mania, melancholy, dementia and paranoia. Aristotle also supported the organic origin of all the physical and mental diseases. Plato, on the other hand, did not. He considered all the psychological problems as inevitable manifestations of the human mind, which are not influenced by external factors. Plato's view, that the source of our perception of reality is the mind and not experience, is reflected in the psychology developed by Kant, the German philosopher of the nineteenth century, and in the theory of the unconscious developed by Freud.

It is interesting that people with conditions of psychological origin such as hysteria sought help in the therapeutic centres of Asclepius. The dreams of both the patient and the person responsible for his or her therapy were interpreted in the belief that dreams reflected the psychological condition of the patient. Plato and Aristotle were followed by Epicurus and Zenon. They created schools and communities of philosophy which were influenced by their ideals and their behavioural patterns. The principle of both these schools was the importance of experience for the development of psychism. The psyche was believed to be a blank, colourless and shapeless mass at birth (Roback 1992).

With the conquests of Alexander, Greek thinking expanded through the rest of the world. The philosophers after Aristotle were not preoccupied by psychological issues. On the contrary, they were interested in political and ethical matters. In particular, the stoics, sceptics, epicureans and cynics mainly treated the ways of becoming independent of the natural world (Lundin 1991).

Today psychology has changed. Still, we must consider the first transformations that established, formed and enriched it during the Athenian fifth century, when many principal ideas were discovered. The individual gained importance in a democratic environment, where medicine and history were born, and the power of Athens was established. At the same time, the changes, inventions and disputes of the past and the hopes for the future were concentrated and expressed. Psychology is part of that great movement of discoveries. Its evolution guides us even now (Romilly 1992).

The discovery of psychology by the Greeks has a particular meaning today, since psychology has become one of the most important sciences. It has been deeply revised by Freud and the psychoanalysts who followed. Furthermore, it has played an important role in the emergence and development of the subsequent psychotherapeutic approaches.

PSYCHOTHERAPY YESTERDAY

When psychotherapy emerged as a science in Germany in the middle of the nineteenth century, it was defined as the analysis of consciousness. At that time, consciousness was considered to be composed of structural elements closely associated to processes within the sense organs. This kind of psychology was fought from all sides and for various reasons. A general criticism was that the mind cannot be investigated through scientific methods, because each mind bears its own particularities. Freud was strongly critical. He compared the mind to an iceberg, whose smaller part is above the water and represents the conscious, while the largest part is beneath the water and represents the unconscious world of invisible forces that control the conscious thoughts of the individual.

For more than forty years, Freud investigated the unconscious through 'free association'. He developed an integral theory of personality and a therapeutic technique for dealing with mental illness. Through this theory, Freud became one of the most controversial and influential figures of the twentieth century.

Freud's interest in psychoanalysis started from neurology. At that time, psychology was dissociated from philosophy and began to develop as an individual science. Freud became interested in both sciences. During his youth, he had also shown an interest in history and literature. His interest in these disciplines is said to have led him to the idea of 'free association' (Fancher 1973).

As a student, Freud had used a book of psychology which strongly influenced his theory. The book referred to Johann Herbart (1776–1841), a philosopher of the nineteenth century. According to Ernest Jones (1953), Freud was influenced by Herbart in using free association as a therapeutic technique, as well as in developing the conflict between the conscious and the unconscious mind. The concept of regression, this cornerstone of psychoanalysis, was adopted by Freud from the writings of Schopenhauer (1788–1860) (Lundin 1991).

Freud was not particularly interested in typical issues of interest for psychologists (sensations, perception, learning). His psychology was a psychology of the personality, which was equally important both in theory and in practice. Some theories and systems were developed by academic psychologists through experiments and observations. Psychoanalysis, however, emerged and developed in a medical and clinical environment. Most of the subsequent psychotherapeutic models have been somehow influenced by the psychoanalytic theory, representing the intellectual movement of Freud's time (1856–1939) when there was a trend towards the physical and biological sciences (Lundin 1991).

More than any other system *psychoanalysis* has influenced other intellectual developments, such as art, drama, sociology, and anthropology as well as psychology. One could say that no other theory of personality had a greater impact on the intellectual life of the twentieth century. A great many individuals who are not psychologists have read Freud's books which can be found everywhere (Lundin 1991).

As a system of thought and as a technique for dealing with mental illness, psychoanalysis continues to evolve and remains a steady, reliable and growing discipline of study and treatment (Corsini 1979). However, we should consider that all forms of mental illness cannot possibly be dealt with by psychoanalysis, which requires the co-operation of patients with a relatively healthy ego, with sufficient motivation for change and the ability to deal with themselves. With the right selection of patients, psychoanalysis can offer help, so that the patients will find the appropriate solution and overcome their internal conflicts (Corsini 1979).

From the early 1920s, Freud's name was known worldwide and his ideas were equally widespread. Many believed that Freud's psychology included all of modern psychology. For years, psychologists were seen as investigators of unconscious motives. Orthodox Freudians have constituted an important and active school.

Many forms of psychotherapy have since appeared. Some have vanished, others persist and continue to exert influence. In 1911, Adler founded his own psychoanalytic theory and therapeutic system, individual psychology. Unlike Freud, who had emphasized the biological nature of man, Adler regarded man as a social being, influenced by the social environment (Lundin 1991). His therapeutic method leads the neurotic person to understand his or her mind and the collective symbols hidden behind his or her behaviour (Lundin 1991). In 1914, Carl Jung founded his own movement of analytical psychology, which preserved some of Freud's ideas and evolved into an independent system. Jung supported empiricism and considered himself to be an observer of psychological issues.

Although Freud did not develop a theory on ego psychology, he was the first to deal with the ego. His interest is apparent in his books *Group Psychology and the Analysis of the Ego* (1921); *The Ego and the Id* (1923), and *Inhibitions, Symptoms and Anxiety* (1926). However, his daughter, Anna Freud, defined the concept of the ego in her book *The Ego and the Mechanisms of Defence* (1936). Hartman, who is considered the father of modern ego psychology, studied Freud's writings for the origins of the concepts of the ego. He expanded the psychology of the ego to the theory of adaptation in 1939, presenting it in 1958. Hartman brought ego psychology to its highest level. His theory became the starting point for Jacobson, Mahler, Spitz and many others who based their theories on his.

The theorists of ego psychology focused on the psychological and physical interaction between the infant and its primary environment, the mother. They claimed that the pathology of adulthood expresses a dysfunction or regression to a pre-Oedipal stage of development, where communication is pre-verbal, mainly physical, and refers to the primal relationship and communication with the maternal figure. Any disturbance to the mother–infant relationship leads to unsuccessful developmental phases which result in serious pathology such as psychosis and psychological and physical disorders (Blanck and Blanck 1974: 19–25).

The theory of object relations resulted in a shift of interest from the instinctual drive to the bond between the self and its objects. Melanie Klein (1952) was one of the earliest architects of this theory. Winnicott expanded Klein's theory and spoke about the 'environmental mother' and the importance of the child's interpersonal surroundings. Among the concepts he developed are those of 'holding' and 'good enough mother' (Winnicott 1965).

During 1970, the concept of self emerged. Heinz Kohut focused his work on self disorders and developed self psychology, according to which the relationship with the self is the basis of the reconstructive process and the main objective of psychotherapy (Kohut 1971).

Behaviourism is an important theory of psychology which appeared in 1913. John Watson attempted to define psychology as a 'purely objective experimental field of natural science'. Its theoretical goal is the 'prediction and control of behavior' (Watson 1913). Some of Watson's influences were Greek naturalism, French materialism of the eighteenth and nineteenth centuries, Darwin's determinism, Pavlov's conditioned reflex, and functionalism (Lundin 1991). Watson followed Aristotle's psychology, which was dominated by dualism, a separation of mind and body. In 1919, he denied the existence of the mind and consciousness and in 1925 he rejected completely the concept of instinct at the human level (Lundin 1991).

Behavioural psychotherapy consists of two systems of treatment. Behavioural therapy is based on the work of Wolpe (1973) and follows a classical conditioning model. Behavioural modification is based on the work of Skinner (1953) and is derived from operant conditioning (Corsini 1979). According to Eysenck, the aim of therapy is 'to get rid of the symptom', in order to eliminate neurosis (Eysenck and Rachman 1965 in Corsini 1979: 231). This is one of the main differences from other theories of psychotherapy, especially psychoanalytic therapy.

Initially this method had to deal with problems related to poor study habits, as well as more complex problems related to personality. During the 1970s and 1980s, behaviour therapy introduced new techniques for schizophrenics (Paul and Lentz 1977) and special programmes for autistic children (Lovaas 1987).

Humanistic psychology was suggested by Abraham Maslow in 1962. It became the 'third force' in psychology, after psychoanalysis and behaviourism. It is influenced by ancient Greek and Latin writings of art and philosophy (Lundin 1991), by existential psychology and existential philosophy. Humanistic therapy focuses not on the 'cure' of problems, but on the growth, creativity and spontaneity of the individual (Rogers 1979).

The best known is the person-centred therapy developed by Carl Rogers in the 1940s. Rogers was influenced by John Dewey's philosophy, the work of Otto Rank, and Buber's and Kierkegaard's existential ideas. His theory evolved out of his experiences as a psychotherapist. Rogers' therapy is non-directive. The therapist never gives advice, never makes critical or punishing statements, but reflects the client's feelings as they are expressed.

Gestalt therapy blends Freudian concepts and humanistic philosophy as well as Gestalt psychology, founded in the first half of the twentieth century by Wertheimer, Kolher and Kofka (Evans 1978). It was developed by Frederick Perls in 1951, who was trained as a Freudian psychoanalyst.

Perls was influenced by Karen Horney, Wilhelm Reich, Kurt Goldstein and others. The focus of Gestalt therapy is in the awareness of one's experience in the here and now. Cognitive explanations or interpretations are rejected. According to Irma Shepherd (1970), Gestalt therapy is effective with socialized individuals such as neurotics, phobics or depressives. She advises Gestalt therapists to avoid work with severely disturbed or psychotic individuals. Existential psychotherapies assist clients in learning to express themselves. They emphasize an awareness of the client's own subjective experience and the belief that the human relationship is of great importance for healing.

During the twentieth century, there was a great development in *group psychology* and *group psychotherapy*. It became necessary during and after the two world wars, especially during the Second World War, because large numbers of people were suffering from the social, political and economic difficulties of those periods. However, it is obvious that the advantages of group psychotherapy are not only financial. Yalom points out that, in a group setting, people discover that their problems are acceptable. Members gain comfort and courage from the support of the group (Yalom 1975).

According to their theoretical orientation, some group therapists stress the importance of social and communicational factors. They believe that groups can be effective. Others consider group procedures as an extension of individual therapy (Clarkson and Pokorny 1994). There is an impression that group psychotherapy is a broad and controversial therapeutic model, quite vague in its title, content, aim and the effectiveness of its methods.

Nevertheless, a great number of approaches have been developed in the United States and in Europe, and in particular, in the United Kingdom after 1940. After the First World War, Freud spoke about group psychology in *Group Psychology and the Analysis of the Ego* (1921), but he did not expand his theory to a therapeutic use. Gestalt psychology and Kurt Lewin's theory played a very important role in the birth of group psychotherapy.

The beginning of group psychotherapy in the United States is associated with Pratt's experiments in Boston in 1905. He used the 'instructive method' in tuberculosis patients with very effective results. Lazel (1993) used the same method in schizophrenic patients. He believed that the improvement of his patients was due to socialization and discussion among them (Freedheim 1993). At the same time, Moreno introduced psychodrama in Vienna.

The social orientation of Adler's Individual Psychology led to a general interest in group methods. Adler's view, that man cannot be studied in isolation but only in a social context, comes from Aristotle, who refers to man as a '*zoon politicon*', a political animal (Adler 1959). In addition, Lewin's theory was focused on group dynamics. He believed that the group can 'push' individuals towards a change in their behaviour.

The development of group psychotherapy in the United Kingdom helped to develop the group method as a therapeutic approach. In the Military Hospital of Northfield during the Second World War, group psychotherapy and the therapeutic community were formed, enabling the subsequent formation of theory and specific technique (Foulkes 1948, 1990; Main 1946; Pines 1978). Bion, Ezriel and Foulkes participated in the Northfield experiment. Foulkes developed group analysis, an integrated theoretical and therapeutic model which synthesized Gestalt theory and psychoanalysis.

The basic theoretical concepts of group analysis derive from the principles of psychoanalysis, Lewin's field theory and Gestalt psychology (Pines 1983: 267). Foulkes' contact with the sociological views of the School of Frankfurt helped him develop the concept of leadership in the social group. He believed in the social nature of the individual's mind and personality. His philosophy on psychotherapy was that

> psychotherapy is always concerned with the whole person. The human being is a social animal who cannot live in isolation. In order to see him as a whole, one has to see him in a group, either that in which he lives and in which his conflicts arise . . . or in a group of strangers where he can re-establish his conflicts in pure culture. The group is the background, the horizon, the frame of reference of the total situation.
>
> (Foulkes 1974, cited in Foulkes 1990: 271)

Relationships among the members of the group are hierarchical, horizontal or equal. The conductor should function either horizontally as an equal member, or, in very rare cases, vertically. The interplay between horizontal and vertical levels of communication within the group constitutes a maturational process for the members, as they communicate with both the adult part of themselves and the immature and dependent part. Through this interplay, they learn to profit from their own emotional deposits in order to become independent and reinforce the adult part of their personality (Tsegos 1982).

The principles of group analysis have influenced other forms of therapy, such as Family Therapy (Skynner 1977) and the therapeutic community (Clark 1965), as well as training institutions for group analytic psychotherapy such as the formation of the European Group Analytic Training Institutions Network (EGATIN).

Since the appearance of the first *therapeutic community* after the Second World War, many different models have developed in various settings. The group analytic model (Tsegos 1982) is a psychotherapeutic community based on the reconstructive model (Van der Linden 1978). It is extremely effective for patients with severe psychic disturbances, such as psychoses or borderline personalities. Its main characteristic is the combination of psychotherapy and sociotherapy on an equal basis. Each activity pursues its own therapeutic aims, but they are interrelated and complementary in their function. Groups with a psychodynamic orientation are mainly concerned with relating to one's self. Those with a sociodynamic orientation are concerned with relating to others as well as relating to reality. The philosophy of the group analytic model is:

- to become therapeutic for each one of its members, therapists, patients, trainees (Clark 1965);
- to minimize the use of interpretations;
- to become effective in cases of severe emotional disturbance.

PSYCHOTHERAPY TODAY

Through this brief overview of the main psychotherapeutic models as they have evolved and been practised during the twentieth century, we followed the development of psychological thought from Ancient Greece to the present day.

Only a very small part of the work that has been done is presented here. Yet it reveals the influence which philosophy and psychology have had on most psychotherapeutic models, directly or indirectly.

The birth of psychotherapy was an important event in medical and psychological history. It opened a new road for the investigation and understanding of psychic disturbance, which throughout the twentieth century has been approached by fields such as the medical, psychological, philosophical and pharmaceutical. Freud's 'iceberg' uncovered the existence of the roots of psychic life, the unconscious world which motivates our actions. Depth psychology played a very important role in the study and understanding of the pathological expression of the psyche. Social psychology focused on the social factors which may influence the development of pathology, suggesting that the cause of pathology should be sought in the interaction and communication among family members (Georgas 1986) and that therapy should be given in a social environment.

Psychotherapy means 'therapy of the psyche'. According to Aristotle, the psyche is 'the cause and the origin of acting and producing psychic and biological phenomena'. Most medical personnel today treat physical or psychological problems, considering the functioning of the individual's organism as a system. Foulkes (1974) emphasizes in his writings that 'the healthy organism functions as a whole, that the . . . disturbed function is due to the disturbance of the equilibrium of the total situation' and that for an effective therapy 'one must take into account the whole personality and the patient's life situation past and present'. He also stresses that 'this can only be done in terms of Psychology' (Foulkes 1948: 3).

At the end of this century, many questions arise concerning the practice of psychotherapy, such as: 'Who gives therapy?' 'Who gets therapy?' 'Where is it available?' or the most crucial, 'Does psychotherapy work?' There is an abundance of theories, and therapists who follow the procedures prescribed by theory or orientation. However, there is great confusion about what really constitutes psychotherapy. A friend or relative may use words with common sense to comfort someone: is this psychotherapy?

To comment on what we mean by 'therapy' or 'psychotherapy' and in view of the practical difficulties which arise because of the large number of different approaches, I recall Foulkes. He considered that 'the first essential and general aim of all psychotherapy is the move from the symptoms to the problem' (Foulkes 1974: 3). 'Its aim is to develop insight and adjustment' (Foulkes 1948: 164), and it can be 'obtained through the multipersonal relationship, which develops in the group' and 'the awareness the client is obtaining in connection to his problem' (Tsegos 1996).

The range of individuals who seek and could benefit from psychotherapy varies from those with mild to those with more severe disturbances. Clearly there are clients or patients who, before the birth of psychotherapy, were treated with cruelty; those who unfortunately continue to be hospitalized; those who at the edge of the twenty-first century are labelled as 'dangerous' and without the hope of any 'cure' nor the freedom to choose the kind of therapy or therapist they prefer, or even whether or not they want to be 'cured'.

It seems that we tend to forget that there are settings which specialize in the treatment of psychoses, such as psychotherapeutic communities. It is well known that such settings offer patients the freedom to choose the kind of participation they prefer and to decide for their own future.

The emergence of psychotherapy during the twentieth century is associated with advances in therapy and the continuing development of new theories and techniques. However, psychotherapy as a part of our life and culture is related to human activities such as art, religion, politics and financial interests. The social view of illness is defined by medical, therapeutic and diagnostic technology, instead of conceiving the person as an integrated system with inherent potentials. Psychotherapists must take responsibility for shaping therapeutic settings with specific structure, context and content which are acceptable to the patient, respect the patient's needs and allow personal growth. These should be suitable for those with severe disorders, and, most of all, should not remove patients from their own environments.

Does psychotherapy work?

A series of research studies has been completed on psychotherapy during the last decades, in spite of the obvious variety and the ethical and practical difficulties. Most results have shown that the answer is '*Yes, psychotherapy is effective*' (Rosenzweig 1992). Some findings may be summarized:

- The client is the principal determiner of the effectiveness of a given treatment (Lambert 1991).
- Psychotherapy alone is as effective as drugs in treating depression (Nevada School of Medicine and Cleveland Foundation, USA 1996).
- The combination of the therapeutic community and of the analytic group in an open psychotherapeutic centre proved beneficial for patients with affective disorders especially during crisis periods (Open Psychotherapeutic Center, Athens, Greece 1992).
- The psychotherapist's personality plays an important role in the success or failure of any psychotherapeutic intervention (Norcross *et al.* 1988).
- The personal training of the future psychotherapist is a foundation for Freudian training, as well as for many other models of psychotherapy, with the exception of the cognitive behavioural paradigm.
- There is a high correlation between the percentage of drop-outs of patients at the early stages of treatment and the intensity of the life crisis a therapist undergoes (Open Psychotherapeutic Center, Athens 1989).

These results among many others indicate the effectiveness of therapy, especially for patients with severe disturbances. Of course this 'effectiveness' is questioned, but our experience is evidence: 'Psychotherapy works.' It is striking that the therapist's personal therapeutic experience and personality are crucial issues for the quality of practice as well as the quality of training.

PSYCHOTHERAPY TOMORROW

The key word for the future of psychotherapy should be 'quality', both in practising psychotherapy and in training psychotherapists. Research (Norcross 1986) has shown that theoretical differences between the psychotherapeutic approaches to clinical practice are not so important for successful outcomes. On the contrary, the relationship between the therapist and the client has played a very important role. It is obvious that in order to have quality in the practice of psychotherapy we must focus on the *qualities* and the *qualifications* of the psychotherapist.

The role of a psychotherapist is quite fascinating but, as with any other discipline, interest alone is not sufficient for professional practice. Guntrip (1971) stresses the importance of training for psychotherapists. He defines training as 'to stimulate people to think clearly about themselves, their ideas and their way of practising'. Guntrip points out that 'to care for people is more important than to care for ideas' (pp. v–vi). If the therapist acquires a humanitarian attitude, it should lead him to caring and supportive relations with his patients and his colleagues, and to a life-style of high quality. He believes that theory should not dominate the experience with patients. On the contrary, experience should influence the theory which should change to meet emerging needs.

Training

Quality in psychotherapy could be achieved through training. The training of future psychotherapists should take place within an institution with a specific structure and training standards. Training in psychoanalysis is directly linked with its origins and evolution, as formed by Freud and his disciples. In 1920, the Institute of Psychoanalysis of Berlin presented an important training curriculum and structure which is very close to the way modern psychoanalytic institutes function. Ernest Jones' contribution is considered to be equally important. He determined common guidelines and standards for the trainees at each institute, whether they were medical or non-medical psychoanalysts. Training encompasses theory, personal training analysis and clinical supervision.

As in the case of individual psychotherapy, the history of training in group psychotherapy corresponds to its tradition, history and the evolution of group-analytic methods. Training group therapists has been addressed by experts in the United States and Europe. The first professionals, mainly psychologists, differed in their orientation and their philosophy of therapy. The literature shows that in fifty years of group psychotherapy in the United States, there is no widely accepted training model suitable for all approaches. Furthermore, the American

Group Psychotherapy Association does not require the personal therapy of trainees in a group, nor their participation in group therapy with 'real' patients. By contrast, the Canadian Group Psychotherapy Association has higher standards and requirements, including therapy in a group with actual patients.

In Europe, the formation of a specific group-analytic method with a clearly defined therapeutic philosophy, theory and methodology has contributed to the establishment and rapid expansion of group analysis in several countries. The Institute of Group Analysis, London was the basis of this development. It controls and regulates the suitability of those practising group analysis through an integrated training policy of high standards. Foulkes mainly focused first on the therapist and second on the training procedure. Therefore, according to his training principles, the essence of training is the appropriate personal therapy and the acquisition of a specific professional identity, regardless of theoretical or technical knowledge.

The same philosophy and need for a strong and clearly defined identity led to the establishment of the European Group Analytic Training Network (EGATIN), founded in 1988 on the initiative of I.K. Tsegos, President of the Institute of Group Analysis (Athens). It is a 'federation of organizations which offer training programmes in group analysis, which generally consist of personal therapy in a group, theory and supervision'. One of its aims is 'to encourage high standards in group-analytic training programmes through the sharing of expertise and experience between member organizations'.

The European Federation of Psychoanalytic Psychotherapists (EFPP), founded in 1991 within the European Community, has specific minimum training requirements for:

1 Psychoanalytic psychotherapy for individual therapy:
  • minimum three years' training
  • minimum three years, forty hours yearly, for personal individual psycho-analysis
  • theoretical and clinical seminars – 200 hours.
2 Group Analytic Psychotherapy Training:
  • minimum four years' training
  • personal group analytic psychotherapy – at least 240 hours
  • minimum supervision – 180 hours
  • seminars in group analytic and psychoanalytic theory, not fewer than 200 hours.
3 Child and adolescent psychoanalytic psychotherapy training:
  • minimum three years' training
  • personal psychoanalytic psychotherapy
  • clinical experience with supervision
  • theory.

Each candidate's personal suitability and progress is evaluated throughout the training period.

The European Federation of Professional Psychologists' Associations (EFPPA) is in the process of establishing training standards for psychological psychotherapists through its *Task Force on Psychotherapy*. These standards will be the guidelines for the future. EFPPA recommends:

1 Entry: five years' university studies in academic psychology.
2 Two years' experience as a professional psychologist in a health setting.
3 Training: three years' full-time supervision – minimum 150 hours
   • theoretical practice – minimum 400 hours
   • personal training therapy – minimum 100 hours
   • clinical supervisory practice – minimum 500 hours.

Our experience has shown that psychotherapy in the future will not be practised in an isolated, fruitless individual setting but in the rich, social environment of the group. This allows the active participation, interaction and growth of each of its members, as well as the growth of the group. According to Foulkes (1964: 99), group psychotherapy is a difficult discipline for the therapist. He suggests that those 'not gifted for it should better leave it alone' and that 'those with special gifts need years of hard study, penetrating experience to possess a sufficient degree of personal integration to stand up to the emotional storms and havocs they have to live through.'

A training community scheme (Tsegos 1988) could offer many opportunities for clinical experience, as well as for the development and reinforcement of the trainee's personal and professional identity. Future psychotherapists will also have the opportunity to make important changes to themselves, to feel equal in social and professional relationships, to improve their life-style and to practise psychotherapy with high quality skills. If only psychotherapists of such quality enter the twenty-first century.

In conclusion, we could say that the twenty-first century will 'welcome' the discipline of psychotherapy. It has developed by advancing, as well as retracting processes, causing controversy but at the same time gaining acceptance as the discipline which has offered the public a great service. People have begun to understand and accept the role of the psychotherapist and the value and contribution of psychotherapy to society. They are more acquainted with and less afraid to accept their services. The 'stigma' of severely disturbed individuals is decreasing. Psychology has played an important role in the development of this fascinating discipline. It will continue to offer its skills in evaluating, researching and improving the knowledge we already have and in contributing to the developmental process of this scientific and artistic profession. Aristotle's observation and experimental methods will continue to stimulate the investigation of our psyche.

120   *Marina Manthouli*

REFERENCES

Adler, A. (1959) *Understanding Human Nature*, New York: Premier Books.

Aristotle, *On the Psyche (De Anima) I, II*, Athens: Papyros.

Beutler, L.E. and Grago, M. (1994) *Psychotherapy Research*, Washington, DC: American Psychological Association.

Blanck, C. and Blanck, R. (1974) *Ego Psychology Theory and Practice*, New York: Columbia Press.

Bootzin, R.R., Bower, G.H. and Crocker, J. (1991) *Psychology Today, 7th edn*, New York: McGraw-Hill.

Clark, D. (1965) 'The therapeutic community: concept, practice and future', *British Journal of Psychiatry* 3: 947.

Clarkson, P. and Pokorny, M. (eds) (1994) *The Handbook of Psychotherapy*, London: Routledge.

Corsini, R. (1979) *Current Psychotherapies, 2nd edn*, Itasca, IL: Peacock Publications.

Cottle, T. and Whitten, P. (eds) (1980) *Current Perspectives*, New York: New Viewpoints.

European Federation for Psychoanalytic Psychotherapy (EFPP) (1991) *Constitution*.

European Federation of Professional Psychologists' Associations (EFPPA) (March 1991) *Task Force on Psychotherapy*.

European Group Analytic Training Institutions Network (EGATIN) (1988) *Constitution*.

Evans, C. (1978) *Psychology, a Dictionary of the Mind, Brain and Behaviour*, London: Arrow Books.

Eysenck, H.J. and Rachman, S. (1965) *The Causes and Cures of Neurosis*, San Diego: Knapp.

Fancher, R. (1973) *Psychoanalytic Psychology. The Development of Freud's Thought*, New York: Norton & Co.

Foulkes, S. (1948) *Introduction to Group Analytic Psychotherapy*, London: Maresfield.

—— (1964) *Therapeutic Group Analysis*, London: Maresfield.

—— (1974) 'My philosophy in psychotherapy', in E. Foulkes (ed.) *Selected Papers of S.H. Foulkes. Psychoanalysis and Group Analysis*, London: Karnac.

—— (ed.) (1990) *Psychoanalysis and Group Analysis: Selected Papers of S.H. Foulkes*, London: Karnac.

Foulkes, S. and Anthony, J. (1957) *Group Psychotherapy. The Psychoanalytical Approach*, London: Maresfield.

Freedheim, D. (ed.) (1993) *History of Psychotherapy. A Century of Change*, Washington, DC: American Psychoanalytical Association.

Freedman, D.A. (1972) 'On the limits of the effectiveness of psychoanalysis: early ego and somatic disturbances', *International Journal of Psychoanalysis* 53: 363–369.

Freud, S. (1937) *History of Psychoanalysis*, trans A. Koen, Athens: Govostis.

Georgas, G. (1986) *Social Psychology. Volume A*, Athens: University of Athens.

Grotjahn, G. (1978) 'A walk with Michael Foulkes', in L. Wolberg, M. Aronson and A. Wolberg (eds) *Group Therapy 1978: An Overview*, New York: Stratton Intercontinental Medical Books.

Guntrip, H. (1971) *Psychoanalytic Theory, Therapy and the Self*, London: Maresfield Reprints.

Hall, G.H. and Lindzey, G. (1978) *Theories of Personality*, New York: John Wiley & Sons.

Hartman, H. (1939) *Ego Psychology and the Problem of Adaptation*, New York: International University Press.

Jones, E. (1953) *The Life and Work of Sigmund Freud*, Harmondsworth, Middlesex: Penguin.

Kennard, D. (1983) *An Introduction to Therapeutic Communities*, London: Routledge & Kegan Paul.

Klein, M. (1952) *The Ego and the Mechanism of Defense*, trans T. Paradelis, Athens: Kastaniotis.

Kohut, H. (1971) *The Analysis of the Self*, New York: International University Press.

Lambert, M.J. (1991) 'Introduction to psychotherapy research', in L.E. Beutler and M. Grago (eds) *Psychotherapy Research: An International Review of Programmatic Studies*, Washington, DC: APA.

Lazel, D. (1993) 'Psychotherapy in groups', in D. Freedheim, *History of Psychotherapy. A Century of Change*, Washington, DC: American Psychoanalytical Association.

Lovaas, I. (1987) 'Research on training for psychotherapy', in D. Freedheim, *History of Psychotherapy. A Century of Change*, Washington, DC: American Psychoanalytical Association.

Lundin, R. (1991) *Theories and Systems of Psychology*, Lexington, MA: Heath & Co.

Main, T. (1946) 'The hospital as a therapeutic institution', *Bulletin of the Menninger Clinic* 10: 66–70.

Norcross, J.C. (1986) *Handbook of Eclectic Psychotherapy*, New York: Brunnel/Mazel.

Paul, G.L. and Lentz, R.J. (1977) *Psychological Treatment of Chronic Mental Patients*, Cambridge, MA: Harvard University Press.

Pines, M. (1978) 'The contributions of S.H. Foulkes to group analytic therapy', in L. Wolberg, M. Aronson and A. Wolberg (eds) *Group Therapy 1978: An Overview*, New York: Stratton.

—— (1983) *The Evolution of Group Analysis*, London: Routledge & Kegan Paul.

Roback, A. (1992) *History of Psychology*, trans Z. Sarikaw, Thessaloniki: Vanias.

Rogers, C. (1979) 'Person-centered therapy', in R. Corsini (ed.) *Current Psychotherapies*, Itasca, IL: Peacock Publications.

Romilly, J. (1992) *Patience, mon coeur! L'essor de la psychologie dans la litterature Grecque classique*, trans M. Athanassiou, Athens: Asty.

Rosenbaum, M. and Berger, M. (eds) (1963) *Group Psychotherapy and Group Function*, New York: Basic Books.

Rosenzweig, M. (1992) *International Psychological Science*, Washington, DC: American Psychological Association.

Shepherd, I.L. (1970) 'Limitations and cautions in Gestalt approach', in J. Fagam and I.L. Shepherd *Gestalt Therapy Now* (pp. 234–238), Palo Alto, CA: Science and Behavior Books.

Skinner, B.F. (1953) *Science and Human Behavior*, New York: Macmillan.

Skynner, R. (1977) *One Flesh: Separate Persons*, London: Constable & Co.

Tompson, R. (1992) *History of Psychology*, trans D. Apostolopoylos, Athens: Kalvos.

Tsegos, I.K. (1982) 'A psychotherapeutic community in Athens', Windsor Conference of Therapeutic Communities, Windsor.

—— (1988) 'Three training communities', 1st Symposium on Therapeutic Communities, Athens.

—— (1996) 'To mix or not to mix', unpublished paper presented at the EGATIN's Study Days, Muñster, April 1996.

Van der Linden, P. (1978) 'Classification of therapeutic communities', Windsor Conference Paper.

Watson, J.B. (1913) 'Psychology as the behaviorist views it', *Psychological Review* 20: 158–177.

Watson, J.B. and Rayner, R. (1920) 'Conditioned emotional reaction', *Journal of Experimental Psychology* 3: 1–10.

Winnicott, D.W. (1965) *The Maturational Process and the Facilitating Environment, Studies in the Theory of Development*, London: Hogarth Press and Institute of Psychoanalysis.

Wolpe, J. (1973) *The Practice of Behavior Therapy*, New York: Pergamon Press.
Yalom, I. (1975) *The Theory and Practice of Group Psychotherapy*, New York: Basic Books.
Zibborg, G. (1966) *A History of Medical Psychology*, New York: Norton & Co.

8 Psychology and education

A century of challenge for educational psychology

Ingrid Lunt

INTRODUCTION

Education has provided a fertile and long-standing area for the application of psychology, arguably constituting the first coherent area of application with, for example, Witmer's clinic in the USA and Burt's professional work in the UK in the early twentieth century. Furthermore, the social, political and educational tasks of the education system have been widely served by psychology and psychologists. Although the relationship is, on the face of it, straightforward, I will argue that there are complexities and difficulties. However, I have no doubt that there is a wide field open for psychology in education, as indeed continues to be demonstrated by research and practice.

THE NATURE AND SCOPE OF EDUCATIONAL PSYCHOLOGY

A definition of the nature and scope of educational psychology has to take account of the fact that there are two groups of psychologists which claim to apply psychology to education: those psychologists working mainly as researchers in universities, and those psychologists working mainly as practitioners and also known, at least in the USA, as school psychologists; perhaps these could be distinguished as the providers and the users of research findings. In this sense, educational psychology provides a rich field of application, although as I hope to demonstrate, the relationship between the two groups of 'educational psychologists' could be enhanced to the benefit of the discipline.

Psychology as a discipline has held a powerful and influential position in education (e.g. Francis 1985; Hargreaves 1986). Much of educational research and practice has developed from educational psychology, and psychology constitutes the discipline-base for much education theory. Historically, the psychology assumed to be relevant and applicable to education (and to schools) included major psychological topics such as cognitive and emotional development, learning, motivation, theories of intelligence, assessment and mental testing, language and social psychology. The paradigm was a predominantly positivist psychology, with an emphasis on quantitative scientific theories and methodologies. The assumption was that psychology could be applied directly to education and that principles from general psychology could be used to understand the phenomena and processes of teaching and learning.

Francis (1995) has discussed the various ways in which psychology is applied to education through educational psychology and the possible forms which this takes. The difficulty with the relationship between them is linked to some extent to the different philosophies and epistemologies of psychology and education and the way in which psychology has, to a certain extent, imposed its own positivist culture on both educational psychology and educational research.

Yet, from its earlier dominance as a foundation discipline for education, 'as far as British education is concerned, psychology appears to be in a rather sorry state' (Tomlinson 1992). It is perceived as lacking in practical and theoretical relevance (e.g. Hirst 1983; Claxton *et al.* 1985; Desforges 1985; Entwistle 1985), as out of touch with current educational issues (e.g. Claxton 1985), as lacking usefulness (e.g. Hargreaves 1978, 1986; Hastings and Schwieso 1987), as having no impact on practical teaching (e.g. Stones 1988) and it has been replaced in teacher education programmes by courses on 'educational studies' which, in turn, have more recently given way to practice in the classroom (Norwich 1985, 1995; Tomlinson 1992; Wilkinson 1992). In relation to the new model of professional training and teacher preparation, psychological theories are out of fashion; the previous hegemony of psychology has been forced to give way to an ideology of pragmatism and a predominantly anti-theoretical stance. This situation arises both out of current political and professional directions in education (e.g. Lawlor 1990), and out of differing views concerning the status of knowledge, the discipline of psychology and the appropriateness of its methods.

Educational psychology may be said to be caught between the disciplines of education and psychology and is drawn in different directions by their different epistemologies and methodologies. This tension is viewed positively by Francis, who views educational psychology as having developed 'a productive tension between education and psychology, its strength and nature varying with the distance between them and with material changes in each over time' (Francis 1995: 11).

Definition of educational psychology

It is appropriate to ask whether educational psychology is a branch (or application) of general psychology or whether it is a discipline in its own right. Hargreaves suggests that educational psychology is

> tied, like some retarded and over-dependent infant, to the parent discipline of mainstream psychology – its concepts, theories, methodology and the dead weight of its gigantic literature. Educational psychology gives every appearance of being afraid to grow up.
>
> (Hargreaves 1986: 17)

Part of the problem of defining the nature and place of educational psychology arises out of the relationship between psychology and education already mentioned: for example, as long ago as 1898, William James expressed the view that

> psychology is a science and teaching is an art; and sciences never generate arts directly out of themselves. An intermediate inventive mind must make that application, by using its originality.
>
> (William James 1899/1983, quoted in Berliner 1993: 50)

Berliner thus contrasts the 'ethical and concrete' approach of the teacher with the 'abstract and analytical' approach of the psychologist; he suggests that 'our job (as educational psychologists) is to psychologise about educational problems and issues and not simply to bring psychology to education' (ibid., p. 72).

The question of the relationship between educational psychology and psychology has both historical and epistemological aspects. So,

> is educational psychology an engineering science (concerned with) the application of relevant knowledge to the process of education . . . or (is) educational psychology an applied science which should develop its own basic research programs for the creation of a body of knowledge directly relevant to the process of education?
>
> (Mathis *et al.* 1977, quoted in Houtz and Lewis 1994: 4)

According to the first view, educational psychologists would take the theories (and methods) of psychology and conduct psychological research in the field of education, thereby contributing original knowledge to the bases of both psychology and education. According to the second view, educational psychology develops apart from and in parallel with mainstream psychology, but is not an application of psychology, rather taking its identity (and methodology) from its field, education. Thus as Kramer (1987) states: 'the child study movement gave rise to two educational psychology disciplines: school psychology and educational psychology.'

Resnick (1987) is clear that most educational psychologists no longer see their field as an application of mainstream psychology, but rather see themselves as conducting research in real-life settings (for example, classrooms) rather than the laboratory, and with a focus on context and interaction rather than on 'objective' experimentation. This is an important development.

Some of the tensions for educational psychology are illustrated by Glover and Ronning, who write:

> By putting itself as the 'middleperson' who applied the principles of psychology to education, educational psychology has put itself in the position of justifying its existence to the rest of psychology and justifying psychology to education. On the one hand, education has criticised educational psychology for being too theoretical and concerned with research. On the

other hand, psychology has accused educational psychology of being too concerned with applications and not possessing clearly articulated programs of research . . . . The essence of the discipline appears to be such that it will continue to be closely scrutinised by psychologists and educators. These two groups appear to have very different world views and attempts to satisfy both will continue to create stress in the discipline.

(Glover and Ronning 1987: 6)

Whatever its historical and epistemological origins, educational psychology has a long history; as mentioned above, it is widely claimed to constitute the earliest application of psychology (Spielberger 1984; Spurgeon *et al.* 1994; Tomlinson 1992). The first laboratory of applied psychology is said to be the anthropometric laboratory founded by Galton in 1884; a few years later in 1890, Cattell's 'mental test' constituted the earliest practical application.

At this time, educational psychology was perceived to be the application of psychological science to practical concerns, for which at that time education provided a fertile field. There are a number of reasons for this, including the needs of a compulsory schooling system, the administrative needs for selection and categorization and a growing interest in 'technical' aspects of the discipline. Those concerned with its early development claimed to take a scientific approach to human problems in the field of education. In particular the scientific field of differential psychology or individual differences, emerging at that time, both contributed to research and simultaneously served a useful function within the education system. This field of individual differences seemed to make it possible to combine 'science' with 'practice' in the same discipline (and by the same people) and thus to apply principles of scientific psychology to practical problems (see Olssen 1993a, 1993b).

Early textbooks viewed with confidence the relationship between psychology and its application to education; for example, a standard American textbook claims that

> educational psychology serves as a foundational discipline in education just as the physical sciences serve engineering . . . educational psychology can provide some insight into most aspects of educational practice . . . educational psychology serves teachers and education in general by providing help in dealing with . . . problems.
>
> (Gage and Berliner 1975: 3)

Similar confidence is expressed on this side of the Atlantic by Fontana:

> The application of psychology to education has a long and honoured history . . . but it is only during the last sixty years or so that psychology has developed the precision and methodology that allow it to make accurate generalisations about child behaviour, and to provide the teacher with the kind of information necessary . . . (to) make objective professional decisions and judgements.
>
> (Fontana 1988: xi)

In their different ways, these two approaches imply a direct and straightforward relationship between the discipline and its application (to teachers).

More recently, Francis (1995) has suggested that 'an educationally grounded psychological field, developed by psychologists researching educational concerns in education contexts and communicating effectively with teachers, truly deserves the name educational psychology' (p. 16). Francis assumes that these 'psychologists' are applying psychology and using psychological methods and theories to research educational concerns.

However, Child (1985) acknowledges some difficulties in application:

> Educational psychology . . . has always had three main functions. Two we are very familiar with, that is the creation and transmission of knowledge. But the third tends to be undervalued, that is the application of knowledge. . . . Educational psychology needs to recognise the importance of this third function – applying psychology in the service of education.
>
> (Child 1985: 22)

On the other hand, practitioner educational psychologists claim to be doing just this and applying psychology in the service of education:

> Educational psychology is the application of psychological science and theory to the learning and behaviour, social and emotional problems of children and young people in the educational context.
>
> (BPS 1994: 13)

Finally, it seems useful to point out again the distinction made by Wittrock (1992), who argued that, traditionally, research in educational psychology has been conducted from two perspectives, the first practice-oriented, the second theory-oriented, applying principles from general psychology to develop an understanding of educational processes such as teaching and learning.

Academic and practitioner educational psychologists

As noted, there have always been two distinct groups which claim to apply psychology to education: academic (research) and practitioner educational psychologists, sometimes distinguished with different titles of educational and school psychologists (Grinder 1978; Wittrock and Farley 1989; Burden 1994; Francis 1995). Both in the UK and in the US, these two groups appear to lead fairly separate professional lives, with predominantly separate concerns, methods, values, employment contexts and literature. Indeed, an overview of the journals in which members of the two groups tend to publish reveals remarkably little overlap.

Professional organizations differentiate the two groups: within the British Psychological Society the 'scientific' or 'academic' education section is separate from the 'professional' division of educational and child psychology; the

American Psychological Association differentiates Division 15, educational psychology, from Division 16, school psychology, and internationally, the International School Psychologists Association (ISPA) has very different concerns and activities from either the division of educational, instructional and school psychology of the International Association of Applied Psychology (IAAP) or the European Association for Research on Learning and Instruction (EARLI).

In the UK, practitioners working in the school system are always referred to as *educational psychologists* (EPs), but this term is frequently used also to refer to psychologists working in universities in the field of education as academics and researchers. Burden (1994) is keen to differentiate the groups, while leaving no doubt of their common roots in applied psychology:

> Although the terms educational and school psychology are sometimes used interchangeably, they actually represent two different but related schools of applied psychology.
>
> (Burden 1994: 294)

On both sides of the Atlantic, there is an issue over the identity of educational psychology, in part related to the question over its origins and its epistemology referred to above. Wittrock and Farley (1989), though optimistic about its future, nevertheless return repeatedly to the search for its identity; Stones (1970) expresses the difficulty:

> A great problem facing the student of educational psychology is the difficulty of deciding exactly what it is . . . at times the term educational psychology has embraced a strand of theory and practice which owes little if anything to experiment or scientific investigation and yet which confidently provides 'explanations' of aspects of children's behaviour and prescriptive formulas for educational practice.
>
> (Stones 1970: 1)

Educational psychology as a research activity: academic educational psychology

Over the past hundred years, researchers have generated a considerable literature on aspects of teaching and learning. This has perhaps been dominated by what is known as the 'process–product' approach which seeks to identify the nature of relationships between teaching performance and student achievement. A meta-analysis of 8,000 comparative process–product studies reveals nine factors as the chief influences on cognitive, affective and behavioural learning, which may be grouped under the three subheadings of student aptitude, instruction and psychological environments (Fraser *et al.* 1987; and see Gage 1978). Criticism of this kind of research based on its pragmatic and atheoretical nature (Gage and Needels 1989) has led to developments in a more interpretive–meaning tradition, based on more constructivist psychology (e.g. Gergen 1985; and see Kelly

1955). Thus educational psychology has developed through research in motivation (Ames and Ames 1984, 1985, 1989), mediation (e.g. Feuerstein *et al.* 1991; Moll 1991), metacognition (Reeve and Brown 1985), locus of control and attribution theory (e.g. Frieze 1980; Wang 1983) to a greater understanding of how the learner interacts with the learning environment, the psychological situation, and how this interaction may be influenced. Recent developments place self-regulated learning at 'the junction of cognition and motivation' (Boekarts 1996). As Boekarts suggests: 'by adopting the "situated learning" or contextual approach, educational psychologists changed their focus away from studying students' learning abilities and learning outcome to (i) students' capacity to regulate their own learning, and (ii) teachers' skills to create appropriate learning environments' (ibid., p. 100). This provides a most fruitful direction for the future, and a challenge to develop understanding which may have a significant effect on the practice of teaching and learning.

Educational psychology as a practitioner activity: practitioner educational psychology

The profession or practice of educational psychology has always had a service function, usually in relation to the operation and administration of the school system. As such, conflicts over the application of psychology may be inherent in its practice and in the role assigned to professional educational psychologists.

A number of volumes have been devoted to this profession in the UK (Chazan *et al.* 1974; Gillham 1978; Lindsay and Miller 1991; Wolfendale *et al.* 1992; and see Sigston *et al.* 1996), and the USA (e.g. Reynolds *et al.* 1984; Elliott and Witt 1986; Gutkin and Reynolds 1990; Thomas and Grimes 1990).

It is possible to trace a number of changing trends in school psychology. Cyril Burt was appointed to the London County Council in 1913 as the first educational psychologist in the UK (Wall 1956; Hearnshaw 1979; Sutherland and Sharp 1980). The considerable advances which had been made in the fields of individual differences and psychological testing in the early years of this century coincided with developments and requirements in the school system to create the climate for this appointment (Dessent 1978; Quicke 1982; Rose 1985; Pilgrim and Treacher 1992). Although Burt worked very much from a psychometric tradition, he was also aware of its limitations:

> Tests were regarded as but the beginning, never the end, of the examination of the child . . . . The scientist may standardise the method; to apply that method and to appraise the results, demands the tact, the experience and the imaginative insight of the teacher born and trained.

> (Burt 1921: 59)

Nevertheless, the tradition of psychometrics, intelligence testing, and other forms of assessment and testing have dominated this profession from its beginning to the present.

Educational psychology as a profession in the UK and in other countries emerged substantially after the Second World War and has to be seen in the context of the introduction of compulsory schooling and the welfare system of the post-war reconstruction period (Ingleby 1974; Quicke 1982; Rose 1985; Pilgrim and Treacher 1992). EPs were one of the 'new' professions whose knowledge and skills were put to political use in decisions over how to distribute resources. During the 1970s and 1980s, the perceived limitations of both psychometrics and child guidance led to a strong interest in behaviourism (e.g. Becker *et al.* 1975; Ainscow and Tweddle 1979; Wheldall and Merrett 1985), and practitioner educational psychologists devoted themselves to behavioural perspectives of learning programmes, classroom management, child-rearing and curriculum task analysis. During the same period practitioner educational psychologists made a shift from direct work with individual children to more indirect work with other adults, influenced by the ecological perspective (Bronfenbrenner 1979; Lusterman 1985), so-called systems theories (Apter 1978; Burden 1981) and a growth of interest in consultation as a form of service delivery to schools (Caplan 1970; Aubrey 1988). The 1990s have been characterized by an increasing focus within education services on accountability, value for money and standards, within a context of reduced resources. In turn this has led to a 'back to basics' orientation and to pressures on educational psychologists restricting them to more limited, and, according to some, less psychological roles.

Thus, within the UK, and indeed in many other countries, educational psychologists find themselves unsure about the nature of their psychological contribution. The changing employment and legislative contexts in the UK continue to cause the profession to reappraise its role (e.g. Farrell 1989; Burden 1992; Lindsay and Lunt 1993) and indeed the nature of its training (e.g. Farrell and Lunt 1994; Lunt and Farrell 1994; Maliphant 1994). In many countries educational psychologists have a central role in the special education system, where instead of focusing on factors influencing students' learning, they are required to test children for special education programmes and provision. There is therefore a tension for practitioner educational psychologists over their role, and the contribution of psychology within an education service which may appear not to value this discipline. Perhaps as a result of the changes affecting educational psychology services, there appears to be a call for a return to psychological theory, or a call for the injection of psychology into educational psychology (e.g. Gray 1992; Lunt and Farrell 1994; Maliphant 1994):

> The largely unmet challenge for educational psychology and educational psychologists lies in the development of a psychology of schooling. This has the potential to provide a link between two types of educational psychology: the educational psychology which forms part of most teacher education and the educational psychology of practising LEA-based EPs.
>
> (Dessent 1988: 87)

Educational psychology as applied psychology

The relationship between psychology and education raises questions about the nature of educational psychology as applied psychology.

Middleton and Edwards (1985) emphasize that 'a clear relationship between theory and application is fundamental to the development of a discipline that has to be capable of making informed and relevant contributions to issues and problems of the modern world' (p. 146). This point is also made by Sigston (1996), who calls for 'the improvement of dialogue between researchers and practitioners, making better matches between research questions and methodologies, and the use of action research methods by practitioners' (p. 9).

The literature does not always make the distinction between 'applied research' and 'applied practice', i.e. between researchers and practitioners, who, it is argued here, have very different functions, value systems and relationships with the discipline of psychology. For example, a 'service' definition is found in 'applied psychologists are people who, in their jobs, try to use their skills to help other people' (Hartley and Branthwaite 1989: 1), while others do acknowledge a differentiation between applied research and applied practice (Spielberger 1984). There are in several fields two separate groups of applied psychologists, those with a research function (who apply psychology to a research field, for example, education, industry, organizations, cross-cultural studies, transport), and those with a service function (who apply psychology to solve immediate human problems from a face-to-face client perspective; for example, clinical, educational, forensic and occupational psychologists working as practitioners). A question should be asked how far these two groups could be said to exist on a continuum of research and practice, and how far their modes of application are discrete and discontinuous. I consider this question in relation to the education context here.

Let us consider, for the moment, a definition of educational psychology as applied psychology. As noted above, it is possible to distinguish between applied research and applied practice (see Spurgeon *et al.* 1994), and to distinguish further between 'applied' and 'applicable' research (Belbin 1979; Watts 1984). According to Belbin, 'a strong technique orientation favours an applied approach, while a strong problem orientation favours an applicable approach' (p. 242). Within the field of education those engaged in applied research would be mainly the 'academic' educational psychologists (or psychologists of education), engaged in research and in teacher training, while those engaged in applied practice would be mainly the professional educational psychologists working predominantly in local authorities. This is an important distinction to make, since the notion of 'applied' is frequently not distinguished from the notion of 'practical' or 'practitioner'. Both groups lay claim to the application of psychology.

Let us briefly consider the relationship between basic and applied psychology. On the one hand are those who claim a direct relationship between the 'science' or theory and its application (see above and e.g. Davidson 1977; Duckworth

1981; Mittler 1982; Spielberger 1984). According to this view, there is a direct relationship from theory to its application, whether this be in terms of research or in terms of practice. Psychological theory develops first, and application follows from theory. A well-used example is the development and application of behavioural psychology, both in research and in practice (but see Schönpflug 1993: 8, and below). However, Middleton and Edwards (1985) point to a strong tension between pure and applied psychology:

> There is currently a sense in which 'pure' psychology is psychology, while the applied field is the point where psychology meets the real world. Such a conception is ruinous both of theory and of practice.
>
> (Middleton and Edwards 1985: 148)

In 1967 Grace Rawlings claimed to be the first 'applied psychologist' President of the BPS and identified in her presidential address some problems in applying psychology:

> Problems in applying psychology are not different from those experienced in applying other sciences. First the body of scientific knowledge must continue to grow; secondly, so must the perception of its relevance to the study of problems external to it; thirdly, the professional education of those who apply the science has to be furthered and improved; fourthly, there should be feedback of problems for the applied fields to the 'pure' scientists.
>
> (Rawlings 1967: 2)

An alternative view is expressed by Schönpflug, who argues that the separate origins and traditions of basic psychology with its 'ontological orientation' and applied psychology with its 'pragmatic orientation' make them incompatible (Schönpflug 1993, 1994). In contrast to the natural sciences, he is unable to find 'linear progress' from basic psychology to applied psychology, according to a 'two-stage model' 'which claims a foundation of practical work within basic research'. He suggests that applied psychology gradually evolved much earlier than the twentieth century from 'the pragmatic tradition' which embraced concerns such as 'decision making, organisation, production of goods, maintenance, and consumption'. With very separate roots and traditions, 'apparently, basic and applied psychology formed a coalition' (Schönpflug 1993: 21). This coalition enabled universities to recruit students, and practitioners to gain status, and is most clearly evident in psychology curricula and training programmes which require professional (applied) psychologists to have a foundation in basic psychology and espouse the scientist-practitioner model of training. However, in his article, Schönpflug highlights some of the continuing problems for this 'coalition' where 'doubts and complaints, conflicts and tensions indicate a continuing polarisation between basic and applied psychology' (Schönpflug 1993: 23).

Hastings and Schwieso point to the need for caution over claims for the direct applicability of educational psychology:

The generation of such high expectations for educational psychology rests on a belief which is commonly held about the relationship between scientific understanding on the one hand and practice on the other . . . that action follows from theoretical understanding.

(Hastings and Schwieso 1987: 2)

These authors go on to identify a problem for educational psychology; they point out that the main aim of psychology as a science is to 'describe and generate understanding' rather than to 'change or influence things'; although it may be argued that educational psychology is different, since its concerns lie within a field of practice. Most of the literature in this field 'has been concerned more with the development of understanding than with informing practice in any direct way'. Thus, whether one sees psychology as engaged in the search for general laws, or understanding of a more individual and interactionist position (see Francis 1995), the bridge with practice provides a considerable challenge (Mittler 1982). This has not helped the position of psychology as a discipline in initial teacher education. Educational psychology, seeking to maintain its roots and base in psychology as a 'science', finds problematical its applicability to the field of education.

This is a central issue for educational psychology as applied psychology:

Any belief that empirical research will yield findings from which it could be deduced exactly what should be done in any particular context, is fundamentally flawed . . . this does not mean that we think educational psychology has become a service industry and abandoned attempts at generating theories to account for its findings, merely that this has become a less prominent aim.

(Hastings and Schwieso 1987: 3–4)

Schwieso *et al.* (1992) are critical of a model of the relationship between theory and practice which 'suggests that psychological knowledge and understanding can be "applied" by teachers – the technologists – so as to achieve their practical purposes' (p. 112). They suggest, first, that the prime purpose of the discipline (of psychology) is to advance understanding, not practice, and second, that much relevant research in the field (of educational psychology) arises from practical and professional concerns, rather than concerns of basic psychology, and third, that psychology and education should interact mutually to 'use psychology and psychological methodologies in the service of education'.

Francis has traced a chronology of different models of application of psychology to education (Francis 1995). According to the first model, 'one-way traffic', educational psychology is a specialized branch of psychology characterized by selection of content to be transmitted to teachers (education). In the second model, educational psychology is a specialized branch of psychology, 'selecting aspects of general psychology to test in educational contexts before informing psychology of the results and transmitting the content to teachers' (Francis 1995: 11). The third model

> shows a more balanced and autonomous relationship with psychology on the one hand and education on the other where the field develops its own research, drawing on training from psychology but addressing educational problems from a dual perspective. It is a research field in its own right, developing research in educational contexts and submitting it for testing within educational provision.

> (ibid., p. 15)

Francis' fourth, and preferred, model provides an educational psychology which 'truly deserves the name' and is

> an educationally grounded psychological field, developed by psychologists researching educational concerns in education contexts and communicating effectively with teachers.

> (ibid., p. 16)

Thus she defines educational psychologists as 'psychologists at work in education'.

THE FUTURE FOR EDUCATIONAL PSYCHOLOGISTS AS PSYCHOLOGISTS AT WORK IN EDUCATION

What are the future challenges for this group of psychologists? First is the challenge to develop a continuum of research and practice, along which research is informed by practice and practice informed by research. This could be facilitated by institutional changes (such as in professional associations and conferences), and in further co-operation between educational psychologists working in different settings. Second is the task of developing a research agenda which links in with the highly political agenda by which education is informed and yet which retains the integrity and rigor of a scientific discipline. This relates in part to methodological and epistemological issues, in part to the culture of academic and professional communities. Third, there is a need for continued debate and discussion of the place of psychology and its relationship with education; the political threat to the position of disciplines providing the foundation for education theory has also undermined the position of psychology. And yet many of the problems within the education system are centrally addressed by psychology and psychologists.

The twenty-first century on whose edge we stand looks optimistic for educational psychology and educational psychologists. Education has become a highly political issue in most countries, both developed and less developed, and the challenge to understand teaching and learning, classroom and school organization and the factors which affect pupils' development and progress, has never been more urgent. My own view is that one of the most important aspects of the challenge is for the different groups of psychologists who apply psychology in education, whether as researchers or practitioners, or in other roles, to become more familiar with each other's work, values and understanding of psychology, and for them to contribute to the agenda which informs each other's work and practice. In this way, practice may be informed by and contribute to research, and research may become both applied and applicable.

REFERENCES

Ainscow, M. and Tweddle, D. (1979) *Preventing Classroom Failure: An Objectives Approach*, Chichester, Sussex: John Wiley & Sons.

Ames, C. and Ames, R. (eds) (1984) *Research on Motivation in Education, Vol. 1: Student Motivation*, London: Academic Press.

—— (eds) (1985) *Research on Motivation in Education, Vol. 2: The Classroom Milieu*, London: Academic Press.

—— (eds) (1989) *Research on Motivation in Education, Vol. 3: Goals and Cognitions*, London: Academic Press.

Apter, S.J. (1978) *Troubled Children, Troubled Systems*, Oxford: Pergamon.

Aubrey, C. (ed.) (1988) *School Consultancy in the UK*, Lewes: Falmer.

Becker, W.C., Englemann S. and Thomas D.R. (1975) *Teaching 1. Classroom Management*, Chicago: Science Research Associates.

Belbin, E. (1979) 'Applicable psychology and some national problems: a synopsis of the 1978 Myers lecture', *Bulletin of the British Psychological Society* 32: 241–244.

Berliner, D.C. (1993) 'The 100–year journey of educational psychology. From interest, to disdain, to respect for practice', in T.K. Fagan and G.R. Vanden Bos (eds) *Exploring Applied Psychology: Origins and Critical Analyses*, Washington, DC: APA.

Boekarts, M. (1996) 'Self-regulated learning at the junction of cognition and motivation', *European Psychologist* 1, 2: 100–112.

British Psychological Society (BPS) (1994) *Professional Psychology Handbook*, Leicester: British Psychological Society.

Bronfenbrenner, J. (1979) *The Ecology of Human Development*, Cambridge, MA: Harvard University Press.

Burden, R.L. (1981) 'Systems theory and its relevance to schools', in B. Gillham (ed.) *Problem Behaviour in the Secondary School: a Systems Approach*, London: Croom Helm.

—— (1992) 'Educational psychology: a force that is spent or one that never got going?', *The Psychologist* 5, 3: 110–111.

—— (1994) 'Trends and developments in educational psychology. An international perspective', *School Psychology International* 15, 4: 293–347.

Burt, C. (1921) *Mental and Scholastic Tests*, London: Staples.

Caplan, G. (1970) *The Theory and Practice of Mental Health Consultation*, New York: Basic Books.

Chazan, M., Moore, T., Williams, P. and Wright, J. (1974) *The Practice of Educational Psychology*, London: Longman.

Child, D. (1985) 'Educational psychology: past, present and future', in N. Entwistle (ed.) *New Directions in Educational Psychology 1: Teaching and Learning*, Lewes: Falmer Press.

Claxton, G., Swann, W., Salmon, P., Walkerdine, V., Jacobsen, B. and White, J. (1985) *Psychology and Schooling: What's the Matter?*, London: Institute of Education Bedford Way Paper 25.

Davidson, M. (1977) 'The scientific/applied debate in psychology: a contribution', *Bulletin of the British Psychological Society* 30: 273–278.

Desforges, C. (1985) 'Training for the management of learning in the primary school', in H. Francis (ed.) *Learning to Teach Psychology in Teacher Training*, Lewes, Sussex: The Falmer Press.

Dessent, T. (1978) 'The historical development of psychological services' in B. Gillham (ed.) *Reconstructing Educational Psychology*, London: Croom Helm.

—— (1988) 'Educational psychologists and the resource issue', in N. Jones and J. Sayer (eds) *Management and the Psychology of Schooling*, Lewes, Sussex: The Falmer Press.

Duckworth, D. (1981) 'Towards a psychological science that can be applied', *Bulletin of the British Psychological Society* 34: 237–240.

Elliott, S.N. and Witt, J.C. (1986) *The Delivery of Psychological Services in Schools: Concepts, Processes and Issues*, Hillsdale, NJ: Erlbaum.

Entwistle, N. (ed.) (1985) *New Directions in Educational Psychology 1 Teaching and Learning*, Lewes, Sussex: The Falmer Press.

Farrell, P. (1989) 'Educational psychology services: crisis or opportunity?', *The Psychologist* 2, 6: 240–241.

Farrell, P. and Lunt, I. (1994) 'Training psychologists for the 21st century', *School Psychology International* 15: 195–208.

Feuerstein, R., Klein, P.S. and Tannenbaum A.J. (1991) *Mediated Learning Experience: Theoretical, Learning and Psychological Implications*, London: Freund.

Fontana, D. (1988) *Psychology for Teachers*, Leicester: BPS and Macmillan.

Francis, H. (ed.) (1985) *Learning to Teach*, Lewes, Sussex: The Falmer Press.

—— (1995) *Reflections on Psychology and Education. A Valedictory Lecture*, London: Institute of Education.

Fraser, B.J., Walberg, H.J., Welch, W.W. and Hattie, J.A. (1987) 'Syntheses of educational productivity research', *International Journal of Educational Research* 11: 145–252.

Frieze, I.H. (1980) 'Beliefs about success and failure in the classroom', in J. H. Macmillan (ed.) *The Social Psychology of School Learning*, New York: Academic Press.

Gage, N.L. (1978) *The Scientific Basis of the Art of Teaching*, New York: Teachers' College Press.

Gage, N.L. and Berliner, D.C. (1975) *Educational Psychology*, Chicago: Rand McNally.

Gage, N.L. and Needels, N.L. (1989) 'Process–product research on teaching. A review of criticisms', *The Elementary School Journal* 89: 253–300.

Gale, A. (1991) 'The school as organisation: new roles for psychologists in education', *Educational Psychology in Practice* 7, 2: 67–73.

—— (1996) *The Reconstruction of British Psychology*, C.S. Myers lecture given at Annual Conference of BPS, April.

Gale, A. and Chapman, A. (1984) *Psychology and Social Problems. An Introduction to Applied Psychology*, London: John Wiley & Sons.

Gergen, K.J. (1985) 'The social constructionist movement in modern psychology', *American Psychologist* 40, 3: 266–275.

Gillham, B. (ed.) (1978) *Reconstructing Educational Psychology*, London: Croom Helm.

Glover, J.A. and Ronning, R.R. (1987) *Historical Foundations of Educational Psychology*, London: Plenum Press.

Gray, P. (1992) 'Bridging the divide between theory and practice: is there enough psychology in what we do?', *Educational Psychology in Practice* 9, 2: 6–8.

Grinder, J. (1978) 'What 200 years tells us about professional priorities in educational psychology', *Educational Psychologist* 12: 284–289.

Gutkin, T.B. and Reynolds, C.R. (eds) (1990) *The Handbook of School Psychology*, New York: John Wiley & Sons.

Hargreaves, D. (1978) 'The proper study of educational psychology', *AEP Journal* 4, 9: 3–8.

—— (1986) *Psychology and Teaching: A View from the Sidelines*, The Fifth Vernon-Wall Lecture, Leicester: BPS.

Hartley, J. and Branthwaite, A. (1989) *The Applied Psychologist*, Milton Keynes: Open University Press.

Hastings, N. and Schwieso, J. (1987) *New Directions in Educational Psychology 2: Behaviour and Motivation in the Classroom*, Lewes, Sussex: The Falmer Press.

Hearnshaw, L.S. (1979) *Cyril Burt Psychologist*, London: Hodder & Stoughton.

Hirst, P. (1983) *Educational Theory and its Foundation Disciplines*, London: Routledge & Kegan Paul.

Houtz, J. and Lewis, C. (1994) 'The professional practice of educational psychology', *Educational Psychology Review* 6, 1: 1–23.

Ingleby, D. (1974) 'The job psychologists do', in N. Armistead (ed.) *Reconstructing Social Psychology*, Harmondsworth, Middlesex: Penguin.

Kelly, G.A. (1955) *The Psychology of Personal Constructs*, New York: Norton.

Kramer, J.J. (1987) 'School psychology: a developmental report with special attention to educational psychology', in J. A. Glover and R. R. Ronning (eds) *Historical Foundations of Educational Psychology*, London: Plenum Press.

Lawlor, S. (1990) *Teachers Mistaught?*, London: Centre for Policy Studies.

Lindsay, G. and Lunt, I. (1993) 'The challenge of change', *The Psychologist* 6, 5: 210–213.

Lindsay, G. and Miller, A. (eds) (1991) *Psychological Services for Primary Schools*, London: Longman.

Lunt, I. and Farrell, P. (1994) 'Restructuring educational psychology training in the UK', *The Psychologist* 7, 6: 268–271.

Lunt, I. and Lindsay, G. (1993) 'Professional psychologists in the United Kingdom: current issues, trends and developments', *European Review of Applied Psychology* 43: 91–98.

Lusterman, D.D. (1985)'An eco-systemic approach to family–school problems', *American Journal of Family Therapy* 13, 1: 22–30.

Maliphant, R. (1994) 'School psychology: restructuring training and expanding professional practice', *The Psychologist* 7, 6: 263–267.

Middleton, D. and Edwards, D. (1985) 'Pure and applied psychology: re-examining the relationship', *Bulletin of the British Psychological Society* 38: 146–150.

Mittler, P. (1982) 'Applying developmental psychology', *Educational Psychology* 2, 1: 5–19.

Moll, L.C. (1991) *Vygotsky and Education*, Cambridge: Cambridge University Press.

Norwich, B. (1985) 'Aspects of the professional socialisation of teachers', in H. Francis (ed.) *Learning to Teach*, Lewes, Sussex: The Falmer Press.

——(1995) 'Statutory assessment and statementing: some challenges and implications for educational psychologists', *Educational Psychology in Practice* 11, 1: 29–35.

Olssen, M. (1993a) 'Science and individualism in educational psychology: problems for practice and points of departure', *Educational Psychology* 13, 2: 155–172.

—— (1993b) 'Educational psychology – its failings and some additional failings: a reply to Joshua John Schwieso', *Educational Psychology* 13, 2: 183–186.

Pilgrim, D. and Treacher, A. (1992) *Clinical Psychology Observed*, London: Routledge.

Quicke, J. (1982) *The Cautious Expert*, Milton Keynes: Open University Press.

Rawlings, G. (1967) 'Problems in applying psychology', *Bulletin of the British Psychological Society* 20, 68: 1–13.

Reeve, R.A. and Brown, A.L. (1985) 'Metacognition reconsidered: implications for intervention research', *Journal of Abnormal Child Psychology* 13, 3: 343–356.

Resnick, L.B. (1987) 'Learning in school and out', *Educational Researcher* 16, 9: 13–20.
Reynolds, C.R., Gutkin, T.B., Elliott, S.N. and Witt, J.C. (1984) *School Psychology: Essentials of Theory and Practice*, New York: John Wiley & Sons.
Rose, N. (1985) *The Psychological Complex*, London: Routledge & Kegan Paul.
Schönpflug, W. (1993) 'Applied psychology: newcomer with a long tradition', *Applied Psychology: An International Review* 42, 1: 5–30.
—— (1994) 'Professional training in psychological departments: a critical analysis', *News from EFPPA* 8, 4: 15–17.
Schwieso, J.J., Hastings, N.J. and Stainthorp, R. (1992) 'Psychology in teacher education: a response to Tomlinson', *The Psychologist* 5, 3: 112–113.
Sigston, A. (1996) 'Research and practice – worlds apart?', in A. Sigston, P. Curran, A. Labram and S. Wolfendale (eds) *Psychology in Practice*, London: David Fulton.
Sigston, A., Curran, P., Labram, A. and Wolfendale, S. (eds) (1996) *Psychology in Practice*, London: David Fulton.
Spielberger, C. (1984) 'Foreword', in A. Gale and A. Chapman (eds) *Psychology and Social Problems. An Introduction to Applied Psychology*, London: John Wiley & Sons.
Spurgeon, P., Davies, R. and Chapman, A. (eds) (1994) *Elements of Applied Psychology*, Switzerland: Harwood Academic Press.
Stones, E. (1970) 'Overview', in E. Stones (ed.) *Readings in Educational Psychology. Learning and Teaching*, London: Methuen.
—— (1988) *Ritual and Reality in Psychology and Teacher Education*, Eighth Vernon-Wall Lecture, BPS: Leicester.
Sutherland, G. and Sharp, S. (1980) '"The fust official psychologist in the wurrld": aspects of the professionalisation of psychology in early twentieth century Britain', *History of Science* 17: 181–208.
Thomas, A. and Grimes, J. (eds) (1990) *Best Practices in School Psychology – II*, Washington, DC: National Association of School Psychologists.
Tomlinson, P. (1992) 'Psychology and education: what went wrong – or did it?', *The Psychologist* 5, 3: 104–109.
Wall, W.D. (1956) *Psychological Services for School*, UNESCO: Institute for Education.
Wang, M.C. (1983) 'Development and consequences of students' sense of personal control', in J.M. Levine and M.C. Wang (eds) *Teacher and Student Perceptions: Implications for Learning*, Hillsdale, NJ: Erlbaum.
Watts, F. N. (1984) 'Applicable psychological research in the NHS', *Bulletin of the British Psychological Society* 37: 41–42.
Wheldall, K. and Merrett, F. (1985) *Positive Teaching: The Behavioural Approach*, London: Allen & Unwin.
Wilkinson, E. (1992) 'Turn back the tide', *The Psychologist* 5, 3: 120–122.
Wittrock, M.C. (1992) 'An empowering conception of educational psychology', *Educational Psychologist* 27: 129–141.
Wittrock, M.C. and Farley, F. (eds) (1989) *The Future of Educational Psychology*, Hillsdale, NJ: LEA.
Wolfendale, S., Bryans, T., Fox, M., Labram, A. and Sigston, A. (eds) (1992) *The Profession and Practice of Educational Psychology*, London: Cassell.

9 Community psychology

A new Gestalt psychology?

J. R. Newbrough^*

Community psychology as a subdiscipline within psychology began in the mid-1960s as an expression of the social justice movement in the United States (Tyler 1996). The name 'community psychology' was chosen to designate a concern for people in settings that needed improvement, and to move beyond the treatment of problematic individual behaviour (Bennett *et al.* 1966). The field grew out of an individualistic clinical orientation and addressed the need for social interventions for mental health problems. It was a newly emergent form of psychology, becoming broader than social psychology and more socially action-oriented than clinical psychology. At the same time, it did not give up its scientific grounding and has been working at keeping a strong connection with science. In this way, community psychology has continued to follow a scientist-professional model inherited from clinical psychology, and has appropriated action research as a way to operationalize that model.

In a new field with the need to be academically respectable, community psychologists have tended to be more person-oriented than concerned with community phenomena (Orford 1992). In order to get some perspective on the research in the field, a research methods conference was held in 1988 in Chicago in which there was an examination of the constraints of the methods and beliefs of traditional psychology (Tolan *et al.* 1990). The papers and discussion made it clear that community psychology had maintained a strong base in traditional methods, and had also moved beyond the paradigm of logical positivism and was engaging in 'adventuresome research'. My contribution to the conversation was to draw attention to Polkinghorne's (1983) work on human science and to argue that it provides the appropriate alternative to positivism for the research of community psychology (Bry *et al.* 1990).

In this chapter, I identify and briefly discuss the historical traditions of community psychology, describe the development of the field as a subdiscipline,

* I found Forrest Tyler's (in press) paper particularly helpful for the historical perspective. The Reflective Practice Group in Nashville provided the postmodern perspective. Paul R. Dokecki, Raymond P. Lorion, Robert T. O'Gorman and Jeanne M. Plas read an earlier draft and offered important feedback. Lynn S. Walker gave extended collegial assistance. I appreciate all their contributions.

and speculate about the role of community psychology in the twenty-first century.

COMMUNITY PSYCHOLOGY IN THE HISTORY OF PSYCHOLOGY

Community psychology draws most directly on the social psychology of Kurt Lewin. Conceptually, the key questions centre around the person-in-context (Orford 1992) and methodologically, the approach is action research (Marrow 1969; Sanford 1970).

Person-in-context

Person-in-context was specified by Lewin in his famous equation, $B=f(P,E)$, (where B=behaviour, P=person, E=environment). This formulation of person–environment fit was Lewin's solution to the part–whole problem raised by Gestalt psychology (Marx and Hillix 1979). For Lewin, the notion of fit was a way to specify functionally the mutual influences of the person and the setting. For me, it offered a way to operationalize Dewey and Bentley's (1949) concept of *transaction*, and an approach for considering how to conduct cross-level analyses (Newbrough 1972).

Community psychology has a part–whole problem represented by the classical formulation of the community as a paradox of the one and the many (Adler and Gorman 1955; Newbrough 1974). Traditionally, psychology is a discipline focused on the individual as the basic scientific reality, rejecting consideration of social groupings as wholes. Rather, social groupings are viewed as the environment for behaviour (see Schoggen 1989 for ways that the environment more specifically impacts behaviour). On the other hand, sociology, starting with Durkheim in 1895, has maintained that social wholes have unitary qualities. Community psychology aspires to connect the two approaches through cross-level analyses and has adopted system and ecology theory to do so.

System theory came into psychology in 1920 with Köhler's book on physical Gestalts, in which he provided a way to understand the whole by defining boundaries and subgroupings within the whole system (Marx and Hillix 1979). Wholes came to be defined 'by the organism being studied, that is, the organism's responses determine what constitutes a meaningful whole' (Marx and Hillix 1979: 174). The next developments were the description of the system as organized into layers or levels of linked functioning (Von Bertalanffy 1950, 1968), and the description of similarities (isomorphism) of functioning across levels (Miller 1965a, 1965b, 1965c). System theory could then resolve the 'holism–individualism' controversy precipitated by Durkheim's assertion of 'social facts' as emergent characteristics of social groups that were not reducible to aggregations of individual behaviour (Polkinghorne 1983).

Bronfenbrenner (1979) was identified by Orford (1992) as illustrating the usefulness of system theory with his ecology of nested systems. He starts, as

Lewin did, with the person as the central focus in the micro-system, and then works upward through three additional layers (meso-system, exo-system and macro-system). These provide the categories to consider the complexity of an entire community and to specify more structurally what Long (1958) described as 'an ecology of games'.

Community psychology, armed with the conceptual tools of system theory/ecology theory, can now begin to operationalize the Gestalt belief in the primacy of the whole by considering just how the person-in-community system is structured and operates (cf. Bregman 1976; Murrell 1970; Newbrough and Christenfeld 1974).

Action research

Action research is an approach to research that begins with a problem in context and then brings the theory and methods of science to bear on it (Lewin 1946). The results of the research are put back into practice in context for the purpose of improving and strengthening the participants. It is a practice–theory–practice cycle in which the theories are validated by application. This contrasts with traditional positivist research that follows a theory–practice–theory cycle, validating the theory in patterns of data (McKernan 1991).

Lewin was strongly influenced by American pragmatic philosophy. James, Dewey and Peirce contributed the action orientation, use of reflection, the community of knowers and the commitment to promoting democratic values through research (Marrow 1969). Adelman (1993) reported that 'Lewin and his students conducted quasi-experimental tests in factory and neighborhood settings to demonstrate, respectively, the greater gains in productivity and in law and order through democratic participation rather than autocratic coercion' (p. 5). Lewin was interested in helping socially marginal groups to overcome the effects of exploitation and oppression. This was a strong theme in the Swampscott Conference (Bennett *et al.* 1966) and has been a foundational principle of community psychology. For Lewin, social science was a means to help resolve social conflicts and to empower groups of people in the community.

> Action research gives credence to the development of powers of reflective thought, discussion, decision and action by ordinary people participating in collective research on 'private troubles' (Wright Mills 1959) that they have in common.
>
> (Adelman 1993: 8)

Human science

Human science is an approach more appropriate than logical positivism to the postmodern period, and one into which community psychology fits comfortably. Polkinghorne (1983) has identified human science as an area that comes out of the Geisteswissenschaften Movement of nineteenth-century Germany and has the same roots as Gestalt psychology. Dilthey, Stumpf's predecessor at Berlin and a principal figure in the movement, argued that the research should be devoted to understanding life experience 'both in its individual manifestations and in its social expressions' and that, in addition to the perception of physical objects, one should study meanings (Polkinghorne 1983: 32). Dilthey specified nine main assumptions about human behaviour that seem contemporary for community psychology:

- Humans are embodied social beings, and therefore a balance should be maintained between studies of the physiological bases of behavior and experience and studies of the structures of life experience.
- The life experience is a structural whole that affects and modifies its various parts.
- The life experience expresses itself in various ways, including facial expressions, gestures, postures, actions, spoken and written languages, and artistic expressions.
- The most substantial sources of knowledge about the life experience are the expressions of life – the pictures painted, the letters written, the poems and stories composed, and the institutions created.
- The life categories that give coherence to a person's expression of life are not necessarily explicitly present to their awareness at the time the expression is produced.
- Since humans are psychosocial beings, they cannot understand life in isolation; they understand it only in the context of social relations and cultural influences that intersect at particular times and places.
- Life is historical, and as individuals manifest life, it changes. Consequently, an unchanging human nature cannot be assumed. The structures of meaning evolve in a one-way process, so that they are different in various historical periods.
- Life is found at the level of meaningful experience. If human science concentrates on a lower level, with less complex and more easily isolated phenomena (such as sensations, instincts, and reflexes), then the very subject matter of the human sciences – life itself – will be missed.
- In addition to explanations in which individual events are subsumed under laws usually causal in nature, human science needs 'detailed, searching description of complex, mental phenomena and human behavior'.

                    (Rickman, quoted in Polkinghorne 1983: 32)

These characteristics describe the realm of enquiry for community psychology; a realm which includes all aspects of human life, not just those apprehended positively by the senses. The object of enquiry in human science is to identify and understand the life world (Polkinghorne 1983).

Whether or not community psychology identifies itself as a human science (Bry *et al.* 1990), it faces the major epistemological problem of post-positivist research, namely how to decide among knowledge claims where there is no absolute basis for certainty. Polkinghorne (1983) offers three overlapping solutions: through reasonableness, through trial and error, and through plural epistemologies.

Reasonableness implies that a decision is made on the basis of all the evidence available. One constructs the most probable interpretation and enters it into a process of discourse, the object of which is 'to reach a discursively realized, rational statement' (Polkinghorne 1983: 246).

Trial and error refers to learning from experience through a cycle of invention and trial. Peirce believed that 'knowledge is the community's attempt to understand the work. Method does not give truth; it corrects guesses. These guesses are revised and, over time, come to a closer approximation of the reality which always remains beyond the reach of human awareness' (Polkinghorne 1983: 251).

Plural epistemologies refers to communities of interpreters. Polkinghorne (1983) argues that

> the comparison and interaction of contexts or systems of inquiry allows for an understanding that is greater than any one point of view. . . . Because knowledge is not automatically the result of direct experience, but is a human construct, the comparison of various constructs can lead to an increase in the depth of understanding.
>
> (Polkinghorne 1983: 251)

Community psychology recognized this problem in the discussion at the 1988 Chicago Conference, where it was noted that the field needs to embrace the widest possible range of methodologies and designs. Methods in a complex world must be more complete and sophisticated than psychometrics and experimental designs (Shadish 1990a, 1990b).

Dokecki (1992) formulated a human science methods paradigm for community psychology (see Table 9.1) and argued that all four types of enquiry should be considered when attempting to obtain a 'full understanding' of a problem. Since each of us typically does not undertake all four types of enquiry on particular problems, the field should provide the means to ensure that all types are conducted. This is a very important point, the implication of which is that enquiries should be complete, and it is the responsibility of the community of enquirers to ensure that a full set of methods is brought to bear on important

Table 9.1 A human science methodological framework for community psychology

Scope of enquiry	Type of enquiry	
	Quantitative–impersonal	*Qualitative–personal*
Micro-level	Experimental and functional studies	Interpretive studies
Macro-level	Systems-analytic studies	Worldview studies

Source: Adapted from Dokecki (1992)

social problems. Individual 'projects' are necessary to the scientific enterprise, but not sufficient. When important areas of knowledge develop, the community of knowers should bear some responsibility to see that they are explored fully.

THE DEVELOPMENT OF THE FIELD OF COMMUNITY PSYCHOLOGY

Community psychology as a discipline has developed an orientation and a set of methods that was described by Rappaport (1977). Orford (1992) has summarized them in Table 9.2 as eight principles which characterize the field. While these principles come from community mental health, they apply equally well to the more general mission of social change through social intervention that was expressed at the Swampscott Conference (Bennett *et al.* 1966).

As a discipline, community psychology has developed through at least three phases and has come into a fourth where it is facing the definition of its social mission (see Table 9.3).

Phase 1 (1965–1968), the establishment period, began in 1965 with a conference at Swampscott, Massachusetts, on the education of psychologists for community mental health (Bennett *et al.* 1966). It was sponsored by the US

Table 9.2 The principles of community psychology

1 *Assumptions about causes of problems*
   An interaction, over time, between person and social settings and systems, including the structure of social support and social power.

2 *Levels of analysis*
   From micro-level to macro-level, especially at the level of the organization and the community or neighbourhood.

3 *Research methods*
   Include quasi-experimental designs, qualitative research, action research and case study methods.

4 *Location of practice*
   As near as possible to the relevant, everyday social context.

5 *Approach to planning services*
   Proactive, 'seeking out', assessing needs and special risks in a community.

6 *Practice emphasis*
   On prevention rather than treatment.

7 *Attitude to sharing psychology with others*
   Positive towards formal and informal ways of sharing including consultation.

8 *Position on working with non-professionals*
   Strongly encouraging of self-help and non-professionals and seeks to facilitate and collaborate.

Source: Adapted from Orford (1992)

Table 9.3 Phases of development of community psychology

Phase 1 (1965–1968) Establishment around a vision.
Issue: Whether to separate from clinical psychology?
Conference: Swampscott, 1965

Phase 2 (1968–1975) Development of the conceptual foundation.
Issue: Does it warrant subdisciplinary status in the academy?
Symposium: Austin, 1968

Phase 3 (1975–1988) Development of the work.
Issue: What are the training models?
Conference: Austin, 1975
Issue: Is the work scientific and academically respectable?
Conference: Chicago, 1988

Phase 4 (1988–) The societal role.
Issue: What is the intellectual centre of the field?
Mechanism: Woods Hole Task Force

National Institute of Mental Health to consider how to train clinical psychologists for working in comprehensive community mental health centres (Smith and Hobbs 1966). The occasion for this training concern was the passage of the Community Mental Health Act of 1963 that proposed the elimination of all congregate mental hospitals over the next twenty years, and the building of more than 2,000 local community mental health centres that would provide a comprehensive set of twelve services to the population in designated catchment areas of 75–200,000 persons (Bloom 1984). The plan developed as part of the Kennedy Administration's response to the report of the Joint Commission for Mental Illness and Health (1961).

The conference delegates were aware of the current view that social conditions contributed substantially to mental health problems (cf. Hollingshead and Redlich 1958; Hughes *et al.* 1960; Srole *et al.* 1962) and wished to address these social conditions more directly. They found the community mental health definition to be too narrow and proposed instead a much broader way of conceptualizing the role of community psychology – namely social interventions both for the improvement of a person's life experience and for the improvement of organizational functioning.

The initial problem was to get this new definition accepted by the discipline. This was accomplished by getting a Division of Community Psychology (Division 27) in the American Psychological Association formally established in Autumn 1967 (Iscoe and Spielberger 1970).

A symposium was held at the University of Texas at Austin in Spring 1967 to conceptualize the field, to provide some models for training and to provide a 'presence' as a subdiscipline prior to the 1967 meeting of the American Psychological Association (Iscoe and Spielberger 1970). The papers at the symposium were clearly grounded in community mental health but contained additional social emphases to distinguish the new area. Five university graduate training programmes (George Peabody College for Teachers, University of Rochester, City University of New York, Yale University, University of Colorado) and four multidisciplinary training programmes (University of Texas, Duke University Medical Center, Boston University, Florida State University) were described to provide training models for the field.

Phase 2 (1968–1975), the development of the conceptual foundation, followed from the Austin Symposium. In Autumn 1967, the division appointed a Task Force on Community Mental Health to develop position papers on research and practice (Rosenblum 1971) and began a monograph series (Adelson 1972). Golann and Eisdorfer (1972) assembled a *Handbook of Community Mental Health*. The leadership of the division were actively involved in the Vail Conference on 'Levels and patterns of professional training in psychology' in 1973. A number of papers were written for the conference including one in which I described community psychology as 'a new holism' (Newbrough 1973). The *American Journal of Community Psychology* was established in 1973 as the official journal of Division 27 and the *Journal of Community Psychology* began in 1974. The first textbook in the field was published by Zax and Specter (1974). The *Annual Review of Psychology* began the first chapter in its regular triennial coverage of the field (Cowen 1973). There was a major amount of work during this phase which established the conceptual base for the discipline.

The division was also very active organizationally in promoting the field. The Austin Conference in 1975 was the first national conference on training for the field (Iscoe *et al.* 1977). Funded by the National Institute of Mental Health, the field had arrived as a subdiscipline worthy of support in the eyes of the government and a panel of scientific reviewers. The manifest agenda for the conference was to deal with a differentiating training field by sharing the various approaches and to work on integrating some of them into models. The latent agenda was to deal with the differentiation of interest groups within the field which were finding their voices but were not being heard: the black psychologists, the Hispanic psychologists, the women psychologists, and the newcomers (graduate students and recent graduates). Both goals were achieved, and the field moved into the next phase.

Phase 3 (1975–1988) was a period of development and expansion. Three new textbooks were produced (Heller and Monahan 1977; Mann 1978; Rappaport 1977). The introductory courses then had a variety of perspectives on which to draw. The journals began to publish special issues on topics of major interest in the field.

This period was heavily influenced by two governmental events. The Carter Administration established The President's Commission on Mental Health headed by Rosalynn Carter. Community psychologists were centrally involved in the work of the Commission; preventive mental health was their primary focus. Based on the work of the Commission (President's Commission 1978), a national mental health act was passed in 1980 that set out an ambitious extension of the 1963 community mental health centres (Bloom 1984).

In 1981, the Reagan Administration took office and moved to have the Congress repeal the Mental Health Act (Bloom 1984). This reflected a deep societal sense that the momentum of social change unleashed in the 1960s needed to be curbed. In addition to the repeal of the Act, there was a narrowing of the definition of mental health to severe mental illness with biological causes. This was to limit funding to the behavioural and social scientists since they tended to find causes for disordered behaviour in the environment, and did not tend to hold those who misbehaved accountable for their behaviour. In society at large, many families with a member being treated for a mental disorder supported the biological causation position because they felt that the current mental health approaches held them responsible (at least in part) for that disorder. They felt very strongly that they were being blamed for situations which were out of their control. These families coalesced into the National Association against Mental Illness, a group of influential citizens who strongly oppose behavioural and social approaches and support biological approaches to mental health.

Community psychology as a discipline became marginalized societally during this period. The change in funding priorities toward the serious mental health and social problems was an opportunity not responded to by the field as a whole. Rather, it reacted by scaling back on externally funded research, working on the evaluation of treatment and intervention programmes, and getting more work published.

The Chicago Conference in 1988 was a turning point to the next phase (Tolan *et al.* 1990). The conference was for the purpose of reviewing the research in the field and distilling the methodology that was appropriate to current research into community phenomena. It was sponsored by the Science Directorate of the American Psychological Association, indicating that the research in this subdiscipline was worthy of consideration and that there was a need for some agreement on the methods for continued research that would move the field forward.

Phase 4 (1988–) was and is concerned with the societal role of the subdiscipline. Community psychology had been mainly inward-oriented since its beginning, even though the Austin Symposium paid considerable attention to the multidisciplinary nature of the work. By 1975, the field seemed headed towards becoming more multidisciplinary, but the conservative political swing in 1981 shifted that effort to survival activities.

At the beginning of this phase, in 1988, the American Psychological Association was faced with a split, with academic experimental psychologists, accustomed to having major influence, deciding to form another organization (the American Psychological Society) that would reflect their values more directly. As a survival move, the leadership of the Division of Community Psychology (Division 27) renamed it the Society for Community Research and Action (SCRA), opened membership to non-psychologists (as well as non-APA psychologists) and established the core meeting as a biennial conference held at a site away from the APA convention and hosted by one of the universities with a strong training programme (see Table 9.4). These meetings have become quite popular and have developed a stronger sense of community in the field. At the same time, SCRA has continued its active membership in the APA.

A radical interest group was established at the biennial conference in Chicago in 1995 by Isaac Prilleltensky and Dennis Fox. The well-attended meetings suggested that critical analysis of society (Held 1980) may have developed to the place where a formal group in the field can be organized. During my tenure as Editor of the *Journal of Community Psychology* (1975–1990), I had been unable to find much interest in socially critical analyses. I have believed from the beginning that the field must have a process for the critical analysis of society if it is to mature.

I urged the field to be concerned with the 'community' side of community psychology (Newbrough 1974, 1984) while I was Editor and during my tenure as president of the division (Newbrough 1980). Heller (1989) has been the other president to emphasize that theme. It has been my belief that the field has been largely ahistorical and has not realized that the modern period came to an end in about 1960 (Newbrough 1992a, 1995; Toulmin 1990). I have taken up the postmodern theme and have begun, with two colleagues, the development of a theory of community called 'The Third Position' (Newbrough 1991, 1992a, 1995). I have joined forces with Dokecki (1992, 1996) who has developed an approach to community praxis called 'The Reflective-Generative Practitioner'. We are working, with Robert O'Gorman, a religious educator, on developing the theory through a praxis of community development in a local Catholic parish (O'Gorman *et al.* in press).

The field has become increasingly international with an interest group being active throughout Phase 4, reporting periodically in *The Community Psychologist*, the divisional newsletter. There has been the development of a strong community psychology interest group in Latin America in the Interamerican Society of Psychology, and interest groups in Australia, Germany, Italy, New Zealand and Spain. A number of conferences have been held in recent years outside the US. The discipline is spreading worldwide and is oriented to

Table 9.4 Biennial conferences in community psychology

Year	Place
1987	University of South Carolina
1989	Michigan State University
1991	Arizona State University
1993	College of William and Mary
1995	University of Illinois at Chicago
1997	University of South Carolina

social interventions, particularly participatory action research and programme evaluation for policy purposes (Wingenfeld and Newbrough, in press). Major differentiations are underway in each country since the discipline is so dependent on context (Kingry-Westergaard and Kelly 1990).

THE CHALLENGES OF THE TWENTY-FIRST CENTURY

As the year 2000 approaches, community psychology is being drawn into a consideration of its role for the twenty-first century. Globalization of market economies has opened the door to massive social change. Supported by the rapid expansion of the computer-based communication systems, people all over the world are experiencing new information and sensing new opportunities. Businesses are restructuring and relocating. Many people are underemployed or without jobs. Bellah, Madsen, Sullivan, Swidler and Tipton (1985) described the effects of this change as creating massive pressures on all of the social institutions to change: political, economic, religious, educational and welfare. People find that the institutions do not meet current needs adequately and have begun to speak out about that. As they find their voices, it becomes apparent that their values are in conflict.

This is the differentiating phase of social change, what Lewin called 'unfreezing'. At this time, multiculturalism in the US has become a reverse melting-pot phenomenon. The new groups wish to maintain their traditions, and to have schools which teach the old ways in the native language. They have become politically influential, taking initiatives that are counter to the dominant position. Diversity will undoubtedly be the most salient social issue of the twenty-first century (Trickett *et al.* 1994; Tyler, in press).

Diversity, while it provides for more potential adaptive alternatives for an uncertain future, also yields conflict that has been impossible for the political leaders to deal with effectively. Moynihan (1993) in *Pandaemonium* describes this situation as many voices, none of whom seems willing to listen and engage in dialogue. One of the reasons for this is that the decision-making processes are designed for melting-pot purposes – to produce decisions in the face of divergent views. *Robert's Rules of Order* (Robert 1967) are coercive. Minority voices lose their ability to speak after the voting since the procedures were not intended to work out compromises that everyone can live with. Most modern political systems, built to engender a melting-pot, have not developed alternatives to majority voting that would more effectively handle differences and conflict. The current system is a coercive strategy that forces the losers to accept their losses and live with them, and does not provide for working through conflict by deliberation. Some indigenous cultures, such as the Maori of New Zealand (Ritchie 1992), have figured out how to develop a process of discussion – that may use intermediaries, that may have ceremonial trials of combat, and that takes whatever time is necessary to work out a mutually agreeable solution.

To make the society work, procedures will be required that are regarded as fair by all parties, and that offer justice and respect. Underneath the need to manage diversity is the more basic challenge of institutional change. Fairness is the salient theme; people find the modern ways to be working unfairly. Conservative groups are bringing traditional forms forward, wanting to reinstate them since they have worked and are familiar. Liberal groups tend to be silent, aware that their social philosophies have yielded the institutions that are now insufficient to the task.

Community in the twenty-first century

Community theory has developed through two phases (Kirkpatrick 1986). First, it was the face-to-face living arrangements of the tribe or the village. Tönnies (1957) called this 'Gemeinschaft'. Second, the development of large cities led to more formalized and differentiated living patterns. This Tönnies called 'Gesellschaft community'. The second phase has yielded a fragmented society with loss of community at the local level and loss of the sense of the common good (Bellah *et al.* 1985).

Kirkpatrick (1986) described the need for the next phase to emphasize the 'mutual-personal' aspects of human relationships. This should be characterized by respect and fairness. I have developed a 'third-position' approach to community that is an attempt to follow Kirkpatrick's lead (Newbrough 1991, 1995). It is a blend of traditional and modern approaches with the addition of a third consideration – the principle of justice. This will require new social forms to be invented, ones that emphasize procedures that will be inclusive. All interests will have to come to the table and stay there for the duration (Newbrough 1995).

The metaphor that I use for the social integration process is Dewey's notion of community as conversation (Schultz 1969). The task is to get the various parties to the 'conversational table'. As Bellah *et al.* (1985) suggest, the focus will have to be on institutional reform. The context for this in the US is exemplified by several recent social reform movements. Common Cause emerged from the 1960s and continues as a force to improve the institutions of government. The communitarian movement began in the 1980s to emphasize the matter of social responsibility to conserve community. Perot's Reform Party came forward in the 1990s as a broad-based political movement expressing the concerns of the middle and working classes who wanted change in the political parties. Similarly, the major issues for the political parties in the 1996 national election centred around welfare, health and educational reform. All of these signal the social ferment and opportunity for which community psychology has wished.

The opportunity for community psychology

Community psychology, throughout the first three phases, has been very committed to being a subdiscipline of psychology. The parent discipline has been so committed to the science of the modern period (logical positivism) that both science and practice have been constrained. The fourth phase has opened community psychology in the US to the possibility that some strategic moves could lead towards a new discipline.

I believe that psychology as a whole will have to deal with the tension between the human science and natural science paradigms, and I expect to see an eventual split into two psychologies. Were that to happen, community psychology would have a way to remain as part of one of the psychologies.

Whether or not that happens, community psychology has taken three steps that could be preparatory to the development of a new human science discipline: change in the definition of the professional role; redefinition of research as interdisciplinary action research, and preliminary work on the integration and development of the science.

Professional role

The Swampscott Conference defined the professional role as 'participant-conceptualizer' to differentiate it from 'scientist-practitioner'. Tyler *et al.* (1983) described a variation as 'resource-collaborator'. Dokecki (1996) and I (Newbrough 1992b, 1995) have described the role as 'reflective-generative practice'. Whatever the title, the role is changing from hierarchical expert to collaborative professional using the action-research process to transform people and social institutions.

Interdisciplinary work

The Chicago Conference (Tolan *et al.* 1990) recognized the need for a focus on social problems, in contrast to theory-driven research, and the need for community psychologists to be part of team approaches. The redefinition of the Division of Community Psychology into the Society for Community Research and Action explicitly opened the professional organization to interdisciplinary membership. The challenge to the leadership now is to move beyond the professional centrism of the field.

Integration of the science

The field began under the umbrella of community mental health. The concepts that have been differentiated are social support, prevention, empowerment and psychological sense of community. The Chicago Conference identified a similar differentiation of methods and stated the need to begin to have a cumulative process of integrating theory, research and method. Kelly (1970) saw the problem early on, and suggested a solution that has worked for the field of oceanography – the Woods Hole Marine Biological Laboratory. It is a social institution that brings people together at the same place every summer for an extended period of time. It has become, both formally and informally, the scientific centre for oceanography.

The society has begun a Woods Hole process in the establishment of the biennial university-based conferences. But they have remained short-term exchanges dealing with matters abstractly and superficially. They cannot address the need for a more sustained process of consolidating method and theory, and getting the professionals in the field working together. In order to pursue this latter purpose, I have described the theme as 'a location-based community research center' and have persuaded the society to establish a task force to pursue the idea for community psychology (Newbrough 1995). Currently, the questions are whether it should be limited to community psychology and located in only one place.

CONCLUSION

Community psychology in the US has arrived at a time of major opportunity. The challenge is substantial and requires some courageous moves. My fear is that the field has become institutionalized to the point that it will not take advantage of the opportunities for which it has been preparing itself. My hope is that, with the external context moving in the right direction, and with the internal moves having prepared the field, community psychology can take leadership in the development of a new human science.

REFERENCES

Adelman, C. (1993) 'Kurt Lewin and the origins of action research', *Education Action Research: An International Journal* 1: 7–24.

Adelson, D. (ed.) (1972) *Man as the Measure: The Crossroads*, New York: Behavioral Publications.

Adler, M.J. and Gorman, W. (1955) *The Great Ideas: A Synopticon of Great Books of the Western World* (Vol. II), Chicago: Encyclopaedia Britannica.

Bellah, R.N., Madsen, R., Sullivan, W.M., Swidler, A. and Tipton, S.M. (1985) *Habits of the Heart: Individualism and Commitment in American Life*, New York: Harper & Row.

Bennett, C.C., Anderson, L.S., Cooper, S., Hassol, L., Klein, D.C. and Rosenblum, G. (1966) *Community Psychology: A Report of the Boston Conference on the Education of Psychologists for Community Mental Health, May, 1965*, Boston: Boston University Press.

Bloom, B.L. (1984) *Community Mental Health: A General Introduction* (2nd edn), Monterey, CA: Brooks/Cole.

Bregman, H.L. (1976) 'Depressed mood: a community psychology study', unpublished doctoral dissertation, North Carolina State University, *Dissertation Abstracts International* 37, 3043B (University Microfilms No. 76–28, 461).

Bronfenbrenner, U. (1979) *The Ecology of Human Development: Experiments by Nature and Design*, Cambridge, MA: Harvard University Press.

Bry, B., Hirsch, B., Newbrough, J.R., Reischel, T.M. and Swidler, R.W (1990) 'Hypothesis generation: criteria for knowing', in P. Tolan, C. Keys, F. Chertok and

L. Jason (eds) *Researching Community Psychology*, Washington, DC: American Psychological Association.

Cowen, E.L. (1973) 'Social and community interventions', *Annual Review of Psychology* 24: 423–472.

Dewey, J. and Bentley, A.F. (1949) *Knowing and the Known*, Boston: Beacon Press.

Dokecki, P.R. (1992) 'On knowing the community of caring persons: a methodological basis for the reflective-generative practice of community psychology', *Journal of Community Psychology* 20: 26–35.

—— (1996) *The Tragi-comic Professional: Basic Considerations for Ethical Reflective-generative Practice*, Pittsburgh, PA: Duquesne University Press.

Golann, S. and Eisdorfer, C.E. (eds) (1972) *Handbook of Community Mental Health*, New York: Appleton Century Crofts.

Held, D. (1980) *Introduction to Critical Theory: Horkheimer to Habermas*, Berkeley, CA: University of California Press.

Heller, K. (1989) 'The return to community', *American Journal of Community Psychology* 17: 1–16.

Heller, K. and Monahan, J. (1977) *Psychology and Community Change*, Homewood, IL: Dorsey.

Hollingshead, A.B. and Redlich, F.C. (1958) *Social Class and Mental Illness: A Community Study*, New York: John Wiley & Sons.

Hughes, C.C., Tremblay, M.-C., Rapoport, R.N. and Leighton, A.H. (1960) *People of Cove and Woodlot: Communities from the Viewpoint of Social Psychiatry*, New York: Basic Books.

Iscoe, I. and Spielberger, C.D. (eds) (1970) *Community Psychology: Perspectives on Training and Research*, New York: Appleton Century Crofts.

Iscoe, I., Bloom, B.L. and Spielberger, C.D. (eds) (1977) *Community Psychology in Transition: Proceedings of the National Conference on Training in Community Psychology*, Washington, DC: Hemisphere.

Joint Commission on Mental Illness and Health (1961) *Action for Mental Health*, New York: Basic Books.

Kelly, J.G. (1970) 'Antidotes for arrogance: training for community psychology', *American Psychologist* 25: 524–531.

Kingry-Westergaard, C. and Kelly, J.G. (1990) 'A contextualist epistemology for ecological research', in P. Tolan, C. Keys, F. Chertok and L. Jason (eds) *Researching Community Psychology: Issues of Theory and Method*, Washington, DC: American Psychological Association.

Kirkpatrick, F. (1986) *Community: A Trinity of Models*, Washington, DC: Georgetown University Press.

Lewin, K. (1946) 'Action research and minority problems', *Journal of Social Issues* 2: 34–46.

Long, N. (1958) 'The local community as an ecology of games', *American Journal of Sociology* 64: 251–261.

McKernan, J. (1991) *Curriculum Action Research: A Handbook of Methods and Resources for the Reflective Practitioner*, New York: St Martin's Press.

Mann, P. (1978) *Community Psychology: Concepts and Applications*, New York: Free Press.

Marrow, A.J. (1969) *The Practical Theorist: The Life and Work of Kurt Lewin*, New York: Basic Books.

Marx, M.H. and Hillix, W.A. (1979) *Systems and Theories in Psychology* (3rd edn), New York: McGraw-Hill.

Miller, J. G. (1965a) 'Living systems: basic concepts', *Behavioral Science* 10: 193–237.

—— (1965b) 'Living systems: structure and process', *Behavioral Science* 10: 337–379.

—— (1965c) 'Living systems: cross-level hypotheses', *Behavioral Science* 10: 380–411.

Moynihan, D.P. (1993) *Pandaemonium: Ethnicity in International Politics*, New York: Oxford University Press.

Murrell, S.A. (1970) *Community Psychology and Social Systems: A Conceptual Framework and Intervention Guide*, New York: Behavioral Publications.

Newbrough, J.R. (1972) 'Concepts of behavior disorder', in S. Golann and C.E. Eisdorfer (eds) *Handbook of Community Mental Health*, New York: Appleton Century Crofts.

—— (1973) 'Community psychology: a new holism', *American Journal of Community Psychology* 1: 201–211.

—— (1974) 'Editorial opinion: community psychology: some perspectives', *Journal of Community Psychology* 2: 204–206.

—— (1980) 'Community psychology and the public interest', *American Journal of Community Psychology* 8: 1–17.

—— (1984) 'Editorial 1984 – prospects for the field of community psychology', *Journal of Community Psychology* 12: 91–98.

—— (1991) 'Hacia una teoria de la comunidad para la psicología comunitaria' ('Toward a theory of community for community psychology'), *Interamerican Journal of Psychology* 25: 1–22.

—— (1992a) 'Community psychology in the postmodern world', *Journal of Community Psychology* 20: 10–25.

—— (1992b) 'The postmodern professional: reflective and generative practice', *Interamerican Journal of Psychology* 27: 1–22.

—— (1995) 'Toward community: a third position', *American Journal of Community Psychology* 23: 9–37.

Newbrough, J. R. and Christenfeld, R.M. (1974) *Community Mental Health Epidemiology: Nashville. A Feasibility Study for a Program to Monitor Depressed Mood in the Local Community* (Final report on Grant MH-20681 to the Center for Epidemiologic Studies, National Institute of Mental Health), Nashville, TN: John F. Kennedy Center for Research on Education and Human Development, George Peabody College of Vanderbilt University.

O'Gorman, R.T., Newbrough, J.R. and Dokecki, P.R. (in press) 'Community generation and transformative social change: communiogenesis in the context of a Catholic parish', in L. Diamond and D.C. Klein (eds) *Transformative Social Change*, Alexandria, VA: NTL Institute.

Orford, J. (1992) *Community Psychology: Theory and Practice'*, Chichester, Sussex: John Wiley & Sons.

Polkinghorne, D. (1983) *Methodology for the Human Sciences: Systems of Inquiry*, Albany, NY: SUNY Press.

President's Commission on Mental Health (1978) *The Report: Vol. I*, Washington, DC: US Government Printing Office.

Rappaport, J. (1977) *Community Psychology: Values, Research and Action*, New York: Holt, Rinehart & Winston.

Ritchie, J. (1992) *Becoming Bicultural*, Wellington, New Zealand: Huia Publishers.

Robert, H.M. (1967) *Robert's Rules of Order*, New York: Pyramid Books.

Rosenblum, G. (1971) *Issues in Community Psychology and Preventive Mental Health*, New York: Behavioral Publications.

Sanford, N. (1970) 'Whatever happened to action research?', *Journal of Social Issues* 26: 3–23.

Schoggen, P. (1989) *Behavior Settings: A Revision and Extension of Roger Barker's Ecological Psychology*, Stanford, CA: Stanford University Press.

Schultz, F.M. (1969) 'The concept of community in the philosophy of John Dewey', unpublished doctoral dissertation, Indiana University, Bloomington, IN.

Shadish, W.R. Jr (1990a) 'Defining excellence criteria in community research', in P. Tolan,

C. Keys, F. Chertok and L. Jason (eds) *Researching Community Psychology: Issues of Theory and Method* (pp. 9–22), Washington, DC: American Psychological Association.

—— (1990b) 'What can we learn about problems in community research by comparing it with program evaluation?', in P. Tolan, C. Keys, F. Chertok and L. Jason (eds) *Researching Community Psychology: Issues of Theory and Method*, (pp. 214–223), Washington, DC: American Psychological Association.

Smith, M.B. and Hobbs, N. (1966) 'The community and the community mental health center', *American Psychologist* 21: 499–509.

Srole, L., Langer, T.S., Michael, S.T., Opler, M.K. and Rennie, T.A.C. (1962) *Mental Health in the Metropolis: The Midtown Manhattan Study*, New York: McGraw-Hill.

Tolan, P., Keys, C., Chertok, F. and Jason, L. (eds) (1990) *Researching Community Psychology*, Washington, DC: American Psychological Association.

Tönnies, F. (1957) *Community and Society* (Gemeinschaft und Gesellschaft), trans. C.P. Loomis, East Lansing MI: Michigan State University Press.

Toulmin, S. (1990) *Cosmopolis: The Hidden Agenda of Modernity*, New York: Free Press.

Trickett, E.J., Watts, R.J. and Birman, D. (eds) (1994) *Human Diversity: Perspectives on People in Context*, San Francisco, CA: Jossey-Bass.

Tyler, F.B. (1996) 'Community psychology in the United States: an evolving history', in A. Palmonari and B. Zarni (eds) *Manuale de Psicologia de Communita* (pp. 157–204), Bologna, Italy: Societa Editrice Il Molino.

Tyler, F.B., Pargament, K.I. and Gatz, M (1983) 'The resource collaborator role', *American Psychologist* 38: 388–398.

Von Bertalanffy, L. (1950) 'The theory of open systems in physics and biology', *Science* 111: 23–29.

—— (1968) *General System Theory*, New York: Braziller.

Wingenfeld, S. and Newbrough, J.R. (in press) 'Community psychology in international perspective', in J. Rappaport and E. Seidman (eds) *Handbook of Community Psychology*, New York: Plenum.

Zax, M. and Specter, G.A. (1974) *An Introduction to Community Psychology*, New York: John Wiley & Sons.

10 Critical moments on the edge

Psychological prevention of psychic and somatic
problems, disorders and illnesses

Salli Saari

INTRODUCTION

Sheldon J. Korchin named the first chapter of community psychology 'The Third
Mental Health Revolution' (1976). The field of community mental health or
community psychology is said to be as radical a change in perspective on human
dysfunction and its alleviation as was wrought in earlier times by Pinel, when he
struck the chains from the insane, and by Freud, when he showed that neuroses
are psychologically determined and curable through therapeutic conversations.
As a consequence of the first revolution, the mentally disturbed emerged as sick
people worthy of humane concern. From the second, their conditions were
conceived as psychologically determined and psychologically treatable. The
thrust of the third mental health revolution lies in the quest for prevention of
emotional disorders through social and community interventions aimed at their
social determinants (Korchin 1976; Bellak 1964; Hobbs 1964).

The history of psychological prevention goes back to the 1960s.
Unfortunately all the summaries and general reviews on this topic originate
in the United States. For example, the *Annual Review of Psychology* includes a
chapter on social and community interventions and psychology every third
year since 1973. The reason may be ascribed to the practice of Finnish
psychology libraries, yet I think there is some validity in this finding. European
psychology has not been unified with common trends and contents. I solved the
problem in a subjective way. I have myself been working for thirty years
mainly in the field of preventive psychology. Finland has a very well-developed
public health system, which gives good conditions for preventive work, and has
had a pioneering role in preventive work, both in somatic and mental disorders
and illnesses. I will reflect and compare my own thinking, research results and
experiences with those of American colleagues in developing psychological
prevention.

In the sections that follow I will describe the definition of prevention and its
meaning in the context of preventive work, the developmental stages that can be
seen in preventive psychology, results and experiences of these stages, the

theoretical background on which the work is based, and finally the current status of prevention.

THE CONCEPT AND PRINCIPLES OF PREVENTION

Psychological prevention has been inspired by the example of public health medicine in the conquest of disease. While clinical medicine focuses on the treatment of sick people, public health medicine is aimed at reducing the incidence and prevalence of disease in the population.

Public health workers distinguish between primary, secondary and tertiary prevention and these concepts were commonly used in the field of mental health. *Primary prevention* is aimed at reducing the possibility of the disease in a susceptible population (population-at-risk). *Secondary prevention* attempts to reduce the duration, prevalence or spread of the disease in those already ill. Emphasis is on early detection and early treatment. *Tertiary prevention* seeks to reduce the consequences of the disease among those who have already had it.

To define prevention in these terms reflects the medical model of mental health. The most fundamental and serious failing of the medical model in mental health is the belief in the structural parallelism between the onset, nature and treatment of psychological and physical dysfunction. Cowen (1973) writes that the most disordered human behaviour differs qualitatively from the modal short-term instance of physical dysfunction because it has deeper roots, longer germination periods, broader impact on many aspects of the person's functioning, and it is shaped to a greater extent by significant people, experiences and social institutions in the individual's history.

To prevent emotional or mental disorders effectively, we need to know their developmental process and the interventions to change them. However, 'at this point, our knowledge of the causation of emotional disorders is both limited and gross, as are our techniques and power to effect change, particularly at the broader social levels', wrote Korchin in 1976 (p. 496).

Caplan (1964) has a central role in developing a conceptual model of prevention. He starts with the basic assumption that all human beings need 'supplies' appropriate to their level of development. Deficiences in these supplies can lead to psychological disorders just as insufficient food or wrong foods can result in malnutrition. According to Caplan, physical, psychosocial and sociocultural supplies are needed for healthy psychological development. Physical supplies include food, shelter, protection from harm and sensory stimulation. Psychosocial supplies are those received through interaction with others and include emotional and intellectual stimulation, love and affection, participation in satisfying social encounters, and so on. If the individual does not hold the respect of others or if they manipulate him or her towards their own ends, emotional disorders may result. Finally, sociocultural supplies are those forces which determine the status of the individual and the expectations held by others. In advantaged social groups, individuals have greater input of such supplies, which predicts healthier personality development. In disadvantaged groups, or times of rapid social change, traditional social supports may be undermined and psychological distress is more likely.

Another factor of importance in Caplan's scheme is the central role of crisis resolution. Life crises, whether accidental or developmental, endanger existing adaptation and can lead to mental disorders or provide opportunity for further growth and development. Hence, helping individuals to overcome crisis situations is a critical part of primary prevention.

Caplan (1964) notes that primary prevention efforts are possible both at the level of 'social action' and at that of 'interpersonal action'. The former consists mainly of efforts to influence legislative and social programmes serving welfare, health or educational needs in the larger society; while interpersonal actions are intended to influence individuals, families and community groups through more direct face-to-face interventions. These involve not only helping people in need (as in crisis intervention) but also indirect actions on their behalf through consultation with 'community caretakers' such as teachers, doctors and political leaders, who are important to the lives of many in the community.

In the 1970s, psychologists in Finland had a very lively, rich discussion among themselves. They rejected the medical model of primary, secondary and tertiary prevention. Instead they used the concepts constructive, preventive, care and rehabilitation. The idea was that the focus for psychological knowledge is normal human development and how to promote this development; this leads to a quite different focus of psychological work when compared with prevention.

For example, in preventive work we try to minimize the risks to mental well-being. In counselling university students we psychologists used to focus our attention on the reasons why students were seeking counselling. If we noticed that many students attended for the same reason, we tried to address this cause. In the late 1970s, we noticed that we had as clients many law students and they all had problems with one and the same examination. The students had to pass this examination to be able to continue their studies. Many students had tried several times, halting their studies for a year or two. The problem led to both loss of self-esteem and financial difficulties for many.

We defined this examination as a clear risk to the mental health of many students and suggested that it should be taken in two stages. This was done and the problem disappeared. We had succeeded in diminishing the risk. However, after some years students, teachers and psychologists harshly criticized the fact that university studies had become too fragmented with too many small, detailed examinations. The students did not learn to master broad entities and trends. We noticed that the diminishing risks do not lead always to the desired result. On some occasions it may be better to concentrate on support strategies to reach the goal instead of lowering the aim in order to diminish the risk. In many cases, at least in the field of university studies, the constructive strategy is ultimately more solid than the preventive one.

When we speak of preventive psychology, the concept of mental health is certain to emerge. In American community psychology, discussion focused for many years on the inadequacy of the medical model to mental heath. We in Finland went still further in our theoretical citicism. In the 1970s, some psychologists argued that we should reject the concept of mental health as being intellectually and theoretically impoverished, and instead describe concrete psychological processes and mechanisms.

The theoretical background of preventive psychology

The social and community approach to mental health criticized traditional clinical psychology for its purely individual and psychotherapeutic focus in both its theoretical approach to mental health and its interventions. 'Clinical theorising, derivative practice, and research all mirror the implicit assumption that the time to initiate help is when a person experiences problems, sometimes grave, recognizes them and/or is rendered ineffectual by them', Cowen writes in 1973 (p. 424). By contrast, traditional clinical psychologists have been critical of social and community psychology and the possibilities of prevention. The basis of their criticism is psychoanalytic theory which gives very limited possibilities of prevention of emotional disorders. The only theoretically based preventive interventions are those applied to parents of infants and small children and even these have not been found to be very effective.

The roots of preventive psychology are based on the role of social and environmental factors in the development of personality and emotional disorders. The findings of large epidemiological studies indicate that individuals in lower socioeconomic groups have higher mortality, morbidity and disability rates across a wide array of illnesses (Syme and Berkman 1976). Kenneth Heller writes in his review of social and community intervention that we still do not know what accounts for this general susceptibility (1990). While there is abundant evidence that social and environmental conditions influence mortality, morbidity and psychological well-being, the process by which these effects occur and the most potent ingredients among various stressors and resources are still largely unknown.

This general formulation is also reflected in the common operating assumption of prevention-oriented psychologists that the incidence of psychological disorder should be viewed as a direct function of environmental stressors inversely related to environmental resources.

Albee (1982) presented a general equation: incidence of psychological disorder = (organic factors + stress)/(coping skills + self-esteem + support groups). This equation represents an interactionist view of the onset of disorders in that organic factors, coping skills and self-esteem represent personal attributes, while stress and social support are environmental characteristics. In this and in similar models (Cohen *et al.* 1986), facets of social support and various learned coping behaviours are said to moderate the effects of environmental stress.

Elias (1987) accepted the general theoretical overview described above, but suggested an important macro-level reformulation. Albee's model is criticized for being person-centred and not sensitive to either situational differences or a developmental perspective. Elias proposed that: likelihood of disorder in a population = (stressors and risk factors in the environment)/(socialization practices + social support resources + opportunities for connectedness). While the Elias reformulation does not consider individual vulnerability, it has greater heuristic value because it focuses on modifiable environmental stressors and resources (Heller 1990). For example, socialization practices can be improved by parenting courses or by supportive and educational outreach projects to parents (Olds 1988). The support resources can be increased by the development of mutual help organizations whose purpose is to counter isolation and loneliness (Levine 1988).

The influence of constitutional and environmental variables in mental health and personality development has usually been investigated by correlational studies in which a linear relationship between these factors has been assumed. However, the correlations found in these studies are quite low, around 0.2 (Dohrenwend 1974; Coleman 1973; Holmes and Rahe 1967; Holmes 1970; Rahe 1974). That means that about 4 to 5 per cent of the variance can be explained by these factors, not enough to support preventive interventions.

Psychologists confronted this dilemma following initial enthusiasm for preventive interventions. It was difficult to accept the research results of minimal influence of environmental and social factors. In 1976, I started a prospective follow-up study to investigate the nature of the mediating process of internal personality factors in the influence of environmental factors on mental health (Saari 1979, 1981; Saari and Majander 1985). The focus of the study was how to explain changes in mental health and personality development. Its theoretical basis was grounded in developmental psychology and stress theory. The first stage of the study was conducted when a random sample of 1,004 university students started their studies, the second stage after three years and the third stage after eight years, in 1983.

One of the mediating personality factors studied was self-esteem. The results of the study showed that the model of mediation is different when self-esteem is high. Similar external conditions and similar stress factors can lead to completely different developmental outcomes in mental health. When self-esteem is high, the stress factors are experienced as challenges, which leads to an increase in feelings of competence. When self-esteem is low the same level of stress and the same stress factors are experienced as paralysing, which heightens stress reactions and gives rise to psychiatric symptoms.

The results of this prospective follow-up study helped to explain the low correlations found between mental health measures and environmental and social factors. Our findings also indicated that primary interventions aimed at preventing emotional disorders by trying to change the community and its social and environmental circumstances often prove ineffective. The interaction among these factors is highly complex. Effective preventive interventions must be focused more directly.

Although the aim of this longitudinal study was to give a better theoretical basis to effective preventive interventions, it led to a crisis in psychological prevention. It is apparent that external living conditions, life stress and environmental circumstances are radically mediated by personality factors such as self-esteem, leading to different subjective experiences. Thus, while there may be political and humane reasons in favour of extensive community development interventions, they are not based on theoretical knowledge supported by psychological research.

The end product of this crisis in psychological prevention is the growth of more scientifically based and more effective preventive interventions anchored in psychological research and theory. The field of health psychology is a good example of this development. In Finland, we have rejected mental health or emotional disorders as the targets of prevention. Psychological interventions are aimed at specific targets. Both the psychological process which is changed by the intervention and also its outcomes are clearly identified. I will describe below these psychological interventions in traumatic stress and crisis, which is a new model widely applied in Finland and the Nordic European countries.

THE DEVELOPMENT AND CONTENT OF PSYCHOLOGICAL PREVENTIVE INTERVENTIONS: AN HISTORICAL OVERVIEW

The phase of political discussion and creation of professional resources

The first preventive psychological work was the education of the population about the availability and content of mental health services in the 1950s. The 1960s and the early 1970s were a time of overall growth in preventive approaches. Public health ideology greatly emphasized the value of preventive work and this belief was reflected in both somatic and mental health policy. The preventive approach was based on the criticisms of disorder- and illness-focused models of mental health. The traditional disorder-focused approach was found to be ineffective and unfair. It was argued, too, that there will never be sufficient professional and economic resources to cover the need of psychotherapy in the community.

In psychology and mental health, prevention was focused on so-called primary prevention. As Korchin (1976) writes, any social programme which increases the quality of life, fosters education or social welfare, improves medical care or increases job opportunities provides in principle physical, psychosocial and sociocultural 'supplies' required and is, in a way, preventive in nature. Sceptical psychologists argued that this is in fact a political task rather than psychological prevention. A second criticism was that the influence of social and community factors on psychic disorders has not been scientifically proven. Any relationships expressed in correlations are so weak that they cannot support the design of psychological interventions. The result of this comprehensive discussion on the possibilities of psychological prevention was a significant increase in professional resources allocated to psychological prevention. The psychologists engaged in this work, especially primary prevention, soon noticed that they had little influence on social inequity and conditions in the community. They had to find other models to do so.

Action phase

Legal, professional and economic conditions for effective psychological preventive work were created in the late 1960s and early 1970s. It was time to turn these resources into action. Many task-oriented preventive interventions and projects were carried out in the 1970s. Disappointments in primary prevention across society led to more focused preventive projects. The fundamental role of families and small groups in personality development was noticed and interventions often involved parent education programmes, prenatal instruction, and various forms of family crisis interventions. Such programmes were usually based in well-baby clinics or other paediatric services to bring them to families who would not seek help from mental health services. The critical task was to help in redirecting parental efforts before serious problems emerged with their children (Felner *et al.* 1983; Korchin 1976).

Preventive work with adolescents often recognized the peer group as a socializing agency. Programmes directed towards the control of delinquency and drug abuse, as well as less extreme problems of adolescent development, focused on this group. Training of support individuals or tutors from the peer group to give social support and to take collective responsibility for each other has been one form of preventive work.

A typical psychological prevention project of this phase was carried out in the Student Health Service in Helsinki in collaboration with Student Theatre and eight student associations in 1975 to 1976. This project exemplified the loose connection to psychological theory or research and strategies for planning, implementing and follow-up which were typical of this phase of development. By contrast, its complexity, richness and originality of ideas were not typical. It was known that many students were either lonely or had problems in their human relationships, especially intimate relationships. Psychologists started the project by co-producing with Student Theatre a performance on problems in human relationships entitled 'Love, suffer and . . .', named after a very well-known Finnish tango, 'Love, suffer and forget!'

Psychologists wrote a short pamphlet on human relationships and ways of solving problems in intimate relationships, including the results of a study of sexual behaviour and experiences among university students. The pamphlets were distributed at each performance, at which a social gathering was held with entertainment planned by psychologists and leaders of the eight student associations. The purpose was to teach student leaders how to organize and promote social occasions where people can learn to know each other and create situations conducive to open discussion. Leaders were asked to gather information on how many students took part in the events, noting those who had previously never attended association meetings. More than a hundred students took part on each occasion, compared with typical attendance by between forty and fifty students, and one-fifth of these were first-time attenders. The project was widely publicized and praised by professionals and theatre critics alike. I am sure, however, when I appraise the results of the project now, that the only long-term effect was in the minds of those who carried out the project and felt it to be rewarding and successful.

During this phase, initiatives in secondary prevention were also actively undertaken. Their aim was to reduce the prevalence of emotional disorders through early diagnosis and prompt, effective treatment. The core assumption was that incipient problems can be detected through early signs and that interventions at that point can head off greater problems in the future. It was further assumed that treatment of mental disorder is easier, faster and economical at an early stage of the illness. Secondary prevention involves widespread screening of people who do not seek help or may even be asymptomatic at the moment when research is undertaken and efforts are made to bring them quickly to appropriate clinical or counselling services.

The first aim of the longitudinal study of university students described earlier was to develop a screening method for early mental health problems to be combined with somatic screening. All university students were invited to this screening in the first year of their studies and more than 80 per cent accepted. Results showed that it was possible to screen the students who had mental health problems at an early stage or who were at high risk of these problems validly and with high reliability. However, difficulty arose in planning early interventions. The first problem was that these students were not well motivated to use the mental health and counselling services as they had been advised. The second problem was that mental health professionals accustomed to working with highly motivated patients with serious symptoms and problems did not know what to do with these students. The professionals did not have sufficient skills to carry out individual preventive work (Saari 1979, 1981). These are problems familiar to other researchers studying secondary prevention through screening processes (Korchin 1976).

Screening 5-year-old children was a second preventive process widely applied in Finland in the 1970s and early 1980s. It was carried out in child guidance centres and almost all 5-year-old children took part each year. Its aim was to identify children who were delayed in their psychological development in order to prevent learning and social problems when they started school at the age of 7. Some were referred to special screening services (psychological, speech therapy, etc.) while others were offered special training programmes to be carried out at home with parents. This very successful screening programme was terminated some years ago due to the economic depression and the cut in public health services.

Crisis centres offering round-the-clock access are another form of secondary prevention, and these are currently one of the most popular models in social and community mental health in the United States (Caplan 1964). Like screening, they are approaches to early intervention. In some crisis centres mental health professionals give all the help needed and in others mutual help is an important form of giving help. The walk-in crisis centres are based on the same idea of early intervention as screening.

Self-help groups and mutual help models (Gesten and Jason 1987) developed as the social and community mental health movement grew (Iscoe and Harris 1984). In the decade from the end of the 1970s to the beginning of the 1980s there were over 500,000 mutual help groups including fifteen million people in the United States (Riessman 1985). The rationale for the groups is that individuals who have some common problem (overweight, depression, grief, bulimia, etc.) gather together to help each other by sharing their problems and giving social support. Some mutual help groups report promising results. The emerging strength and scope of the mutual help movement presents both an opportunity and a dilemma for mental health professionals. Effective alliance with such grassroots efforts may strengthen their impact and broaden the base of support for mental health services. To do so requires an uncommon sharing of control and degree of collaboration. Research designs that respect the groups' voluntary quality are needed. Tampering in the name of training may also diminish the spontaneity and intimacy critical to such groups' functioning (Gesten and Jason 1987). Finally, professional support for mutual help may have the unintended consequences of accelerating governmental cutbacks in mental health budgets (Pilisuk and Minkler 1985) and providing an excuse for 'blaming the victim' (Ryan 1971).

Consultation is emerging as one of the major techniques in psychological prevention (Bellak and Barten 1969; Iscoe and Harris 1984; Korchin 1976). Consultation is an indirect method of effecting change through other professionals, for example, teachers, nurses and medical doctors. By consultation, mental health professionals can influence a large number of people in their normal surroundings and circumstances. Consultation spread during the golden years of psychological prevention and has retained its status even in the years of economic depression and ideologic depression of psychological prevention.

In the earlier section on definitions in preventive psychology, I criticized the concept of primary prevention and favoured the concept of constructive psychological intervention. This notion appears in articles and books on social and community interventions in the United States (Gesten and Jason 1987; Felner *et al.* 1983; Heller 1990). These perspectives and interventions concentrate on enhancing social problem-solving skills and strengthening the person's ability to cope with life crises.

Gesten and Jason (1987) concluded that

a wide variety of preventively oriented competence building technologies are now available. Future efforts will be strengthened by clear specification of training activities, as well as examination of the extent to which specific program components and aquired competencies relate to measured adjustment gain. Assessing outcomes in terms of wellbeing or positive affect as well as reduction in psychopathology also merit consideration in light of the nonclinical nature of participants, and partial independence of these adjustment dimensions.

(Gesten and Jason 1987: 436)

The theoretical, ideological and resource crisis in preventive psychology

After two decades of preventive work, enthusiasm and faith in the possibilities of psychological prevention have diminished. This crisis among specialists, at once both theoretical and ideological, occurred at the same time as both Europe and the United States encountered economic depression. The experts did not have enough motivation and strength to counter the cutbacks in preventive services and interventions. The resources of preventive programmes diminished significantly and a phase of professionally planned intervention programmes to prevent the development of psychological disorders and mental illness came to an end.

Scientific psychological prevention

As is often the case, such a crisis prompted the growth of preventive psychology. Psychologists no longer focused on the development of emotional disorders nor on preventive mental health interventions. They began work to prevent suicides, the onset of lung cancer through helping people to stop smoking, heart disease through helping people to control their weight, and so on. The aims of psychological prevention became more exact and interventions were based on theory with precise knowledge of the processes to be changed and of the psychological techniques to achieve change.

Health psychology offers a good example of this development in psychological prevention. Research in somatic medicine and in the disease process of many common diseases has identified a central role for human behaviour. Psychological knowledge on how to produce the desired behavioural changes became a great challenge to health psychologists and their intervention programmes. One of the most widely cited and successful prevention programmes aims at reducing the risk of heart disease (Cohen *et al.* 1986; Egger *et al.* 1983; Puska *et al.* 1985). These programmes generally operate over several years on a community-wide basis. Typically, they use mass media intensively, attempt to change a wide range of behaviours and evaluate programme effectiveness through quasi-experimental designs that compare intervention communities to demographically similar control communities who receive no intervention. These programmes have demonstrated reductions of between 9 and 15 per cent in the risk for heart disease (Levine *et al.* 1993; Maccoby and Alexander 1980).

Similar large-scale programmes have been applied to reducing smoking, stress and substance abuse (Gesten and Jacobs 1987; Winett *et al.* 1989). Typically in programmes multiple methods are used to reach the target population and strengthen the effect of the intervention. These programmes use mass media, small group discussions and face-to-face services. The role of psychologists lies in planning the programmes, choosing the methods, training personnel who carry out the programme, and following up the outcomes of the interventions. Psychological methods have also been used among people who have already got a disease to help them change their behaviour in living with it (Albino 1983; Johnson 1980).

These health psychology programmes have an important contribution to make at a broader level by helping to change the *zeitgeist* and thereby affect social norms concerning health-related behaviours (Levine *et al.* 1993). In many countries, a change of social norms has in addition made it politically possible for governments to enact legislation which in turn supports the aims of health behaviour interventions.

Scientifically based interventions have also been applied in the field of mental health. One example of this kind of psychological prevention is work in Finland with traumatic crisis and critical incidents. Its aim is to reach the psychological victims of traumatic incidents, defined as all major or smaller accidents, fires, drowning, suicides, violent deaths and violent occasions, and also normal sudden deaths such as heart attacks or 'cot deaths' or sudden infant death. Psychological victims of a disaster are the survivors, the people left behind following a death – children, parents, other relatives, friends, colleagues, schoolfriends and teachers. Other victims are eye-witnesses to the incident, rescue staff – firemen, emergency staff, policemen, ambulance drivers, doctors and nurses – and other health personnel. Those who caused the accident or incident and people close to them may also be victims. A sudden, unexpected death or sometimes also near-death situation has a strong psychological impact on all the people who were close to the dead person or who are actual witnesses to the event. In other words, the entire community immediately surrounding the victim counts as psychological victims of the disaster.

The work started in 1989, the year when the first local crisis team was founded. In a few years it has developed very quickly and is highly respected by the public, by politicians and decision makers and by health professionals. The work has also had effects on social norms. Through it, knowledge of psychological aspects of human beings has increased and attitudes to psychological phenomena have become more accepting. This development has happened mainly due to the psychological work done in major disasters.

The basis of these preventive interventions is the scientific fact that disasters and critical incidents produce severe and long-term reactions, symptoms and problems for about 30 per cent of the psychological victims of the disaster. These reactions can develop into long-term psychological or somatic illnesses, and also find expression in legal disputes. Psychological interventions carried out by local crisis teams aim to prevent these after-effects of traumatic events. In almost every municipality in Finland, there is a crisis team consisting of psychologists, medical doctors, public health and other nurses, social workers and church workers. Membership of the team is voluntary, but the work done for the team is regarded as part of the members' normal working hours. In other words, the local authorities have prioritized work aimed at the prevention of psychological trauma. Members of the crisis team are on call around the clock usually for a week at a time. In addition, they organize and lead psychological debriefing sessions. Before embarking on this work, crisis team members are given special psychological training. Many of the crisis teams have an opportunity for regular supervision. For major disasters there is a special team of forty psychologists throughout Finland with considerable expertise in traumatic crises. It has organized psychological aid for the victims of all major disasters.

The guiding principle behind acute crisis intervention is that help must be provided immediately after the event. An active search must identify those in need of help. This must be available and flexible and it must reinforce the victims' sense of coping. In practice, the police, the emergency personnel in hospitals and health centres and firemen have a duty to inform the crisis team about the accident, suicide, sudden death or other critical incident. The team members contact the victims of the disaster to speak with them and encourage them to undergo psychological debriefing. They both give and arrange immediate social support. It is assumed that every person who is the psychological victim of some disaster has a right to psychological debriefing and its benefits.

Psychological debriefing is a special method widely used to help the victims of the disaster to overcome their reactions. Its purpose is to prevent after-effects such as post-traumatic stress disorders by systematically reviewing in detail exactly what happened and also the impressions, thoughts and feelings of the victims. Debriefing also aims to reinforce group spirit and a feeling of solidarity, to activate social support and to normalize reactions. It should be carried out between twenty-four and seventy-two hours after the traumatic event. The time of the debriefing session is very important because of the psychological process going on in the victims' minds. In the reaction phase of the process, people are open and have an urge to raise very difficult emotional thoughts and feelings in the discussion. If the debriefing session takes place too late, it may be impossible to go in depth into difficult personal topics and the results are much poorer.

I have labelled this chapter 'Critical moments on the edge: psychological prevention of psychic and somatic problems, disorders and illnesses'. In work with traumatic crises there are critical moments that dramatically define the future of the victims. If the traumatic event and experience are not worked through in the mind of the victim and if psychological aid comes too late, it can mean considerable suffering, personality change and, in the worst cases, development of somatic or mental illness.

CONCLUSION

Psychologists meet much human suffering in their work. They must also face the discrepancy between the need for mental health services and the possibilities for help. Given this perspective, the development of psychological prevention and the community mental health movement is easy to understand.

Even when the scientific basis of psychological prevention was poor, psychologists had to believe that it was possible to prevent emotional disorders and psychic illnesses. In theory, the most effective prevention is to induce change in the factors producing these disorders. To counterbalance psycho-analytic theory, which focused on inner conflicts of the personality and early childhood to explain the roots of emotional disorder, psychologists who took the challenge of prevention seriously overemphasized the role of environmental, social and community factors in the etiology of emotional disorders.

Research findings as well as the practical experiences of psychological prevention and its poor results create scepticism about the possibility of preventive work in general and also the role of environmental factors in the development of mental health. Research yielded new knowledge about the complex interaction and mediating processes with personality factors. However, the model was too complicated to be used as a basis for preventive interventions, and a split in the field of prevention arose. This breakup of the basis of psychological prevention proved fruitful. One outcome was scientifically based psychological preventive programmes with clear and concrete aims. Knowing how to change the psychological process, and the optimal time to effect change, helps to target the needs of individuals who require intervention. The science of psychology has reached a developmental level which permits us to identify the critical moments on the edge and also to affect on which side of the edge individuals find themselves in the future.

REFERENCES

Albee, G.W. (1982) 'Preventing psychopathology and promoting human potential', *American Psychologist* 37: 1043–1050.

Albino, J.E. (1983) 'Health psychology and primary prevention: natural allies', in R.D. Felner, L.A. Jason, J.N. Moritsugu and S.S. Farber (eds) *Preventive Psychology. Theory, Research and Practice*, New York: Pergamon Press.

Bellak, L. (1964) 'Community psychiatry: the third psychiatric revolution', in L. Bellak (ed.) *Handbook of Community Psychiatry*, New York: Grune & Stratton.

Bellak, L. and Barten, H.H. (1969) *Progress in Community Mental Health*, New York: Grune & Stratton.

Caplan, G. (1964) *Principles of Preventive Psychiatry*, New York: Basic Books.

Cohen, R.Y., Stunkard, A. and Felix, M.R. (1986) 'Measuring community change in disease prevention and health promotion', *Preventive Medicine* 15: 411–473.

Coleman, J.C. (1973) 'Life stress and maladaptive behavior', *American Journal of Occupational Therapy* 27, 4: 169–180.

Cowen, E.L. (1973) 'Social and community interventions', *Annual Review of Psychology* 24: 423–472.

Dohrenwend, B.P. (1974) 'Problems in defining and sampling the relevant population of stressful life events', in B.S. Dohrenwend and B.P. Dohrenwend (eds) *Stressful Life Events. Their Nature and Effects*, New York: John Wiley & Sons.

Egger, G., Fitzgerald, W., Frape, G., Monaem, A. and Rubinstein, P. (1983) 'Results of large scale media antismoking campaign in Australia: North Coast "Quit for Life" programme', *British Medical Journal* 287: 1125–1128.

Elias, M.J. (1987) 'Establishing enduring prevention programs: advancing the legacy of Swampscott', *American Journal of Community Psychology* 15: 539–553.

Felner, R.D., Jason, L.A., Moritsugu, J.N. and Farber, S.S. (1983) *Preventive Psychology. Theory, Research and Practice*, New York: Pergamon Press.

Gesten, E.L. and Jason, L.A. (1987) 'Social and community interventions', *Annual Review of Psychology* 38: 427–460.

Heller, K. (1990) 'Social and community intervention', *Annual Review of Psychology* 41: 141–168.

Hobbs, N. (1964) 'Mental health's third revolution', *American Journal of Orthopsychiatry* 34: 822–833.

Holmes, T.S. (1970) 'Adaptive behavior and health change', medical thesis, Seattle: University of Washington.

Holmes, T.R. and Rahe, R.H. (1967) 'The social readjustment rating scale', *Journal of Psychosomatic Research* 11: 213–218.

Iscoe, I. and Harris, L.C. (1984) 'Social and community interventions', *Annual Review of Psychology* 35: 333–360.

Johnson, S.B. (1980) 'Psychosocial factors in juvenile diabetes', *Journal of Behavioral Medicine* 3: 29–35.

Korchin, S.J. (1976) *Modern Clinical Psychology*, New York: Basic Books.

Levine, M. (1988) 'An analysis of mutual assistance', *American Journal of Community Psychology* 16: 167–183.

Levine, M., Toro, P.A. and Perkins, D.V. (1993) 'Social and community interventions', *Annual Review of Psychology* 44: 525–558.

Maccoby, N. and Alexander, J. (1980) 'Use of media in lifestyle programs', in P.O. Davidson and S.M. Davidson (eds) *Behavioral Medicine: Changing Health Lifestyles*, New York: Brunner/Mazel.

Olds, D.L. (1988) 'The prenatal/early infancy project', in R. H. Price, E.L. Cowen, R.P. Lorion and J. Ramos-McCay (eds) *Fourteen Ounces of Prevention: A Casebook for Practitioners*, Washington, DC: APA.

Pilisuk, M. and Minkler, M. (1985) 'Social support: economic and political considerations', *Social Policy* 16: 6–11.

Puska, P., Nissinen, A., Tuomilehto, J., Salonen, J.T. and Koskela, K. (1985) 'The community-based strategy to prevent coronary heart disease: conclusions from the ten years of the North Karelia Project', *Annual Review of Public Health* 6: 147–193.

Rahe, R.H. (1974) 'The pathway between subjects' recent life changes and their near-future illness reports: representative results and methodological issues', in R.S. Dohrenwend and B.P. Dohrenwend, (eds) *Stressful Life Events. Their Nature and Effects* (pp. 73–86), New York: John Wiley & Sons.

Riessman, F. (1985) 'New dimensions in self-help', *Social Policy* 15: 2–5.

Ryan, W. (1971) *Blaming the Victim*, New York: Random House.

170   *Salli Saari*

Saari, S. (1979) 'Terveystarkastukset ehkäisevän mielenterveystyön muotona. Mielenterveysseulan kehittämistyö' ('Health screening as a form of preventive mental health. Development of a mental health screening procedure'), *Ylioppilaiden terveydenhoitosäätiön tutkimuksia ja selvityksiä* 2/1979, Helsinki.

—— (1981) 'Mielenterveyden muutoksen ennustaminen ja selittäminen kolmen ensimmäisen opiskeluvuoden aikana' ('Prediction and explanation of the changes in students' mental health during the first three university years'), *Ylioppilaiden terveydenhoitosäätiön tutkimuksia ja selvityksiä* 10/1981, Helsinki.

Saari, S. and Majander, H. (1985) 'Seurantatutkimus mielenterveyden kehittymisestä. Ulkoisten elämänolojen välittymismallin tarkastelua' ('A follow-up study on the development of mental health: examination of external living conditions and their mediation'), University of Helsinki, Department of Psychology, Research Reports No.2, Helsinki.

Syme, S.L. and Berkman, L.F. (1976) 'Social class, susceptibility and sickness', *American Journal of Epidemiology* 104: 1–8.

Winett, R.A., King, A.C. and Altman, D.G. (1989) *Health Psychology and Public Health: An Integrative Approach*, New York: Pergamon Press.

11 Flight from science
Alternative medicine, postmodernism and relativism

Adrian Furnham

INTRODUCTION

Is the growth and popularity of complementary and alternative medicine a flight from science? Are thousands of people turning their lower back pains on modern high-technology medicine, perhaps the greatest achievement of the twentieth century, because of ignorance and disillusionment? Are these seekers after new, different (and unproven) treatments naive (or sophisticated) followers of the new relativistic and postmodern philosophy of our age? Or are the millions who dabble in complementary medicine simply 'shopping' for a good deal, being intelligent and educated consumers of better care?

Complementary (alternative) medicine is now widely used throughout the developed world. The major complementary therapies, such as acupuncture, homoeopathy, herbalism and osteopathy, are extensively used and increasingly accepted (BMA 1993). In the United Kingdom, Fulder and Munro (1985) found that in 1981, complementary consultations averaged 19,500 per 100,000 people – 6.5 per cent of general practice consultations. Acupuncture, chiropractic and osteopathy were the most popular specialities, with about two million consultations per year each. Overall, about 1.5 million people (2.5 per cent of the population) were receiving courses of treatment in a single year. Thomas *et al.* (1991) estimated that their more restricted group of professionally registered complementary practitioners undertook four million consultations per year, roughly one for every fifty-five patient consultations with an NHS general practitioner.

In Europe, studies suggest that between one-third and one-half of the adult population have used complementary medicine at some time. Where self-medication with homoeopathic and herbal remedies is included in the definition (for studies in Belgium, Finland and France), approximately one-third of people have had complementary treatment in the previous year (Lewith and Aldridge 1991; Sharma 1992). In the USA, Eisenberg *et al.* (1993) have recently found that more visits are made to providers of unconventional therapy (which includes the more widely known complementary therapies) than to all US primary care physicians (general practitioners). The expenditure on unconventional therapies was comparable to that spent on all hospitalizations in the US. Eisenberg *et al.*'s (1993) definition 'commonly used interventions neither widely taught in US medical schools nor generally available in US hospitals' (p. 247) included all the major complementary therapies, vitamin and mineral supplements, and other complementary remedies. Also included, however, were taking exercise and relaxation techniques – hardly unconventional. The results exaggerate the use of truly unconventional therapies, but nevertheless show a widespread use and acceptance.

What do the main alternative/complementary therapies have in common? Aakster (1986) believes that they differ from orthodox medicine in terms of five things. Inevitably, these sorts of contrasts exaggerate both the differences and the within-group homogeneity, but are worth considering:

- *Health*: Whereas conventional medicine sees health as an absence of disease, alternative medicine frequently mentions a balance of opposing forces (both external and internal).
- *Disease*: The conventional medicine interpretation sees disease as a specific, locally defined deviation in organ or tissue structure. Alternative and complementary practitioners stress many wider signs, such as body language indicating disruptive forces and/or restorative processes.
- *Diagnosis*: Regular medicine stresses morphological classification based on location and etiology, while alternative interpretations often consider problems of functionality diagnostic.
- *Therapy*: Conventional medicine often aims to destroy, demolish or suppress the sickening forces, while alternative therapies often aim to strengthen the vitalizing, health-promoting forces. The latter therapies seem particularly hostile to chemical therapies and surgery.
- *Patient*: In much conventional medicine the patient is the passive recipient of external solutions, while in alternative medicine the patient is an active participant in regaining health.

Aakster (1986) attempted to elucidate what he called three main frames of medical thinking. The first he called the *pharmaceutical* model, which sees disease as a demonstrable deviation of function or structure and can be diagnosed by careful observation. The causes of disease are mainly germ-like and the application of therapeutic technology is all-important. The *integrational* model resulted from technicians attempting to reintegrate the body. Further, this approach was not afraid of allowing for psychological and social causes to be specified in the aetiology of illness. The third model was labelled *holistic* and does not distinguish between soma, psyche and social. Further, it stresses total therapy and holds up the idea of a natural way of living.

Aakster (1986) is sceptical, not cynical. He believes that orthodox medicine can, and has, become too ideological and rigid. He sees a place for 'alternative' theories, primarily in challenging accepted assumptions. Further, alternative approaches help to focus on suffering rather than on technology, and how human problems can be solved by human means. He also argues that 'alternative approaches bring back into our care system simplicity, safety, individual responsibility and autonomy' (p. 270). It may be expected that the application of alternative approaches, with their emphasis on health-strengthening forces and life-style, means that our expensive, highly complex and almost unmanageable health systems might be replaced by a 'more horizontally organised, smaller, professional care system, of lower complexity on a reduced scale' (p. 272).

What of alternative practitioners themselves? To what extent are they a homogenous group? How do they react to evaluative studies? What do they really believe? The growth in the number and acceptance of complementary and alternative medical practitioners means that they are now far from being a 'fringe'. There is clearly both a demand and a supply set of factors that has accounted for their meteoric rise. Patients demand more satisfying and sophisticated doctor–patient relationships and seem less satisfied with naive 'scientism' and the side-effects of drugs. Alternative practitioners have been quick to respond to the growth in individualism, consumerism and emphasis on self-responsibility for health.

While there have been various papers that have examined orthodox medical practitioners' and students' perceptions, Cant and Calnan (1991) looked at alternative practitioners. They were particularly interested in how they see their role; how they believe it should develop; how they feel it should exist within an orthodox medical framework, and their thoughts about the future.

Predictably, these 'alternative' practitioners resist being lumped together in a homogenous group. Overall, they believed patients turn to them as a last resort, not because they reject the 'medical model', but rather the 'system' which has delayed and frustrated them. The results showed that while most practitioners sought collaboration with the medical profession, they did not seek integration, preferring to keep their identity. Most groups wanted to establish associations and training standards so that they would not have to be subordinate to orthodox medicine but form a separate and autonomous domain. Most sought validation and legitimation by the government in order to gain credence in the medical field. Most seemed optimistic, envisaging themselves as expanding and accruing credibility and acceptability. Certainly, what Cant and Calnan's qualitative study has clearly shown is that there remain very important differences between the amorphous groups that have been categorized as complementary or alternative medical practitioners.

There is also a growing interest in complementary medicine within the health professions. Questionnaire studies have examined the attitudes of orthodox medical students and practitioners (Reilly 1983; Wharton and Lewith 1986; Anderson and Anderson 1987; Furnham *et al.* 1995), and found high rates of interest and knowledge, and referral of patients to complementary medicine.

The reasons for this increased interest and use of complementary medicine are not well understood, though many opinions have been offered. Some have suggested that the move towards complementary medicine represents a 'flight from science' (Smith 1983) or credulous faith in occult or paranormal phenomena (Skrabanek 1988; Baum 1989). Orthodox practitioners have delighted in attacking the theory and evidence from complementary medicine. Good empirical studies, published in respectable journals, appear to confirm the belief that much of complementary medicine is merely a placebo effect.

Knipschild (1988) studied iridology and noted that the presence of an inflamed gall-bladder containing gallstones is said to be easily recognized by certain signs in the lower lateral part of the iris of the right eye. Knipschild made stereo colour slides of the patients – half with the disease and half without. These slides were then shown to five iridologists, all leaders in their field, two of whom were medical doctors. They were asked to rate each patient's probability for having gall-bladder disease on a 7–point scale from 'definitely' to 'definitely not'. The iridologists estimated the prevalence of disease to be 56 per cent, which was nearly correct. However, it seemed that the iridologists could not distinguish between cases and controls. Moreover, they were highly inconsistent. Knipschild concluded that iridology is not a useful diagnostic aid. Knipschild (1988) sent the report to the five iridologists who complained that it is difficult to evaluate the iris without other medical information, including the size of both irises. They suggested that other diseases, apart from that of the gall-bladder, manifest more clearly in the iris. He also sent the study to eighty-three authors, and published it in orthodox and alternative medical magazines. He asked them to state their belief in iridology before and after reading the paper. Certainly belief dropped significantly after reading the report, but less so among alternative practitioners than orthodox ones.

Attacks on alternative medicine come from many quarters. Skrabanek (1988), who has made a special practice of attacking acupuncturists, has presented the sceptical and cynical set of objections that are well known. He claims that it is often difficult to evaluate any complementary practitioner's health claims because they lack a clear diagnosis. He focuses his criticism on procedures as diverse as Christian Science and psychic surgery. He attacks homoeopathy for treating not the disease but the problem; his complaint against osteopathy is poor reliability and diagnosis; while his attack on acupuncturists is based on the idea that its success is due entirely to the placebo effect.

Stalker and Glymore (1989) are particularly critical of the 'holistic' theories which they claim contain a 'reactionary impetus to return the practice of medicine to the practice of magic and to replace logic and method with occultism and obfuscation' (p. 23). For instance, they believe the much-repeated trivial and banal thesis that 'mental states affect physical states, and physical states affect mental states' is self-evident and that no one doubts it. Further, it is equally true and acknowledged that a variety of factors including sociopolitical, economic and environmental, affect health. They do view the implicit belief that all states of health are psychosomatic as simply wrong, but even if it were so, it would simply call for the scientific method to investigate the claim. They conclude:

At the base of the litany that each person must be treated as unique, that every part of the body is interdependent on every other part, and that body and mind are inseparable is the claim that holistic practitioners are absolved from demonstrating causal relations between their treatments and alleged therapeutic gains. They are under no obligation, they believe, to reconcile their claims about therapy with what is known about the causal pathways of the body. Their emphasis on the power of the mind is part theme and part tactic; the mind is supposed to be able to exert its power on parts of the body without regard to the laws of nature. The holistic practitioner sees the body in much the same way that magicians of old viewed the universe. The body becomes the last bastion of magic.

(Stalker and Glymore 1989: 24)

THE POSTMODERNIST ARGUMENT

Various sociologists have speculated on contemporary lay views of modern medicine (Bakx 1991; Williams and Calnan 1996). Many of these papers are theoretical rather than empirical, and if empirical, usually report qualitative rather than quantitative results. Hence they are not 'bottom-up' ideas or evidence from a representative sample of patients, but 'top-down' speculation as to what lay people think and why. Many argue that in the West we are now in a new 'postmodern era' in which people see themselves, professionals and their world differently. They are more sceptical of orthodox medicine and much happier to entertain alternative therapies.

There has long been a debate on the medical model and the medicalization of social issues referring to the way in which medical jurisdiction, concepts and control have expanded to many social issues. There are various theories as to why this has occurred, but agreement as to its consequences: medicalization undermines and withdraws the public's self-determination and exercises both increased social control and surveillance over ordinary people's bodies and lives. This is the argument of Foucault (1979) and others, but which has been challenged by some who believe the opposite, namely that we are currently witnessing the rise of de-medicalization (Turner 1987). Indeed, Strong (1979) waggishly suggested that it is medical sociology that is expansionist and imperialist in hyping alternative models and control mechanisms. Medical expansionist hegemony has been replaced by social science doing the same thing.

Williams and Calnan (1996) have attempted to summarize succinctly the views of Giddens and other influential theorists interested in contemporary social life. One idea from this school is that currently, all beliefs and practices (including medical) are subject to systematic examination, critical scrutiny and revision. Certainly, medicine is becoming more fragmented as it becomes more specialized and certain sectors are more sympathetic to a more holistic, biographical model, rather than a viral, biological approach. It is also true that much research medicine sees knowledge as tentative and corrigible, not because it is challenged by those with different epistemologies, but rather, quite simply, because it is assumed that new discoveries are made rapidly.

In the West, people live longer and in a more pain-free environment. Yet there is increasing ambivalence about modern technological medicine such as transplantation surgery, new reproductive technologies and the widespread use of modern drugs. Fewer and fewer 'health consumers' are passively duped by medical ideology. Medicine is at once a fountain of hope and despair because of what writers call *reflexivity* – the routine incorporation of new ideas into social relations and practices. Further, growing concern about *risk* encourages a subtle balance between active trust and radical doubt in medical experts. Finally, the *media* attempt a demystification role in putting modern medical practices on trial by encouraging the audience to be the jury. While the media could at the same time be accused of increasing mystification, there seems no doubt that it has educated the public to look critically at its treatment.

From the postmodernist perspective, there is a greater critical distance between modern medicine and the lay populace. Lay people are acquiring more sophisticated technical knowledge which makes them more educated and demanding consumers. Postmodernist critiques clearly ask more questions than they answer. Thus, Williams and Calnan note:

> In conclusion, in this world of uncertain times, one thing remains clear: namely that lay people are not simply passive or active, dependent or independent, believers or sceptics, rather they are a complex mixture of all these things (and much more besides). Without wishing to sound too post-modern, reality, in truth, is a mess, and we would do well to remember this as we edge ever closer to the twenty-first century!
>
> (Williams and Calnan 1996: 1619)

But does this postmodernist analysis explain the attraction of complementary medicine? It seems better at explaining, or at least describing possible causes for the disillusionment with contemporary, orthodox medicine – the so-called flight from science – rather than the movement towards contemporary practitioners. Indeed, it is possible to argue that the sceptical, risk-orientated views of the postmodern individual should lead them to be distrustful of complementary medicine rather than to embrace it. Some complementary medicine philosophy, although clearly heretical to modern orthodox scientific thought, has all the absolutist hallmarks of the latter and should therefore in principle be unappealing to postmodern people!

THE RISE OF RELATIVISM

The rise of philosophic, aesthetic and moral relativism from the late 1960s has been dramatic, though the epistemological relativists and absolutists (or universalists) have been sparring for years. According to Harre and Krausz (1996), there are two versions of relativism:

- *Scepticism* – which holds that no point of view is privileged, no description is true, and no assessment of value is valid;
- *Permissiveness* – which holds that all points of view are equally true and privileged, all descriptions are true and all assessments of value are equally valid.

It may be that the use of the terms 'alternative' and 'complementary' medicine reflect this difference. Those who use and prefer the title 'complementary medicine' nearly always assert the permissive view – the idea that different (even conflicting) descriptions and explanations can both be true, such that orthodox and complementary medicine can, and should, happily thrive side by side.

The absolutists also have subtle differences. Harre and Krausz (1996) list three features of the absolutists' beliefs:

- *Universalism*: there are beliefs and entities which are true in all contexts, at all times, for all peoples;
- *Objectivism*: there are beliefs and entities which exist independently of the point of view, corpus of beliefs, or conceptual scheme held to, and employed by, any particular person or society;
- *Foundationalism*: there is a common set of basic statements and existents (axioms) incapable of further analysis, out of which all other existents are constructed.

Relativists, according to Harre and Krausz (1996), negate all three of these doctrines. The philosophical position that appears to have grown in popularity and which has migrated from arts, through social science to science discipline ideas, is that of discursive relativism. This asserts that there are many theories for every phenomenon and many descriptions possible for the same event. In everyday language, the tenets of this approach, according to Harre and Krausz (1996) are:

- Languages are never completely inter-translatable;
- There are indefinitely many incompatible theories for each database, meeting the same criteria of acceptability;
- There are indefinitely many irreconcilable systems of moral and aesthetic values.

Arguments proliferate as to the key notions such as inter-translatability, incompatibility, irreducibility, and so on, and are spelled out in different ways. This general philosophical foundation for all discursive relativisms can be condensed into four negative theses:

- There could be no universal language adequate to a common human world;

- There could be no common unified theory universally applicable in all contexts at all times;
- There could be no definite system of descriptive categories picking out a common range of natural and social phenomena;
- There could be no universal moral/aesthetic principles viable in all cultures at all times.

(Harre and Krausz 1996: 8).

They go on to point out that relativism can be topic- or issue-specific. Four typical areas are:

- *Semantic relativism*: relativity of meaning to language; a word cannot be translated into another language without loss of meaning, and some words cannot be translated at all; for example, *amae*, a Japanese word used for a unique, locally defined emotion, has no equivalent in English. Its meaning can only be grasped indirectly;
- *Ontological relativism*: relativity of existence to conceptual systems; for example, electric fluids existed for Franklin, but not for us; witches existed for the Azande and not for us;
- *Moral relativism*: relativity of moral worth to societies and epochs; sex before marriage was once held to be wrong, but is not generally considered so now;
- *Aesthetic relativism*: relativity of aesthetic value to cultures and epochs; for example, the music of classical Chinese opera might well be judged cacophonous relative to the standards of Bel Canto.

(Harre and Krausz 1996: 23–24)

As philosophers are wont to point out, one can find weak and strong, coherent and inconsistent, absolutists and relativists. Harre and Krausz (1996) have delineated four types:

- *Strong absolutism (or dogmatism)*: Universalism with Objectivism and Foundationalism.
- *Moderate absolutism*: Universalism with Objectivism but without Foundationalism.
- *Moderate relativism*: Anti-universalism with Objectivism but without Foundationalism. Anti-universalism with Foundationalism but without Objectivism.
- *Strong relativism (or anarchism)*: Anti-universalism with anti-Objectivism and anti-Foundationalism.

This level of philosophical debate is not to be found in the alternative and complementary medicine literature. Nevertheless, the ideas have 'percolated down' to many practitioners. The ideas of moral and aesthetic relativism have been popular since the 1960s, but ontological relativism is now 'catching on'. While practitioners of orthodox medicine have been schooled in the unquestioning, absolutist model, complementary practitioners are exposed to relativist thinking. Curiously, the former are rendered vulnerable in arguments with the latter through lack of philosophic education and practice at debate. Many orthodox practitioners are rendered completely helpless when faced with relativist arguments, many of which can be forcefully articulated. Further, the sight of the mighty orthodox practitioners bewildered by philosophic discourse is amazingly attractive to the relatively powerless relativists who may 'adopt' relativist positions more out of spite than commitment.

While it may be true that some complementary practitioners espouse a version of relativism, albeit a poorly articulated version (and most orthodox practitioners are in some form absolutists), it does not seem to be the case that their patients divide along these lines. This is partly due to the lack of philosophic education on the part of patients. In fact, if anything, many patients feel more secure with the absolutist certainty in knowledge and practice. What complementary medicine patients do espouse are holistic rather than atomistic approaches to medical care.

Yet there is increasing evidence that complementary patients seek out the *idiographic* ideology implicit in alternative medicine. Ideas of individual uniqueness and of contextualization sit well with their worldview. On the other hand, many orthodox patients appear happy with the *nomothetic* approach of orthodox medicine. Cassiletti (1988) recognized that the popularity of a particular therapy is, in part, a function of how well it fits into the sociocultural context of the time. Thus, the liquid preparations popular at the turn of the century fitted well with the pharmaceutical bottled medicines available at the time. Today, 'metabolic' and 'immuno-enhancing' therapies like diet, self-care, vitamins and internal cleansing reflect the social trends and values of our time. Cassiletti believes that there are five underlying social trends of our time that render certain treatment popular. They are as follows:

- Various rights movements (including patients' rights);
- Consumer movements that shift patients from the dependent role to a partnership/active consumer role;
- Holistic medicine movement;
- Self-care and fitness emphases;
- Disaffection with, and mistrust of, organized medicine.

Our belief in the power and supremacy of the individual and our overriding need to understand and control leads us to the 'mind has the power to heal' philosophy. Our frustration in our lack of ability to cure and control various diseases leads to attempts to achieving control, healing and understanding via less intrusive or toxic therapies. The argument is functional: patients are attracted to alternative therapies whose ideologies fit the current *zeitgeist*. Hence their attractiveness and popularity is currently a function of the sociocultural theories of our time, which are predominantly relativistic.

Canter and Nanke (1989) argue that homoeopathy, like health psychology, attempts to classify individuals into types. Through intensive psychometric work on thirty-six homoeopathic patients, and informed by Jungian theory, they categorized patients into four groups as described in Table 11.1. Such typologies are interesting, but they can be unhelpful. To some extent, there is a paradox in a group of professionals at once asserting uniqueness and then categorizing. Certainly, typologies may help observation and the formulation and listing of hypotheses. They are also, however, rather dangerous, because they may encourage practitioners to assume that once people have been categorized, they fulfil all the behaviours associated with that type.

Canter and Nanke (1989, 1991) believe that the scientific-practitioner model for medical and psychological practitioners has both benefits and drawbacks, that is, even those well within the orthodox (absolutist) camp can be concerned about the double-blind, placebo, controlled-trial approach. Conflicting priorities, moral concerns about withholding treatment from control group subjects, problems about isolating single factors when multiple factors seem to be operating, the difference between clinical and statistical significance, practical difficulties, the problem of loading at group (aggregated) versus individual differences and the preference for quantitative over qualitative data mean that the medical/psychological scientist/practitioner is rare. Canter and Nanke believe

Table 11.1 Homoeopathic classification of patients

	Scientific/rational	*Humanistic/sensing*	*Mystical/intuitive*	*Religious/moral*
World governed by	fixed natural laws; rational orderly processed	human purposes and actions	factors beyond human understanding	divine purposes
World explained by	science will explain everything	can only understand in terms of own experience	no absolutes – depends on how you look at things	spiritual values necessary to make sense of world
Better world if	growth of scientific knowledge	growth of humanitarian principles	shared vision of the future	return to religious values
People should	pay more attention to facts than to opinions	spend more time living, less time thinking	attend more to broad perspective, less to details	attend more to values, less to practical matters
My life explained by	there is a rational explanation for everything in my life	my life only has the meaning I give it	my life is a small part of a wider plan	there is a spiritual purpose behind everything in my life
Decisions made	on the basis of understanding of the facts	on the basis of what feels right in the situation	on the basis of hopes for the future	on the basis of moral values
My friends	think the same as I do	are in the same position as me	share same ideals as I do	share same moral values as I do
Best way to prepare for the future	set clear goals and plan carefully	live to the full today	keep an open mind about possibilities	live in harmony with the environment

Source: Canter and Nanke 1989

that we need a broader view of science and that there are some research priorities for complementary medicine:

- All clinical judgements need to be demonstrably reliable (over time, across judges);
- Basic clinical questions have to be asked:
  - Does the treatment work (not discounting spontaneous remission)?
  - Do some patients get worse as a result of treatment?
  - How long does the treatment last?
  - What evidence is there of comparative effectiveness?
  - What are the causal mechanism/the active ingredients in the treatment?
  - What is the explanation?
  - Which, if any, therapist factors are important?
  - What patient characteristics predict what?

There is no doubt that this list of questions is fundamental. What is not clear, however, is how they can be tested without reference to the more standard experimental methods of clinical trials, double-blind procedures and so on.

Canter and Nanke (1991) note that despite no convincing evidence, prefrontal lobotomies and ECT were used because of patients' positive responses. They argue that the popularity of alternative medicine does suggest that there is a very important process occurring in the patient–practitioner interaction which bears investigation.

SOCIOLOGICAL PERSPECTIVES

Sociological perspectives on health suggest that political factors play a large part in the popularity of various forms of medicine. For instance, McKee (1988) notes that while holistic critiques of Western medicine suggest it is too bioreductionist, so the holistic health movement can be accused of promoting both an *individualistic* rather than a social analysis of health and a *victim-blaming* ideology which serves to transfer the burden of health costs from the state and corporations to the individual.

She argues that holistic health serves the interest of capital accumulation, while Western medicine promotes capitalism. The old conspiracy theories run thus: the short-term treatment of disease is profitable and medical practice is oriented to crisis intervention and pathology correction, not prevention or health maintenance. The bio-reductionist model is accepted, not the social-environmental model. McKee feels that the holistic medicine supporters have neglected to criticize orthodox medicine on these grounds, though their contrasting view of health should give them this wider perspective. She appears to lament the fact that the holistic medicine movement has not helped forge a strong, anti-capitalist people's health movement!

It certainly seems a change for the alternative therapists to be tarred with the same brush as orthodox medicine and then be asked to join an even more extreme and discredited movement! Inevitably, sociologists want an analysis of the conflict and rivalry between orthodox and alternative medicine at a socioeconomic and political level.

Faced with many synonyms to describe non-orthodox medicine such as alternative, complementary, fringe, natural, non-conventional and marginal, Bakx (1991) chose the term 'folk' because it reflects two themes: it is relevant to culture and it reflects the fact that people have and make choices.

Yet Bakx is interested in explaining the 'eclipse' of folk medicine in Western society. He chose the word 'eclipse' rather than 'demise' or 'disappearance' because eclipses are cyclical and temporary, and what is unorthodox today may become the orthodoxy of tomorrow. In fact, Bakx does not see the eclipse of folk medicine but its opposite – providing a viable and valuable alternative. His analysis is sociopolitical: he believes the crisis of biomedicine, the changes in advanced capitalism, the awareness of green issues to be all part of the growth of a postmodern economy and society. Thus in the views of this sociologist, sociological forces have increased dissatisfaction with biomedicine and increased the cultural gap between doctors and patients.

WHAT IS THE ATTRACTION OF ALTERNATIVE MEDICINE?

Why should the strange, varied, contradictory and bizarre collection of alternative/complementary/non-allopathic treatments mesmerize sophisticated Western populations who have the technological sophistication of modern medicine available to them? Taylor (1985) answered the question by focusing on the doctor–patient encounter and the nature of the relationship between practitioner and client which the alternative system offers. She recognizes the differences between the various therapies surrounded by the 'holistic' label and the fact that they share no common epistemological basis. Yet they are distinguished and distinguishable from orthodox medicine in their emphasis on the subjective experience of the patient and the insistence that all therapists should focus on the whole person, not just the disease. By contrast, and somewhat unfairly, Taylor (1985) argues that scientific medicine sees the human body as a machine, like any other, which needs servicing. Patients, who are cases, should not distract the doctor by their unique personal feelings and experiences.

Using contrasts, Taylor (1985) argues that the orthodox doctor is teacher and facilitator, while the alternative practitioner is therapist. Too many people have become accustomed to the sort of medicine which 'relies on magic bullets administered by harassed physicians who cannot distinguish us one from another as we flow from waiting room to examination room to billing office' (p. 197). Orthodox medicine concentrates on sickness and alternative medicine concentrates on wellness. Alternative practitioners seem to characterize orthodox medical practices as technological and aggressive and their own as natural and non-invasive. Yet as Taylor notes:

There seems to be little that is 'natural' or 'non-invasive' about the acupuncturist's technique of sticking needles into various parts of the anatomy. Some kinds of alternative specialists train in schools which do not look very different from medical schools, go into private practice and, when their services are recognised as competitive with mainstream medicine, their prices become competitive too.

(Taylor 1985: 197)

Taylor examines the ever-more familiar ground of why therapies are growing in popularity. The usual reasons are suggested:

- A change in the cultural mood (*zeitgeist*);
- Medicine has not changed and still sees itself as 'restoring people to productivity within a certain form of society';
- Alternatives expand and contract in popularity in proportion to the successes and failures of conventional medicine;
- Fear of iatrogenic diseases which are problems which stem from medical intervention and drugs which are supposed to cure, but in fact exacerbate, the problem.

But Taylor argues that the failures, cost and uneven distribution of modern medicine alone cannot account for the rise in alternative medicine because they do not explain *recent* interest when cost and access are enduring problems; and consumers indeed have to pay more for alternative medicine which is not covered by the state or by insurance.

It is the *simultaneous* dissatisfaction/disaffection with orthodox medicine and the attraction of alternative medicine which seems to have most explanatory power. The rise and fall of different healing systems is contingent in large part on the changing nature of the medical encounter. When medicine can promise neither relief nor cure, the quality of the individual doctor–patient relationship is paramount. The consumer movement, the women's movement and the more general demand for participation all focused on the medical encounter, but traditional medical schools and practising doctors resisted populist demands and the pressure for democratization and customer service. Not only did medicine resist change, but for many there was a perceptible deterioration of the medical encounter. Malpractice lawsuits have made doctors more cautious; there are fewer generalists and more specialists so a long-term relationship is less likely; and the increase in technological 'breakthroughs' has alienated many 'modern' patients. Patients have neither a 'voice option' in the medical encounter, nor an 'exit option' to leave. Changing doctors, getting second opinions, paying for insurance are very difficult for most, hence patients have to confront the many problematic aspects of the relationship with an orthodox medical doctor. What the modern patient wants, and appears not to be getting, is:

- Being treated with respect: crowded waiting rooms, being patronised and being processed are common complaints;
- Being treated as a more educated consumer, but still being met by a wall of clinical autonomy and a refusal to share information;
- Not being faced by doctors who have nothing to offer and nothing to do either because treatments don't work or because the best policy is judged to be to do nothing;
- A consumer contract with equal responsibilities, and not the experience of many patients that doctors do not trust them to make appropriate decisions about their health care.

Thus for Taylor, medicine is a relationship. The fate of complementary medicine is determined not so much by the proven efficacy of its methods but rather by orthodox practitioners being either unwilling or unable to deliver what the modern patient wants.

For Lynse (1989), there are two reasons why patients choose alternative medicine: push and pull. *Disappointment* with currently available health care and *curiosity*. He uses a historical example to argue three points. First, alternative practitioners use new, unaccepted controversial concepts. It is possible that a new theoretical framework will make it possible to reinterpret pre-scientific concepts and pseudo-scientific explanations within an acceptable framework. Second, empirical data in support of alternative therapies may be impossible to understand against the background of the prevailing paradigm; that is, effects have not been well recorded or documented, *but are real*. Third, the development of a new paradigm provides the opportunity for reinterpreting pre-scientific terms and data in a new light. For instance, nineteenth-century medicine saw illness in terms of an imbalance of bodily fluids; hence the use of bleeding. It was difficult for doctors to accept the paradigm change to a more modern approach. Lynse argues that theoretical and professional interests conspire against the acceptance of an alternative therapy.

THE EMPIRICAL LITERATURE

There are a number of possible reasons for turning to complementary medicine. Some patients are 'pushed' because they may have become dissatisfied with orthodox medicine, rejecting its reliance on high technology, wary of the dangers of invasive techniques and the toxicity of many drugs. Others are 'pulled' because while they may retain a belief in the value and effectiveness of orthodox medicine, at least in certain areas, they find some aspects of complementary medicine attractive. They may regard it as especially efficacious for some conditions, as dealing more with the emotional aspects of illness, or as having a spiritual dimension that is not seen as important in orthodox medicine.

One of the first studies to ask why people choose alternative therapy was done by Moore *et al.* (1985). They asked sixty-five patients at a Centre for Alternative

Therapies why they chose to attend. Most came for pain alleviation or allergies to be cured. Although they reported having a good relationship with their doctor, most were unhappy about the failure of regular medicine. Nearly half felt rushed and that their doctor did not understand their problems. Interestingly, this obviously self-selected group of patients were well informed about alternative medicine through friends and the media. Attendance did not increase this knowledge but two-thirds believed their treatment worked. Interestingly, expectation of success correlated with outcome. Despite the obviously self-fulfilling placebo effect, this study suggests that the authors failed to explore any mechanism or process behind the data.

There have been some empirical attempts to understand the popularity of alternative medicine. In an interesting and perhaps unique study, Finnegan (1991) interviewed thirty-eight patients in-depth from the 300 or so visiting a general centre specializing in complementary medicine. From the demographic information which he collected, he found support for the generally held view that a high proportion of the patients had long-term chronic ailments, had been unable to find a conventional diagnosis for their symptoms, and seemed unresponsive to conventional treatment. In other words, the primary motivation was the failure of conventional medicine to bring about a satisfactory improvement in their condition. He found evidence for two distinct types of patients: those who turn to alternative medicine as a last resort and are neither interested in, nor embrace, its philosophy, and those who are more committed to belief and ideology than the alleviation of their personal suffering. Perhaps with a much bigger sample, a few further interesting nuances might have been discovered.

What reasons do patients give for visiting a complementary health practitioner? Budd *et al.* (1990) looked at 197 British patients: forty visiting an acupuncturist and 107 an osteopath. In all, 58 per cent of the acupuncture and 83 per cent of the osteopathy patients said the treatment was suggested by a doctor, while 13 per cent and 12 per cent respectively said it was because it was suggested by a family member or friend. Few said it was because they were interested in the treatment, but 20 per cent of acupuncture and 26 per cent of osteopathy patients said it was because it was readily available. The only major difference between the two groups was that whereas only 3 per cent of the osteopathy patients said they sought the treatment 'as a last resort', 27 per cent of the acupuncturists said this was the case for them. The research also showed that acupuncturists treated a wider range of conditions than did an osteopath, who treated mainly musculo-skeletal problems, joint and muscle strain. It certainly appears that these patients supported by the National Health Service were not pulled by the philosophy or reputation of complementary medicine, but chose it because their doctor recommended it and it was available. Clearly, the availability and cost of treatment makes a big difference as to when and why people use it.

In a series of programmatic studies, Furnham, Vincent and colleagues investigated why patients of complementary medicine chose their preferred practitioner (Furnham 1986, 1993, 1994, 1997; Furnham and Bhagrath 1992; Furnham and Forey 1994; Furnham and Kirkcaldy 1995; Furnham *et al.* 1995; Furnham *et al.* 1995; Vincent and Furnham 1994, 1995; Vincent *et al.* 1995). In their work, Furnham has speculated on ten possible reasons why people choose complementary medicine, which include:

- Disillusionment with (the hegemony of) orthodox biomedicine (in general)/ (never fulfilled its promise);
- Anti-science, anti-establishment (postmodernist virus) beliefs about professionals practising 'scientific medicine';
- Fear (of the power) of professionals' doubts about motives;
- Dissatisfaction with orthodox techniques when dealing with everyday chronic problems (backache);
- The philosophy of (some) complementary medicine therapies (whole person, non-intrusive, 'psychological');
- Simply 'shopping for health' and being prepared to try anything once; experimentation in the market place;
- Internal locus of control needs to take more responsibility for (all aspects of) health (health-consciousness);
- Offering the unstable the possibility of morbid self-interest and less limited therapist time and attention;
- Different health beliefs and theories as to the aetiology, manifestation and cure of illness (health belief model);
- Consistent advice from significant others about the efficacy of complementary medicine.

Furnham (1997) surveyed the empirical evidence from the dozen or so empirical studies under five headings as described in the next section.

Anti-orthodox medicine

Possible reasons that have been posited include disillusionment with the hegemony of orthodox medicine (in general) which is seen as never having reached its nineteenth-century promise. Allied to this 'explanation' is the possible reason that prospective patients, imbued with anti-science, anti-establishment, postmodernist theory, reject 'scientific' medicine and the orthodox, positivist theory upon which it is based. While it is possible that this explanation may be used to explain why some people are both attracted to, but primarily flee from, orthodox medicine, the programmatic studies have revealed that this group is very small. Confined to the more articulate, educated, relatively fit middle class, theoretical or epistemological reasons do not account for much of the variance when explaining choice of complementary medicine. Further, it is possible that patients and clients develop 'theories' of their choice and rationalizations for their behaviour *post hoc*; that is, after, rather than before, they made their choice. However, it is possible that anti-orthodox philosophic ideas do change the *zeitgeist*, which in turn influences patients' perception of both orthodox and complementary medicine.

Dissatisfaction and/or fear of orthodox professionals

There is considerably more evidence to support the type of explanation which holds that patients of complementary practitioners have had bad experiences of orthodox doctors, but there are also equivocal studies which show that alternative patients are not disgruntled with alternative medicine (Donnelly *et al.* 1985). These experiences come in a number of forms: first, that the doctor does not seem to take the time or care to 'fully understand' the patient; that is, that patients feel they are being *processed* too quickly by the orthodox medical system (Hewer 1983). They feel cheated: possibly their expectations of a consultation are inappropriate and unreasonable; they may be presenting with obvious psychosomatic or trivial complaints which busy orthodox doctors cannot deal with. A second reason for dissatisfaction lies in the patient's perception that the doctor and his or her cure/therapy simply does not work. In other words, their chronic condition, most frequently back pain, gets no better and that the orthodox practitioner, for all his or her training and the advancement of modern medicine, is unable to deal with the problem. Third, there are patients who fear orthodox medical practitioners. They fear their power and their methods which some see as too technological and insufficiently sensitive to individual differences. Surgeons frequently epitomize the all-powerful, even brutal, side of medicine. Studies on health locus of control show that orthodox medical patients have more faith in their practitioner, but take less responsibility for their own health. It really revolves around the issue of trust and the extent to which patients believe their practitioners can and do help them.

The philosophy of complementary medicine

It has been argued that some patients are attracted to specific branches of complementary medicine because of its philosophy; that is, the types of explanation it gives for health and illness. This is particularly the case when explanations are both holistic and psychological, or simply 'new age' ideas around mental and physical self-betterment, esoteric teaching and contemplative practice (Levin and Coreil 1986). Just as people choose and read newspapers that confirm their political views, so people may seek out practitioners whose 'philosophy' fits their own. Once again, while this may in part be true, it is perhaps too cognitive an explanation, particularly if people are chronically sick and seeking relief from pain. It does not appear to be the case that complementary medicine patients have some noticeably different health belief models compared to similar patients who are exclusive users of orthodox medicine (Furnham 1997).

Morbid self-interest and neurosis

Cynics from the orthodox medicine camp have been known to explain the behaviour of complementary patients as a manifestation of neurosis. That is, that neurotic, psychosomatic patients are drawn to the psycho-babble and talking/touching cures of some complementary practitioners precisely because it is a case of psychologically disturbed people getting psychological help. The evidence is equivocal on this point, and a number of studies have shown the incidence of actual psychiatric morbidity (cases) to be higher in complementary medicine patients. Yet it could be that chronic, painful illness which appears both progressive and incurable leads to a higher incidence of neurosis and the search for alternative treatments. There does seem to be evidence that people with a specific demographic and sociological profile seek out alternative medicine; but whether or not they are neurotic remains unclear.

Shopping for health

Few patients are exclusive users of one branch of complementary medicine. As the above studies have shown, most people have an understanding that certain types of complementary medicine are ideally suited to specific complaints. These include acupuncture for migraine, osteopathy for back pain, homoeopathy for allergies, and so on. Equally, they believe orthodox medicine to be by far the most efficient for problems associated with broken bones and bleeding. The more health options there are available, the more people shop for health, trying out various solutions or cures for different conditions. This seems particularly true of very health-conscious people.

Do patients tell their doctor about their use of alternative and complementary therapies? Many studies show an increase in the use of alternative medicine along with the growth of 'consumer sovereignty' in health care decisions. Yet Murray and Shepherd (1993) believe there is evidence that while patients use orthodox and non-orthodox treatments at the same time, they do not inform either practitioner about the other. Thus they found evidence that patients sense the traditional antipathy between the medical profession and alternative therapists and hence are reticent about disclosing their use of the latter's treatment to the former. They believe this has important implications for all GPs and they forcefully conclude:

> If general practitioners are to recognise alternative practitioners as potential allies, and if the patients are to continue to use orthodox and alternative treatments in combination, then these areas of concern must be confronted.
>
> (Murray and Shepherd 1993: 988)

CONCLUSION

Angry, sarcastic and dismissive articles by otherwise sober, disinterested orthodox medical practitioners who argue that the increasing numbers of patients going to complementary medical practitioners are irrationally fleeing from science are clearly misplaced. To some extent, medical education and practice has not taken cognizance of the changing beliefs and needs of patients. Patients in the West are better consumer educated and more demanding. For various reasons, including economic, orthodox medicine has not been able to adapt to their needs. But complementary practitioners have.

In fact, as various studies have shown, doctors (physicians) are not hostile to complementary medicine (Ernst *et al.* 1995; Furnham 1993). They see complementary medicine as moderately effective and useful, though many remain uncertain about its proven effectiveness.

The ordinary patient, even those who are sophisticated, does not know about randomized controlled trials, and the database on the efficacy of herbalism, homoeopathy or chiropractic. But they do pay attention to the media and friends, and when faced with a chronic problem are happy to try out new approaches.

A central concern of all health promotion and education is to de-medicalize the health services and empower the patient. Many branches of complementary medicine share similar goals with health educators, the critical appraisal of orthodox medicine as well as encouraging patients both to choose specific practitioners (and practices) for specific problems, as well as to take responsibility for their health. Complementary medicine patients may therefore be better health-educated than those using the orthodox medicine sector exclusively.

Patients' 'theories of illness' may relate, importantly, to compliance with medical advice. There is considerable interest in, and attendant research concerned with, compliance in medical settings. Some studies have suggested that health beliefs, specifically lay theories of health, are important determinants of compliance. Thus patients are more likely to remember and follow advice that fits in with their theory. Hence the importance of understanding, and where appropriate enriching or altering, lay theories of health. However, lay people are as likely to influence and educate each other as they are to follow specialist professional advice. Indeed, for some people it is lay practitioners, rather than specialist or complementary, who have more source credibility when discussing health issues. Thus health educators may wish to focus on the educative role of all practitioners of complementary medicine.

REFERENCES

Aakster, C. (1986) 'Concepts in alternative medicine', *Social Science and Medicine* 22: 265–273.

Anderson, E. and Anderson, P. (1987) 'General practitioners and alternative medicine', *Journal of the Royal College of General Practitioners* 37, 295: 52–55.

Bakx, K. (1991) 'The "eclipse" of folk medicine in Western society', *Sociology of Health and Illness*, 13: 17–34.

Baum, M. (1989) 'Rationalism versus irrationalism in the care of the sick: science versus the absurd' (Editorial), *Medical Journal of Australia* 151, 11–12: 607–608.

BMA (1993) *Complementary Medicine*, Report of the Board of Science and Education.

Budd, C., Fisher, B., Parruder, D. And Price, L. (1990) 'A model of co-operation between complementary and allopathic medicine in a primary care setting', *British Journal of General Practice* 40: 376–378.

Cant, S. and Calnan, M. (1991) 'On the margins of the medical market place? An exploratory study of alternative practitioners' perceptions', *Sociology of Health and Illness* 13: 46–66.

Canter, D. and Nanke, L. (1989) 'Emerging priorities in complementary medical research', *Complementary Medical Research* 3: 14–21.

—— (1991) 'Psychological aspects of complementary medicine'. Paper presented at Keele University, January.

Cassiletti, B. (1988) 'The social implications of questionable cancer therapies', *Cancer* 63: 1247–1250.

Donnelly, W., Spykerboer, S. and Thong, Y. (1985) 'Are patients who use alternative medicine dissatisfied with orthodox medicine?' *Medical Journal of Australia* 142: 539–541.

Eisenberg, D., Kessler, R.C. and Foster, C. (1993) 'Unconventional medicine in the United States', *New England Journal of Medicine* 328: 246–252.

Ernst, E., Resch, K-L. and White, A. (1995) 'Complementary medicine: what physicians think of it', *Archives of International Medicine* 155: 2405–2408.

Finnegan, M. (1991) 'The Centre for the Study of Complementary Medicine: an attempt to understand the popularity through psychological, demographic and operational criteria', *Complementary Medical Research* 5: 83–88.

Foucault, M. (1979) *Discipline and Punishment*, Harmondsworth, Middlesex: Penguin.

Fulder, S.J. and Munro, R.E. (1985) 'Complementary medicine in the United Kingdom: patients, practitioners and consultations', *Lancet* 2, 8454: 542–545.

Furnham, A. (1986) 'Medical students' beliefs about five different specialities', *British Medical Journal* 293: 1067–1680.

—— (1993) 'Attitudes to alternative medicine: a study of the perception of those studying orthodox medicine', *Complementary Therapies in Medicine* 1: 120–126.

—— (1994) 'Explaining health and illness', *Social Science and Medicine* 39: 715–725.

—— (1997) 'Why do people choose and use complementary therapies?', in E. Ernst (ed.) *Complementary Medicine: An Objective Approach* (pp. 71–88), London: Butterworth-Heinemann.

Furnham, A. and Bhagrath, R. (1992) 'A comparison of health beliefs and behaviours of clients of orthodox and complementary medicine', *British Journal of Clinical Psychology* 32: 237–246.

Furnham, A. and Forey, J. (1994) 'The attitudes, behaviours and beliefs of patients of conventional vs complementary (alternative) medicine', *Journal of Clinical Psychology* 50: 458–469.

Furnham, A. and Kirkcaldy, B. (1995) 'The health beliefs and behaviours of orthodox and complementary medicine clients', *British Journal of Clinical Psychology* 25: 49–61.

Furnham, A. and Smith, C. (1988) 'Choosing alternative medicine: a comparison of the beliefs of patients visiting a GP and a homeopath', *Social Science and Medicine* 26: 685–687.

Furnham, A., Hanna, D. and Vincent, C. (1995) 'Medical students' attitudes to complementary medical therapies', *Complementary Therapies in Medicine* 3: 212–219.

Furnham, A., Vincent, C. and Wood, R. (1995) 'The health beliefs and behaviours of three groups of complementary medicine and a general practice group of patients', *Journal of Alternative and Complementary Medicine* 1: 347–359.

Harre, R. and Krausz, M. (1996) *Varieties of Relativism*, Oxford: Blackwell.

Hewer, W. (1983) 'The relationship between the alternative practitioner and his patient', *Psychotherapy and Psychosomatics* 40: 172–180.

Knipschild, P. (1988) 'Looking for gall bladder disease in the patient's iris', *British Medical Journal* 297: 1578–1581.

Knipschild, P., Kleijnen, J. and Ter-Riet, G. (1990) 'Belief in the efficacy of alternative medicine among general practitioners in The Netherlands', *Social Science and Medicine* 31, 5: 625–626.

Levin, J. and Coreil, J. (1986) '"New Age" healing in the US', *Social Science and Medicine* 23: 889–897.

Lewith, G.T. and Aldridge, D.A. (1991) *Complementary Medicine and the European Community*, Saffron Walden, Essex: C.W. Daniel.

Lynse, N. (1989) 'Theoretical and empirical problems in the assessment of alternative medical technologies', *Scandinavian Journal of Social Medicine* 17: 257–263.

McKee, J. (1988) 'Holistic health and the critique of Western medicine', *Social Science and Medicine* 26: 775–785.

Moore, J., Phipps, K., Marcer, D. and Lewith, G.T. (1985) 'Why do people seek treatment by alternative medicine?' *British Medical Journal* 290: 28–29.

Murray, J. and Shepherd, S. (1993) 'Alternative or additional medicine? An exploratory study in general practice', *Social Science and Medicine* 37: 983–988.

Reilly, D.T. (1983) 'Young doctors' views on alternative medicine', *British Medical Journal* 287, 6388: 337–339.

Sharma, U. (1992) *Complementary Medicine Today: Practitioners and Patients*, London: Routledge.

Skrabanek, P. (1988). 'Paranormal health claims', *Experientia* 44, 4: 303–309.

Smith, T. (1983) 'Alternative medicine' (Editorial), *British Medical Journal* 287, 6388: 307–308.

Stalker, D. and Glymore, L. (1989) (eds) *Examining Holistic Medicine*, Buffalo, NY: Promotheus.

Strong, P. (1979) 'Sociological imperialism and the medical profession', *Social Science and Medicine* 13: 199–211.

Taylor, R. (1985) 'Alternative medicine and the medical encounter in Britain and the United States', in J. Salmon and W. Warren (eds) *Alternative Medicine: Prejudice and Policy Perspectives* (pp. 191–221), London: Tavistock.

Thomas, K.J., Carr, J., Westlake, L. and Williams, B.T. (1991) 'Use of non-orthodox and conventional health care in Great Britain', *British Medical Journal* 302, 6770: 207–210.

Turner, B. (1987) *Medical Power and Social Knowledge*, London: Sage.

Vincent, C. and Furnham, A. (1994) 'The perceived efficacy of orthodox and complementary medicine', *Complementary Therapies in Medicine* 2: 128–134.

——(1995) 'Why do patients turn to complementary medicine? An empirical study', *British Journal of Clinical Psychology* 35: 37–48.

Vincent, C., Furnham, A. and Willsmore, M. (1995) 'The perceived efficacy of complementary and orthodox medicine in complementary and general practice patients', *Health Education Research* 10: 395–405.

Wharton, R. And Lewith, G. (1986) 'Complementary medicine and the general practitioner', *British Medical Journal* 292: 1498–1500.

Williams, S. and Calnan, M. (1996) 'The "limits" of medicalization? Modern medicine and the lay populace on "late" modernity', *Social Science and Medicine* 42: 1609–1620.

12 One hundred years of work and organizational psychology
Progress, deficiencies and promise

Bernhard Wilpert

INTRODUCTION

It seems appropriate to deconstruct some expectations which may be raised by the title of this chapter. What follows is not an attempt to do justice to the full richness of the century of history of work and organizational psychology (W/O). Many colleagues better prepared to tackle the intricacies of historiography have already dealt with that task aptly and comprehensively. I shall consult their works or refer to them as needed. Furthermore, do not expect an unbiased, objective and even-handed treatment of our field from me. Being European of German extraction, though also partly trained in the traditions of the United States, the influence of personal and scientific socialization will be reflected in what I am going to say. In addition, it is impossible to forgo one's own present scientific preoccupations when dealing with the past and future problems and challenges of our discipline.

In short, I confess and claim an eclectic bias. I feel justified to do so by the foresight of the editors of this volume who invited me to present 'a personal view of the strengths and weaknesses, the achievements and failures of the last 100 years of psychology in the area of work and organizational psychology and include [my] estimation and recommendations as to where psychology might go in this area in the next century'. What else might be expected after such a radical call for idiosyncrasy but a radical and personal reflection?

FUNDAMENTAL UNITY OF WORK AND ORGANIZATION

The division of work is basic to work. Adam Smith was not the first theoretician to discuss this division from a social science perspective, but he secured for himself a most important place in all subsequent discussions of the subject. He illustrates in the first pages of his *opus magnum, The Wealth of Nations* (1776), that the division of labour facilitates each worker's production of 4,800 needles instead of twenty. His example is too well known to repeat. Adam Smith held that the use of appropriate machines together with the division of work is the central motor of any economic development, thereby encouraging increased aptitude of workers and saving time. Division of labour is thus the central principle of all economic development and societal welfare, ultimately promoted by the natural human inclination to exchange one utility for another to satisfy personal needs.

John Stuart Mill goes a step further. With reference to Wakefield he points out in his book *Principles of Political Economy* (1848) that division of labour is governed by a more comprehensive law. The *combination* of work is the law describing how several individuals co-operate in order to achieve the same task or a set of different tasks.

Durkheim completes what may be called the trinity of early social scientific theorists of work. Division of labour, for Smith a cause of economic development and for Mill a central element of socially organized production, obtains a particular dignity in Durkheim's thinking. For him, the division of labour is the critical condition of the person's individuation as well as socialization. It is the source of civilization and even a fundamental law of history based in biology. In one of his major works, *On The Division of Labour* (1893), Durkheim attempts to answer the basic question of how the individual personality relates to social solidarity: 'How come that an individual, while becoming ever more autonomous, depends ever more on society?' (Durkheim 1977: 78). He makes the well-known distinction between mechanic and organic solidarity. The former emerges as a natural consequence of similarities among people, such as race or language. Organic solidarity results from the division of labour, in which individual differences among people are important. It 'is possible only if each has an activity field which he owns, i.e. when he is a personality' (1977: 444). And it is exactly that individuation which relates individuals inescapably to society by making them mutually dependent. As R. König once said, Durkheim the sociologist *par excellence* and arch-enemy of the psychologist Tarde thus becomes 'psychologist against his own will' (König 1978: 134). He overcomes at its very beginnings the historical accident which divided psychology from sociology, an accident for which he was not least instrumental.

For Durkheim, the division of labour is the basis of not only *societal* but also *moral* life. Pathologies – such as the forced division of labour which takes no account of the talents of people and limits their 'action space' – must be avoided (Durkheim 1977: 430):

> This happens in enterprises where the tasks are divided in a manner (such) that the activity of each worker sinks below the level it normally should have.
> (Durkheim 1977: 433)

Durkheim was a critic of fragmenting work even before its incarnation by Taylor, a theme so elegantly and aptly elaborated by Marx.

Citing classical theorists on work, who preceded the era of work/ organizational psychology, grounds my central argument and thus overcomes what I consider to be a mortal sin of psychology. This sin is to have separated work from organization through focusing either on individuals and their immediate tasks or on organizations and their properties. Rather, I claim that individual work can be appraised only when it is embedded within an organizational context.

Heinz Franke, a German organizational psychologist, developed a radical way of thinking about work within organizations. Regrettably, his work was unfinished due to his untimely death. Franke held that received traditions in psychology which focus on the individual are inappropriate. By contrast, he urged us to 'develop a concept of the individual which takes account of the interactive duties (*Verpflichtetheit*) of the individual from its [*sic*] very beginning' (Franke 1978: 337). Schmidt elaborates this notion, emphasizing co-operation:

> The form of co-operation is the interface between the transformation process and the social system of work. The specific configuration of co-operative work relations directly reflects the specific configuration of natural, technical and human resources. . . . The form of co-operation . . . is the generative mechanism of the entire edifice of the social system of work.
>
> (Schmidt 1991: 80)

Next to the essentially *organizational* nature of work, its anthropological significance must also be considered. Lewin (1920), in one of the early criticisms of Taylorism, articulated this dual aspect succinctly. Work is, on the one hand, always the yoke of effort and labour, the instrumental means needed for survival. Its value is gauged according to the economic advantages it offers to the worker. On the other hand, work is necessary, because without it life is empty and incomplete. Work is rooted in an undeniable life value, providing meaning and substance:

> Because work is life itself, that is why one wants to bring all life energy to it and wants it to be effective. This is why one wants work to be rich and wide, manifold and not cripplingly narrow. Therefore, there is love of work in it, creativity, dynamics and beauty. It should not hinder development potential, but should bring it to full realisation. Progress in work procedures should not result in reduction of work time, but in increasing life value of work, it should make it richer and more in line with human dignity.
>
> (Lewin 1920: 11ff.)

We have here an early formulation of anthropological–philosophical axioms which were later so beautifully expressed in Hannah Arendt's treatise *The Human Condition* (1958). Arendt described the dual nature of work. It is both drudge or labour, and a creative act.

These theoretical bases of the intrinsic *organizational* characteristics of any work linking the individual to society and of the fundamental *anthropological* significance of work for the individual are also the tenets of psychologists such as Rubinstein (1977), who stressed work as a basic human activity which inescapably relates individuals with each other. From each of these theoretical notions of work I derive my yardsticks to evaluate how the main phases of W/O psychology coped with the challenges confronting it.

CRITICAL CHALLENGES

It has become quite fashionable to identify phases in the historical developments of both work and organizational psychology. Recent textbooks do so according to different conceptions of the individual – economic, social, self-actualizing and complex (Ulich 1991). Others define phases in terms of major developmental characteristics such as the activities of pioneers, the expansion of knowledge, stabilization or the profession's role in a science of intervention (Greif 1983). In this chapter, I choose five phases as follows.

The human motor

Rabinbach (1988), in his masterful treatment of the history of ideas in work sciences, views Taylorism as an extension of the machine concept. According to this view, human work is an integral part of a production machine, providing the critical energetic principle. Taylorism was soon assailed by dire and justified criticisms from various psychological perspectives (Lahy 1916; Lewin 1920; Stern 1921; Lang and Hellpach 1922). However, Taylor's lasting impact rests on three achievements:

• a first comprehensive attempt to study work scientifically;
• a coherent philosophy of work organization;
• a successful increase in industrial productivity.

Taylor may thus be considered to be the father of time and motion studies, the first major attempts to deal with work processes using an analytical, scientific perspective.

Whether Taylor's intentions to arrive at 'appropriate work-loads' are mere lip-service paid to lofty humanitarian principles, and whether these drastic measures of dividing up of work are due to his own achievements or to those of his disciples, are moot questions. Nevertheless, it is clear that some of the extreme consequences of Taylorism challenge the curative and preventive activities of work/organizational psychologists even today (Ulich 1989). Taylor's central notion distinguished the vertical division of workers' dispositive, managerial and execution tasks and the horizontal sharing out of tasks among workers. Both are organizational principles of dividing work.

Aptitudes and selection

Taylor's influence fell on fertile ground, nurturing the growth of the subdiscipline *psychotechnics*. While Taylor's analytical approach was still an integral part of a comprehensive organizational thinking, previous workers in psychotechnics concentrated on individual work tasks and their requisite qualification demands. Fed by notions of experimental and differential psychology as well as by assumptions of innate competencies, we note the expansion of vocational aptitude testing and the use of intelligence and performance tests for vocational guidance and placement. For several decades, these activities created the basis for public recognition of applied psychology as a socially useful discipline.

There was also public support for an extremely important contribution to the further institutionalization and professionalization of the young field, namely the foundation of a large number of institutes of psychotechnics within and outside universities. Between 1918 and 1926, virtually all industrialized countries created such centres of applied psychology, followed by the creation of various learned journals covering the field of psychotechnics and applied psychology (Greif 1991). At about the same time, first initiatives for a comprehensive international co-operation emerged. Thus, in 1920, the first international congress of psychotechnics was held in Geneva under the presidency of Claparède. Claparède later became the first president of the International Association of Psychotechnics. This was renamed in 1952 the International Association of Applied Psychology (IAAP) and is the oldest and largest international psychological association with individual membership and comprehensive scope.

This period of development achieved lasting and salient effects in our discipline. A set of professional core competencies – for example, assessment techniques – and a positive trend in institutionalization and professionalization were the results. A negative aspect on the balance sheet was the fact that all this took place with a relative neglect of organizational issues. Attempts to include aspects of industrial organization (*Betriebsorganisation*) in the agenda (Moede 1930) remained rather perfunctory.

Social dynamics

This state of affairs changed with the new regime of human relations which focused clearly on social dynamics in the work place. The story of what went on – and what did not (Parsons 1974) – in the Hawthorne works of Western Electric has often been told. Suffice it to say that for the right or wrong reasons the Hawthorne experiments established more than any other research the importance of social factors in the theory and practice of work/organizational psychology. The topic was raised again with better theoretical underpinnings by the Michigan School, particularly with the seminal work of Katz and Kahn (1966). They defined an organization as a network of roles, standardized behaviour patterns which are expected from any person functionally related to others. Katz and Kahn view the relationships between individuals in work as overriding in importance. Despite criticisms of their metatheory (Greif 1983), their approach facilitates the systematic analysis of such important dynamic aspects in the life of work organizations as role conflicts, role stress, power relations and well-being.

Advocates of human relations tend to ignore two critical domains. Typically, they do not consider technology crucial to the understanding of behaviour within organizations. Second, their focus remains centred on organizations, in spite of claims that they consider them to be open systems.

Sociotechnics

This shortcoming was overcome by the work of creative scholars at the Tavistock Institute of Human Relations with their *open sociotechnical systems* approach. The works of Emery, Trist, Herbst, Miller, Rice and Bamforth in the 1940s and 1950s prepared the ground for a new paradigm which influenced thinking about work and organizations in the decades which followed. These theorists not only emphasize interpersonal relations in work settings and their intimate links to organizational structures. They also focus on the triad formed by individual–technology–organization, searching for an optimal fit among the three. Attending to these aspects was a necessary condition for developments within our discipline which could cope with the later emerging themes of organizational design as well as environmental factors. Any organizational output – whether a product, quality, safety, job satisfaction, or good decision making – results from a complex interaction of the social, organizational and technical components of a given subsystem. Environmental opportunities and constraints may have an impact on any of these three components. Evidence for the theoretical and practical utility of the socio-technical systems approach abounds. Many hundreds of research and organizational design projects applying this approach have been conducted throughout the world (Eijnatten *et al.* 1994).

It goes without saying that sociotechnical thinking implies a quantum leap in addressing complexity. Such thinking depends on theoretical concepts which take into account various system levels. We do so infrequently because we often lack the holistic conceptualizations and operational use, both of which we require. This is particularly true for organization–environment relations (Wilpert 1992). While we know that important societal and work-related values are changing, necessarily influencing work behaviour (MOW 1987; Super and Sverko 1995), it is not at all clear how we can guide management appropriately in applying such insights. Similarly, we know from research on industrial democracy (IDE 1981, 1993) that formal laws and regulations predict participation levels in organizations. But it is not at all clear what advice we ought to give to managers and policy makers on how to reach optimal levels of worker involvement in organizational decision making. In epistemological terms we face the towering task of developing the appropriate correspondence rules which allow us to relate findings on different systems levels (Franke 1978: 343). We face a task analogous to deciphering a palimpsest, reading several possibly related layers of scriptures on the same scroll (Schmidt 1991).

Social constructions and inter-organizational fields

Perusing some of the recent work/organizational psychological literature reveals two further thematic shifts (Wilpert 1995). The first is a growing recognition that organizations must be viewed as social constructions; the second, a growing concern with inter-organizational relations (Sydow 1996).

Both approaches herald new perspectives on the life of organizations. The understanding of organizations as entities which must continually be created and re-created in terms of socially shared meanings and symbol systems owes much to cultural anthropology and appear as the more radical epistemological shift of the two. It has important methodological implications inasmuch as meanings of objects and processes can be revealed better through anthropological methods such as participant observation, recording informal conversations and recording legends, myths and histories than through traditional standardized instruments. Connected with the approach is the hope of gaining inside views and an understanding of organizations accompanies the use of these methods.

The resolute focus on inter-organizational relations has been familiar to us for quite some time (Levine and White 1961; Aldrich 1979). In recent years it has gained momentum partly from development of the sociotechnical paradigm and formal network analysis (Burt 1980) and partly in response to business trends of globalization and organizational networking.

The social construction perspective focuses on the internal life of organizations. By contrast, the inter-organizational perspective focuses outwards. Each offers promise rather than achievement at present. Each declares itself open to sister disciplines of psychology and by so doing highlights a further significant challenge to our subdiscipline: interdisciplinary thinking and co-operation.

THE PRESENT: A CRITICAL EDGE

Two worthy colleagues concerned with professional and scientific developments within our discipline opened a recent paper on *Work Psychology in Europe* with a lapidary statement: 'The 1990s is a critical decade for Work/Organizational psychology' (De Wolff and Shimmin 1994: 333). These authors present the responses of twenty-four scholars and practitioners throughout Europe who evaluated seven different possible scenarios for the development of work/ organizational psychology. De Wolff and Shimmin point out that two overriding dynamics seem to shape present development: the emergence of European scientific and professional networks and the expressed need for multidisciplinary approaches.

Founded in the 1980s, organizations such as the European Federation of Professional Psychological Associations (EFPPA), the European Network of Organizational and Work Psychologists (ENOP) and the European Association of Work and Organizational Psychology (EAWOP) are now being consolidated. Each facilitates greater international exchange and co-operation in scientific endeavours and practice. They support annual symposia (ENOP); biannual congresses (EFPPA, EAWOP); distribution of newsletters; publication of a journal intended to bridge science and practice (EAWOP); international exchanges of students and teachers (ENOP); interdisciplinary European summer schools (ENOP), and workshops for scholars from work/organizational psychology and related fields (ENOP). Such efforts reflect growing international awareness and the need to marshal resources so as to meet the challenges posed by the trend towards European unity. Creating a European curriculum of university teaching of work/organizational psychology and establishing equivalence of certificates and diplomas seem to be particularly relevant for the future growth and identity of the field (Roe *et al.* 1994).

In all these efforts we are literally dancing on the edge. I am not afraid that we might fall off the edge, but we are at an important crossroads in the development of work/organizational psychology (Roe 1995) and we may or may not meet the challenges ahead with success. The decisive question seems to be whether we offer real service to a wider Europe which includes the Central and Eastern European countries. The changes taking place in that part of the world are profound. They especially affect work-related values, attitudes and behaviours to a hitherto unmatched extent. The need for work/organizational psychology to foster suitable transition and its capacity to do so are paramount. Small but significant contributions may be seen in the efforts of ENOP to provide university libraries in Eastern and Central Europe with standard reference books, and of IAPP to waive dues for Eastern European colleagues joining international networks.

LOOKING AHEAD

We are also on the edge in terms of entering the immediate future, the new millennium. Recent papers (Kuhlmann 1995; Cascio 1996) try to answer the question, 'Whither industrial and organizational psychology in a changing world of work?' The articles deal with dramatic changes at the end of our century and focus on the possibilities of adequate reactions from work/organizational psychology in the twenty-first century. Our economies are undergoing drastic deregulation of industries such as civil aviation, banks and communication which had formerly been nationalized. This process unleashes new waves of international competition, compounded by international merger activities – for example, French and German Telecom. Thus employees find themselves in immediate and direct competition with workers in Singapore, Korea, the United States and Japan. 'Downsizing' is the likely answer to the question of how to increase competitiveness. Unemployment, breakage of existing social networks, dilution of traditional industrial relations systems and income reduction are the results.

Accordingly, the relevant issues for work/organizational psychology are as follows:

- changes in organizational structures (smaller units in network organizations);
- dominance of technicians rather than workers as the elite among employees;
- need for multiple competencies;
- obsolescence of seniority in favour of competence having market value;
- changes in management roles: visionary management, industrial democracy, semi-autonomous work groups, workers and managers exchanging jobs, managers become coaches, facilitators, mentors; flatter hierarchies;
- empowerment of workers: increased responsibility, flexibility, new learning, self-management, new esteem and demand for workers in the company;
- work in international teams;
- drastic increases of the work-force in service sectors.

Everyone with a trained work/organizational psychological ear will immediately respond: '*Yes, that's it!*' These are some of the central issues. They imply new tasks in work analysis, personnel selection, assessment and training, organizational development and the evaluation of change.

By way of illustration I shall detail two aspects with overriding importance for work/organizational psychology and society: assessment, and the division of work.

Assessment

One strength of work/organizational psychology since its very beginning has been the demonstrated ability to analyse work demands and the corresponding aptitude of an individual to do the job as required. The literature abounds with validated psychometric tests purporting to predict a person's likelihood of success in a given post or profession. This was part and parcel of the public recognition of work/organizational psychologists. So far so good, we might say, and go on with business as usual. However, what if the very nature of the demands should change? We know from many studies showing converging results that by the end of this decade every second work place will be affected by the introduction of computers. New demands on 'intellective' work activities and information processing emerge to replace the former, sensual handling of work objectives (Zuboff 1988).

Further, we know that the half-life of knowledge is shrinking steadily. People must learn new work methods more quickly and flexibly. The motto is, learning how to learn. To work effectively in continuously shifting work teams requires more social competencies. Changes in attitudes and values reveal themselves in rising levels of creative capability, self-reliant planning and task execution. Since we have yet to conceptualize or to operationalize these new demands, how can we use traditional instruments, validated for different purposes, to predict our success in meeting them? In the past we assumed the relative stability of work demands, and therefore that these could be matched with an individual's relatively stable work-related aptitudes. Now we are faced with the task of selecting individuals who can adapt to changing demands over a lifetime. We must conclude that our revered portfolio of assessment techniques is becoming increasingly obsolete. This is tantamount to saying that we are in danger of losing our central competencies as work/organizational psychologists. Indeed, we are dancing on the edge.

The answer to this problem asserts itself. In many ways we must begin again. New work analytic studies must elucidate the psychologically relevant changes in work settings. New demands must be conceptualized and translated into categories of required qualifications. New diagnostic tools for selection, placement and performance evaluation must be developed. I cannot think of any discipline other than ours which is more qualified to do this job. I see this as one of the most important priorities for the agenda of work/organizational psychology at the transition from the twentieth to the twenty-first century. It is truly fundamental because it is the basis for similar challenges in the areas of vocational education and training, personnel and management development, design of effective incentive structures, and organizational development. We cannot achieve adequate solutions to these challenges without a close co-operation between psychologists in academia and in practice.

Division of work

Politicians and economists tell us that 'it is historically proven that new technologies do not kill jobs' (President of the French Republic at the G7–meeting in Lille, April 1996). I hear the message, but I do not believe it. From our own research I know of companies which increased their productivity by 200 to 300 per cent by introducing new technologies. The Chief Executive Officer of one company proudly told us that no employee was made redundant after this achievement. But nobody was hired in addition either! The company simply externalized the labour market consequences of its productivity increases. Others act through 'downsizing'. Thus unemployment becomes rampant in all our countries.

In contrast to economists and politicians I claim that the reverse is the case. Unemployment no longer results from economic cycles but from technical progress and ensuing productivity increases. At least in my country, the daily news about unemployment figures and the imminent erasure of positions is staggering. Some time ago I read in the newspapers published on a single day the following alarming news of job losses:

- Postal services – abolition of 60,000 jobs in 1994
- Telecom – 10,000
- German automotive industry – 90,000
- European automotive industry – 400,000

- Women pushed out of the labour market
- 30–35 million unemployed in Western Europe
- Unemployment rates of 40 per cent or higher in some groups or regions.

I see a split in European societies which separate those who still have a work place from those who do not. The proportion of those deprived of a job is increasing. Some speak of a two-thirds society; that is, one in which two-thirds live on the sunny side and the remainder in the shade. Our societies are marked by a gap of social justice when we consider the distribution of work. Politicians and economists lack sufficient courage or trust in people to tell them that this problem is going to remain with us for quite some time to come.

And yet, our societies define themselves as work societies. Many decades ago, Hannah Arendt (1958), for many the most important German woman philosopher of our century, heralded the problem of a society without work:

> The modern age has carried with it a theoretical glorification of labour and has resulted in a factual transformation of the whole society into a labouring society. The fulfilment of the wish (not needing to work), therefore . . . comes at a moment when it can only be self-defeating. . . . What we are confronted with is the prospect of a society without labour, that is, without the only activity left to them. Surely, nothing could be worse.
>
> (Arendt 1958: 4–5)

Work still serves the central function of providing meaning in life, and individual and social identity. Our own findings suggest the validity of this thesis without proving it conclusively (MOW 1987). It becomes even more credible when our findings are complemented by qualitative research results (Baethge *et al.* 1988; Super and Sverko 1995).

Further, the increased participation of women in paid employment adds another ingredient. Women have from childhood been less thoroughly socialized than men through traditional work ethics. For them, economic independence and personal autonomy seem to be even more significant as intrinsic motivational forces. Thus, rather than identifying a reduction in the subjective significance of work, we may say:

> For large groups of employees, not the least for women, the opposite dynamics seem to be operating today in that the professional (work) role has and continues to have an integral function in the construction of personal identity.
>
> (Baethge 1991: 10)

Cassen, the French social critic, observed even more emphatically that full citizenship (*citoyenneté*) is constituted through participation in the labour market. It is work which provides meaning to life. Hence, it is not so much a question whether work-related values decrease today, but how to cope with ever diminishing opportunities to work (Cassen 1993).

CONCLUSION

The growing contradiction between the objective reduction in the demand for active, human work and the continued high subjective importance of working requires revolutionary concepts. With this concluding thesis I draw on the foregoing observations about sociotechnical changes in work settings in the industrialized countries and the consequences for the labour market. It seems that various dimensions of work-related values are changing in certain ways, particularly work motives and social norms. There is growing interest in meaningful, fulfilling work apart from its continued function as income generator. But change is reflected also in the increased importance of how time is spent outside of paid work/leisure.

The epochal and spectacular rises in productivity and concomitant industrial restructuring have led to a drastic reduction in the demand for labour. This has led today to the unemployment of twenty million people in the European Union, more than forty million in all of Europe. Tomorrow there are likely to be even more people unemployed. Appeals to work more and to work harder, and arguments in favour of investing more in new technologies with the hope of fighting unemployment, will only serve to heighten the dilemma. After all, where will industrialists invest? They will invest in technologies which enhance productivity and save work in order to become more competitive internationally. The consequence: less demand for labour.

We have to take note, however, of the predictions of some labour economists (Rürup 1994) of changes in labour; for example, less child-bearing and an increase in the proportion of those aged 60 years and over in the population will drastically reduce the potential work-force in our countries by around the year 2010. This pattern will lead to a shortage of available labour. Against this contention I maintain that it is written on the wall that large parts of our population will be deprived of work in both the short and the long run. The trend towards labour-saving competitive technologies will not and cannot be reversed.

Therefore, revolutionary rethinking is needed, for three reasons:

- Revolutionary rethinking is necessary with regard to a more sensible, more just distribution of work.

I am talking here about a rationale for a new division of work which is rather different from Durkheim's *'Things being as they are'*. This can be done only through further reductions in the time individuals work and consequently through the creation, or rather maintenance, of work places. Reducing the hours of work across the board will not achieve this end by itself. In some sectors we have a lack of qualified workers, while in others we have an abundance. Hence, reductions in working time must be accompanied by retraining programmes. Such new distributions of work ought to be complemented by extending the notion of work to other domains of society.

For example, there is work which must be done but which has not yet achieved the status of paid work – environmental protection, care for the old and sick, anti-racist activities, and so on.

• Revolutionary rethinking is necessary with regard to the redistribution of surplus value created by work.

We have to develop new concepts for the redistribution of the fruits of work, because it is an unbearable prospect to see that they only benefit those who happen to be in a work place and leave out those who suffer from not finding work. Unless we find solutions here we will undoubtedly have large-scale social unrest and explosive developments. One solution might be a guaranteed minimum income for all adults.

• Revolutionary rethinking is necessary with regard to the 'construction of a civilisation of liberated time' (Gorz 1993).

The alarming increase in unemployment in industrialized countries can no longer be abated through economic growth. The hopeless and desperate search for full employment under given criteria for the distribution of work and its fruits impedes the search for new models governing free time. What is required is to seize the opportunity to develop concepts for a better use of self-directed time in the face of a decline in the amount of hetero-determined time in traditional workplaces.

The challenge for work/organizational psychology today and tomorrow, therefore, presents itself in both domains: the traditional world of paid work and its contribution to a better, more human use of leisure time.

REFERENCES

Aldrich, H. (1979) *Organizations and Environment*, Englewood Cliffs, NJ: Prentice-Hall.
Arendt, H. (1958) *The Human Condition*, Chicago: The University of Chicago Press.
Baethge, M. (1991) 'Arbeit, Vergesellschaftung, Identität – zur zunehmenden normativen Subjektivierung der Arbeit', *Soziale Welt* 1: 6–19.
Baethge, M., Hantsche, B., Pellul, W. and Voskamp, U. (1988) *Jugend: Arbeit und Identität*, Koln: Opladen.
Burt, R.S. (1980) ' Models of network structure', *Annual Review of Sociology* 6: 79–141.
Cascio, W.F. (1996) 'Whither industrial and organizational psychology in a changing world of work?' *Administrative Science Quarterly* November: 928–939.
Cassen, B. (1993) *Le Monde Diplomatique*, March, No. 468, Vol. 38.
De Wolff, C. and Shimmin, S. (1994) 'Complexities and choices: work psychology in Europe', *European Work and Organizational Psychologist* 4, 4: 333–341.
Durkheim, E. (1977) *Über die Teilung der sozialen Arbeit*, Frankfurt: Suhrkamp.
Eijnatten, F.M. van, Eggermont, S.J.C., de Goffman, C.T.A. and Mankoe, I. (1994) *The Socio-Technical System Design (STSD) Paradigm*, Eindhoven: Eindhoven University of Technology.
Franke, H. (1978) 'Organisationspsychologie als wissenschaftliche Disziplin', in A. Mayer (ed.) *Organisationspsychologie* (pp. 332–349), Stuttgart: Poeschel.
Gorz, P. (1993) *Le Monde Diplomatique*, March.
Greif, S. (1983) *Konzepte der Organisationspsychologie*, Bern: Huber.

—— (1991) 'Geschichte der Organisationspsychologie', in H. Schuler (ed.) *Lehrbuch der Organisationspsychologie* (pp. 15–48), Bern: Huber.

IDE International Research Group (1981) *Industrial Democracy in Europe*, Oxford: Oxford University Press.

—— (1993) *Industrial Democracy in Europe Revisited*, Oxford: Oxford University Press.

Katz, D. and Kahn, R.L. (1966) *The Social Psychology of Organisations*, New York: John Wiley & Sons.

König, R. (1978) *Emil Durkheim zur Diskussion*, Munchen: C. Hauser.

Kühlmann, T.M. (1995) 'Arbeits- und Organisationspsychologie: Gedanken zu ihrer Lage und ihren Zukunftschancen', *Report Psychologie* 20, 3: 10–19.

Lahy, J.M. (1916) *Le système Taylor et la physiologie du travail professionel*, Paris: Masson.

Lang, R. and Hellpach, W. (1922) *Gruppenfabrikation*, Berlin: Springer.

Levine, S. and White, P.E. (1961) 'Exchange as a conceptual framework for the study of organizational relationships', *Administration Science Quarterly* 5: 583–601.

Lewin, K. (1920) 'Die Sozialisierung des Taylorsystems', *Schriftenreihe praktischer Sozialismus* 4: 3–36.

Mill, J.S. (1870) *Principles of Political Economy*, London: Longmans, Green, Reader & Dyer.

Moede, W. (1930) *Lehrbuch der Psychotechnik*, Berlin: Springer.

MOW International Research Team (1987) *Meaning of Working*, London: Academic Press.

OECD (1994) *The OECD Jobs Study: Facts, Analysis, Strategies*, Paris: OECD.

—— (1995) *The OECD Jobs Study: Implementing the Strategy*, Paris: OECD.

Parsons, H.M. (1974) 'What happened at Hawthorne? New evidence suggests the Hawthorne effect resulted from operant reinforcement contingencies', *Science* 138: 922–933.

Roe, R.A. (1995) *Work & Organizational Psychology at the Cross-roads. A European View*, Keynote lecture, 4th European Congress of Psychology, Athens, 2–7 July.

Roe, R.A., Coetsier, P., Lévy-Leboyer, C., Peiro, J.M. and Wilpert, B. (1994) 'The teaching of work and organizational psychology in Europe: towards the development of a reference model', *European Work and Organizational Psychologist* 4, 4: 355–365.

Rubinstein, S.L. (1977) *Grundlagen der allgemeinen Psychologie*, Berlin: Volk und Wissen.

Rürup, B. (1994) 'Arbeit der Zukunft – Zukunft der Arbeit', in H. Hoffmann and D. Kramer (eds) *Arbeit ohne Sinn? Sinn ohne Arbeit?* (pp. 35–50), Weinheim: Beltz Athenäum.

Schmidt, K. (1991) 'Cooperative work: a conceptual framework', in J. Rasmussen, B. Brehmer and J. Leplat (eds) *Distributed Decision making –Cognitive Models for Cooperative Work*, Chichester, Sussex: John Wiley & Sons.

Smith, A. (1924) *Der Reichtum der Nationen*, Leipzig: Alfred Kroner.

Stern, E. (1921) *Angewandte Psychologie*, Leipzig: Teubner.

Super, D. and Sverko, B. (eds) (1995) *Life Roles, Values, and Careers*, San Francisco, CA: Jossey-Bass.

Sydow, J. (1996) 'Inter-organizational relations', in M. Warner (ed.) *International Encyclopedia of Business and Management*, London: Routledge.

Ulich, E. (1989) 'Historische Ausgangspunkte', in S.Greif, H. Holling and N. Nicholson (eds) *Arbeits- und Organizationspsychologie* (pp. 19–32), München: Psychologie Verlags Union.

—— (1991) *Arbeitspsycholgie*, Stuttgart: Poeschel.

Wilpert, B. (1992) 'Organization–environment relations – towards overcoming limited perspectives in organizational psychology', in J. Misumi, B. Wilpert and H. Motoaki

(eds) *Organizational and Work Psychology*, Proceedings of the 22nd International Congress of Applied Psychology, Vol. 2, pp. 66–88.
—— (1995) 'Organizational behavior', *Annual Review of Psychology* 46: 59–90.
Zuboff, S. (1988) *In the Age of the Smart Machine*, New York: Basic Books.

13 The coming of age of the psychology of thinking and reasoning

Ruth M. J. Byrne

THE PSYCHOLOGY OF THINKING AND REASONING

If we are to understand any aspect of individuals – their personalities, emotional problems, everyday likes and dislikes – we need to understand their mental life. Thinking is the pinnacle of human mental life and it has attracted psychological investigation for most of this century (for an introductory review, see Eysenck and Keane 1995, chapters 15–17). Contemporary research on thinking covers a wide range of mental activities, from reasoning and problem solving to creativity and daydreaming (e.g. Johnson-Laird 1988). Within the study of thinking in general, the study of rational thought in particular has occupied pride of place. Many of the issues that psychologists confront in attempting to understand the nature of thinking are best illustrated by considering the specific example of the nature of reasoning (e.g. Oakhill and Garnham 1995), and reasoning research will be my primary focus in this chapter.

The achievements of almost a century of psychological research on thinking and reasoning are evident in the contemporary study of the topic in the 1990s. I will begin this chapter by outlining the current state of the art in research on the psychology of reasoning. I hope to show that there is now a clear and well-developed science of thinking and reasoning. The cognitive science of reasoning embraces the research endeavours not only of cognitive psychology but also of philosophy and logic, linguistics, artificial intelligence, neuroscience and anthropology within its interdisciplinary brief and it is characterized by many of the hallmarks of a well-established science. The theoretical basis of the field is clear-cut:

- well-specified theories to account for a broad range of experimentally reliable phenomena are implemented in computer programs (e.g. Johnson-Laird and Byrne 1991; Rips 1994);
- competing and empirically falsifiable theories guide the broad research programme of the field and their predictions are tested in rigorous experimentation (e.g. Evans *et al.* 1993, Chapter 3);
- the theories make novel predictions about new phenomena and as a result

they lead to the discovery of previously unsuspected aspects of human reasoning. The experimental basis of the field is also clear-cut;

- experimental testing relies on a wide and representative repertoire of tasks, which includes tasks that rely on inferences based on sentential connectives such as hypothetical and disjunctive deductions, inferences based on quantifiers such as categorical syllogisms, and inferences based on relations such as spatial and temporal deductions;
- the experimental measures are precise and replicable, and they include the frequency of correct conclusions, the nature of errors, the latency to respond and the retrieval of arguments and conclusions.

The alternative contemporary accounts of deduction cover a broad range of deductive thought, including hypothetical reasoning, quantificational reasoning, relational reasoning and meta-deductive reasoning. They provide their own answers to the enduring questions about human reasoning: Are people capable of rational thought? Why do people make mistakes when they try to reason? Why is logical thinking swayed by emotions?

Along with these clear successes in the study of thinking and reasoning, there have been equally clear failures. It seems that everyone has his or her own favourite list of things that the cognitive science of thinking has failed to do, and among these lists some points of agreement recur:

- research on thinking has been fragmented into artificially separated and unnecessarily isolated topics (e.g. Eysenck and Keane 1995);
- little systematic contact has been made between theories of cognition and emotion and the relation between them remains opaque (e.g. Gilhooly 1996);
- there is no general capture of everyday thinking – for example, there is as yet no principled extension of theories of formal reasoning to the domain of informal inference;
- successes in understanding well-defined topics such as problem solving and logical inference have been outweighed by failure, albeit failure by neglect, in understanding topics such as imaginary thinking or daydreaming.

There are probably very few cognitive scientists who would dispute the validity of these criticisms. What *is* disputed is what these weaknesses reveal about the cognitive science approach and its future prospects in understanding thinking. I suspect that many cognitive scientists would agree that these failures merely reflect the need to be able to walk before trying to run, as I hope to demonstrate in the next section. It makes sense to first construct theories that are empirically falsifiable and computationally modelled for the set of robust research findings that have been gathered over the past century in, for example, formal reasoning. Only when this task has been achieved is it possible to extend the theories from their central base into less well-charted terrain, for example, daydreaming. I will suggest that the cognitive science of reasoning is on the cusp of this development as we approach the new millennium: there are the beginnings of forays from safe topics such as deduction and problem solving to more challenging topics such as everyday inference and imaginary thinking. Of course, an alternative view is that the failure of cognitive science to provide an account of topics such as daydreaming or imagination reveals a more damaging flaw in its scope and potential. To choose between these alternative interpretations, we need to examine the history of the psychology of thinking and reasoning to see how it has reached its current point. After the initial sketch of the current state of the art in reasoning, I will outline some developments in the history of research on reasoning that may shed light on the nature of its current drawbacks.

The study of deductive reasoning in the 1990s

Psychologists who study deduction want to know whether people are rational or not. The issue of human rationality is of more than theoretical interest – it has important practical consequences for everyday life. Imagine you are working in a nuclear power plant during an emergency and your job is to work out what is going wrong. Suppose you know the following general rule:

1 If the test is to continue, the turbine must be rotating fast enough to generate emergency power.

Suppose the computer monitoring system informs you that the turbine is not rotating fast enough. What should you infer? The valid inference, called a *modus tollens* inference, is that the test cannot continue. But people have difficulty making the valid *modus tollens* inference. In the real life example here, the nuclear power plant workers did not make the valid inference that the test could not be continued. As a result partly of this inferential difficulty, they did not discontinue the test in time and the Chernobyl nuclear disaster occurred with worldwide implications (Johnson-Laird 1994a; Medvedev 1990; Reason 1990). Establishing which inferences cause people difficulty can lead to the development of aids to inference to overcome detected human inferential frailties. How do people make inferences like the *modus tollens* one, and what is the source of their errors when they go astray? People are affected by their limited working memories, their background knowledge and familiarity with the topic, their beliefs and their emotional response to it (Evans *et al.* 1993 has a detailed review of alternative viewpoints on the sources of errors in reasoning).

The main issue that exercises researchers on deductive reasoning in the 1990s concerns the nature of the mental representations and cognitive processes that underlie inferential competence and performance. To understand how people reason, we need to know what processes occur when they make a correct inference, and how these processes are corrupted when they make an error. The processes concerned may be unconscious processes in the Helmholtzian sense, processes that may occur outside of conscious awareness and to which people may have no introspective access (e.g. Johnson-Laird 1988). Several alternative theories of human deduction have been developed since the early 1980s and much of the current research on deduction attempts to distinguish between these theories. I will outline the primary tenets of the two theories which purport to have sufficient scope to account for the complete range of deductive inference, and which have received the most empirical attention since the early 1980s.

Rules versus models

The traditional view is that reasoning depends on rules of inference that operate by virtue of their form (e.g. Braine 1978; Rips 1983). The formal rule theory proposes that an inference such as the example in 1 above has the following syntactic structure:

2   If p then q
    not-q

The theory proposes that reasoners rely on comprehension processes to recover the logical skeleton of the argument, and they reach a conclusion by constructing a mental derivation, applying syntactic inference rules from their mental repertoire. The repertoire includes simple valid rules, such as the *modus ponens* rule:

3   If p then q
    p
    Therefore q

The mental derivation of the inference in 1 (above) proceeds by the following steps:

i	If p then q	(premise 1)
ii	not-q	(premise 2)
iii	Suppose p	(supposition-creating rule)
iv	Therefore q	(by application of *modus ponens* rule to premises in i and iii).
v	q and not-q	(by application of a conjunction rule, conjoining premises in iv and ii)
vi	Therefore not-p	(*reductio ad absurdum*, from contradiction in v, and supposition in iii)

The theory proposes that there is no inference rule corresponding directly to the *modus tollens* inference and so the derivation requires a number of steps and the application of a number of inference rules; as a result, it is a difficult inference to make and reasoners can go astray. The mental representations proposed by the theory are abstract inference rules and the cognitive processes are procedures that construct mental derivations of conclusions (Braine and O'Brien 1991; Rips 1994). The theory predicts that inferences that require few steps in their derivation (such as the *modus ponens* inference illustrated in 3 above) are easier than inferences that require many steps in their derivation (such as the *modus tollens* inference illustrated in 2 above). It proposes that reasoners are rational by virtue of their mental repertoire of valid inference rules. Errors, in particular errors that arise from the influence of beliefs or emotions due to the content or context of the inference, may arise because the interpretational component which parses the argument to its underlying logical skeleton may process the information to an inappropriate logical form.

An alternative view of the process proposes that reasoning depends on the construction and manipulation of mental models (Johnson-Laird 1983; Johnson-Laird and Byrne 1991). The model theory proposes that the inference in 1 (above) is made by first constructing a mental model, that is, a mental representation that corresponds to the structure of the world rather than to the structure of the language used to describe the world. Reasoners construct a model of the premise in 1 earlier:

t   f

    . . .

where the diagram captures the idea that the test is to be continued by 't' and the idea that the turbine is rotating fast enough by 'f'. The content of the set of models may include background knowledge about what a reactor looks like, how it works, what processes generate electricity, and so on; to understand the process of inference our primary concern is not the content of the models but their structure. There may be other alternative situations to that represented in the first model where the test is to be continued and the turbine rotates fast enough, and so the second model, represented by the ellipsis '. . .' in the diagram, captures the idea that individuals make a mental note that there may be alternatives. The theory proposes that reasoners represent as little information as possible explicitly because of the constraints of working memory. (In fact, the models require further footnotes to spell out the nature of the other models in the implicit set, and for these more technical details see Johnson-Laird and Byrne 1991; Johnson-Laird *et al.* 1992).

The further information in the second premise that the turbine is not rotating fast enough is also represented in a model:

not-f

where 'not' is a propositional-like tag to represent negation (see Johnson-Laird and Byrne 1991). The procedures that combine models have difficulty in adding this model to the set of models of the first premise because there is no explicit match. The models of the first premise must first be 'fleshed out' to be more explicit:

t   f
not-t   not-f
not-t   f

212 Ruth M. J. Byrne

One 'conditional' interpretation of the first premise is that it is consistent with three alternative models: in one the test is to be continued and the turbine is rotating fast enough, in the other two the test cannot be continued, and in one of these situations the turbine is not rotating fast enough, in the other it is. Another 'biconditional' interpretation of the assertion is that it is consistent with just the first two situations. Regardless of which interpretation a reasoner comes to, the information from the second premise can be matched to only one of the models in the fleshed out set – the second model – and it rules out any further consideration of the other models. The second model supports the valid conclusion that the test cannot be continued.

The theory proposes that inferences that require few models (such as the *modus ponens* inference, which can be made from the initial set of models without any need to flesh out the models to be more explicit) are easier than inferences that require multiple models, such as the *modus tollens* inference, because of the constraints of working memory. The theory proposes that reasoners' errors are consistent with keeping in mind just a subset of the models. These predictions have been corroborated in a variety of domains of deduction (Johnson-Laird and Byrne 1991). The theory proposes that the mental representations are models, and the cognitive processes are procedures that manipulate models. The mental logic which underpins human rationality contains no formal inference rules, but instead rules that construct and revise mental models. The theory proposes that reasoners are rational by virtue of the semantic principle that a conclusion is valid if there are no counter-examples to it. Errors, in particular errors that arise from the influence of beliefs or emotions due to the content or context of the inference, arise because of the nature of the models that reasoners construct, the limitations of working memory, and the influence of background knowledge on the ability to flesh out models or to rule out models.

These two alternative accounts have been pitted against each other, as well as against other more circumscribed theories, such as the proposal that reasoning depends on domain-specific inference rules (Cheng and Holyoak 1985) or on superficial heuristics (Evans 1989). Much of the research on reasoning in the 1990s consists of trying to establish the scope and limitations of these alternative theories to explain a wide range of well-established phenomena of deduction. The task of ascertaining the truth of the alternative theories has taken place in two ways: first, experimental evidence has been gathered that could potentially falsify the theories. For example, alternative theories have been pitted against each other by comparing problems which require, for example, many inference rules but few models, to problems which require few inference rules but multiple models (Byrne and Johnson-Laird 1989, 1992; Byrne and Handley 1997; Byrne *et al.* 1995a; Johnson-Laird and Byrne 1989; Johnson-Laird *et al.* 1989, 1992). Second, the theories have been computationally modelled; that is, the primary tenets of each theory have been implemented in a computer program: the program makes the same sorts of inferences that people make and the same sorts of errors, by using the types of representations and processes that the theory proposes people use (for examples of computer simulations, see Johnson-Laird and Byrne's 1991 'Propsych', and Rips' 1994 'Psycop'). The use of computational modelling does not prove that the theory is an accurate version of what goes on in people's heads, but it does prove that the theory is sufficiently well specified and coherent to be realized in a physical system.

Rules versus models in the suppression effect

Consider an example of the disagreement that arises between rule theorists and model theorists. Rule theorists propose that the only rules in the mental repertoire are simple valid inference rules (Braine and O'Brien 1991). But people sometimes make inferences that are fallacious. For example, they tend to make the following inference:

4 If the test is to be continued, the turbine must be rotating fast enough to generate emergency power.
  The test cannot be continued.
  Therefore the turbine must not be rotating fast enough.

The inference is fallacious on a conditional interpretation of the assertion because there may be alternatives in which the test cannot be continued even though the turbine is rotating fast enough. In 1983, Rumain, Connell and Braine argued that individuals make such fallacies only if they have overinterpreted the first premise to mean that there are no alternatives. Provided that these alternatives are made clear to individuals, they will resist the fallacies; for example:

5 If the test is to be continued, the turbine must be rotating fast enough to generate emergency power.
  If there is a genuine emergency, the turbine must be rotating fast enough to generate emergency power.
  The test cannot be continued.
  What, if anything, follows?

Given such explicit alternatives, individuals resist the fallacy and say that it is not possible to make a deduction, that is, in this example, it is not possible to say whether or not the turbine is rotating fast enough. Rule theorists concluded from this sort of evidence that people do not have a rule corresponding to the fallacy in their minds, because it can be suppressed.

In 1989, I showed that the valid inferences can be suppressed in exactly the same way. Individuals make the simple valid *modus ponens* inference effortlessly:

6 If the test is to be continued, the turbine must be rotating fast enough to generate emergency power.

The test is to be continued.
Therefore, the turbine must be rotating fast enough to generate emergency power.

Making the inference requires reasoners to assume that any background conditions have also been met. Provided that these background conditions are made clear to individuals, they will resist making even the simplest valid inference:

7 If the test is to be continued, the turbine must be rotating fast enough to generate emergency power.
   If the safety procedures are followed, the turbine must be rotating fast enough to generate emergency power.
   The test is to be continued.
   What, if anything, follows?

Individuals who are given these sorts of additional antecedents resist the valid inference and say that it is not possible to make a deduction; that is, in this example, it is not possible to say whether or not the turbine is rotating fast enough – it depends on whether the safety procedures are being followed. By parity of argument with rule theorists we can conclude that people do not have a rule corresponding to the valid inference in their minds either, because it too can be suppressed. The suppression of the *modus ponens* inference does not cast doubt on its validity as an inference, but it does cast doubt on the notion that reasoners have a mental rule corresponding to the inference which operates by virtue of its form alone.

The suppression effect illustrates the role of background knowledge in thinking and reasoning and it shows that we need a full account of how people interpret a situation and how they retrieve relevant information from memory if we are to understand their inferential abilities. Experiments on the suppression of the valid inferences have shown that it may depend on judgements that reasoners make about the certainty of the information upon which they base their inferences (Stevenson and Over 1995), it may depend on the saliency of relevant information in memory (Chan and Chua 1994), and it may depend on the comprehension of the relation between certain kinds of information (Byrne and Johnson-Laird 1992). Experiments that I have carried out recently in collaboration with Orlando Espino and Carlos Santamaria from the University of La Laguna, in Tenerife, Spain indicate that it may depend on the construction of a coherent set of models (Byrne *et al.* 1997). The debate between theorists about the consequences of the suppression effect (Byrne 1991; Politzer and Braine 1991) illustrates the need for theories of reasoning to provide an account of comprehension as well as reasoning proper (Fillenbaum 1993).

In summary, the current state of the art in the psychology of reasoning reflects the existence of several alternative theories of deduction. These theories are well developed, as their computational simulations testify, and they are potentially falsifiable, as their conflicting experimental predictions testify. They provide alternative perspectives on the nature of human reasoning, and on the central issues of rationality, errors in reasoning, and the influence of content and context. These theories emerged in the early 1980s only after many preceding decades dedicated to establishing a core set of phenomena in the field. I will turn now to a brief consideration of this historical backdrop.

A CENTURY OF RESEARCH ON THE PSYCHOLOGY OF REASONING

The history of human interest in our own reasoning stretches back at least 2,000 years to the writings of Plato and Aristotle. This 2,000-year heritage overshadowed the nature of research in the new experimental psychology of deduction as it emerged around the turn of this century (Storring 1908). Early work on the psychology of deduction had as its primary goal a comparison of human thought to logic, and in particular to the prescriptions of specific logical systems, such as Aristotelian categorical syllogisms (Wilkins 1928; Woodworth and Sells 1935) and an investigation of departures from logical prescriptions as a result of the influence of attitudes and beliefs (Janis and Frick 1943; Morgan and Morton 1944). As a result, research on reasoning in the early decades of the twentieth century focused on comparing the inferences reasoners made with the standards set by logics (notwithstanding the hiatus in research on mental processes during the behaviourist era and the notable exception of the Gestaltists' focus on problem solving). In the 1950s and 1960s the task of describing basic phenomena of reasoning was achieved in a variety of deductive domains, including syllogistic inference (Chapman and Chapman 1959), relational inference (De Soto *et al.* 1965; Huttenlocher 1968; Clark 1969), and sentential inference (Wason 1959; Johnson-Laird and Tagart 1969). Researchers began to examine the role of content and context (Fillenbaum 1974; Staudenmayer 1975) and to formulate general theories of inference (Inhelder and Piaget 1958; Henle 1962; Wason and Johnson-Laird 1972).

The groundwork was laid during the 1970s for the emergence of psychological theories from under the shadow of many centuries of philosophical thought. During this time, there was a steady accumulation of a wealth of robust empirical findings (Potts 1972; Taplin and Staudenmayer 1973; Revlis 1975; Roberge 1977; Evans 1977; Johnson-Laird and Steedman 1978), a concerted attempt to delineate the role of content, especially in Wason's selection task (Wason 1966; Johnson-Laird *et al.* 1972; Manktelow and Evans 1979), and an examination of individual strategies in reasoning (Johnson-Laird 1972; Trabasso *et al.* 1975). It was not until the early 1980s that large-scale theories of inference with the scope to encompass deduction in different domains emerged, not only of the formal inference-rule variety (Braine 1978; Rips 1983) but also of a model-based variety (Guyote and Sternberg 1981; Johnson-Laird 1983).

In short, the psychology of reasoning has adopted the characteristics of the prevailing *zeitgeist*: research in the early part of the century concentrated on describing experimental performance in keeping with the preoccupation with the idea of a natural science approach to human behaviour. Research in the late–middle decades was ground-clearing, establishing what the basic robust phenomena of deduction are in a broad and wide variety of situations and with different contents and contexts. In some cases rigorous and precise, if small-scale, information-processing accounts of specific task performance were provided. But it was not until research in the latter decades of the century that there emerged large-scale theories to account for the wealth of data, to predict new phenomena, and to be tested experimentally and modelled computationally.

My argument is that the current state of what is known and what is not known in the psychology of thinking is one that we have inherited from our psychological ancestors. If there had been decades of research and thousands of journal articles published describing the results of countless experimental findings on the nature of, say, daydreaming, as there has been on the nature of logical reasoning, then it is very probable that the flagship cognitive science theories in the 1990s would be theories of daydreaming rather than of logical reasoning. It is probable that contemporary criticism would question the plausibility of extending our theories of daydreaming to the more difficult field of logical thinking, instead of vice versa. The choice throughout much of the early part of the twentieth century to focus on logical thinking instead of, say daydreaming, probably owes as much to the availability of ready-made views from logic and to the desire of the fledgling science of psychology to address 'serious' questions, as it does to the enduring importance of the issue of whether or not people are rational.

A current discernible aim in the psychology of reasoning is to extend theories developed to account for deduction to related and more everyday sorts of thinking. One possibility is that logical thinking and other sorts of thinking, such as daydreaming, have nothing in common and require wholly separate sorts of theories. Another possibility is that they are related and share at least some aspects in common and a full account of thinking requires the formulation of a unified theory (Newell 1990; Anderson 1993). The latter viewpoint seems more plausible given a consideration of economy and parsimony – how could our minds be so constructed that we could slip seamlessly and effortlessly from, say, logical thinking to daydreaming and vice versa, if these mental activities were supported by wholly separate and different sorts of architecture and mechanisms? The quest for unified theories has become the holy grail of the 1990s psychology of thinking (Eysenck and Keane 1995). Like any holy grail it may not be attainable, and like any quest such reservations are poor deterrents to its pursuit.

THE FUTURE OF RESEARCH ON THINKING AND REASONING

The volume of research on the psychology of deduction outstrips research on everyday thinking, such as daydreaming or imaginary thought. After considerable research investigation of the core phenomena in deduction, the theoretical development to account for the phenomena has proceeded apace. A similar phase of investigation is required of the core phenomena in other areas such as daydreaming and imagination. Once robust phenomena are identified in these domains, attempts can be made to expand theories of deduction to account for findings in such related fields. Revisions may be required and possibly the abandonment of certain theories may result. Is it possible that a general theory of thinking may develop systematically from a central point such as deduction to encompass other sorts of thinking? Already there are glimpses of this steady extension – the model theory of deduction has begun to be extended to the related domains of probabilistic thinking (Johnson-Laird 1994b), predictive thinking (Rodriga *et al.* 1992), decision making (Legrenzi *et al.* 1993), and imaginary counterfactual thinking (Byrne, in press; Byrne and Tasso 1994; Byrne *et al.* 1995b). To illustrate this extension I will now turn to the example of imaginary counterfactual thinking.

Imaginary counterfactual thinking

When we muse about the past or speculate about the future, we often imagine that an event did not happen and, in keeping with this mutation, we alter aspects of the situation that led to the now-undone event, or that followed from it. For example, an investor who has lost money on stocks and shares may think 'if only . . .' and complete this thought by imagining that he or she had invested elsewhere (Kahneman and Tversky 1982). Our *counterfactual* musings may be designed to help us work out the causes and effects of aspects of a situation (Hofstadter 1979) and to guide us in learning from our mistakes or our good fortune (Roese 1994), and they give rise to a range of emotions including regret, disappointment, hope and relief (Johnson 1986; Landman 1987).

When individuals are required to think about what might have been, they undo aspects of the actual situation in a principled manner. For example, they tend to change exceptional events rather than normal ones (Gavanski and Wells 1989; Kahneman and Tversky 1982); they change actions rather than inactions (Kahneman and Tversky 1982; Landman 1987; although see Gilovich and Medvec 1994); they change events within voluntary control rather than outside it (Girotto *et al.* 1991); they change the first event in a causal sequence rather than subsequent events (Wells *et al.* 1987); and they change the most recent event in a sequence of independent events (Miller and Gunasegaram 1990). The most mutable aspect of a scenario may be identified by the ease with which alternatives can be generated; this availability heuristic – the ease with which instances come to mind, either retrieved or constructed – plays a role in many inferential situations (Kahneman and Tversky 1982). It may be easier to construct counterfactual alternatives by deleting unlikely events and replacing them with more normal ones, rather than by adding unlikely events in the place of normal ones, because unlikely events spontaneously retrieve their normal counterparts (Kahneman and Miller 1986).

Consider the temporality effect which has been observed in a number of situations. Miller and Gunasegaram (1990: 1111) gave subjects the following scenario:

8   Imagine two individuals (Jones and Cooper) who are offered the following very attractive proposition. Each individual is asked to toss a coin. If the two coins come up the same (both heads or both tails), each individual wins $1,000. However, if the two coins do not come up the same, neither individual wins anything. Jones goes first and tosses a head; Cooper goes next and tosses a tail. Thus, the outcome is that neither individual wins anything.

Most subjects judged that it was easier to undo the outcome by the alternative of Cooper tossing a head, rather than Jones tossing a tail. They also believed that Cooper would experience more guilt, and would be blamed more by Jones. Logically neither party should be considered more mutable than the other since the event is one of chance. Miller and Gunasegaram suggest the temporality effect may underlie many everyday judgements, such as the tendency for blackjack players to be averse to playing on the last box, for teams to sport their faster runner last in a relay race, and for people to wager more on their predictions than their postdictions.

We have suggested that the temporality effect arises from key processes in the construction of mental models (Byrne *et al.* 1995b, 1996a). Suppose individuals construct a model in which they explicitly represent the factual situation that is described and, when they must think of ways in which the outcome could have been different, they consider the counterfactual possibilities that are implicit in their models. For example, they may initially construct an explicit model of the factual situation to represent the coin-toss scenario given above and their models of the counterfactual situation may be wholly implicit as follows:

factual: Jones – head   Cooper – tail
counterfactual: . . .

Individuals may even annotate their models further to indicate the outcomes that follow from each alternative situation (Byrne *et al.* 1996a):

factual:	Jones – head	Cooper – tail	*lose*
counterfactual:	Jones – head	Cooper – head	*win*
	Jones – tail	Cooper – tail	*win*
	Jones – tail	Cooper – head	*lose*

However, the temporality effect indicates that when individuals think of counterfactual alternatives they tend to *partially* flesh out their initial models, and the result is consistent with just one of the three counterfactual alternatives:

factual: Jones – head   Cooper – tail
counterfactual: Jones – head   Cooper – head

. . .

and the remaining counterfactual models are represented in an implicit way only. Why do individuals construct this particular counterfactual alternative?

We suggest that they do not consider the counterfactual alternative in which the players both lose (the last in the fully fleshed out set given above) because it does not undo the outcome of losing the game. There are two counterfactual alternatives that do succeed in undoing the outcome, the second and third in the fully explicit set of models above. We suggest that only one of these two counterfactual alternatives constitutes a *minimal* mutation (Byrne *et al.* 1996a). We suggest that the earlier event provides the context for the interpretation of the subsequent events, and the model is defined as being about heads, say, if heads is the first toss in the game. Models may be 'anchored', just as they are in numerical domains, by the earlier information – as demonstrated, for example, by the observation that reasoners asked to estimate quickly the answer to $8 \times 7 \times 6 \times 5 \times 3 \times 2 \times 1$ produce larger estimates than those asked to estimate the answer to $1 \times 2 \times 3 \times 4 \times 5 \times 6 \times 7 \times 8$ (Kahneman and Tversky 1982). Individuals may *initialize* their models by the first event (Byrne *et al.* 1996a), and because they construct minimal models that represent as little information as possible explicitly, the earlier event may be conferred the status of contextualizing the model to constrain the interpretation of subsequent events and their representation in the models.

In collaboration with Alessandra Tasso from the University of Padua in Italy, Susana Segura and Pablo Berrocal from the University of Malaga in Spain, and Ronan Culhane and Patrick McAlinney from the University of Dublin, Trinity College, Ireland, I have carried out a series of experiments to examine this model-based interpretation of the temporality effect (see Byrne *et al.* 1996a; 1996b). In one series of experiments we decoupled the initializing role of the first event from its contributing position in the target sequence (Byrne *et al.* 1995b, 1996a). We gave subjects scenarios based on the following sort of story:

9 Imagine two individuals (Jones and Brady) who take part in a television game show, on which they are offered the following very attractive proposition. Each individual is given a shuffled deck of cards, and each one picks a card from their own deck. If the two cards they pick are of the same colour (both from black suits or both from red suits) each individual wins £1,000. However, if the two cards are not the same colour, neither individual wins anything.

Jones goes first and picks a black card from his deck. At this point, the game-show host has to stop the game because of a technical difficulty. After a few minutes, the technical problem is solved and the game can be restarted. Jones goes first again, and this time the card that he draws is a red card. Brady goes next and the card that he draws is a black card. Thus, the outcome is that neither individual wins anything.

The technical hitch device enables us to decouple the contextualizing role of the first (pre-hitch) event, and its (post-hitch) role in the target plays. In the version shown in 9 (above), the pre-hitch and post-hitch plays differ and the temporality effect was eliminated – subjects undid the first event as often as the second. The first target play no longer has an initializing role in the model and so it is no longer immutable; as a result, either play is mutable. In a second version of the story, the pre-hitch and post-hitch plays were the same and in this case we observed the standard temporality effect. These results rule out a number of alternative possibilities, including the possibility that people undo the more recent event because it is more available or 'fresh' in working memory, or is readily accessed by a backward search through the entries to working memory. On this account, the temporality effect would be observed in both versions of the story, because the more recent event is the same in each.

This example of research on imaginary counterfactual thinking shows how the mechanisms developed to account for one domain of thinking, deductive inference, can be extended to account for another domain of thinking, counterfactual thinking. Of course, on the way to constructing a unified theory of thinking it is possible that at any juncture the entire edifice might collapse. But the example illustrates that it may be possible to have a unification of the fragmented areas of thinking eventually. It also illustrates that an account of the relation between cognition and emotion may emerge from the extension of theories of thinking to areas of thought that are linked closely with emotion. It may be possible that in the next hundred years, the psychology of thinking and reasoning will be characterized by a set of alternative unified theories of thinking that captures a wide range of formal and informal thinking, from deduction to daydreaming, in a single coherent framework.

REFERENCES

Anderson, J.R. (1993) *Rules of the Mind*, Hillsdale, NJ: Lawrence Erlbaum Associates.

Braine, M.D.S. (1978) 'On the relation between the natural logic of reasoning and standard logic', *Psychological Review* 85: 1–21.

Braine, M.D.S. and O'Brien, D.P. (1991) 'A theory of IF: a lexical entry, reasoning program, and pragmatic principles', *Psychological Review* 98: 182–203.

Byrne, R.M.J. (1989a) 'Suppressing valid inferences with conditionals', *Cognition* 31: 61–83.

—— (1989b) 'Everyday reasoning with conditional sequences', *Quarterly Journal of Experimental Psychology* 41A: 141–166.

—— (1991) 'Can valid inferences be suppressed?', *Cognition* 39: 71–78.

—— (1996) 'Towards a model theory of imaginary counterfactual thinking', in J. Oakhill and A. Garnham (eds) *Mental Models in Cognitive Science: Essays in Honour of Phil Johnson-Laird*, Hove, Sussex: Erlbaum, Taylor & Francis.

Byrne, R.M.J. and Handley, S.J. (1997) 'Reasoning strategies for suppositional deductions', *Cognition* 62: 1–49.

Byrne, R.M.J. and Johnson-Laird, P.N. (1989) 'Spatial reasoning', *Journal of Memory and Language* 28: 564–575.

—— (1992) 'The spontaneous use of propositional connectives', *Quarterly Journal of Experimental Psychology* 44A: 89–110.

Byrne, R.M.J. and Tasso, A. (1994) 'Counterfactual reasoning: inferences from hypothetical conditionals', in A. Ram and K. Eiselt (eds) *Proceedings of the Sixteenth Annual Conference of the Cognitive Science Society,* Hillsdale, NJ: Erlbaum.

Byrne, R.M.J., Espino, O. and Santamaria, C. (1997) 'The suppression effect', manuscript in preparation.

Byrne, R.M.J., Handley, S.J. and Johnson-Laird, P.N. (1995a) 'Reasoning from suppositions', *Quarterly Journal of Experimental Psychology,* 45: 915–944.

Byrne, R.M.J., Culhane, R. and Tasso, A. (1995b) 'The temporality effect in thinking about what might have been', in J. Moore and J. Lehman (eds) *Proceedings of the Seventeen Annual Conference of the Cognitive Science Society,* Hillsdale, NJ: Erlbaum.

—— (1996a) 'Context alters temporal mutability in imaginary counterfactual thinking', manuscript submitted for publication.

Byrne, R.M.J., Segura, S., McAlinney, P. and Berrocal, P. (1996b) 'Temporal event order in counterfactual thinking about what might have been', manuscript submitted for publication.

Chan, D. and Chua, D. (1994) 'Suppression of valid inferences: syntactic views, mental models, and relative salience', *Cognition* 53: 217–238.

Chapman, L.J. and Chapman, J.P. (1959) 'Atmosphere effect re-examined', *Journal of Experimental Psychology* 58: 220–226.

Cheng, P. and Holyoak, K. (1985) 'Pragmatic reasoning schemas', *Cognitive Psychology* 17, 391–416.

Clark, H.H. (1969) 'Linguistic processes in deductive inference', *Psychological Review* 76: 387–404.

Copi, I.M. (1982) *Introduction to Logic* (6th edn), London: Macmillan.

De Soto, C.B., London, M. and Handel, S. (1965) 'Social reasoning and spatial paralogic', *Journal of Personality and Social Psychology* 2: 513–521.

Evans, J.StB.T. (1977) 'Linguistic factors in reasoning', *Quarterly Journal of Experimental Psychology* 29: 297–306.

—— (1989) *Bias in Human Reasoning: Causes and Consequences,* Hove, Sussex: Erlbaum.

Evans, J.StB.T., Newstead, S. and Byrne, R.M.J. (1993) *Human Reasoning: The Psychology of Deduction,* Hillsdale, NJ: Erlbaum.

Eysenck, M. and Keane, M.T. (1995) *Cognitive Psychology: A Student's Handbook,* Hove, Sussex: Erlbaum.

Fillenbaum, S. (1974) 'Or: some uses', *Journal of Experimental Psychology* 103: 913–921.

—— (1993) 'Deductive reasoning: what are taken to be the premises and how are they interpreted?', *Behavioral and Brain Sciences* 16: 348–349.

Gavanski, I. and Wells, G.L. (1989) 'Counterfactual processing of normal and exceptional events', *Journal of Experimental Social Psychology* 25: 314–325.

Gilhooly, K.J. (1996) *Thinking: Directed, Undirected and Creative,* London: Academic Press.

Gilovich, T. and Medvec, V.H. (1994) 'The temporal pattern to the experience of regret', *Journal of Personality and Social Psychology* 67: 357–365.

Girotto, V., Legrenzi, P. and Rizzo, A. (1991) 'Event controllability in counterfactual thinking', *Acta Psychologica* 78: 111–133.

Guyote, M.J. and Sternberg, R.J. (1981) 'A transitive chain theory of syllogistic reasoning', *Cognitive Psychology* 13: 461–525.

Henle, M. (1962) 'On the relation between logic and thinking', *Psychological Review* 69: 366–378.

Hofstadter, D.R. (1979) *Godel, Escher, Bach: An Eternal Golden Braid,* New York: Basic Books.

Huttenlocher, J. (1968) 'Constructing spatial images: a strategy in reasoning', *Psychological Review* 75: 550–560.

Inhelder, B. and Piaget, J. (1958) *The Growth of Logical Thinking*, New York: Basic Books.

Janis, I. and Frick, F. (1943) 'The relationship between attitudes towards conclusions and errors in judging the logical validity of syllogisms', *Journal of Experimental Psychology* 33: 73–77.

Johnson, J. (1986) 'The knowledge of what might have been: affective and attributional consequences of near outcomes', *Personality and Social Psychology Bulletin* 12: 51–62.

Johnson-Laird, P.N. (1972) 'The three term series problems', *Cognition* 1: 58–82.

—— (1983) *Mental Models*, Cambridge: Cambridge University Press.

—— (1988) *The Computer and the Mind*, London: Fontana.

—— (1994a) 'The psychology of deduction', paper delivered to the Trinity Week Academic Symposium, Trinity College, Dublin University.

—— (1994b) 'Mental models and probabilistic thinking', *Cognition* 50: 189–209.

Johnson-Laird, P.N. and Byrne, R.M.J. (1989) '*Only* reasoning', *Journal of Memory and Language* 28: 313–330.

—— (1991) *Deduction*, Hove, Sussex, and Hillsdale, NJ: Erlbaum.

—— (1993) 'Models and deductive rationality', in K.I. Manktelow and D.E. Over (eds) *Rationality: Psychological and Philosophical Perspectives*, London: Routledge.

Johnson-Laird, P.N. and Steedman, M. (1978) 'The psychology of syllogisms', *Cognitive Psychology* 10: 64–99.

Johnson-Laird, P.N. and Tagart, J. (1969) 'How implication is understood', *American Journal of Psychology* 2: 367–373.

Johnson-Laird, P.N., Byrne, R.M.J. and Schaeken, W. (1992) 'Propositional reasoning by model', *Psychological Review* 99: 418–439.

Johnson-Laird, P.N., Byrne, R.M.J. and Tabossi, P. (1989) 'Reasoning by model: the case of multiple quantification', *Psychological Review* 96: 658–673.

Johnson-Laird, P.N., Legrenzi, P. and Legrenzi, M. (1972) 'Reasoning and a sense of reality', *British Journal of Psychology* 63: 395–400.

Kahneman, D. and Miller, D. (1986) 'Norm theory: comparing reality to its alternatives', *Psychological Review* 93: 136–153.

Kahneman, D. and Tversky, A. (1982) 'The simulation heuristic', in D. Kahneman, P. Slovic and A. Tversky (eds) *Judgement under Uncertainty: Heuristics and Biases*, New York: Cambridge University Press.

Keane, M.T., Ledgeway, T. and Duff, S. (1994) 'Constraints on analogical mapping: a comparison of three models', *Cognitive Science* 18: 387–438.

Landman, J. (1987) 'Regret and elation following action and inaction: affective responses to positive versus negative outcomes', *Personality and Social Psychology Bulletin* 13: 524–536.

Legrenzi, P., Girotto, V. and Johnson-Laird, P.N. (1993) 'Focussing in reasoning and decision-making', *Cognition* 49: 37–66.

Manktelow, K.I. and Evans, J.StB.T. (1979) 'Facilitation of reasoning by realism: Effect or non-effect?', *British Journal of Psychology* 70: 477–488.

Medvedev, Z.A. (1990) *The Legacy of Chernobyl*, Oxford: Blackwell.

Miller, D.T. and Gunasegaram, S. (1990) 'Temporal order and the perceived mutability of events: implications for blame assignment', *Journal of Personality and Social Psychology* 59: 1111–1118.

Miller, G.A. and Johnson-Laird, P.N. (1976) *Language and Perception*, Cambridge: Cambridge University Press.

Morgan, J.J.B. and Morton, J.T. (1944) 'The distortion of syllogistic reasoning produced by personal convictions', *Journal of Social Psychology* 20: 39–59.

Newell, A. (1990) *Unified Theory of Cognition*, Cambridge, MA: Harvard University Press.

Oakhill, J. and Garnham, A. (1995) *Thinking and Reasoning*, Oxford: Oxford University Press.

Politzer, G. and Braine, M.D.S. (1991) 'Responses to inconsistent premisses cannot count as suppression of valid inferences', *Cognition* 38: 103–108.

Potts, G.R. (1972) 'Information processing strategies used in the encodings of linear orderings', *Journal of Verbal Learning and Verbal Behavior* 11: 727–740.

Quinton, G. and Fellows, B.J. (1975) '"Perceptual" strategies in the solving of three term series problems', *British Journal of Psychology* 66: 69–78.

Reason, J. (1990) *Human Error*, Cambridge: Cambridge University Press.

Revlis, R. (1975) 'Two models of syllogistic inference: feature selection and conversion', *Journal of Verbal Learning and Verbal Behavior* 14: 180–195.

Rips, L.J. (1983) 'Cognitive processes in propositional reasoning', *Psychological Review* 90: 38–71.

—— (1994) *The Psychology of Proof*, Cambridge, MA: MIT Press.

Roberge, J.J. (1977) 'Effects of content on inclusive disjunction reasoning', *Quarterly Journal of Experimental Psychology* 29: 669–676.

Rodriga, M.J., De Vega, M. and Castaneda, J. (1992) 'Updating mental models in predictive reasoning', *European Journal of Cognitive Psychology* 4, 141–157.

Roese, N.J. (1994) 'The functional basis of counterfactual thinking', *Journal of Personality and Social Psychology* 66: 805–818.

Rumain, B., Connell, J. and Braine, M.D.S. (1983) 'Conversational comprehension processes are responsible for reasoning fallacies in children as well as adults: IF is not the biconditional', *Developmental Psychology* 19: 471–481.

Stalnaker, R.C. (1968) 'A theory of conditionals', in N. Rescher (ed.) *Studies in Logical Theory*, Oxford: Basil Blackwell.

Staudenmayer, H. (1975) 'Understanding conditional reasoning with meaningful propositions', in R.J. Falmagne (ed.) *Reasoning: Representation and Process*, New York: John Wiley & Sons.

Stevenson, R. and Over, D. (1995) 'Deduction from uncertain premises', *Quarterly Journal of Experimental Psychology* 48A: 613–643.

Storring, G. (1908) 'Experimentelle Untersuchungen uber einfache Schlussprozesse', *Archiv fur die Gesamte Psychologie* 11: 1–27.

Taplin, J.E. and Staudenmayer, H. (1973) 'Interpretation of abstract conditional sentences in deductive reasoning', *Journal of Verbal Learning and Verbal Behavior* 12: 530–542.

Trabasso, T., Riley, C.A. and Wilson, E.G. (1975) 'The representation of linear order and spatial strategies in reasoning: a developmental study', in R.J. Falmagne (ed.) *Reasoning: Representation and Process*, New York: John Wiley & Sons.

Wason, P.C. (1959) 'The processing of positive and negative information', *Quarterly Journal of Experimental Psychology* 11: 92–107.

—— (1966) 'Reasoning', in B.M. Foss (ed.) *New Horizons in Psychology*, Harmondsworth: Penguin.

Wason, P.C. and Johnson-Laird, P.N. (1972) *Psychology of Reasoning: Structure and Content*, London: Batsford.

Wells, G.L., Taylor, B.R. and Turtle, J.W. (1987) 'The undoing of scenarios', *Journal of Personality and Social Psychology* 53: 421–430.

Wilkins, M.C. (1928) 'The effect of changed material on the ability to do formal syllogistic reasoning', *Archives of Psychology* 16: 102.

Woodworth, R.S. and Sells, S.B. (1935) 'An atmosphere effect in syllogistic reasoning', *Journal of Experimental Psychology* 18: 451–460.

14 The history of the concept of goals

Peter M. Gollwitzer

Research and theorizing on goals and their effects on thought, affect and behaviour have become very popular in social psychology, as documented by many recently edited books (e.g. Frese and Sabini 1985; Gollwitzer and Bargh 1996; Halisch and Kuhl 1987; Kuhl and Beckmann 1985; Pervin 1989) and review chapters (e.g. Gollwitzer and Moskowitz 1996; Karniol and Ross 1996; Karoly 1993). The reasons for this are manifold. Some are rooted in theoretical developments in the psychology of motivation (see Heckhausen 1991; Geen 1995; Gollwitzer 1990, 1993; Kuhl 1984) which has moved beyond explaining the choice of actions to the wilful control of actions. This new interest in volition has led to the embracing of the goal concept, as goals are at the starting point of any volitional control of action.

But the renaissance of the concept of goals is also promoted by recent developments in the field of social psychology known as 'social cognition'. First, following William James' (1890) observation that 'my thinking is first and always for the sake of my doing', it is increasingly recognized that much of people's thinking is to control their actions. Second, the metaphor that governs current theorizing on human information processing is changing from the 'faulty computer' or the 'cognitive miser' to the 'flexible strategist' (Fiske 1993). All this has created a tremendous interest in issues of volition. Thus the goal concept, allowing a cognitive analysis and being at the core of the volitional control of behaviour, is also embraced by researchers interested in social cognition.

HISTORICAL BACKGROUND

According to the behaviourists, goal-directed behaviour is easily recognized by a number of observable features. Besides persistence, the main feature mentioned by Tolman (1925), researchers pointed to the appropriateness of goal-directed behaviour in the sense that the goal-directed organism adopts an effective course of action in response to variations in the stimuli connected with the goal. If, for instance, one route to goal attainment is blocked, another course of action to the same goal is taken. Or if the goal changes in its location (for example, a rat trying to escape a cat), the goal-directed organism (i.e. the cat) readily adapts to these changes by actions that correspond to the variations of the goal. Finally, besides persistence and appropriateness, goal-directed organisms are also found to show hyperactivity when exposed to the stimuli associated with a previously experienced goal. This restlessness is commonly referred to as searching for the goal.

The behaviourists spelled out the observable features of goal-directed behaviour (i.e. persistence, appropriateness and searching); but what qualifies as an actual goal? Goals specify powerful incentives, where incentives are defined as objects and events that affect an organism's behaviour radically and reliably (such as food, sexual stimulation, sudden loud noise, and so forth). Whether an object or event is treated as a goal or an incentive, however, depends solely on the investigator's perspective on the organism's behaviours. If the investigator selects a certain incentive as the reference point for the description of behaviour, this incentive becomes a goal. In the behaviourist tradition, the reference point for goal-directed behaviour is apparently not the intention or the goal set by the organisms themselves (see Bindra 1959).

The reference point of modern goal theories is, in contrast to the behaviouristic view, the internal subjective goal. Goal-directed behaviour is studied in relation to goals held by the individual (for example, a person's goal to stop smoking serves as a reference point for his or her efforts to achieve this goal). Research questions focus on whether and how setting personal goals affects a person's behaviours. This theoretical orientation has its own historical precursors which reach back far beyond the heydays of behaviourism. William James (1890), in his *Principles of Psychology*, included a chapter on the will, in which he discussed the following questions: How is it possible that a behaviour that a person intends to perform (i.e. has been set as a goal by this person) fails to be executed? James referred to such problems as issues of the *obstructed will*, but he also raised questions related to what he called issues of the *explosive will* (i.e. how is it possible that an undesired behaviour is performed even though we have set ourselves the goal to suppress it?).

James' theorizing rests on the assumption that behaviour can potentially be regulated by a person's resolutions (or intentions or subjective goals) even though in certain situations and at certain times it may be difficult for such resolutions to come true. In any case, the individual's subjective goal is the reference point for the goal-directed action and not a powerful incentive focused on by an outside observer (or scientist). The question raised by James is whether people meet their goals in their actions, not whether their actions towards an incentive carry features of persistence, appropriateness and searching.

A further prominent historical figure in theorizing about subjective goals and their effects on behaviour is William McDougall. In his *Social Psychology* (1931) he was so intrigued by the issue of purposeful or goal-directed behaviour that he proposed a novel psychological theorizing (i.e. hormic psychology – see McDougall 1931). McDougall explicitly saw the reference point for goal-directed behaviour in a person's subjective purpose or goal. He postulated that subjective goals guide a person's behaviour. This guidance is thought to be achieved through cognitive activity that pertains to the analysis of the present situational context and the envisioned event or goal state to be realized. Furthermore, progress towards and attainment of the goal are seen as pleasurable experiences, and thwarting and failure are seen as painful or disagreeable. With respect to the observable features of goal-directed activity, however, McDougall referred to the same aspects as the behaviourists (for example, persistence and appropriateness).

In the history of German psychology, the issue of goal-directedness of behaviour played a particularly prominent role and resulted in an intensive exchange of opinions. This controversy began at the beginning of this century and lasted up to the 1930s. The main protagonists were Ach on the one hand (for a summary, see Ach 1935), and Lewin (1926) on the other. In an attempt to establish a scientific analysis of the phenomenon of volitional action or willing (*Willenspsychologie*), Ach employed a very simple experimental paradigm. Subjects were trained to respond repeatedly and consistently to specific stimuli (for example, numbers or meaningless syllables) with certain responses (for example, to add or to rhyme, respectively). When these responses had become habitual, subjects were instructed to employ their will and execute antagonistic responses (for example, to subtract or read, respectively). Ach discovered that forming the intention to respond to the critical stimuli with an antagonistic response helps 'to get one's will'.

The theorizing on how an intention achieves the reliable execution of the intended action was based on the concept of *determination*. Ach assumed that linking in one's mind an anticipated situation to a concrete intended behaviour creates what he called a determination, and that this determination in turn would urge the person to execute the intended action once the specified situational stimulus is encountered. The strength of the determination should depend on how concretely people specify the intended action and the respective situation; concreteness was thought to intensify determination. Moreover, the intensity of the act of intending (willing) should also increase determination, because intensive willing induces a heightened commitment ('I really will do it!'). Determination was expected to elicit directly the intended behaviour without a person's conscious intent to get started. Ach speculated that determination may affect perceptual and attentional processes so that the specified situation is cognized in a way which favours the initiation of the intended action.

Kurt Lewin (1926), who scornfully termed Ach's ideas a 'linkage theory of intention', proposed a 'need' theory of goal striving. Intentions, like needs, assign a valence (in German: *Aufforderungscharakter*) to objects and events in people's social and non-social surroundings. For a person who intends to mail a letter (i.e. Lewin's favourite example!), a mailbox entices (or at least calls or reminds) him or her to deposit a letter, very much like food entices a hungry person to eat. Because needs can be satisfied by various types of behaviours which may all substitute for each other in terms of reducing need tension (for example, eating fruit, vegetables, bread, and so forth), many different intention-related behaviours qualify for satisfying the quasi-need associated with an intention. The amount of the tension associated with the quasi-need was assumed to directly relate to the intensity of a person's goal strivings. The exact amount of tension may vary. First, it is affected by the degree of quasi-need fulfilment (i.e. tension comes to a final rest only when the goal is achieved), but it is also thought to depend on the strength of relevant real needs (i.e. superordinate drives and general life goals) and how strongly these are related to the quasi-need. For a person with strong affiliative needs but weak achievement needs (or professional goals) a mailbox, for example, acquires more valence when someone intends to send off letters inviting people to a party, as compared to sending out a job application.

MODERN GOAL THEORIES

Many of the ideas on goal-directed behaviours, as presented by James, McDougall, the German 'psychology of will', and to a lesser degree the behaviourists, have been adopted by modern goal theories. In order to arrive at a comprehensive presentation of the many different theories, I have grouped them according to aspects of similarity which has led to two major categories:

- Content theories of goal striving, which attempt to explain differences in goal-directed behaviours and their consequences in terms of what is specified as the goal by the individual. In other words, differences in goal content are expected to drastically affect a person's behaviours.
- Self-regulation theories of goal striving, which attempt to explain the volitional processes that mediate the effects of goals on behaviour. As we will see, there are two different types of self-regulation theories, one of a more motivational, the other of a more cognitive nature.

GOAL CONTENT THEORIES

Goal contents vary because goals may be challenging or modest, specific or vague, abstract or concrete, proximal or distal, with a negative or positive outcome focus, and so forth. But goals may also cover different themes and issues since they can be based on different needs and incentives. Moreover, the type of implicit theory the individual holds regarding the functioning of the subject matter involved further determines goal content. Goal content theories analyse the effects of differences in goal content on goal-directed behaviour and the consequences of these behaviours. The research strategy adopted by goal content theorists compares the effects of goals varying on a dimension of interest (for example, specific vs. vague goals, goals based on autonomy needs vs. goals based on material needs) on a relevant dependent variable (for example, quantity or quality of performance).

Goal specificity

The prototype of a goal content theory is *goal setting theory*, first put forth by the organizational psychologists Locke and Latham (for a summary, see Locke and Latham 1990). The theory was meant to offer applied psychologists a 'theory of work motivation that works'. The basic thesis is that challenging goals that are spelled out in specific terms have a particularly positive effect on behaviour. In more than 400 mainly experimental studies (a count conducted by Locke and Latham in 1990), challenging specific goals were superior to modest specific goals as well as to challenging vague goals (i.e. 'do your best' goals). A typical study conducted in a work setting may serve as an example (Latham and Yukl 1975). Woodworkers were sent out to the forest equipped with goals with different contents or no goals at all. Challenging goals (i.e. standards above what can be achieved with normal effort expenditure) led to a higher productivity as observed in the no-goal control group when goals were formulated in specific terms (for example, number of trees to be cut). Specific non-challenging goals implying modest standards failed to increase productivity, as did challenging but vague goals, such as 'do your best'.

Needs as sources of goals

For Locke and Latham (1990), it is not the differences in sources (for example, different needs, or self-set vs. assigned goals) that matters. What matters is whether goal content is formulated in a challenging specific format or in a non-specific and non-challenging (modest) way. In other words, Locke and Latham focus on structural features of goal content (i.e. specificity and challenge) and not on whether the goal is based on one source or another. Deci and Ryan (1991) have criticized this point of view by stating that not all goals are 'created equal'. According to Deci and Ryan, goals affect a person's behaviour differently depending on what kind of need is the source of a person's goal setting. If, for instance, two students in an art class are confronted with the possibility of creating an interesting painting, Student A may set herself the goal of pleasing her parents, whereas Student B focuses on his intrinsic joy in creating an interesting piece of work. Based on their *self-determination theory*, Deci and Ryan postulate that goals in the service of autonomy, competence and social integration needs lead to better performances in the sense of greater creativity, higher cognitive flexibility, greater depth of information processing and more effective coping with failure. Deci and Ryan argue that the respective needs are assumed to further autonomous, self-determined and authentic goal striving. This positive kind of goal activity is contrasted with a less effective, negative kind, which is unreflectively controlled from outside (for example, goal assignments by authorities) or from inside (for example, goal setting based on feelings of obligation).

Implicit theories as sources of goals

A further goal content theory is suggested by Dweck (1991) (see also Elliott and Dweck 1988). Dweck's theory focuses on achievement goals and postulates a distinction between learning goals and performance goals. The source of goal setting is a person's implicit theory about the nature of ability – not a person's needs, as asserted by Deci and Ryan. Whether in a given achievement situation people set themselves either one or the other type of goal depends on whether they hold an entity theory (i.e. they believe that the amount of ability is fixed and cannot be easily changed) or an incremental theory (i.e. they believe that the amount of ability can be improved by learning). People with such drastically different theories about the nature of ability set themselves quite different types of goals in achievement situations. Entity 'theorists' try to find out via task performance how capable they are, thus making inferences on the amount of their respective talent. They set themselves performance goals. But incremental 'theorists' want to know where and why they are making mistakes in order to learn how to improve – they set themselves learning goals. These distinct types of goals have important behavioural consequences, in particular when it comes to coping with failure. For individuals with performance goals, negative outcomes signal a lack of intelligence and thus result in helpless reactions (for example, low persistence). People with learning goals, on the other hand, view setbacks as cues to focus on new behavioural strategies. Their behaviour is oriented towards mastering the causes of the setback.

Further goal content differences

Before ending the section on goal content theories, two important structural differences between types of goal contents need to be mentioned. The first is discussed by Bandura and Schunk (1981) and relates to the time frame of goal attainment. Proximal goals relate to what one does in the present or the near future, whereas distal goals point far into the future. Bandura and Schunk observed that proximal goals improved children's arithmetic attainments. This effect was mediated by an increase in the children's strength of self-efficacy and intrinsic interest in mathematics. Apparently, distal goals are too far removed in time to guide a person's actions effectively, as they fail to provide small successes that promote self-efficacy and interest.

A second important difference in the framing of goals has recently been introduced by Higgins *et al.* (1994) and pertains to the valence of one's goal pursuit. Achievement goals with a positive outcome focus (i.e. goals that focus on the presence or absence of positive outcomes) favour task performance, whereas goals with a negative outcome focus (i.e. goals that focus on the presence or absence of negative outcomes) undermine it. In addition, individuals with chronic discrepancies between their actual and ideal selves (i.e. people who fall short of their ideals) are found to prefer positive outcome focus goals, whereas individuals with actual/ought self-discrepancies (i.e. people who fall short of their duties) prefer the negative outcome focus goals.

SELF-REGULATION THEORIES OF GOAL STRIVING

As experience tells us, there is often a long way from goal setting to goal attainment. Having set a goal is often just a first step towards goal attainment and requires that a host of implementational problems are solved successfully. These problems are manifold, as they pertain to initiating goal-directed actions and bringing them to a successful ending. To solve these problems effectively, the individual needs to seize good opportunities to act, ward off distractions, flexibly step up efforts in the face of difficulties, bypass barriers, compensate for failures and shortcomings and negotiate conflicts between goals. Self-regulation theories analyse how the individual effectively solves these problems of goal implementation. Often they focus on one of these problems in particular and ignore the others. But all of them try to propose general principles that apply to the problems of implementation of all goals despite differences in context.

The model of action phases

Nuttin (1980), in defining the central features of a motivational goal theory, argued that goals and action plans are not simply cognitions that specify standards or reference points. Rather, goals and plans are cognitively explicated and elaborated needs. Whereas goals describe desired events and outcomes, plans specify how one intends to attain these events and outcomes. The intensity of goal-directed actions is thought to be determined by the individual's motivation to reach the goal, and by the instrumentality of the plan on which these actions are based.

In their model of action phases, Heckhausen and Gollwitzer (Heckhausen and Gollwitzer 1987; Gollwitzer 1990; Heckhausen 1991) followed Nuttin's prescription of a motivational goal theory and explicated it in more detail. The model assumes that a person's motives and needs produce more wishes and desires than can possibly be realized. Therefore, the individual is forced to make a choice, which is preceded by deliberating the feasibility and desirability of these wishes and desires. Only a few of the feasible and attractive wishes are chosen for implementation and thus turned into goals. Whether goal-directed behaviours are initiated in a given situation depends on the desirability and feasibility of the goal, but also on the perceived suitability of the present situational context. All this is considered in relation to the desirability and feasibility of other competing goals that also press for realization in the given situation, and to possible future situational contexts that may be more or less suitable than the one at hand.

The model takes a comprehensive temporal (horizontal) view of the course of goal pursuit which extends from the origins of a person's wishes and desires to the evaluation of attained outcomes. It is suggested that the course of goal pursuit entails four different, consecutive action phases. At each of these phases people are expected to face a qualitatively distinct task which needs to be accomplished in order to promote goal completion. The first of these tasks, which is accomplished in the *pre-decisional phase*, is deliberating wishes in light of the evaluative criteria of feasibility and desirability, in order to arrive at a decision on whether to act on one's wishes. A positive decision transfers the wish or desire into a binding goal, which is accompanied by a feeling of determination or obligation. Accordingly, the next task to be solved is to promote the initiation and successful execution of goal-directed action. This may be simple when the necessary goal-directed actions are well-practised and routine, or complex when we are still undecided about where and how to act. In complex cases, the execution of goal-directed action needs to be prepared. The action phases model refers to this period prior to the initiation of goal-directed action as the *pre-actional phase*. To advance further on the way from wishes to action, the individual reflects and decides on *when, where, how* and *how long* to act, thus creating plans for action.

With the initiation of goal-directed behaviours, the individual enters the *actional phase*. The task associated with this phase is bringing goal-directed behaviours to a successful conclusion. For this purpose it is necessary that the individual readily responds to situational opportunities and demands. He or she should jump at all opportunities that allow progress towards the goal, and when differences and hindrances are encountered, should readily increase his or her efforts. This responsiveness to situational opportunities and demands promotes goal achievement. The final action phase is called *post-actional*. Here the task is to evaluate one's goal achievement. This is done by comparing what has been achieved with what has been desired.

Action phases and mind-sets

The primary objective of the action phases model is to identify the typical problems people encounter in their goal pursuits. Thereby it has stimulated theoretical concepts that help to understand people's functioning at the various stages of goal pursuit. One of these is the concept of mind-set. Gollwitzer (1990) suggests that different mind-sets (i.e. general cognitive orientations with distinct features) should emerge when a person addresses the distinct tasks associated with the various action phases. These mind-sets should be endowed with those cognitive features that facilitate the respective tasks and are thus functional to task completion.

By initiating the mind-sets that correspond to the action phases they are currently pursuing, people can effectively promote their goal pursuits. Studies conducted on the mind-sets associated either with deliberating one's wishes and desires (i.e. the deliberative mind-set of the pre-decisional phase) or with planning the initiation of goal-directed actions (i.e. the implemental mind-set of the pre-actional phase) support this idea. When subjects are asked to engage in intensive deliberation of whether to turn an important personal wish or desire into a goal, a cognitive orientation (i.e. the *deliberative mind-set*) with the following features originates. Subjects become more open-minded with respect to processing available information. Heeded information is processed more effectively and even peripheral information is encoded (Heckhausen and Gollwitzer 1987). Second, desirability-related information is processed more effectively than implementation-related information (Gollwitzer *et al.* 1990b). Finally, with respect to desirability-related information, the pros and cons of making a decision are analysed in an impartial manner (Beckmann and Gollwitzer 1987). Moreover, feasibility-related information is analysed in a relatively objective, non-illusionary way (Gollwitzer and Kinney 1989; Taylor and Gollwitzer 1995). This cognitive orientation (i.e. the deliberative mind-set) should facilitate the making of 'good' (i.e. realistic) goal decisions, because it prevents perceiving wishes and desires (i.e. the potential goals) as more desirable or feasible than they actually are.

When subjects are asked to plan the implementation of an important personal goal or project, a cognitive orientation (i.e. the *implemental mind-set*) with quite different attributes originates: subjects become closed-minded in the sense that they are no longer distracted by irrelevant information (Gollwitzer 1996). They are also effective in processing information related to implementation-related issues (for example, the sequencing of actions – see Gollwitzer *et al.* 1990b). Moreover, desirability-related information is processed in a partial manner favouring pros over cons (Beckmann and Gollwitzer 1987), and feasibility-related information is analysed in a manner that favours illusionary optimism. This optimism extends to the perceived control of uncontrollable outcomes (Gollwitzer and Kinney 1989), to a person's self-perception of important personal attributes (for example, cheerfulness, academic ability, sensitivity to others, self-respect, drive to achieve, leadership ability), and to the perceived vulnerability to both controllable and uncontrollable risks (for example, developing an addiction to prescription drugs or losing a partner to an early death, respectively) (Taylor and Gollwitzer 1995). Finally, the implemental mind-set elevates people's moods and self-esteem. The mind-set effects on self-perception and perceived vulnerability to risk, however, are not mediated by mood or self-esteem changes (see Taylor and Gollwitzer 1995). All the listed features of the implemental mind-set should facilitate goal achievement as they allow the individual to cope effectively with classic problems of goal implementation, such as being distracted with irrelevant things, doubting the attractiveness of the pursued goal, or being pessimistic about its feasibility.

Implementation intentions vs. goal intentions

A second concept stimulated by the action phases model is that of implementation intentions (Gollwitzer 1993). It relates to a particular form of planning where the individual commits him- or herself to perform a certain goal-directed behaviour when a particular situation is encountered. Implementation intentions take the format of 'I intend to do x when situation y is encountered', thus linking an anticipated future situation (opportunity) to a certain goal-directed behaviour. Implementation intentions are different from goal intentions. The latter take the format of 'I intend to achieve x', whereby the x specifies a desired end-state, which may be the execution of a desired concrete behaviour or the attainment of a desired outcome.

Implementation intentions constitute a powerful strategy to overcome problems of goal realization. First, forming implementation intentions increases a person's commitment to the respective goal intention (Gollwitzer *et al.* 1990a). Second, it helps people to get started with goal-directed actions. Goal intentions that are furnished with implementation intentions are completed about three times more often than mere goal intentions (Gollwitzer and Brandstätter, in press). Because implementation intentions spell out links between situational cues and goal-directed behaviours, it is assumed that by forming such intentions people pass on the control of goal-directed behaviour to environmental cues, which facilitates the initiation of goal-directed actions. On a micro-level of analysis, it is hypothesized that the mental representation of the specified situational cues becomes highly activated, thus making these cues more easily accessible. Results of various experiments support this view (for a summary, see Gollwitzer 1993, 1996). Situational cues specified in implementation intentions were more easily detected and remembered, as well as more readily attended to than comparable non-intended situations. Moreover, it is hypothesized that implementation intentions create strong associative links between mental representations of situations and actions that are commonly only achieved through repeated and consistent acting in these situations. Accordingly, the initiation of the intended goal-directed behaviour in the presence of the critical situation should resemble the initiation of a habitual response. Indeed, various experiments demonstrate that the goal-directed behaviours specified in implementation intentions are initiated swiftly and effortlessly in the presence of the critical situation. In addition, the subliminal presentation of the critical situation suffices to activate cognitions that guide the intended behaviour.

In summary, forming an implementation intention is an act of will that changes conscious control of goal-directed action over to direct, environmental control (Bargh and Gollwitzer 1994). The situational stimuli specified in implementation intentions become direct elicitors of goal-directed action.

Competing goal pursuits

Kuhl (1984) (for a recent summary, see Kuhl and Beckmann 1994) focuses on self-regulatory processes that contribute to goal achievement in the face of competing action tendencies. Following Atkinson and Birch's (1970) theorizing on the dynamics of action, it is assumed that at any given point many different action tendencies, both waxing and waning in strength, co-exist. For an ordered action sequence to occur, Kuhl assumes that a current guiding goal has to be shielded from competing goal intentions. He terms this shielding mechanism *action control* and differentiates a number of different, but compatible control strategies, such as attention control, emotion control, motivation control and environment control. Through environment control, for instance, the individual prevents the derailing of an ongoing goal pursuit by removing any competing temptations or enticements from the situational context in which goal pursuit is to occur. Whether and how effectively these strategies are employed depends on the current control mode of the individual. An *action-oriented* person concentrates on the planning and initiation of goal-directed action, responds flexibly to the respective contextual demands, and employs the listed control strategies effectively. Things are quite different with a *state-oriented* person. This person cannot disengage from competing incomplete goals and is caught up in dysfunctional persevering thoughts, directed at past or future successes or failures.

Researchers on goals are becoming increasingly aware of the fact that goals are not created in isolation. People set themselves many goals, and these goals may come into conflict with each other. When goals are short term, the process of shielding an ongoing goal pursuit from competing others seems most important. Other self-regulatory processes are needed, however, when the conflicting goals are enduring, such as self-defining goals (Wicklund and Gollwitzer 1982), personal strivings (Emmons 1989) or life tasks (Cantor 1994). Emmons and King (1988) observed that conflict between and within personal strivings is associated with poor well-being. Conflict was found to relate to negative affectivity and/or physical symptomatology. Emmons (1996) argues that creative integrations of a person's strivings might reverse the negative effects of conflict. The observation that so-called generativity strivings (i.e. strivings which demand both the creating and giving up of a product) are associated with higher levels of subjective well-being is cited in support of this idea, as generativity may be understood as the creative blending of intimacy strivings and power strivings.

Conflict between goals has also been discussed in the theoretical framework of life tasks (Cantor and Fleeson 1994). Life tasks, such as doing well academically, exert specific influences on behaviour as they are interpreted differently over the life course and across situational contexts. Life tasks are often confronted with difficulties, frustrations, anxieties and self-doubts, and the individual's style of appraising these hindrances leads to a typical pattern of action goals aimed at overcoming these obstacles. For instance, college students who worry about their abilities when they experience failure (i.e. outcome-focused individuals – see Harlow and Cantor 1994) may, in a strategic effort to meet their academic life task, turn for reassurance to others whom they regard as confidantes and encouragers. In this case, social goals are put in the service of academic goals.

Goals and discrepancy reduction

If one considers a person's goal pursuit as an issue of discrepancy reduction, a host of further self-regulatory processes can be identified. Discrepancy reduction theories of goal pursuit do not conceive of goals as something attractive (i.e. specifying a positive incentive corresponding to some vital need) that pulls the individual in the direction of goal attainment. The set goal only specifies a performance standard. Prototypical are Bandura's (1991) ideas on the self-regulation of action. According to Bandura, goals have no motivational consequences *per se*; they only specify the conditions that allow a positive or negative self-evaluation. If the set goal is attained through one's actions, a positive self-evaluation prevails, whereas staying below one's goal leads to a negative self-evaluation. Thus the individual is pushed by the negative self-evaluation associated with the discrepancy, and he or she is pulled by the anticipated positive self-evaluation that is 'intrinsically' linked to closing the gap between the *status quo* and the goal (i.e. the performance standard).

These basic ideas imply that goals stimulate effortful acting towards goal attainment (what Bandura refers to as high performance motivation) only when people cognize a discrepancy between the *status quo* and the set goal. Bandura therefore proposes attaining frequent feedback as a powerful measure to stimulate goal pursuit. Moreover, people are expected to engage in efforts to reduce the experienced discrepancy only when they have acquired a strong sense of self-efficacy with respect to the required actions. Doubts about possessing the capabilities necessitated by these actions undermine a person's readiness to act on the goal.

Bandura's ideas remind one of control theory as suggested by Carver and Scheier (1981). Stimulated by Miller *et al.* (1960), Carver and Scheier apply a control theoretical framework to the study of goal-directed action. The central conceptual unit of their analysis is the negative feedback loop. In a negative feedback loop a reference criterion is compared with a perceptual input in a comparator. If there is a difference between the two, a signal is generated (i.e. an error is detected). The detected error elicits behaviour that reduces the discrepancy between the reference criterion and the perceptual input. Following Powers' (1973) proposal that behaviour is organized hierarchically, Carver and Scheier assume a cascading loop structure. A positive affective response as a consequence of goal attainment is not assumed however, nor is the detection of error associated with negative affect. Rather, the speed of progress towards a goal is seen as the source of positive or negative feelings in a person's goal pursuit. The intensity of these feelings is regulated again in a feedback loop: if the speed meets a set reference criterion, positive feelings emerge amd vice versa (Carver and Scheier 1990).

Automatic goal pursuits

The goal theories discussed so far characterize a person's goal striving as an intentionally controlled, conscious and reflective endeavour. Goal choice demands the conscious weighing of pros and cons, and goal implementation necessitates reflective thinking about how to realize the goal. As mentioned above concerning implementation intentions however, people can strategically switch from conscious control of goal-directed actions to direct control of action by the environment (Gollwitzer 1993). This helps an individual in difficult circumstances to attain desired ends. But there is another type of environmental control of goal-directed actions, which is spelled out in Bargh's (1990) automotive theory. It is suggested that strong mental links develop between the cognitive representations of situations and the goals the individual chronically pursues within them. As a consequence of this repeated and consistent pairing in the past, these goals become automatically activated when the individual enters the relevant situation. The automatically activated goal then guides behaviour within the situation, without the individual choosing or intending that particular line of action. There may have been a deliberate choice of the goal in the past, but this conscious choice is now bypassed. The situational cues directly guide the person's goal-directed actions (Bargh and Gollwitzer 1994).

SUMMARY

Research stimulated by modern theorizing on goals has discovered the following about goal pursuits. First, it makes a difference how people frame their goals and what is the content of their goals. How people formulate their achievement goals – in specific or vague terms, challenging or modest, proximal or distal, as a performance goal or a learning goal, approach or avoidance goal – affects how successfully they will behave in a respective achievement situation. Similarly, whether people's personal strivings or life goals are based on one type of need or another determines how successfully they go through their lives in terms of psychological and physical well-being. Future research on goal content theories should ask questions about further important goal content dimensions.

Second, goal striving is recognized as a volitional, self-regulatory endeavour. Classic theorizing on motivation (Atkinson 1964; McClelland 1951; Nuttin 1980; Weiner 1972) construes goal pursuit as an issue of need satisfaction. A person's needs are conceived of as the ultimate source of goals because needs (for example, the need for affiliation) produce wishes and desires that specify attractive incentives. The demands of situational contexts determine what becomes a person's action goal because, depending on the situation present, certain actions are seen as more instrumental than others for the satisfaction of one's needs (i.e. acquiring the respective incentives). Following this line of thought, it is tempting to assume that the intensity of a person's goal pursuit is exclusively determined by the strength of a person's respective need and the instrumentality of the pursued goal-directed behaviours.

Modern goal theories do not deny that people's needs or motives affect their goal pursuits; nor do they rely solely on motivational determinants of goal pursuit. The focus of modern goal theories is on the superimposed self-regulatory strategies. These strategies are assumed to help the individual overcome the many problems of goal implementation. Even when goals are highly attractive and the respective action plans are highly instrumental, people may still experience problems with getting started, warding off distractions, compensating for shortcomings, and negotiating conflicts between goals. In this sense, modern goal theories have returned to the theories of Ach, James and McDougall, which were prevalent prior to the heyday of motivational need theories (Atkinson 1958). Today, goal pursuits are again seen as subject to volition and modern goal theorists attempt to identify those volitional (wilful) strategies that make a person's goal-directed efforts most successful.

Future research on the self-regulation of goal pursuit should continue to search for effective mental strategies and ask questions of when these are employed and on what cognitive processes they are based. Two issues deserve enhanced attention in future research. The first extends to the termination of goal pursuit, the second to the self-defensive aspects of self-regulation. With regard to the self-regulation of disengagement from goals, we still observe a scarcity of theorizing. Although Klinger (1975) offered a stage theory of disengagment that describes the phases of a person's giving up on an incentive, there should be more theorizing and research on both the conditions that trigger disengagement and the self-regulatory processes that promote it (Oettingen 1996).

Second, most self-regulation theories of goal pursuit portray the individual as non-defensive. The individual attempts to achieve personal goals with the best of his or her efforts. But people do not only have to serve their goals, they also need to protect their self-esteem. As Jones and Berglas (1978) pointed out in their research on self-handicapping, people often undermine the attainment of an achievement goal in an effort to protect self-esteem. Future research should therefore try to explore how people integrate self-regulatory strategies of goal pursuit with self-defensive strategies aimed at the protection of self-esteem (Baumeister 1996).

REFERENCES

Ach, N. (1935) 'Analyse des Willens', In E. Abderhalden (ed.), *Handbuch der biologischen Arbeitsmethoden (Vol. 6)*, Berlin: Urban und Schwarzenberg.
Atkinson, J.W. (1958) *Motives in Fantasy, Action, and Society*, Princeton, NJ: Van Nostrand.
—— (1964) *An Introduction to Motivation*, Princeton, NJ: Van Nostrand.
Atkinson, J.W. and Birch, D. (1970) *The Dynamics of Action*, New York: John Wiley & Sons.

Bandura, A. (1991) 'Self-regulation of motivation through anticipatory and self-reactive mechanisms', in R.A. Dienstbier (ed.) *Nebraska Symposium on Motivation Vol. 38* (pp. 69–164), Lincoln: University of Nebraska Press.

Bandura, A. and Schunk, D.H. (1981) 'Cultivating competence, self-efficacy and intrinsic interest through proximal self-motivation', *Journal of Personality and Social Psychology* 41: 586–598.

Bargh, J.A. (1990) 'Auto-motives: pre-conscious determinants of social interaction', in E.T. Higgins and R.M. Sorrentino (eds) *Handbook of Motivation and Cognition Vol. 2* (pp. 93–130), New York: Guilford Press.

Bargh, J.A. and Gollwitzer, P.M. (1994) 'Environmental control of goal-directed action: automatic and strategic contingencies between situations and behaviour', in W. Spaulding (ed.) *Nebraska Symposium on Motivation Vol. 41* (pp. 71–124), Lincoln: University of Nebraska Press.

Baumeister, R. (1996) 'Self-regulation and ego threat: motivated cognition, self-deception, and destructive goal setting', in P.M. Gollwitzer and J.A. Bargh (eds) *The Psychology of Action* (pp. 27–47), New York: Guilford Press.

Beckmann, J. and Gollwitzer, P.M. (1987) 'Deliberative vs. implemental states of mind: the issue of impartiality in pre- and postdecisional information processing', *Social Cognition* 5: 239–279.

Bindra, D. (1959) *Motivation*, New York: Ronald Press.

Cantor, N. (1994) 'Life task problem solving: situational affordances and personal needs', *Personality and Social Psychology Bulletin* 20: 235–243.

Cantor, N. and Fleeson, W. (1994) 'Social intelligence and intelligent goal pursuit: a cognitive slice of motivation', in W. Spaulding (ed.) *Nebraska Symposium on Motivation Vol. 41* (pp. 125–180), Lincoln: University of Nebraska Press.

Carver, C.S. and Scheier, M.F. (1981) *Attention and Self-regulation: A Control-theory Approach to Human Behaviours*, New York: Springer-Verlag.

—— (1982) 'Outcome expectancy, locus of attribution for expectancy, and self-directed attention as determinants of evaluations and performance', *Journal of Experimental Social Psychology* 18: 184–200.

—— (1990) 'Origins and functions of positive and negative affect: a control-process view', *Psychological Review* 97: 19–35.

Deci, E.L. and Ryan, R.M. (1991) 'A motivational approach to self: integration in personality', in R. Dienstbier (ed.) *Nebraska Symposium on Motivation Vol. 38* (pp. 237–288), Lincoln: University of Nebraska Press.

Dweck, C.S. (1991) 'Self-theories and goals: their role in motivation, personality and development', in R. Dienstbier (ed.) *Nebraska Symposium on Motivation Vol. 38* (pp. 199–255), Lincoln: University of Nebraska Press.

Elliott, E.S. and Dweck, C.S. (1988) 'Goals: an approach to motivation and achievement', *Journal of Personality and Social Psychology* 54: 5–12.

Emmons, R.A. (1989) 'The personal strivings approach to personality', in L.A. Pervin (ed.) *Goal Concepts in Personality and Social Psychology* (pp. 87–126), Hillsdale, NJ: Erlbaum.

—— (1996) 'Striving and feeling: personal goals and subjective well-being', in P.M. Gollwitzer and J.A. Bargh (eds) *The Psychology of Action* (pp. 313–337), New York: Guilford Press.

Emmons, R.A. and King, L.A. (1988) 'Conflict among personal strivings: immediate and long-term implications for psychological and physical well-being', *Journal of Personality and Social Psychology* 54: 1040–1048.

Fiske, S.T. (1993) 'Social cognition and social perception', *Annual Review of Psychology* 44: 155–194.

Fiske, S.T. and Taylor, S. (1991) *Social Cognition (2nd edn)*, New York: McGraw-Hill.

Frese, M. and Sabini, J. (1985) *Goal-directed Behaviour: The Concept of Action in Psychology*, Hillsdale, NJ: Erlbaum.

Geen, R.G. (1995) *Human Motivation*, Pacific Grove, CA: Brooks/Cole Publishing Company.

Gollwitzer, P.M. (1990) 'Action phases and mind-sets', in E.T. Higgins and R.M. Sorrentino (eds) *Handbook of Motivation and Cognition Vol. 2* (pp. 53–92), New York: Guilford Press.

—— (1993) 'Goal achievement: the role of intentions', in W. Stroebe and M. Hewstone (eds) *European Review of Social Psychology Vol. 4* (pp. 141–185), Chichester, Sussex: John Wiley & Sons.

—— (1996) 'The volitional benefits of planning', in P.M. Gollwitzer and J.A. Bargh (eds) *The Psychology of Action* (pp. 287–312), New York: Guilford Press.

Gollwitzer, P.M. and Bargh, J.A. (1996) *The Psychology of Action: Linking Cognition and Motivation to Behaviour*, New York: Guilford Press.

Gollwitzer, P.M. and Brandstätter, V. (in press) 'Implementation intentions and effective goal pursuit', *Journal of Personality and Social Psychology*.

Gollwitzer, P.M. and Kinney, R.A. (1989) 'Effects of deliberative and implemental mind-sets on the illusion of control', *Journal of Personality and Social Psychology* 56: 531–542.

Gollwitzer, P.M. and Kirchhof, O. (in press) 'The willful pursuit of identity', in J. Heckhausen and C.S. Dweck (eds) *Motivation and Self-regulation Across the Life-span*, New York: Cambridge University Press.

Gollwitzer, P.M. and Moskowitz, G.B. (1996) 'Goal effects on action and cognition', in E.T. Higgins and A.W. Kruglanski (eds) *Social Psychology: Handbook of Basic Principles* (pp. 361–399), New York: Guilford Press.

Gollwitzer, P.M., Heckhausen, H. and Ratajczak, H. (1990a) 'From weighing to willing: approaching a change decision through pre- or postdecisional mentation', *Organizational Behaviour and Human Decision Processes* 45: 41–65.

Gollwitzer, P.M., Heckhausen, H. and Steller, B. (1990b) 'Deliberative vs. implemental mind-sets: cognitive tuning toward congruous thoughts and information', *Journal of Personality and Social Psychology* 59: 1119–1127.

Halisch, F. and Kuhl, J. (1987) *Motivation, Intention and Action*, Berlin: Springer-Verlag.

Harlow, R.E. and Cantor, N. (1994) 'The social pursuit of academics: side-effects and "spillover" of strategic reassurance seeking', *Journal of Personality and Social Psychology* 66: 386–397.

Heckhausen, H. (1991) *Motivation and Action*, Heidelberg: Springer-Verlag.

Heckhausen, H. and Gollwitzer, P.M. (1987) 'Thought contents and cognitive functioning in motivational versus volitional states of mind', *Motivation and Emotion* 11: 101–120.

Higgins, E.T., Roney, C.J.R., Crowe, E. and Hymes, C. (1994) 'Ideal versus ought predilections for approach and avoidance: distinct self-regulatory systems', *Journal of Personality and Social Psychology* 66: 276–286.

James, W. (1890) *Principles of Psychology*, New York: Holt.

Jones, E.E. and Berglas, S. (1978) 'Control of attributions about the self through self-handicapping strategies: the appeal of alcohol and the role of underachievement', *Journal of Personality and Social Psychology* 4: 200–206.

Karniol, R. and Ross, M. (1996) 'The motivational impact of temporal focus: thinking about the future and the past', *Annual Review of Psychology* 47: 593–620.

Karoly, P. (1993) 'Mechanisms of self-regulation: a systems view', *Annual Review of Psychology* 44: 23–52.

Klinger, E. (1975) 'Consequences of commitment to and disengagement from incentives', *Psychological Research* 82: 1–25.

Kuhl, J. (1984) 'Volitional aspects of achievement motivation and learned helplessness: toward a comprehensive theory of action control', in B.A. Maher and W.A. Maher (eds) *Progress in Experimental Personality Research* (pp. 99–171), New York: Academic Press.

Kuhl, J. and Beckman, J. (1985) *Action Control: From Cognition to Behaviour*, New York: Springer-Verlag.

—— (1994) *Volition and Personality*, Göttingen: Hogrefe.

Latham, G.P. and Yukl, G.A. (1975) 'Assigned versus participative goal setting with educated and uneducated wood workers', *Journal of Applied Psychology* 60: 299–302.

Lewin, K. (1926) 'Vorsatz, Wille und Bedürfnis', *Psychologische Forschung* 7: 330–385.

Locke, E.A. and Latham, G.P. (1990) *A Theory of Goal Setting and Task Performance*, Englewood Cliffs, NJ: Prentice-Hall.

McClelland, D.C. (1951) *Personality*, New York: William Sloane Associates.

McDougall, W. (1931) *Social Psychology*, London: Methuen.

Miller, G.A., Galanter, E. and Pribram, K.H. (1960) *Plans and the Structure of Behaviour*, New York: Holt, Rinehart & Winston.

Nuttin, J. (1980) *Motivation, Planning, and Action*, Leuven, Belgium: Leuven University Press.

Oettingen, G. (1996) 'Positive fantasy and motivation', in P.M. Gollwitzer and J.A. Bargh (eds) *The Psychology of Action* (pp. 236–259), New York: Guilford Press.

Pervin, L.A. (1989) *Goal Concepts in Personality and Social Psychology*, Hillsdale, NJ: Erlbaum.

Powers, W.T. (1973) *Behaviour: The Control of Perception*, Chicago: Aldine.

Taylor, S.E. and Gollwitzer, P.M. (1995) 'Effects of mind-set on positive illusions', *Journal of Personality and Social Psychology* 69: 213–226.

Tolman, E.C. (1925) 'Purpose and cognition: the determinants of animal learning', *Psychological Review* 32: 285–297.

Weiner, B. (1972) *Theories of Motivation*, Chicago: Markham.

Wicklund, R.A. and Gollwitzer, P.M. (1982) *Symbolic Self-completion*, Hillsdale, NJ: Erlbaum.

15 Visual perception at the edge of the century

Géry d'Ydewalle[*]

Although studies on perception have always been an important area of research in psychology, its research prominence and focus have changed as a function of the history of psychology. The founders of our science were heavily involved in perception research, partly due to the heated debate concerning the necessity of distinguishing sensory and perceptual experiences. While some scholars (particularly Helmholtz 1867/1962) claimed that our perceptual experience is built or constructed from our sensations, others claimed that the distinction between sensation and perception is an artificial one and that we can only reach our sensory feelings through a process of abstraction. The debate emerged in all fields of perception but it was particularly evident when trying to explain visual depth perception. While Hering (1878/1964) advocated a direct fusion of the images from the two eyes into a single image which he calls the Cyclopean eye, Helmholtz defended the position that the two images are separately processed, and much later in the processing, there is a merging through higher-order 'unconscious inferences'.

The advent of behaviourism between the First and Second World Wars put perception research at rest in North America, with a few notable exceptions in the field of psychophysics (see Boring 1942). Gestalt psychology in Europe provided a wealth of new phenomena but the explanatory basis (in particular, the innateness and physiological basis of visual illusions) has since not been well accepted. The classic work of the Gestalt School on perceptual organization was restricted to demonstrations of a number of phenomena like figure–ground segregation and the role of different grouping principles or so-called Gestalt laws, without much concern for the underlying perceptual mechanisms (only referring quickly to a possible physiological basis) or for the functional role of these phenomena in the wider context of other kinds of processing taking place in the visual system. As to the sensation–perception discussion, Gestalt psychology strongly defended the abstract nature of the sensations, focusing research on the holistic nature of our perceptual experience: the perceptual experience is more than and different from the sum of all our sensations.

[*] I wish to acknowledge in the writing of this chapter the collaboration of Anja Daems, Peter De Graef, Paul van Diepen, Karl Verfaillie, Johan Wagemans and Martine Wampers.

The early stages of cognitive psychology in the 1950s, as, for example, the 'New-Look' psychology, gave perception research an additional new issue: the importance of top-down versus bottom-up processes. The new issue was somewhere related to the sensation–perception distinction: when one acknowledges the impact of higher-order cognitive processes, one implicitly accepts the distinction. Not surprisingly, the cognitive psychologists gave more importance to top-down processes. However, as with Gestalt psychology, cognitive psychologists largely restricted their research activities to demonstrations of top-down influences, without serious attempts to provide detailed scrutinies of the nature of the underlying processes.

Top-down approaches were then strongly qualified by Gibson's influence, leading to theories of direct perception; that is, perception without any inferential steps, intervening variables or associations. Perception was then a direct function of stimulation to be conceived as physical energy to which the sense organs respond. Gibson (1950) believed in 'invariance' of perception, whereby the environment provides an active organism with a continuous and stable flow of information.

Somewhere, perception psychology reached a point where no substantial theoretical progress could be expected. Several theories were advanced which tried to provide convincing and corroborating evidence for their viewpoint (top-down vs. bottom-up approaches; direct vs. indirect perception theories, etc.). However, more substantial progress was made in the research fields of memory and attention in the early 1960s, and this progress was made possible by the advent of the information-processing approach and the emergence of a new umbrella science, cognitive science. While the information-processing research focused heavily on unravelling underlying mental processes, the cognitive science approach, with its links to artificial intelligence, brought forward yet a further a new research issue, the nature of mental representations. It is partly with the background of these two developments (research on information processing and mental representations) that Marr's (1982) book on 'Vision' was so particularly welcome among psychologists working in the field of perception research. It is worthwhile noting that the subtitle of his book explicitly refers to the two issues of processing and representation: '*A Computational Investigation into the Human Representation and Processing of Visual Information*'.

To introduce Marr here in a nutshell is next to impossible. Suffice it to emphasize that raw sensory data are assumed to go through several successive levels of representations before reaching a fully-fledged three-dimensional representation of the outside world (raw primal sketch, full primal sketch, 2.5–D and 3–D representations), as subjectively experienced in our perception. To reach a particular level of representation, a variety of computational processes is assumed, and those processes have been the focus of much recent empirical research. Many details of Marr's analyses are now either changed, rejected or confirmed. What is more important for the psychology of perception is the influence of their programmatic nature: Marr's book launched a concerted effort and a renewed interest in the field, not only among psychologists but also (or rather primarily) among neuroscientists and computer vision people. We do believe that Marr's computational framework, with its emphasis on processing and several levels of representations, will continue to be very influential beyond the present century, and we will illustrate the scope of his influence in some current research interests at the Laboratory of Experimental Psychology in Leuven, Belgium.

As an example of recent work on perceptual organization with a strong computational flavour, consider the work on grouping by proximity in dot lattices. A dot lattice consists of a collection of dots that are regularly spaced at equal distances along two directions. Kubovy (1994) has classified dot lattices into six different categories depending on two parameters, the relative length of the vectors in the two directions and the angle separating them. In Kubovy and Wagemans (1995), sixteen different lattices, sampled uniformly from the space of all possible lattices, were presented briefly in random orientations. Observers were asked to indicate the orientation of the strips that they saw most clearly by clicking a mouse button on one of four fields corresponding to the four shortest vectors in the preceding stimulus pattern. In this way, Kubovy and Wagemans were able to calculate relative choice frequencies and to quantify the degree of perceptual ambiguity by means of the Shannon (1948) and Wiener (1948) measure of entropy. Furthermore, they were able to show that the strength of grouping by proximity diminishes as a decaying exponential function of distance. Additional analyses and new experiments revealed that grouping strength depends only on the distance between dots, not on the larger context of the whole lattice, despite the fact that lattices tend to look quite different based on their symmetries. This goes against the dominant belief in Gestalt psychology that the whole differs from the sum of the parts and that parts should behave differently when embedded in different wholes.

As another example, consider some recent research on the detection and use of symmetry. Although experimental work in the 1970s and 1980s was aimed at testing the effect of a large number of variables (such as orientation, eccentricity and density) on the visual system's sensitivity to global structure in patterns (see Wagemans 1995 for a review), this research tended to neglect the fact that bilateral mirror symmetries in planar patterns are only rarely viewed head-on: most often we look at such patterns from an oblique angle in such a way that our retinal images contain skewed symmetries. Skewing makes it harder to detect symmetry because certain properties are destroyed but skewing also introduces constraints on the possible three-dimensional orientation of the underlying plane. Skewing indeed disrupts the pre-attentive detectability of mirror symmetry in dot patterns (Wagemans *et al.* 1991, 1992, 1993). However, some conditions allow skewed symmetry to be perceived as perfect mirror symmetry at a specific orientation in depth (Wagemans 1992, 1993).

A major achievement of human vision is that we are able to recognize objects from many different angles surprisingly well, considering the large effects that viewpoint changes bring about in the actual patterns we have available on our retinas. One of the possible sources of information the visual system could use to solve this problem are those properties in the image that are perfectly or relatively stable under the set of transformations that occur as a result of viewpoint changes. Mathematically, it is well known what these invariant properties are for different sets of transformations (see Van Gool *et al.* 1994 for some background) and computer vision work has made much use of them in the last few years (e.g. Van Gool *et al.* 1995). One set of predictions derived from this mathematical approach is concerned with the minimal information that is needed to be able to compare two planar patterns under a restricted set of transformations. For example, for affine transformations (in which perspective compression is disregarded, as if patterns are viewed from a large distance) at least four points are required to determine shape equivalence. Human perceivers are indeed able to match simple planar patterns consisting of four dots, each under a set of affine transformations (Wagemans *et al.* 1994). Some specific findings were hard to understand from the assumption that observers compare patterns through a mental transformation process to undo the physical transformation. It is more likely that human perceivers rely on salient visual properties such as concavity/convexity and (quasi-)parallelism or (quasi-) collinearity when they are available (see Kukkonen *et al.* 1996). When these are not available, a slower and more laborious process must be used which probably relies on quantitative invariants (such as affine-invariant co-ordinates). Even when the performance levels themselves vary with the parameter values of the transformation, this need not imply that invariants are not used (see Wagemans *et al.* 1996).

Another example of recent work inspired by this mathematical framework is concerned with the distinction between perspective transformations and more general projective transformations. Mathematically, perspective transformations form a special subset within the group of projective transformations but they do not form a group, and therefore do not have their own invariants. In experiments comparing the perceptual effects of perspective versus projective transformations (Wagemans *et al.*, in press), human perceivers dealt almost as well with projective deformations as with perspective deformations. In a task with random distractors, projective transformations were identified almost as well as perspective transformations, and in a direct comparison task, perspectively related patterns were only slightly preferred over projectively related ones. Once more, this seems to support the importance of invariants compared to alternative information sources or perceptual strategies.

One major question which was put forward by Marr is how the visual system integrates several sources of information in order to achieve object perception. Information integration also forms the quintessence of another problem faced by the visual system: the retinal image of the outside world is continuously changing as a function of the movements of the eye, head and body. Indeed, about four times each second, a human observer makes a saccadic eye movement to bring new information in high-resolution central vision. At present, it is not clear how visual information is integrated across saccades. One technique used to investigate trans-saccadic integration changes the displayed stimulus during the observer's saccadic eye movement, so that the information available during the pre-saccadic fixation is different from the information in the post-saccadic fixation. Due to saccadic suppression (i.e. the intake of information being suppressed during saccades), detection that something has changed can only be based on the integration of pre-saccadic and post-saccadic information. Verfaillie *et al.* (Verfaillie, in press; Verfaillie *et al.* 1994) used this technique to examine trans-saccadic integration during the perception of biological motion. Although the available stimulus information in biological-motion perception is confined to a small number of lights attached to the joints of a moving actor, the human visual apparatus readily interprets the stimulus as a moving biological creature performing a particular action. Verfaillie focused on two issues concerning trans-saccadic integration. The first issue can be associated with the action component of a biological-motion stimulus (for example, the action of walking): does the visual system anticipate the future event-course across saccadic eye movements (see also Verfaillie and d'Ydewalle 1991)? The second topic is the nature of the object representation that is carried across saccades: what object attributes are transferred from one fixation to the next? Verfaillie *et al.* (1994) observed that intrasaccadic changes in the image-plane position of the biological-motion walker were hard to detect (see also Verfaillie, in press), whereas changes in the figure's in-depth orientation were readily noticed, indicating that the object representation that is transferred across saccades is relatively independent of the stimulus object's position, while it incorporates aspects of the object's orientation.

Verfaillie (1993) collected further converging behavioural evidence. In a serial two-choice reaction-time task, subjects had to discriminate between a point-light walker and a similar distracter. Reliable short-term priming effects were established in consecutive trials, but only when priming and primed walkers had the same in-depth orientation. On the other hand, the orientation-dependent priming effect was not tempered when priming and primed walkers differed on other characteristics (such as their position in the visual field). The findings support the hypothesis that recognition of a point-light walker is accomplished by accessing an orientation-dependent, but high-level (i.e. position-independent) object representation (Verfaillie 1992; Verfaillie and Boutsen 1995).

While Verfaillie's main work focused on the representational integration between two successive fixations, Van Diepen and Wampers carried out studies on the integration within a single fixation, particularly when viewing real-world situations, such as a kitchen or a playground. While viewing a scene, people mainly fixate information-rich areas, such as object locations. During a fixation the eyes do not move, and information is extracted from the fixated object. Fine details can only be rapidly processed by the central part of the retina (the fovea);

accordingly a fixation is used to register details allowing object identification. As the saccadic eye movements from one fixation to another are not programmed to random positions in the image but to areas of interest (objects), some processing of peripheral information necessarily occurs during the preceding fixation.

To study the perceptual processes during scene perception, new eye-contingent display change techniques were developed to manipulate the information available to the fovea while maintaining peripheral information, or vice versa (Van Diepen 1996; Van Diepen *et al.* 1994). In the so-called 'moving mask paradigm', foveal information is masked at a preset onset delay following the beginning of each fixation. The mask is removed again at the end of the fixation, to reappear at the new fixation position, again after the preset onset delay. By varying the mask onset delay, it can be estimated how long it takes to register foveal information. Van Diepen *et al.* (1995) applied the moving mask paradigm to scene perception and concluded that the initial 45 to 75 ms of a fixation were sufficient to register enough foveal information for object identification. These findings are in agreement with the results of a moving mask experiment in reading (Rayner *et al.* 1981). They found that during reading, foveal information can be acquired within the first 50 ms of a fixation.

Peripheral information extraction was studied using the 'moving window paradigm'. In this paradigm, a window containing unmanipulated image information is centred on the actual fixation position and moves in synchrony with the eyes. One can manipulate the information that is available outside the window (i.e. peripherally) to see what kind of information is used in peripheral vision. This question was investigated by Wampers *et al.* (1996). The unmanipulated image appeared within the window in all conditions. In the experimental conditions, either a lowpass or a highpass version of a scene was presented outside the window. The lowpass version preserved global form and luminance information but contained no detailed information; the highpass version maintained edge information at the expense of luminance information; and in the control condition, the unmanipulated image appeared outside the window. Subjects had to explore the scenes in the context of a search task. Contrary to expectations based on acuity limitations in the periphery of the human eye, a better performance in the highpass condition was obtained compared with the lowpass condition. The following explanation was provided. While detailed information cannot be processed in peripheral vision, the visual system can detect where detailed information can be found in the periphery. Since detailed information is mainly found at object locations, subjects can localize objects immediately in the highpass condition. This is not possible in the lowpass condition since only coarse information can be found in the entire periphery.

The time course of peripheral information extraction was investigated by varying the moment at which different kinds of peripheral information were made available during a fixation. Van Diepen and Wampers (1996) presented either a lowpass, a bandpass or a highpass version of a scene outside the fixation window during the first 100 ms of each fixation. After this period, the manipulated image was replaced by the normal image. In the control condition, the normal image appeared outside the window during the whole fixation. Within the fixation window, unmanipulated information was again presented in all three conditions. Performance did not differ between the experimental and control conditions suggesting that peripheral information is not processed during the first part of a fixation. In a similar experiment, the periphery changed after the first 100 ms of a fixation, while the unmanipulated image was presented during the initial part of the fixation. There was again no difference between the experimental conditions and the control condition. This is quite surprising, for one would expect that peripheral information is especially useful during the last part of a fixation when a saccade target has to be selected, but can be explained by a temporal integration of peripheral information throughout the fixation.

De Graef addressed the more general question of whether the perception of the scene indeed affects the recognition of the objects in the scene. For this purpose, De Graef developed a new research paradigm, involving the presentation of natural scenes in which selected target objects appear normally or in violation of their typical semantic or spatial relations to the rest of the scene. The scenes also included a variable number of non-objects, and subjects were instructed to explore the scene in order to count the number of non-objects. During the subject's search, fixation times are recorded for the target objects that are incidentally fixated. With this paradigm, De Graef *et al.* (1990, 1992) repeatedly demonstrated that contextually violated objects are fixated longer and/or more frequently, which suggests that they are harder to identify. Note that these effects are insensitive to full instruction about the nature of the contextual anomalies as well as to extensive training on the anomalous stimuli, indicating that there can be no simple explanation in terms of surprise (De Graef and Tant 1995).

Human observers frequently encounter other human beings who are engaged in many different actions which in turn consist of an even greater variety of body postures. Perceiving and identifying these actions and body postures is therefore a major task of the human visual system. This task is not straightforward, however. Depending on the orientation and position of the acting body towards the observer, different instances of a particular action or pose may produce very different retinal images, but nevertheless will have to receive identical labels. For example, the action commonly known as 'running' must be recognized as such, whether the orientation of the body is to the left, to the right, towards or away from the observer.

The problem the visual system faces here is of course similar to the orientation-invariance problem in object perception in general, but in the case of action or pose identification, it acquires an additional dimension. Due to their non-rigid nature, human bodies can have an infinity of possible three-dimensional representations that can all project on to many different two-dimensional retinal images. Categorizing a stimulus object as a human body requires abstraction of the body's two-dimensional projection and of the specific three-dimensional arrangement of the body parts. Identifying a body action or pose, on the other hand, also involves transcending the particular two-dimensional projection of the body pose, but does not necessitate abstracting away from the spatial relations between the parts. On the contrary, action or posture identification boils down to categorizing a particular three-dimensional representation of a human body as a specific pose or action phase. The question then becomes whether or not the representations, that are computed to match the stored models of body actions or poses for identification purposes, are orientation-dependent.

There is some neurophysiological (e.g. Perrett *et al.* 1989) and psychological evidence (e.g. Verfaillie 1993) suggesting that the representations which mediate the recognition of the human body are viewpoint-specific. The representations underlying action identification, however, have not yet received much attention. In a series of long-term priming experiments, Daems and Verfaillie (1996) addressed this issue. Priming refers to the observation that prior viewing of a stimulus facilitates later recognition. The effect can last over a relatively long period of time and presumably results from the persistent activation of the pre-semantic representations that mediate recognition. As such, characteristics of these representations are assumed to modify priming effects. Thus if the stored representations of human actions and body poses are orientation-dependent, priming effects should be orientation-dependent as well.

In the first experiment, subjects had to name various actions and poses that were shown in side views or straight-ahead views. Identification performance was better with same-view primes than with different-view primes. A second experiment investigated whether this result could be due to the fact that the two different views of a posture did not always share the same visible body parts. To minimize visibility differences, mirror images of the side views were used as primes in the different-view condition. Again, different-view (mirror-image) primes were less effective in increasing recognition performance than same-view primes. In a further experiment, a forced choice reaction time task was used instead of a naming task. Subjects had to distinguish normal human body poses from impossible poses as quickly as possible. For the normal poses, the viewpoint-dependent priming effect was replicated: reaction times were faster after a same-view than after a different-view prime. The different-view and the no-prime condition did not differ significantly, suggesting that mirror-image primes did not produce priming. Also, there was no priming in the case of the impossible poses, even when an identical same-view picture was used as prime. In conclusion, the findings suggest that the representations that are computed to match the stored models of actions and body postures are orientation-dependent.

The above research examples from the Leuven Laboratory of Experimental Psychology hopefully provide convincing materials to illustrate how the computational approach from Marr, or more generally the information processing paradigm, has the potential to enrich considerably research on perception. They also demonstrate how such a framework can integrate top-down and bottom-up processes, despite Marr's original emphasis on bottom-up mechanisms, leaving the cognitive processes for further investigation.

The recent advent of connectionism does not really change the picture. Connectionism gives only minor attention to visual perception, and as a whole discards top-down cognitive influences. There are of course some notable exceptions modelling top-down and bottom-up interactions, for example the interactive activation model. However, despite some initial (and convincing) successes in modelling psychological processes, we feel that connectionism is already out of the field of visual perception.

After such a history, in what direction is perception research likely to go in the next century? We believe that more attention will be given to unravelling the power of human visual perception by analysing more complex visual events, moving from psychophysical studies on simple visual patterns to fully-fledged capturing of important visual events. Based on the former work within the information-processing paradigm, scrutinizing the basic processes will push the field well beyond the more illustrative studies of Gestalt psychology, cognitive psychology or a Gibsonian direct approach.

REFERENCES

Boring, E.G. (1942) *Sensation and Perception in the History of Experimental Psychology*, New York: Appleton Century Crofts.

Daems, A. and Verfaillie, K. (1996) 'Viewpoint-dependent priming effects in the perception of human actions and body postures', *Psychological Reports No. 192*, Leuven: Katholieke Universiteit Leuven, Laboratory of Experimental Psychology.

De Graef, P. and Tant, M. (1995) 'Attentional distribution and context effects in the perception of everyday scenes', Eighth European Conference on Eye Movements, Derby, UK.

De Graef, P., Christiaens, D. and d'Ydewalle, G. (1990) 'Perceptual effects of scene context on object identification', *Psychological Research* 52: 317–329.

De Graef, P., De Troy, A. and d'Ydewalle, G. (1992) 'Local and global contextual constraints on the identification of objects in scenes', *Canadian Journal of Psychology* 46: 490–509.

Gibson, J.J. (1950) *The Perception of the Visual World*, Boston, MA: Houghton Mifflin.

Helmholtz, H.L.F. von (1867/1962) *Handbook of Physiological Optics*, New York: Dover.

Hering, E. (1878/1964) *Outline of a Theory of the Light Sense*, Cambridge, MA: Harvard University Press.

Kubovy, M. (1994) 'The perceptual organisation of dot lattices', *Psychonomic Bulletin and Review* 1: 182–190.

Kubovy, M. and Wagemans, J. (1995) 'Grouping by proximity and multistability in dot lattices: a quantitative Gestalt theory', *Psychological Science* 6: 225–234.

Kukkonen, H.T., Foster, D.H., Wood, J.R., Wagemans, J. and Van Gool, L. (1996) 'Qualitative cues in the discrimination of affine-transformed minimal patterns', *Perception* 25: 195–206.

Marr, D. (1982) *Vision: A Computational Investigation into the Human Representation and Processing of Visual Information*, San Francisco, CA: Freeman.

Perrett, D.I., Harries, M.H., Bevan, R., Thomas, S., Benson, P.J., Mistlin, A.J., Chitty, A.J., Hietanen, J.K. and Ortega, J.E. (1989) 'Frameworks of analysis for the neural representation of animate objects and actions', *Journal of Experimental Biology* 146: 87–113.

Rayner, K., Inhoff, A.W., Morrison, R.E., Slowiaczek, M.L. and Bertera, J.H. (1981) 'Masking of foveal and parafoveal vision during eye fixations in reading', *Journal of Experimental Psychology: Human Perception and Performance* 7: 167–179.

Van Diepen, P.M.J. (1996) 'A Pixel-resolution video switcher for eye contingent display changes', *Psychological Reports No. 198*, Leuven: Katholieke Universiteit Leuven, Laboratory of Experimental Psychology.

Van Diepen, P.M.J. and Wampers, M. (1996) 'Scene exploration with Fourier filtered peripheral information', submitted for publication.

Van Diepen, P.M.J., De Graef, P. and d'Ydewalle, G. (1995) 'Chronometry of foveal information extraction during scene perception', in J. M. Findlay, R. W. Kentridge and R. Walker (eds) *Eye movement Research: Mechanisms, Processes and Applications* (pp. 349–362), Amsterdam: Elsevier.

Van Diepen, P.M.J., De Graef, P. and Van Rensbergen, J. (1994) 'On-line control of moving masks and windows on a complex background using the ATVista Videographics Adapter', *Behavior Research Methods, Instruments, and Computers* 26: 454–460.

Van Gool, L., Moons, T., Pauwels, E. and Oosterlinck, A. (1995) 'Vision and Lie's approach to invariance', *Image and Vision Computing* 13: 259–277.

Van Gool, L., Moons, T., Pauwels, E. and Wagemans, J. (1994) 'Invariance from the Euclidean geometer's perspective', *Perception* 23: 547–561.

Verfaillie, K. (1992) 'Variant points of view on viewpoint invariance', *Canadian Journal of Psychology* 46: 215–235.

—— (1993) 'Orientation-dependent priming effects in the perception of biological motion', *Journal of Experimental Psychology: Human Perception and Performance* 19: 992–1013.

—— 'Transsaccadic memory for the egocentric and allocentric position of a biological-motion walker', *Journal of Experimental Psychology: Learning, Memory, and Cognition*, in press.

Verfaillie, K. and Boutsen, L. (1995) 'A corpus of 714 full-color images of depth-rotated objects', *Perception and Psychophysics* 57: 925–961.

Verfaillie, K. and d'Ydewalle, G. (1991) 'Representational momentum and event course anticipation in the perception of implied periodical motions', *Journal of Experimental Psychology: Learning, Memory, and Cognition* 17: 302–313.

Verfaillie, K., De Troy, A. and Van Rensbergen, J. (1994) 'Transsaccadic integration of biological motion', *Journal of Experimental Psychology: Learning, Memory, and Cognition* 20: 649–670.

Wagemans, J. (1992) 'Perceptual use of nonaccidental properties', *Canadian Journal of Psychology* 46: 236–279.

—— (1993) 'Skewed symmetry: A nonaccidental property used to perceive visual forms', *Journal of Experimental Psychology: Human Perception and Performance* 19: 364–380.

—— (1995) 'Detection of visual symmetries', *Spatial Vision* 9: 9–32.

Wagemans, J., Lamote, C. and Van Gool, L. 'Shape equivalence under perspective and projective transformations', *Psychonomic Bulletin and Review*, in press.

Wagemans, J., Van Gool, L. and d'Ydewalle, G. (1991) 'Detection of symmetry in tachistoscopically presented dot patterns: effects of multiple axes and skewing', *Perception and Psychophysics* 50: 413–427.

—— (1992) 'Orientational effects and component processes in symmetry detection', *Quarterly Journal of Experimental Psychology* 44A: 475–508.

Wagemans, J., Van Gool, L. and Lamote, C. (1996) 'The visual system's measurement of invariants need not itself be invariant', *Psychological Science* 7: 232–236.

Wagemans, J., Van Gool, L., Swinnen, V. and Van Horebeek, J. (1993) 'Higher-order structure in regularity detection', *Vision Research* 33: 1067–1088.

Wagemans, J., De Troy, A., Van Gool, L., Foster, D.H. and Wood, J.R. (1994) 'Minimal information to determine affine shape equivalence', *Psychological Reports No. 169*, Leuven: Katholieke Universiteit Leuven, Laboratory of Experimental Psychology.

Wampers, M., Van Diepen, P.M.J. and d'Ydewalle, G. (1996) 'The use of coarse and fine peripheral information during scene perception', submitted for publication.

16 On the edge of consciousness

Pre-attentive mechanisms in the generation of anxiety

Arne Öhman

INTRODUCTION: CONSCIOUSNESS AND ATTENTION

The James legacy

Close to the last turn of a century, William James (1890/1950) suggested that 'my experience is what I agree to attend to' (p. 402). His treatment of attention therefore linked it closely to consciousness. In his view, attention was 'the taking possession by the mind, in clear and vivid form, of one out of what seem several simultaneously possible objects or trains of thought. Focalization, concentration, of consciousness are of its essence. It implies withdrawal from some things in order to deal effectively with others' (pp. 403–404).

The behaviourist revolution put attention (now understood as 'stimulus control') far down on the list of psychological research priorities, where it rested inconspicuously for the first half of the twentieth century. However, almost exactly at mid-century, it was brought back to the agenda of experimental psychology, primarily by British investigators (e.g. Cherry 1953; Broadbent 1958). The following decades have witnessed an enormously expanded volume of research on attention in neuroscience (e.g. Näätänen 1992), in cognitive psychology (e.g. Parasuraman and Davies 1984), and, more recently, in clinical psychology (Wells and Matthews 1994).

Nevertheless, some observers have questioned whether the quantitative expansion corresponds to qualitative improvements in understanding. Writing for a volume of the *Annual Review of Psychology* dated close to a century after James' book, Johnston and Dark (1986) described how their bewilderment increased, sometimes to the level of 'despair and panic', the more they read of the contemporary literature on attention, and how they, in such moments, had to turn to William James for new hope and inspiration. In concluding their chapter, they questioned whether the psychology of attention had made any significant progress beyond the milestone provided by James.

I think that this conclusion is overly pessimistic. One reason for the (arguably) limited growth in the understanding of attentional processes during this century may be that psychologists have taken an unnecessarily limited view of this topic. Attention has been viewed as a distinct process of its own, as a cold, rational process where computer analogues have loomed large when it comes to theoretical analyses. With regard to empirical studies, attentional phenomena have been examined in relation to arbitrary stimuli in arbitrary tasks, with few explicit considerations of ecological validity. For example, because isolated words are easy to work with, they have provided the dominating material for research on attention even though they are a very special class of stimuli in a broader biological perspective. In contrast, this chapter has as one of its primary points of departure what Lang *et al.* (1997) called 'natural selective attention'; that is, attention to stimuli that may have been recurrently encountered by our distant forefathers as they foraged Pleistocene savannas in small groups of genetically related individuals.

As with many other psychologists, those investigating attention have typically adhered to what has become known as the 'Standard Social Science Model' (Pinker 1994; Tooby and Cosmides 1992). According to this model, a fundamental task of psychology is to understand the general mechanisms by which the impact of culture on individuals is mediated. As culture is given a primary role, and biology is seen as secondary, studying arbitrary stimuli in arbitrary situations has been taken to guarantee the generation of general empirical laws whose validity is unconstrained by the specifics of the actual experimental set up (cf. Seligman 1970).

The empiricist view of psychology promoted by the Standard Social Science Model has recently been challenged by a nativist perspective anchored in evolutionary biology, which argues that psychological mechanisms have been structured into domain-specific modules by evolutionary history (Tooby and Cosmides 1992). Language provides one of the best examples: there are innate language-specific mechanisms in the human brain that structure all human language to show universal similarities (Pinker 1994). Other examples include early parent–child interaction (e.g. Bowlby 1969), partner selection (e.g. Buss and Schmitt 1993) and human fears and phobias (e.g. Öhman *et al.* 1985). Viewed in this broader evolutionary perspective, attentional phenomena are seen as the effect of functional behaviour systems that have evolved as solutions to specific adaptive problems. In particular, natural selective attention results from the need to prioritize specific inputs when faced with challenges that may promote or threaten the transport of genes between generations.

The spotlight metaphor

Conscious attention is often represented as a focused spotlight that brightly illuminates a limited, specific part of the environment, or recalls an item from memory. This is an appealing metaphor that brings to mind images of light beams searching through empty dark space like Second World War air-defence spotlights trying to locate hostile bombers in the sky. Viewed in this way, however, the metaphor is apt to become misleading. The conditions of the psychological laboratory may indeed be arranged to provide as empty a background as the peaceful night sky for the objects to which the research participants are expected to attend, but in the natural environment organisms do not operate under the assumption that what is outside the attentional spotlight is just empty homogenous space. Rather, the typical situation is more like using a focused flashlight in a familiar but dark room. We know at least implicitly which the non-illuminated objects are and where they are located, and we may even be able to find our way around the room unassisted by the light. Furthermore, when the flashlight happens to move across an important object so that a glimpse of it becomes briefly visible at the edge of the beam, this may be sufficient for its identification. The familiarity of the environment outside the attentional beam is of critical importance when attention is shifted from one aspect of the environment to another. Because the spotlight is moved to a familiar object, the perceptual apparatus can be primed to receive a particular pattern of stimulation, which then greatly facilitates its identification even if it has to be based on a very brief glimpse. In some respects, the situation is illustrated by the phenomenon of 'blind-sight' (Weiscrantz 1986): people with damage to the visual cortex effectively lack an attentional spotlight because they are unable consciously to perceive shapes and patterns. Yet they are able to perceive some aspects of objects such as their movement in space.

From this perspective, the attentional spotlight would not be expected to dance capriciously around among objects in a personally determined dark space, but the dance would be structured in systematic patterns of movements depending on the current concerns of the person. But then, to paraphrase Yates, if attention is the dance, who is the dancer, and how can we tell the dancer from the dance? I shall argue that it is emotion that is the dancer. What I am essentially proposing is an effect theory of attention (cf. Johnston and Dark 1986: 68–70), where attention is controlled by currently activated emotional systems. The emotions that I shall be dealing with, furthermore, are assumed to be functionally shaped by evolution.

ATTENTION AND EMOTION

A functional perspective on emotion

Essentially, emotions can be understood as action sets (Lang 1984), as preparations to act in one way rather than another. A fundamental dimension is that of approach/avoidance, ranging from a readiness to stay in the situation and engage in its potentialities to abandoning it because of the threats and dangers it implies (Lang *et al.* 1990). An important point with emotions is that they allow for flexibility in the interaction between organism and environment. In effect, a primary function of emotion has been described as the decoupling of stimuli and responses (Scherer 1994). Rather than the rigid stimulus–response relationship of signal stimuli and fixed action patterns, emotions in many contexts allow flexible use of environmental support to achieve desired outcomes. For example, children, who because of emotional distress need the safe base offered by their parents, can approach them by their own locomotion, whether by crawling, walking or running, or by vocal gestures that propel the parent to come rushing in to provide support and comfort. Viewed in this perspective, emotions become means to regulate behaviour in relation to agendas set by biological evolution. Thus, the critical tasks that had to be mastered by our distant forefathers who eventually delivered genes to the next generation are embedded in emotion. They include, for example, finding and consuming food and drink, finding shelter, seeking protection and support from conspecifics, asserting oneself among conspecifics and getting their attention, satisfying curiosity, getting access to, and engaging with, sexual partners, and avoiding and escaping life-threatening events. These are all activities that are structured by emotions. In a biological perspective, therefore, emotions can be understood as a clever means shaped by evolution to make us want to do what our ancestors had to do successfully to pass genes on to future generations (e.g. Öhman 1996).

Viewed in this functional perspective, the emphasis in the psychology of emotion is shifted from the unique phenomenology of human feeling to action tendencies and response patterns that we share with more or less distant relatives in the animal world. Thus, rather than conceptualizing emotion as a central feeling state more or less imperfectly mirrored in verbal reports, physiological responses and expressive behaviour, the evolutionary perspective views emotion as complex responses that include several partly independent components (see Öhman and Birbaumer 1993, for a more thorough discussion of some key conceptual issues in the study of emotion). The psychological phenomena that we dub 'emotional' occur in situations that are significant to the person, either for phylogenetic or ontogenetic reasons. They are related to verbal responses implying affective appraisal and evaluation of the situation. At the behavioural level, emotional phenomena are manifested, for example, as approach or avoidance tendencies (e.g. Lang *et al.* 1990) or non-instrumental (i.e. 'overflow') characteristics of behaviour (Frijda 1986). Finally, because emotions recruit often vigorous action tendencies, they are associated with behavioural energetics and arousal processes, which become accessible for scientific study through psychophysiological measures, such as electrodermal activity and heart rate. In this perspective, the verbal, behavioural and physiological components of emotions should not be understood as alternative avenues to unitary internal states presumably isomorphic with phenomenological experience, but as loosely coupled and dissociable components of a complex emotional response (Lang 1993).

The signal function of emotion

Even though the functional focus of this evolutionary perspective on emotion is on the organization of action, emotions have pervasive effects on all types of psychological processes, from perception to cognition, to motivation, to learning, and so on. Indeed, the function of an emotion has to extend from systems for parsing the environment to flexible action patterns if it is to promote stable behavioural strategies which will eventually be favourably evaluated by natural selection. Successful strategies not only imply efficient action but also the ability to receive critical information from the environment. To guarantee this, emotion governs attention. Indeed, many theorists agree that emotions have important 'signal functions' that prompt the organism to focus attention on particular aspects of the surroundings (e.g. Folkman *et al.* 1979; Hamburg *et al.* 1975; Izard 1979, 1991). For example, as stated by Izard (1979), 'a particular emotion sensitizes the organism to particular features of its environment . . . [and] . . . ensures a readiness to respond to events of significance to the organism's survival and adaptation' (p. 163). This sensitization function is coupled to a powerful disrupt-and-reset function, the emotional counterpart of which is surprise (Izard 1991) and the purpose of which is to redirect the activity of the organism towards the encountered significant stimulus.

In many respects these functions of emotion are similar to those ascribed to the orienting reflex (Öhman 1987; Sokolov 1963). Through the automatic capture of attention by stimuli that are significant to the organism, processing of the stimulus is shifted from an automatic, parallel stimulus–analysis mechanism, to the capacity-limited, serial, and effortfully controlled processing that is often associated with consciousness (Öhman 1979, 1987).

The signal function of emotion implies that we attend to different aspects of the environment when in different emotional states. When in euphoric mood, we may concentrate attentional resources on cues signalling success at the risk of missing task-relevant signals that call for a change in the course of action in order to avoid disaster. When in separation distress, the child's attention may be concentrated on a sound implying that the missing parent is at the door, and when plagued by fear and anxiety, attention becomes biased to focus on threats in the surrounding world (Mathews 1990; Öhman 1993).

Following the peculiar habit of psychologists to devote their interest to the dark rather than the bright side of life, I shall now proceed to review research from my own laboratory and those of other investigators that contributes to the understanding of the emotion-attention dance in the specific emotional context of fear and anxiety. This is a step that does not lack precedence in our discipline. On the contrary, many investigators in the fields of emotion start out by boldly talking about emotion in general, only later to inconspicuously retreat to a specific emotion such as fear. Such a retreat, however, should primarily be understood as tactical. A relatively well-defined phenomenon such as fear is more likely to yield to an empirical analysis than is the often vague empirical connotation of more inclusive but less well-defined constructs such as emotion. If we are successful in this more specific context, we may then have developed tools for a more effective pursuit of the overall strategy: to conquer the citadel of emotion (see LeDoux 1994 and Öhman 1994, for further discussion of this issue).

Fear, anxiety and attention

Fear is a specific emotion that is central to several important evolutionary-derived behavioural systems. Öhman *et al.* (1985) analysed fear within two such systems, a predatory defence system and a social submissiveness system. Thus, in this perspective, fear operates to bring organisms away from predators and to promote yielding in the face of dominant conspecifics. One can argue that these two types of fear have important differences (Öhman 1986), but they also have a common core. Fear can be understood as a negative or aversive, highly activated emotional state, which prompts avoidance of, and escape from, situations that threaten the survival or well-being of organisms. To achieve the evolution-selected outcome, avoidance, the organism must have perceptual systems that are able to locate stimuli related to threat wherever they occur in the perceptual field. Clearly, there is a premium on speed: fast identification of threat allows early activation of defences, which may put the potential victim out of reach of the striking predator or the moody authority figure before any damage can happen. Defined in this way, fear is an emotion associated with active and potentially successful coping with threats. When coping efforts fail, escape is thwarted, and the organism is left in a situation of uncertain uncontrollability, fear is replaced by anxiety (Epstein 1972). Thus, fear and anxiety are viewed as of common evolutionary descent which gives them a common core, but they also differ profoundly with respect to behavioural outlets: for anxiety there is none that is effective, but for fear a potentially successful coping option is available.

The evolutionary perspective implies that stimuli which have been associated with threat throughout mammalian evolution should be easily connected to fear and anxiety and that, as emotion-provoking, they should be effective and automatic attention-catchers. The analyses presented by Öhman *et al.* (1985) suggest that evolutionary fear-relevant stimuli are likely to be found among threatening beasts and men. Specifically, we shall concentrate on what may be termed the prototypes of animal fears, snakes and spiders (Öhman 1986; Öhman *et al.* 1985), and on equally prototypical facial gestures conveying anger and dominance (Dimberg and Öhman 1996; Öhman and Dimberg 1984). The first hypothesis to be examined, therefore, is straightforward: evolutionary relevant threat stimuli should be very effective in capturing attention. A subsidiary hypothesis is that this process of attention-capturing should be automatic in the sense that it does not require extensive intentional cognitive processing.

TESTING THE HYPOTHESIS WITH FACIAL THREAT STIMULI

The face-in-the-crowd effect

In an innovative study, Hansen and Hansen (1988) exposed subjects to complex matrices of visual stimuli with the task of pressing different buttons depending on whether all stimuli in a matrix were similar, or whether it included a deviant stimulus. In support of the evolutionarily derived hypothesis, they reported that subjects were faster to locate a deviant angry face in a background crowd of happy faces than vice versa. This 'anger superiority effect', furthermore, was reported to be unaffected by the size of the background crowd, which was taken as support for attributing it to an automatic 'pop-out' effect of pre-attentive origin. In other words, this implies that the effect had its origin at the edge of conscious attention. In line with the previously developed argument, Hansen and Hansen (1988) proposed that angry faces were located by parallel processing mechanisms that automatically picked out the target, whereas the location of happy faces required a post-attentive serial search. In agreement with the evolutionary scenario, this interpretation suggested that evolutionarily significant threat stimuli were automatically located in a complex visual display by the observer.

However, there are several problems with this interpretation. First, in the initial experiment reported by Hansen and Hansen (1988), error rates were exceedingly high, which implies that the reported RTs were based on very few trials. Second, an error of experimental design confounded the report of the pop-out effect. In this experiment, only one angry and one happy face was used, and the angry face had a characteristic shadow, which appears to account for the pop-out effect (Purcell *et al.* 1993). Finally, subjects were quicker at deciding that a deviant target was *not* present in a matrix of happy than in a matrix of angry faces. Consistent with other data (e.g. Kirouac and Doré 1984), this finding suggests that the angry faces were harder to process than the happy ones, perhaps because happy faces are much more prevalent in the environment of the typical subject population for this type of experiment, namely college students (Bond and Siddle 1996). Later reports that response latencies to angry targets were affected by location of the target in the matrix (Hampton *et al.* 1989) rather suggest that sequential search strategies were also used in the search for angry targets. Consequently, the shorter latency for angry targets in happy crowds in fact could be attributed to more efficient processing of the background happy faces, i.e. to post-attentive rather than pre-attentive mechanisms (Hansen and Hansen 1994). Thus, the original Hansen and Hansen (1988) data cannot be invoked as support for automatic selection of threatening stimuli.

Revisiting the face-in-the-crowd effect: schematic stimuli

The original Hansen and Hansen (1988) data are clearly important and interesting and they are worth pursuing further. In my laboratory, we have performed a series of studies aimed at a further elucidation of the face-in-the-crowd effect. A strategical first choice in this research was to use schematic rather than real faces. Real faces are complicated to use because they do not allow direct control of their physical features. For example, angry faces are more similar to neutral control faces than are happy faces, which may explain why happy faces are often more quickly found among neutral ones than are angry faces (e.g. Byrne and Eysenck 1995). With schematic faces, on the other hand, threatening and non-threatening faces can be constructed so that their physical difference from a neutral face is identical. By using schematic faces, furthermore, we should be able to determine more exactly which facial features are critical for a potential angry superiority effect.

As a methodological avenue to delineate the critical feature of threatening symbolic faces, Aronoff *et al.* (1988) collected threatening masks from a wide assortment of cultures and defined features that were common to most of them. Such features included static aspects of faces such as pointed ears, and dynamic features such as frowning eyebrows. Many of the features isolated as dynamic characteristics of facial threat by Aronoff *et al.* (1988) conformed to findings reported from studies of schematic faces by McKelvie (1973). Specifically, his data indicated that frowning eyebrows were critical for negative evaluation of faces and for perception of anger in a face. Based on these findings we constructed facial stimuli in which several features such as eyebrows, mouths, eyes and cheek-bones could be independently manipulated. In a series of rating studies we found that these features appeared to be hierarchically structured in an affective space defined by the semantic differential dimensions of evaluation, activity and potency. First, frowning eyebrows made faces cluster within an area of affective space that could be characterized as negatively evaluated, potent and highly activated, whereas faces with the opposite eyebrow (i.e. raised in the middle) were clustered in a positively evaluated area of the affective space. These clusters were divided into subclusters by the mouth (happy or sad), and these subclusters, in turn, were further split depending on the shape of the eye, and so on.

On the basis of these findings, we selected threatening, non-threatening and neutral faces for use in the type of visual search paradigm developed by Hansen and Hansen (1988). In the first experiment we exposed subjects to 3×3 matrices of schematic faces of which half showed identical facial expressions (neutral, threatening (angry) or non-threatening (happy)). In the remaining half of the trials, one of the nine faces showed a deviant expression: angry against a neutral background, happy against a neutral background, angry against a happy background, happy against an angry background, and neutral against any of the expressive backgrounds. The deviant stimulus occurred equally often at all positions in the matrix. Exposure times were for 1 or 2 seconds. The subjects pressed one button if all faces were the same and another one if there was a deviant stimulus in the matrix.

The results showed a powerful overall effect of threat in the detection time for deviant stimuli. Regardless of background condition, detection was faster for threatening (angry) than for non-threatening (happy) stimuli. However, finding a neutral face among angry or happy faces was still faster, because of the distinct physical difference between targets and distractors in this condition. The background condition interacted with exposure time. With a neutral background, detection of the threatening face was faster both with 1- and 2-second exposures.

With the opposite expression background (non-threatening with a threatening deviant; threatening with a non-threatening deviant), however, the faster detection of threatening faces was evident only at the longer interval. Similar to the fast detection of neutral deviants against backgrounds of angry or happy faces, this implies that the difficulty of the perceptual discrimination was important. When it was easy, i.e. when the background had horizontal features and the targets diagonal ones, a 1-second exposure was sufficient to get the anger superiority effect. However, when the perceptual discrimination was difficult, i.e. both background and targets had diagonal lines, 2 seconds were needed for the anger superiority effect to emerge.

There was no difference in latency to decide that a deviant stimulus was *not* present in matrices of threatening and non-threatening faces, which both took significantly longer than matrices of neutral stimuli. Error rates were low and tended to be lower for threatening than for non-threatening deviants.

In a second experiment, we varied the size of the matrix, from 2×2 to 5×5 pictures. The task of the subjects was to look for deviant threatening and non-threatening stimuli against backgrounds of neutral stimuli. Thus, in this experiment the conditions were arranged for *consistent mapping* of target and distractors. That is to say, targets never occurred as distractors and vice versa. According to Shiffrin and Schneider (1977), this arrangement facilitates automatic detection of the targets. The results showed a strong effect of target size on the latency to decide that no deviant stimulus was present, which implies that the subjects searched sequentially through the matrix before they finally decided that no target was present. However, both for the threatening and the non-threatening targets there was hardly any effect of target size up to the 4×4 matrix, and then a slowing at the 5×5 matrix. As the overall size of the matrix was not controlled, the latter result may depend on the need to move the eyes in order to scan the whole matrix in the 5×5 condition. Again, however, detections were significantly faster for threatening than for non-threatening targets. These results imply that the apparent pop-out effect in identifying the targets was due to the physical difference between targets and distractors, i.e. where only the target involved diagonal and curved lines. In spite of this joint basis for a pop-out effect, however, the subjects nevertheless were faster with threatening than non-threatening facial displays.

These results show quite clearly that a threatening facial display is more rapidly detected against a background crowd of faces than are non-threatening displays. None of the confounding factors that becloud interpretation of the original Hansen and Hansen findings were present in this study. Error rates were low, there was no confounding factor favouring the threat condition, and subjects were as fast to detect that a deviant stimulus was not present in a matrix of threatening faces as in matrices of non-threatening faces. Thus these results provide support for the hypothesis that humans in general are particularly effective in discovering threatening stimuli in their surroundings.

Facial threat and anxiety

One may wonder whether emotion is critical to the effects reported with our schematic facial stimuli. The happy and angry faces were physically very similar, as both had diagonal lines for eyebrows and curved lines for mouths, and the eyes were simply inverted from one expression to the other. This made both expressions differ to the same degree from neutral faces. Nevertheless, the subjects were consistently faster in finding the angry face in the crowd, even though we know nothing about whether they actually responded emotionally to the expressions. One way to clarify this finding would be to use a subject population likely to respond emotionally to the threatening stimulus and then see whether they would be faster than normal in finding a deviant threatening face. Such an experiment still remains to be done in our laboratory, but there are recent data available from other investigators, starting from the premise that anxiety is associated with a generalized bias to focus attention on threatening words (e.g. MacLeod 1991; Mathews 1990).

Byrne and Eysenck (1995) have examined detection latencies for real angry and happy faces against a background of neutral faces or faces of the opposite expression. Highly anxious subjects were faster than subjects low in anxiety to find angry faces against a background of neutral faces, whereas the two groups did not differ in latency to find happy faces against a neutral background. When the background consisted of angry faces, anxious subjects were slower to find happy faces than were non-anxious subjects, suggesting a powerful distracting effect from angry background faces. These findings suggest that high anxiety enhances the normal bias to be faster with threatening than non-threatening stimuli.

Bradley and Mogg (1996) used normal controls and individuals diagnosed with generalized anxiety disorder or depression as subjects in an attentional experiment using faces as stimuli. A trial started with a 1-second exposure of two faces with different emotional expressions side by side on a screen. Facial expressions included threat, sadness and happiness, as well as a neutral control expression. When the faces disappeared, a probe stimulus emerged, centred at the point where one of the faces had been. The probe occurred equally often after either face and the subjects were required to press a different response key depending on the side of the screen on which the probe was presented. In addition to probe reaction times, eye-movements were measured to determine at which of the two pictures the subjects looked, and with what latency. The results showed a bias of the generalized anxiety disorder patients to look at angry faces, with reliably shorter latencies than for other expressions. Thus, again, these results show that threatening facial stimuli are effective attention-catchers, particularly for persons with anxiety disorder. From these data, it appears that the readiness to respond to threatening cues implied by high anxiety facilitated attention to the threatening faces. Emotion, therefore, appears to drive attention.

FURTHER TESTS WITH THREATENING ANIMAL STIMULI

The snake-in-the-grass effect

The results reviewed in the previous section show quite clearly that facial stimuli implying threat are more effective than non-threatening stimuli in capturing the attention both of normal and anxious subjects. This provides good support for the evolutionary hypothesis suggesting that fear stimuli which have followed humans through their evolution should automatically capture attention. One interesting question raised by these findings is whether similar results would be observed with other classes of evolutionarily fear-relevant stimuli such as pictures of snakes and spiders. Such studies have been performed in my laboratory (Öhman *et al.* 1997).

Subjects were exposed to matrices of pictures of either snakes, spiders, flowers or mushrooms, where in half of the cases all stimuli in the matrix were of the same category, whereas the other half had a stimulus from a deviant category. The subjects were quicker to find a deviant snake or spider among flowers and mushrooms than vice versa. This increase in speed of detection was not accompanied by more errors. On the contrary, there were fewer errors in detecting fear-relevant than fear-irrelevant deviant stimuli. Response latencies were shortest for deviant snakes among background flowers and then for spiders among mushrooms. The longest latencies were found for deviant mushrooms among background snakes, and flowers among spiders. This distribution of detection latencies appears to make ecological sense.

The time to identify a deviant stimulus was generally longer for a large (3×3) than for a small (2×2) matrix, but this effect was, as indicated by a reliable interaction between fear relevance and size of matrix, more obvious when the subject's task was to locate a fear-irrelevant than a fear-relevant target. In fact, separate tests showed a reliable size-of-matrix effect only for fear-irrelevant targets. This failure of matrix size reliably to affect the detection of deviant fear-relevant stimuli among fear-irrelevant background stimuli suggests that attention was automatically drawn to deviant snakes and spiders whereas a more sequential search strategy was used to locate deviant flowers and mushrooms. Thus, these results indicate that fear-relevant stimuli were picked up independently of their position in the perceptual field in a process reminiscent of a pop-out effect of pre-attentive origin.

As with the visual search studies using schematic faces as stimuli, these data cannot be accounted for in terms of the confounding factors plaguing interpretation of the original Hansen and Hansen (1988) studies (see Hansen and Hansen 1994). Because we used categories of stimuli rather than single exemplars for each fear-relevance condition, it is very unlikely that some common confounding factor for all animal stimuli could account for finding shorter latencies to them. Indeed, with our design, one cannot but wonder what stimulus features were used by the visual system to quickly extract that a critical stimulus was present in the display. Second, latencies to decide that a critical stimulus was not present were shorter for the fear-relevant than the fear-irrelevant categories which precludes appeal to faster recognition of the fear-irrelevant stimulus as a basis for the shorter detection latency of deviant fear-relevant stimuli (cf. Hampton *et al.* 1989).

Snakes-in-the-grass: fearful subjects

A similar question to that with regard to the facial stimuli could be raised in the context of biologically fear-relevant animal stimuli: Would subjects fearful of snakes or spiders show a more pronounced bias than non-fearful subjects in detecting such stimuli?

Specific fear questionnaires were administered to a large group of students (of medicine, physical therapy, or optics) and those scoring above the ninetieth percentile in snake fear and below the fiftieth percentile in spider fear, or vice versa, were invited to participate in an experiment. A non-fearful control group, scoring below the fiftieth percentile in both types of fear, was also recruited. These subjects were exposed to the previously described procedure for the second experiment. That is to say, they had 2×2 and 3×3 matrices, half of which had only pictures of flowers, mushrooms, snakes or spiders. The remaining half of the matrices had one picture from a deviant category, i.e. snakes or spiders among flowers or mushrooms, or flowers or mushrooms among snakes or spiders.

The results replicated earlier findings in showing overall shorter reaction times to identify deviant snakes or spiders among flowers or mushrooms than vice versa. Similar to the previous experiments, matrix size had a clear effect on fear-irrelevant stimuli, whereas latencies were as fast with the 2×2 as with the 3×3 matrix for fear-relevant stimuli. Finally, and most importantly, fearful subjects were faster specifically in identifying their feared as opposed to their non-feared fear-relevant stimulus (for example, snake-fearful subjects were faster with snakes than with spiders and vice versa). Thus, having an emotional response connected to the fear-relevant stimulus facilitated its detection.

To sum up, in this section I have described two series of studies which provide converging evidence in support of the hypothesis that evolutionarily relevant threat stimuli are highly effective in engaging attention. Indeed, because the size and complexity of the display did not seem to matter for fear-relevant stimuli, one can argue that finding such stimuli in a complex array of stimuli depends on an automatic process that does not require conscious attention. For both types of stimuli, furthermore, the speed of detection was enhanced for populations of subjects likely to respond emotionally to the target stimuli. Thus, subjects with generalized anxiety disorder showed a bias to direct their attention and respond faster to threatening facial displays, and subjects specifically fearful of snakes or spiders were extremely quick to discover their specific feared stimulus.

PRE-ATTENTIVE ACTIVATION OF PHOBIC FEAR

An important question raised by the demonstration of enhanced attention to threatening stimuli is whether the bias only concerns attention or whether it would also include emotional responding. For example, one possibility is that there is a pre-attentive bias to attend to threat and that, as a result, conscious attention is focused on the threat. Once this has happened, further response is dependent on conscious appraisal of the situation, so that an emotional episode is evoked only if the result of the appraisal implies that fear is justified. The alternative possibility is that not only attention, but also emotion is controlled from the automatic, pre-attentive level. In favour of the latter alternative, evolutionary argument could be invoked to the effect that rapid emotional activation would mobilize resources to deal with the threat and promote early avoidance responses, which would help in surviving the threatening encounter. In fact, there are neural mechanisms to boost this argument. LeDoux (e.g. 1990) has delineated a neural network which may route stimulus information implying threat monosynaptically to the amygdala, thus bypassing the slow multi-synaptic pathway via the cortex, in order to prompt early responding to threats. In this way the emotional response would be activated before the stimulus would be consciously recognized.

The hypothesis that fear activation does not require conscious perception of the fear-eliciting stimulus for its elicitation was tested by Öhman and Soares (1994). They made use of the consistent finding that snake- and spider-phobic subjects show elevated psychophysiological responses to visual representations of their feared object (e.g. Fredrikson 1981; Hare and Blevings 1975; and see Sartory 1983 for a review). For example, Globisch *et al.* (1997) reported that snake- or spider-fearful subjects showed enhanced skin conductance responses, a heart rate acceleration in contrast to a deceleration, and a blood pressure increase to pictures of snakes or spiders as compared to neutral or positively evaluated pictures, even if stimulus durations were very short (150 ms). In addition, startle probe stimuli presented after onset of the feared pictures showed substantial potentiation of the startle blink reflex indicating escape and avoidance inclinations (Lang *et al.* 1990). Thus, these results document that fearful subjects show a pronounced emotional response to feared stimuli.

Backward masking as a method to assure pre-attentive processing

In normal perception, pre-attentive and conscious information processing interact to determine what is eventually perceived. These levels are intimately interwoven. Special methods are therefore needed to tease them apart if one wants to demonstrate that emotional responding can be elicited after only a pre-attentive, automatic analysis of the stimulus in the absence of its conscious recognition. One method to tease apart non-conscious automatic mechanisms of stimulus analysis from conscious appraisal of the stimulus is backward masking.

With this procedure, the conscious recognition of a target stimulus is blocked by an immediately following masking stimulus. The extent to which the target stimulus is perceived is primarily dependent on the interval between the onsets of the target and the masking stimuli, the stimulus-onset-asynchrony (SOA) (Esteves and Öhman 1993). When this interval is short (say, less than 50 ms), the masking stimulus tends to completely block recognition of the target stimulus. Nevertheless, it can be demonstrated that the target stimulus, even though it remains blocked from awareness, influences the person's behaviour (see Bornstein and Pittman 1992, for a review). For example, Marcel (1983) demonstrated that reaction times to identify the colour of patches presented to subjects were affected by preceding colour words even when the words were impossible to recognize because of backward masking.

Esteves and Öhman (1993) and Öhman and Soares (1993, 1994) adapted the backward masking technique for use with emotional stimuli. As masks for common phobic objects, such as pictures of snakes and spiders, Öhman and Soares (1993, 1994) used pictures of similar objects that were cut into pieces and then randomly reassembled and re-photographed so that no central object could be discerned. Esteves and Öhman (1993) examined the effectiveness of facial pictures with a neutral emotional expression as masks for facial pictures portraying effects of anger or happiness.

A forced-choice procedure was used to determine masking effects as a function of the SOA. The subjects were exposed to long series of stimulus pairs, in which the first stimulus served as target and the second as mask. They were required to guess the nature of the target stimulus, and then to state their confidence in the guess. The results showed that the subjects required an SOA of about 100 ms for confident correct recognition of the target stimulus, and there were no differences between the stimulus categories. When the SOA was 30 ms or less, the subjects both performed, and felt that they performed, randomly. These results were stable, irrespective of whether the subjects were randomly selected non-fearful university students or classified as highly fearful or non-fearful on the basis of questionnaire data.

Phobic responses to masked stimuli

Using the backward masking technique, Öhman and Soares (1994) tested the hypothesis that phobic fear can be pre-attentively activated, and thus that more than shifts in attention can be achieved by automatic stimulus analyses. They selected subjects who were either highly fearful of snakes or of spiders (but not of both) as well as non-fearful controls using the method described previously.

These subjects were exposed to two stimulus series consisting of repeated presentations of pictures of snakes, spiders, flowers and mushrooms. In the first series, these target pictures were masked by immediately-following non-recognizable pictures (cut and randomly reassembled) at an SOA producing effective masking (30 ms). In the second series, the targets were presented without masks.

Skin conductance responses were recorded as an index of the physiological response component of fear. In addition, the subjects were exposed to an extra series of pictures in which they were asked to rate their subjective response in terms of valence (like/dislike) activation, and control.

The skin conductance results were very clear. The subjects who were afraid of snakes showed elevated response to snakes compared to spiders and neutral stimuli; the spider-fearful subjects showed specifically elevated responses to spiders, and the non-fearful subjects did not differentiate between the categories, regardless of masking condition. Thus, the results from the masked series were very similar to those from the non-masked series, which suggests that most of the response was pre-attentively recruited.

Interestingly, the psychophysiological findings were paralleled in the ratings of the subjective response to the pictures. Thus, the snake-fearful subjects rated themselves as more disliking, more activated and less in control when exposed to the masked snake pictures than to any other pictures. Similar results were obtained for spider pictures among the spider-fearful subjects, whereas the non-fearful controls did not differentiate between the stimulus categories. Thus, some aspect of the stimulus content became available to the cognitive system even though conscious recognition can be ruled out as a factor behind these findings. Perhaps the subjects were able to use their pre-attentively activated bodily response to guide their ratings.

These results show quite conclusively that conscious perception of the phobic stimulus is not necessary to activate fear in phobics. Masked presentation of the phobic stimulus appeared as effective as non-masked presentation in inducing enhanced SCRs to feared pictures. Thus pre-attentive processing of a phobic stimulus is sufficient to recruit at least part of the phobic response. Not only can fear stimuli recruit attention after a mere pre-attentive analysis of the stimulus array, but fear and anxiety can be activated from stimuli in the environment that are too weak or too peripheral in the perceptual field to enter the focus of conscious attention. When the stimulus information is eventually registered in consciousness, this occurs against a background of rising emotional activation which is likely to shape the appraisal of the stimulus as an emotional one.

CONCLUSION

In this chapter, I have argued that there are emotionally relevant events and objects that may lurk in psychological darkness outside the spotlight of conscious attention. If some of these events should come close to the edge of the attentional beam, a shift of attention is likely to focus on the emotionally relevant event. However, the movement of the attentional beam across perceptual fields is not random but governed by representations in memory about the non-attended terrain, a substantial part of which may be evolutionarily primed.

Depending on the emotional state of the individual, various domains in this terrain are more likely to receive attention than others, partly by evolutionary design. Thus, the dance of the attention spotlight is structured by emotion-regulation systems that have been shaped by evolution so that, independently of conscious intentions, the spotlight is likely to focus on environmental stimuli relevant for survival contingencies, and for promoting the transfer of genetic material to a new generation. In particular, stimuli related to survival threats in the evolutionary ecology of mammals are likely to be effective attention-capturers. This is a proposition that receives extensive empirical support with regard to threatening stimuli, as shown in my review of the literature and from recent research performed in my laboratory. When a fear-relevant stimulus captures attention, an emotional response is immediately and automatically set in motion. This was demonstrated in research using masked presentations of emotionally potent fear stimuli for fearful subjects. In spite of the fact that conscious recognition of the stimuli could be effectively ruled out, the subjects nevertheless showed enhanced skin conductance responses to non-recognized fear stimuli. Taken together, these findings demonstrate the fruitfulness of an evolutionary approach to attentional phenomena, and, by implication, to psychological phenomena in general.

REFERENCES

Aronoff, J., Barclay, A.M. and Stevenson, L.A. (1988) 'The recognition of threatening facial stimuli', *Journal of Personality and Social Psychology* 54: 647–655.

Bond, N.W. and Siddle, D.A.T. (1996) 'The preparedness account of social phobia: some data and alternative explanations', in R.M. Rapee (ed.) *Current Controversies in the Anxiety Disorders* (pp. 291–316), New York: Guilford Press.

Bornstein, R.F. and Pitman, T.S. (eds) (1992) *Perception without Awareness*, New York: Guilford Press.

Bowlby, J. (1969) *Attachment and Loss, Vol. 1: Attachment*, London: Hogarth Press.

Bradley, B.P. and Mogg. K. (1996) 'Eye movements to emotional facial expressions in clinical anxiety', *International Journal of Psychology* 31: 541 (Abstract).

Broadbent, D.E. (1958) *Perception and Communication*, London: Pergamon Press.

Buss, D.M. and Schmitt, D.P. (1993) 'Sexual strategies theory: an evolutionary perspective on human mating', *Psychological Review* 100: 204–232.

Byrne, A. and Eysenck, M.W. (1995) 'Trait anxiety, anxious mood, and threat detection', *Cognition and Emotion* 9: 549–562.

Cherry, E.C. (1953) 'Some experiments on the recognition of speech, with one and with two ears', *Journal of the Acoustical Society of America* 25: 975–979.

Dimberg, U. and Öhman, A. (1996) 'Beyond the wrath: psychophysiological responses to facial stimuli', *Motivation and Emotion* 20: 149–182.

Epstein, S. (1972) 'The nature of anxiety with emphasis upon its relationship to expectancy', in C.D. Spielberger (ed.) *Anxiety: Current trends in Theory and Research (Vol. II)*, New York: Academic Press.

Esteves, F. and Öhman, A. (1993) 'Masking the face: recognition of emotional facial expressions as a function of the parameters of backward masking', *Scandinavian Journal of Psychology* 34: 1–18.

Folkman, S., Schaeffer, C. and Lazarus, R.S. (1979) 'Cognitive processes as mediators of stress and coping', in V. Hamilton and D.M. Warburton (eds) *Human Stress and Cognition: An Information Processing Approach*, Chichester, Sussex: John Wiley & Sons.

Fredrikson, M. (1981) 'Orienting and defensive responses to phobic and conditioned stimuli in phobics and normals', *Psychophysiology* 18: 456–465.

Frijda, N.H. (1986) *The Emotions*, Cambridge: Cambridge University Press.

Globisch, J., Hamm, A.O., Esteves, F. and Öhman, A. (1997) 'Fear appears fast: temporal course of startle reflex potentiation in animal fearful subjects', Paper submitted for publication.

Hamburg, D.A., Hamburg, B.A. and Barchas, J.D. (1975) 'Anger and depression in perspective of behavioral biology', in L. Levi (ed.) *Emotions: Their Parameters and Measurement*, New York: Raven.

Hampton, C., Purcell, D.G., Bersine, L., Hansen, C.H. and Hansen, R.D. (1989) 'Probing 'pop-out': another look at the face-in-the-crowd effect', *Bulletin of the Psychonomic Society* 27: 563–566.

Hansen, C.H., and Hansen, R.D. (1988) 'Finding the face in the crowd: an anger superiority effect', *Journal of Personality and Social Psychology* 54: 917–924.

—— (1994) 'Automatic emotion: attention and facial efference', in P.M. Niedertahl and S. Kitayama (eds) *The Heart's Eye: Emotional Influences in Perception and Attention* (pp. 217–243), San Diego: Academic Press.

Hare, R.D. and Blevings, G. (1975) 'Defensive responses to phobic stimuli', *Biological Psychology* 3: 1–13.

Izard, C.E. (1979) 'Emotions as motivations: an evolutionary-developmental perspective', in H.E. Howe, Jr and R.A. Dienstbier (eds) *Nebraska Symposium on Motivation 1978*, Lincoln: University of Nebraska Press.

—— (1991) *The Psychology of Emotions*, New York: Plenum.

James, W. (1890/1950) *The Principles of Psychology Vol. 1*, New York: Dover.

Johnston, W.A. and Dark, V.J. (1986) 'Selective attention', *Annual Review of Psychology* 37: 43–75.

Kirouac, G. and Doré, F.Y. (1984) 'Accuracy and latency of judgement of facial expressions of emotions', *Perceptual and Motor Skills* 59: 147–150.

Lang, P.J. (1984) 'Cognition in emotion: concept and action', in C.E. Izard, J. Kagan and R.B. Zajonc (eds) *Emotions, Cognition, and Behavior*, New York: Cambridge University Press.

—— (1993) 'The three-system approach to emotion', in N. Birbaumer and A. Öhman (eds) *The Structure of Emotion: Psychophysiological, Cognitive and Clinical Aspects* (pp. 18–30), Seattle: Hogrefe & Huber.

Lang, P.J., Bradley, M.M. and Cuthbert, B.N. (1990) 'Emotion, attention, and the startle reflex', *Psychological Review* 97: 377–395.

—— (1997) 'Motivated attention: affect, activation, and action', in P.J. Lang, R.F. Simons and M.T. Balaban (eds) *Attention and Orienting: Sensory and Motivational Processes*, Hillsdale, NJ: Erlbaum, in press.

LeDoux, J.E. (1990) 'Information flow from sensation to emotion: plasticity in the neural computation of stimulus value', in M. Gabriel and J. Moore (eds) *Learning and Computational Neuroscience. Foundations of Adaptive Networks*, Cambridge, MA: MIT Press.

—— (1994) 'Memory versus emotional memory in the brain', in P. Ekman and R.J. Davidson (eds) *The Nature of Emotion: Fundamental Questions* (pp. 311–312), New York: Oxford University Press.

McKelvie, S.J. (1973) 'The meaningfulness and meaning of schematic faces', *Perception and Psychophysics* 14: 343–348.

MacLeod, C. (1991) 'Clinical anxiety and the selective encoding of threatening information', *International Review of Psychiatry* 3: 279–292.

Marcel, A. (1983) 'Conscious and unconscious perception: an approach to the relations between phenomenal experience and perceptual processes', *Cognitive Psychology* 15: 238–300.

Mathews, A. (1990) 'Why worry? The cognitive function of anxiety', *Behaviour Research and Therapy* 28: 455–468.

Näätänen, R. (1992) *Attention and Brain Function*, Hillsdale, NJ: Erlbaum.

Öhman, A. (1979) 'The orienting response, attention, and learning: an information processing perspective', in H.D. Kimmel, E.H. van Olst, and J.F. Orlebeke (eds) *The Orienting Reflex in Humans* (pp. 443–472), Hillsdale, NJ: Erlbaum.

—— (1986) 'Face the beast and fear the face: animal and social fears as prototypes for evolutionary analyses of emotion', *Psychophysiology* 23: 123–145.

—— (1987) 'The psychophysiology of emotion: an evolutionary-cognitive perspective', *Advances in Psychophysiology* 2: 79–127.

—— (1993) 'Fear and anxiety as emotional phenomena: clinical phenomenology, evolutionary perspectives, and information processing mechanisms', in M. Lewis and J.M. Haviland (eds) *Handbook of Emotions* (pp. 511–536), New York: Guilford Press.

—— (1994) 'The psychophysiology of emotion: evolutionary and nonconscious origins', in G. d'Ydewalle, P. Eelen and P. Bertelsen (eds) *International Perspectives on Psychological Science. Vol. 1: The State of the Art* (pp. 197–226), Hillsdale, NJ: Erlbaum.

—— (1996) 'Preferential preattentive processing of threat in anxiety: preparedness and attentional biases', in R.M. Rapee (ed.) *Current Controversies in the Anxiety Disorders* (pp. 253–290), New York: Guilford Press.

Öhman, A. and Birbaumer, N. (1993) 'Psychophysiological and cognitive-clinical perspectives on emotion: introduction and overview', in N. Birbaumer and A. Öhman (eds) *The Organization of Emotion: Cognitive, Clinical, and Psychophysiological Aspects*, Toronto: Hogrefe & Huber.

Öhman, A. and Dimberg, U. (1984) 'An evolutionary perspective on human social behavior', in W.M. Waid (ed.) *Sociophysiology* (pp. 47–85), New York: Springer-Verlag.

Öhman, A. and Soares, J.J.F. (1993) 'On the automaticity of phobic fear: conditioned skin conductance responses to masked phobic stimuli', *Journal of Abnormal Psychology* 102: 121–132.

—— (1994) 'Unconscious anxiety: phobic responses to masked stimuli', *Journal of Abnormal Psychology* 103: 231–240.

Öhman, A., Dimberg, U. and Öst, L.G. (1985) 'Animal and social phobias: biological constraints on learned fear responses', in S. Reiss and R.R. Bootzin (eds) *Theoretical Issues in Behavior Therapy* (pp. 123–178), New York: Academic Press.

Öhman, A., Flykt, A. and Esteves, F. (1997) '"The snake in the grass effect": visual search for fear-relevant stimuli in a complex display', submitted for publication.

Parasuraman, R. and Davies, D.R. (eds) (1984) *Varieties of Attention*, Orlando: Academic Press.

Pinker, S. (1994) *The Language Instinct*, New York: Morrow.

Purcell, D.G., Stewart, A.L. and Skov, R. (1993) 'The face in the crowd: an effect of a confounding variable', Paper presented at the Convention of the American Psychological Society, Chicago.

Sartory, G. (1983) 'The orienting response and psychopathology: anxiety and phobias', in D. Siddle (ed.) *Orienting and Habituation: Perspectives in Human Research* (pp. 449–474), Chichester, Sussex: John Wiley & Sons.

Scherer, K.R. (1994) 'Emotion serves to decouple stimulus and response', in P. Ekman and R.J. Davidson (eds) *The Nature of Emotion: Fundamental Questions* (pp. 127–130), New York: Oxford University Press.

Seligman, M.E.P. (1970) 'On the generality of the laws of learning', *Psychological Review* 77: 406–418.

Shiffrin, R.M. and Schneider, W. (1977) 'Controlled and automatic human information processing: II. Perceptual learning, automatic attending, and a general theory', *Psychological Review* 84: 127–190.

Sokolov, E.N. (1963) *Perception and the Conditioned reflex*, Oxford: Pergamon Press.

Tooby, J. and Cosmides, L. (1992) 'The psychological foundation of culture', in J.H. Barkow, L. Cosmides and J. Tooby (eds) *The Adapted Mind: Evolutionary Psychology and the Generation of Culture* (pp. 20–136), New York: Oxford University Press.

Weiskrantz, L. (1986) *Blindsight: A Case Study and Implications*, Oxford: Oxford University Press.

Wells, A. and Matthews, G. (1994) *Attention and Emotion: A Clinical Perspective*, Hillsdale, NJ: Erlbaum.

17 Cognitive neuropsychology

The good, the bad and the bizarre

Peter W. Halligan and John C. Marshall

INTRODUCTION

The scientific study of psychology began towards the end of the nineteenth century with the ambitious aim of explaining the mental processes involved in conscious human behaviour. Early pioneers such as Wundt, who founded the first psychological laboratory in Germany, realized that many aspects of mental processing of which we are aware are the product of prior levels of 'unconscious' processing. In this respect, cognitive processing is not dissimilar from the respiratory or digestive systems: we are usually conscious of the inputs and outputs but need medical science to tell us what happens in between. In attempting to fractionate perceptions, decisions and memories into their elementary components by introspection, the early psychologists came to the conclusion that conscious mental processes were augmented by an integrated set of relatively discrete and largely automatic cognitive processes outside phenomenological awareness.

The rise of radical behaviourism in the 1920s resulted, however, in the systematic neglect of these covert psychological processes until the 'cognitive revolution' of the late 1950s. The 'new look' in psychology, neuroscience, linguistics and artificial intelligence made it clear that behaviourist accounts had little or nothing to say about the organization of perception, thought and action (Neisser 1967). Unlike earlier neurological accounts which were concerned with physical structures and neurophysiological processes, information-processing accounts attempted to investigate the cognitive structures and processes that lie between sensory input and behavioural output.

At the same time as the cognitive revolution was unfolding, developments were also taking place in the clinical neurosciences. Clinicians, long interested in the effects of acquired brain damage, had begun to develop a conceptual framework for interpreting the selective psychological impairments that commonly followed damage to the right and left hemispheres. By the end of the nineteenth century, the study of selective impairments in speech production and comprehension (Broca 1861; Wernicke 1874) forced the realization that the left hemisphere was specialized for language and began the overthrow of the 'holistic theory' of brain functioning.

In the early twentieth century, single case investigations drove the initial classification of selective impairments into clinical syndromes such as the different varieties of aphasia, alexia, agraphia, acalculia, visual agnosia, amnesia and neglect. Eventually, as more and more psychologists joined physicians with an interest in cognition, neuropsychology became established as an independent speciality within psychology.

Clinical developments, coupled with the growing acceptance of cognitive psychology and advances in computing and neuroscience, made it possible for psychologists to construct testable functional models of cognitive processes on the basis of observed behavioural effects in the clinic. The emergence of cognitive neuropsychology in the 1970s illustrates the productive synthesis of cognitive psychology and clinical neuroscience in addressing common questions of how the mind/brain works.

This confluence of clinical neuroscience and cognitive psychology permitted fundamental questions about the functional architecture of the mind to be investigated in an experimentally testable way. This, in turn, had the effect of reviving the study of previously neglected areas within psychology, such as consciousness.

For a more comprehensive review of cognitive neuropsychology, the interested reader is directed to Bradshaw and Mattingley (1995); Ellis and Young (1996); Heilman and Valenstein (1993); McCarthy and Warrington (1990); Parkin (1996); Riddoch and Humphreys (1994) and Shallice (1988).

Outline of the chapter

The focus of this chapter is cognitive neuropsychology. Given the exponential growth in the area, this review must be selective. There are three sections:

- The first provides those unfamiliar with the area with a brief overview of some of the theoretical assumptions underlying cognitive neuropsychology.
- The second section considers the contribution of dissociations in cognitive neuropsychology.
- The last section discusses future developments; in particular the potential contribution of functional brain imaging and the recent application of cognitive neuropsychology to psychiatric phenomena.

COGNITIVE NEUROPSYCHOLOGY: THEORETICAL UNDERPINNINGS

Cognitive neuropsychology is an interdisciplinary approach that charts and explains the different types of cognitive impairments observed after brain damage. As a comparatively new speciality, cognitive neuropsychology is characterized by a methodological approach somewhat different from traditional psychology. For example, the forms of aphasia or dyslexia have to be inferred from the behavioural patterns of the patient's performance after an experiment of nature (for example, stroke, tumour and head injury). The patient's performance is then used both to understand the particular cognitive defects after brain damage and to deduce the architecture of the premorbid cognitive subsystems involved.

The approach taken by cognitive neuropsychology conceptualizes complex mental processes in terms of informational processing systems comprising many separate but interconnected subsystems. The informational processing account forms the basic framework in which cognitive processes can be deconstructed and investigated. These models have allowed researchers to consider impairments in terms of damage to specific mechanisms, necessary routes and intermediary processes. An illustration of an informational processing model for visual object recognition is shown in Figure 17.1. This model charts the hypothetical information processing routes from pre-attentive extraction of simple structural properties to post-attentional integration of local or global processing and, finally, the assignment of relevant spatial frames of reference, prior to recognition and naming.

Cognitive neuropsychology is concerned, then, with characterizing how normal cognitive process may be impaired after acquired brain damage. Disorders of higher cortical function are understood in terms of selective breakdown in the information-processing modules that underlie different forms of complex cognitive processing. The goal of cognitive neuropsychology is therefore to interpret patterns of impaired and intact cognitive performance observed in brain-injured patients in terms of damage to modules or components of normal cognitive functioning. An adequate account of a cognitive ability should be able to explain both normal functioning and the possible patterns of breakdown following brain injury. The approach should in turn provide clinicians with a rational framework from which to implement treatment and rehabilitation strategies (Howard and Patterson 1989; Riddoch and Humphreys 1994; Robertson 1994). The validity of these inferences rests in part on conjectures about the link between normal and pathological cognition – the *transparency or locality assumption* (Caramazza 1986, 1992; Farah 1994a); that is, the relationship between impaired performance and normal cognition 'may be transparent in the sense that the hypothesised modifications of the normal processing system are traceable within the proposed theoretical frameworks' (Caramazza 1992). In other words, the effects of brain damage are assumed to lead to local changes in the system and new processing structures are not created as a result of the brain damage. The status of this assumption has been recently questioned by Farah (1994a), Kosslyn and Intriligator (1992) and Robertson *et al.* (1993).

Modularity

The notion that complex cognitive skills such as recognizing familiar faces, speech production, writing, reading or remembering events are carried out by

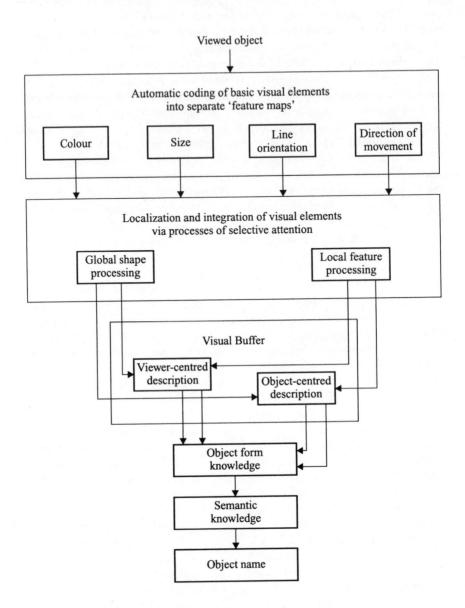

Figure 17.1 Schematic hierarchical model of visual object recognition

Source: From Thaiss and De Bleser (1992)

distinctive modules in local areas of the brain implies that brain damage may produce highly selective impairments of cognition. Indeed, some forms of cognitive neuropsychology are only viable if the hypothetical modules envisaged are both conceptually distinct in terms of the overall cognitive system and spatially distinct in terms of their putative anatomical location (Shallice 1988). Current evidence suggests that while specialized processing areas do exist, most psychological processes are mediated by distributed neuronal assemblies extending over large parts of the brain (Corbetta 1993).

The concept of psychological modularity together with the notion that different mental functions occupy different brain areas (functional specialization) none the less remains a cornerstone assumption of cognitive neuropsychology. The idea of the modular brain can be traced back to the nineteenth-century 'organologist', Franz Josef Gall, whose work anticipated much of modern neuropsychology (Miller 1996).

Modularity permits the possibility of adding, improving or removing select modules without having to redesign the overall system. The publication of Jerry Fodor's book *The Modularity of Mind* in 1983 gave fresh impetus to this discussion when he characterized cognitive modules in terms of automaticity, domain specificity and informational encapsulation. It is assumed that modules generally correspond to localized regions of the brain and carry out their functions independent of other modules. The distinction between modular and central systems implies that mental processes such as beliefs cannot influence the internal operations of modules. The Müller-Lyer illusion (Figure 17.2) provides an illustration. The illusion that the line with the outward extended fins looks longer persists, despite repeated empirical disconfirmation with a ruler!

The components involved in different cognitive processes are often displayed in the form of flow charts or box and arrow diagrams (cf. Figure 17.1). The separate modules and their interconnections in such displays must be shown to conform to the observed empirical patterns of experiments on normal subjects and clinical findings. The box and arrow approach has in turn been used to inform the construction of sensitive diagnostic tests for discrete cognitive impairments after brain damage (Lezak 1995).

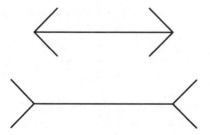

Figure 17.2 An illustration of the Müller-Lyer illusion

The concept of modularity has been further developed by evolutionary psychologists who argue that any attempt to map the putative functional structure of human brain/mind needs to consider the recent technical advances of evolutionary biology. Without such a perspective, it is possible that misleading assumptions may influence cognitive neuropsychology theory (Cosmides and Tooby 1995). If one assumes that the human brain is the result of a highly adaptive process, then the distinctive sets of informational processing modules so far revealed may be viewed as the product of an underlying evolutionary process brought about to perform a particular set of functions. Thus, distinctive mental sub-processes or modules, such as face recognition, comprehension and memory modules, may have been shaped by natural selection in order to solve specific survival problems.

Single case approach

In contrast to traditional neuropsychology, a distinctive characteristic of cognitive neuropsychology is the revival of interest in detailed single case studies (Caramazza and Badecker 1991; McCloskey 1993). Single cases were an important source of neuropsychological evidence in the nineteenth century and are so now. Traditional syndromes, derived as they are from common co-occurrences of selective symptoms, are regarded as too coarse-grained to support differential functional analysis. The emphasis on case studies distinguishes cognitive neuropsychology from traditional clinical neuropsychology. Advocates of the single case approach argue that because brain damage may disrupt cognitive systems in a variety of different ways, individual differences cannot be ignored (Sokol *et al.* 1991). In other words, it is not possible to be sure that any two patients will manifest the same sort of cognitive impairment even after similar naturally occurring lesions. While a reasonable compromise is to carry out a case series, the strength of the single case approach lies in its potential to reveal theoretically interesting dissociations between tasks within subjects that might appear superficially similar in a group study. Significant dissociations between symptoms have often been discovered in patients whom traditional neuropsychology has grouped together as representative of the same syndrome category (Ellis and Young 1996). Single cases are thus preferable to the study of comparatively heterogeneous groups of patients where data must be averaged and where the association of symptoms may be due to anatomical accident rather than functional necessity. Single cases studies must none the less be supplemented by group norms for particular tests, and group studies in their own right are of particular value in investigating associations between symptoms that may be of anatomical significance. A recent discussion of the virtues and limitations of single case methodology can be found in Caramazza and Badecker (1989), Zurif *et al.* (1991) and Robertson *et al.* (1993).

Some limitations of the cognitive approach

The recent explosion of research findings in cognitive neuropsychology has however produced an ever expanding array of fragmented data (e.g. visual neglect: see Halligan and Marshall 1994). Explanations of impaired phenomena in terms of damage to underlying cognitive processes have proven somewhat elusive for many cognitive domains (Ellis 1987). Many current theoretical accounts of cognitive disorders cannot adequately explain some of the most basic clinical findings that have been known for several decades. For instance, in the case of visual neglect, a spatial disorder where patients ignore or neglect one side of space, it still remains unclear why rightward transection displacements on horizontal line bisection are linearly related to stimulus length (Halligan 1995), or why patients transect to the left of true centre with small line lengths (Halligan and Marshall 1988; Marshall and Halligan 1989). Failure to provide an adequate explanation for some of these basic features of neglect has inevitably contributed to the appearance that research in this area is a disconnected patchwork of puzzles and anomalies (Halligan and Marshall 1994).

The seductive reification of syndrome labels (often taken over from traditional neuropsychology) also continues to plague the field. It is still not always recognized that terms such as 'dysphasia' or 'neglect' are not explanations for disordered cognitions but rather shorthand descriptions of the types of behaviour that stand in need of an explanation (Halligan and Marshall 1992). The enterprise should not be to develop theories of neglect, dyslexia or amnesia but rather to characterize the domains of normal spatial cognition, attention, reading and memory in such a way that the observed impairments of such functions are understandable.

DISSOCIATIONS: CARVING COGNITION AT THE SEAMS

If a modular organization underpins normal cognitive processes, then localized neurological damage or 'natural fractionations' in brain-damaged patients can be expected to selectively affect some cognitive functions and not others. Cognitive neuropsychology achieves an understanding of the architecture of cognitive systems by charting dissociations between cognitive tasks that occur in patients with selective brain damage (Shallice 1988). Dissociations constitute one of the main methodological tools for exposing the putative boundaries between cognitive modules. Naturally occurring fractionations or dissociations provide valuable insights into the intact and damaged mechanisms in language (Margolin 1991), amnesia (Cermak 1982), dyslexia (Coslett and Saffran 1994), prosopagnosia (Young 1994) and neglect (Halligan and Marshall 1994). Cognitive neuropsychologists use dissociations to 'carve cognition at its seams', sometimes revealing processes that have remained relatively immune to brain damage. A dissociation occurs when a patient performs normally on one task and badly on another related task. The result suggests the existence of separate cognitive modules responsible for different cognitive operations. However, as indicated by Shallice (1988), single dissociations are open to alternative interpretations. They do not of themselves entail the existence of isolable subsystems and can occur from impairments to different levels or modes of operation within the same subsystem.

Early examples of dissociation involving language were reported by Graves (1851), who (in the *Dublin Quarterly Journal of Medical Science*) described several patients with selective impairments in speech production for proper names. Dissociations between speech comprehension and speech production have also been known for some time. In 1833, Jonathan Osborne reported the case of a 26-year-old language scholar at Trinity College who became aphasic following an 'apoplectic fit'. The case was reported in the *Dublin Journal of Medical and Chemical Science* in an article entitled 'On the loss of the faculty of speech depending upon forgetfulness of the art of using the vocal organs.' Although able to comprehend verbal and written language, the scholar's speech while fluent was so contaminated with paraphasic errors that he was 'treated as a foreigner'. Nevertheless, he made a good recovery of auditory comprehension, and written comprehension, and relatively well-preserved written expression. However, speech repetition remained severely impaired (Margolin 1991).

Double dissociations

Single dissociations do not in themselves imply that two cognitive functions underlying the tasks are necessarily mediated by separate cognitive modules or systems. Task difficulty may explain these dissociations; for example, long-term memory tasks may be more difficult than short-term memory tasks. To avoid this criticism, it is necessary to find patients who show the opposite pattern of results. An example from a category-specific semantic impairment demonstrates this point. In 1984, Warrington and Shallice reported a patient who, while grossly impaired on the identification of pictures of living objects, performed well on similar items depicting inanimate objects. They suggested that their patient suffered from a degradation of the representations for the semantic category of living objects. Three years later in 1987, Warrington and McCarthy reported another patient who showed the converse dissociation: relative impairment when recognizing inanimate objects, normal or near normal when performing on pictures of animate objects. Since the respective impairments were independent of each other, the assumption was that the two types of visual recognition reflected some form of organizational difference in the neural implementation of the underlying semantic system (however, see reviews by Humphreys and Riddoch 1987; Damasio 1990).

Although such 'functional dissociations' are frequently observed in the absence of obvious anatomical counterparts, they are nevertheless considered evidence of two independent processing mechanisms (Shallice 1988). The relationship between dissociable systems and their underlying anatomical mechanisms is not straightforward (Weiskrantz 1989). Although the logic of double dissociations provides a strong form of evidence for the existence of separate modules, the legitimacy of this methodology has also been the subject of discussion (Dunn and Kirsner 1988; Jones 1983; Miller 1993; Shallice 1988).

Reliable dissociations and double dissociations provide the necessary building blocks from which to construct the putative functional architecture of specific cognitive abilities. By making explicit the range and type of cognitive deficits that can give rise to difficulties in perception, memory, language, learning and planning, findings from cognitive neuropsychology have been used to devise rational treatments that can be individually titrated to the individual patient's condition (Riddoch and Humphreys 1994).

IMPLICIT PROCESSING AFTER BRAIN DAMAGE

Some of the most striking functional dissociations in neuropsychology involve those that disconnect conscious or explicit awareness from non-conscious or implicit processing. Brain damage can produce highly selective impairments of awareness and can inform neuropsychological theory regarding the existence of alternative neural mechanisms or pathways. Evidence of implicit psychological processing has been ascertained using at least three different methods: (1) forced choice – where the patient is requested to guess or indicate a preference; (2) evaluating the extent to which selective primes/cues in the affected modality modulate responses on the non-affected side; and (3) by measuring directly the physiological or autonomic responses. In the case of prosopagnosia, patients have demonstrated differential electrical skin conductance or evoked potentials to familiar faces despite an explicit inability to identify them (Bauer 1984; Tranel and Damasio 1985; Renault *et al.* 1989). There is now considerable evidence from many conditions to suggest that implicit processes influence patient behaviour (Milner and Rugg 1992; Schacter *et al.* 1988; Weiskrantz 1991; Young 1994, 1996). In memory disorders, these distinctions have made it necessary to qualify amnesia as an impairment of conscious recollection rather than as a global failure to retain it (Moscovitch *et al.* 1986). There is an extensive literature documenting neuropsychological dissociations in aphasia (Tyler 1992), memory (Moscovitch and Umilta 1991) and reading (Coslett and Saffran 1994).

One of the better known illustrations of implicit processing is 'blindsight' (Weiskrantz 1986), where patients unaware of the stimuli in their blind field can nevertheless indicate (at levels significantly above chance) the location of stimuli when requested to guess. Although unaware of targets in the affected field, some patients, when requested to guess in a forced choice experiment, are able none the less to indicate the location of targets in their blind field by pointing or moving their eyes (Weiskrantz *et al.* 1974). Although these patients may perceive more than would be expected, it is not clear whether 'blindsight' carries any functional benefit for the patient (Weiskrantz 1991).

Evidence of 'blindsight' has also been found using skin conductance (Zihl *et al.* 1980) and altered pupil size (Weiskrantz 1990). Rafal *et al.* (1990) demonstrated that 'unseen' stimuli presented to the 'blind' hemifield had the effect of inhibiting the latency of saccades to the seen stimulus in the intact field. Studies of 'blindsight' indicate that the processing of visual stimuli can take place even though there is no phenomenological awareness by the subject. Anatomical and physiological evidence suggests that some forms of 'blindsight' may rely on intact residual visual ability that is mediated subcortically (Weiskrantz 1986). Other forms may be explained in terms of a disconnection between specialized areas in the visual cortex (Zeki 1993). A recent review of 'blindsight' and related topics can be found in Stoerig (1996).

The question as to whether 'knowing without knowing' can be found in other sensory modalities currently excites much interest. In the tactile modality, reports of 'blind touch' (Lahav 1993; Paillard *et al.* 1983; Rossetti *et al.* 1995) or 'numbsense' (Perenin and Rossetti 1996) and 'deaf hearing' (Michel and Peronnet 1980) have also been reported. These reports lend further support to the concept of multi-channelling of sensory information already well established in the visual system and the realization that perception is not a unitary process. The findings of 'blindsight' are more widely known; less well known but just as striking (since they take place in free vision) are some of the recent clinical dissociations observed with *visual neglect*, a much more common disorder seen after right brain damage. These will be described in more detail in the following section.

Neglect dissociations

Recent studies of left visual neglect have produced a plethora of dissociations suggesting that several different levels of processing can take place in the 'neglected' field after right brain damage without conscious awareness (Halligan and Marshall 1994; Robertson and Marshall 1993). In unilateral neglect, patients seem unable to detect or respond to stimuli in spatial locations contralateral to the damaged cerebral hemisphere. The condition has been reported in the visual, auditory, tactile and olfactory modalities (Halligan and Marshall 1993), although the most extensive investigations concern visuo-spatial neglect. Unlike 'blindsight', which has to be elicited experimentally, left neglect is clinically obvious and is also a major negative prognostic factor reliably associated with poor performance on functional recovery measures (Halligan and Robertson 1992).

Until quite recently, it was generally assumed that patients with neglect had no conscious awareness of objects presented in the neglected field. However, Marshall and Halligan (1988) and subsequently many others (Berti and Rizzolatti 1992; Ladavas *et al.* 1993; McGlinchey-Berroth *et al.* 1996; Mijovic-Prelec *et al.* 1994; Ro and Rafal 1996) showed that, despite unawareness of relevant features on the affected left side, many patients could be influenced by information on the neglected side.

Figure 17.3 The 'Burning House' set of stimuli used in Marshall and Halligan (1988)

The case reported by Marshall and Halligan (1988), patient PS, had sustained a right hemisphere stroke. We presented her simultaneously with two line drawings of a house, one of which had red flames and black smoke emitting from the left-hand side window (Figure 17.3). Requested to make same/different judgements between the two pictures, PS reliably judged the two drawings to be identical. When asked several minutes later to select the house she would prefer to live in however, she reliably chose the non-burning house at a high level of statistical significance, commenting that it was a 'silly question' since both houses were identical. In other words, although PS was unable to report the crucial differences between the two houses (despite free movement of the head and eyes), she nevertheless appeared to process some information in the hemispace contralateral to lesion that influenced her preference judgement (cf. Manning and Kartsounis 1993). Later, more detailed studies by Berti and Rizzolatti (1992) and McGlinchey-Berroth *et al.* (1996), using cross-field matching and priming experiments, showed that implicit perception, up to the level of meaning, was possible in some patients with neglect. In the case of Berti and Rizzolatti (1992), patients who denied seeing anything in the left visual field nevertheless showed significantly shorter reaction times to the right field stimulus for congruent rather than non-congruent conditions.

In a later study, again in a free vision task, we showed evidence of a further type of dissociation between two forms of conscious perceptual awareness. The patient JR (who had severe neglect) was shown hierarchical drawings in which a

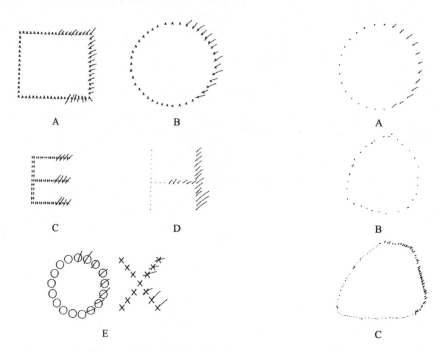

Figure 17.4 Stimuli and patient responses from Marshall and Halligan (1995)
Left: The patient's attempt to cross out the local features of the global forms, having previously correctly named both aspects of each figure.
Right: The patient's attempt to cross out the local features on a predrawn figure (A) to reproduce the figure (B), to draw the figure and to cross out all the local features (C).

large (global) form, such as a geometric figure or an alphabetic letter, was composed of smaller local forms, i.e. dots, circles or letters (Figure 17.4). JR gave accurate verbal reports of the global structure, yet when required to cross out the smaller subfigures, only cancelled those on the right of each global figure. Furthermore, this result was reliably found even after JR herself produced a reasonable global figure (circle) composed of dots. When subsequently requested to cancel out the local parts (i.e. the dots) of her own earlier construction, JR again neglected all the local features on the left (see Figure 17.4)! In other words, conscious perception of the *whole* stimulus did not automatically lead to visual awareness of all the local *parts* thereof. Our conjecture (Marshall and Halligan 1995) was that panoramic or global processing can remain intact to a significant degree in some patients with neglect. In most cases however, global processing of the visual world can no longer be used to direct automatic focal attention to spatial locales that require further focal analysis. Without this ability, local attention which is usually biased to the right will always represent too little of the visual world. Once attention has been focused, the panoramic or global view is lost to conscious awareness. When focal attention is biased to the right as in the case of neglect, the patient is in no position to observe the absence of left-sided input. Even if selective attention can be voluntarily moved leftwards, the necessary guiding framework provided by the global scale is no longer available. Consequently, the patient no longer sees any reason to continue to explore leftwards. In these and other examples, where performance within an individual patient can be normal on one aspect and grossly impaired on another involving the same stimulus seconds later, left neglect may be regarded as a partial disconnection syndrome in which residual processes of the impaired right hemisphere cannot be used to constrain the performance of the intact left hemisphere. In this respect, patients like JR might be described as showing a type of disconnection between two forms of conscious visual awareness.

Collectively, these findings from visual neglect, 'blindsight' and many other conditions indicate the danger of equating phenomenological conscious experience with the operation of the perceptual mechanisms involved. In the absence of phenomenological awareness, there is evidence that many patients when tested indirectly may show some degree of information processing for the stimulus on the affected side as in the case of neglect or 'blindsight'.

FUNCTIONAL IMAGING OF COGNITIVE FUNCTIONS

While clinical neuropsychology was motivated in large part by concerns with anatomical localization of the lesion, recent developments in structural imaging (CT, MRI) have largely rendered this use redundant. However, it still remains important to establish objectively those areas of the brain which have been affected by brain damage. With the advent of functional imaging, neuroscientists are now beginning to chart the functional organization of human cognitive processes in the normal brain. These developments have been made possible by increasingly sophisticated functional neuroimaging techniques, such as PET (Positron Emission Tomography) and FMRI (Functional Magnetic Resonance Imaging), both of which have been used to provide an index of the neural activity in different areas of the brain during selective cognitive tasks. PET in particular has been at the forefront of many recent studies investigating cognitive neuropsychological processes. Measurement of regional cerebral blood flow (rCBF) provides an exciting tool with which to investigate sites of increased cerebral activity that occur upon specific cognitive activations (Nadeau and Crosson 1995).

PET imaging has, to date, confirmed many previous classical neuropsychological findings, particularly the localization of sensory and motor functioning. In addition, it has also provided new findings on the top-down modulation effects of attention (Dupont *et al.* 1993), the functional anatomy of lexical retrieval (Damasio *et al.* 1996), the brain regions responsible for episodic memory (Shallice *et al.* 1994) and the common semantic system for words and pictures (Vandenberghe *et al.* 1996). It has also confirmed the existence of an anterior attentional system in the anterior cingulate (Posner and Petersen 1990) and shown that localized areas in the right frontal lobes are selectively activated during vigilance tasks (Pardo *et al.* 1991).

The advantage of studying cognitive neuropsychology using PET stems from its potential ability to show many active regions of the brain and then, using a 'cognitive subtraction' technique (involving a reference condition), to differentiate these areas of the brain (in normal subjects) activated during specific psychological tasks.

A recent study by Fink *et al.* (1996) serves to demonstrate how PET may be used to augment and extend previous neuropsychological findings. This study was concerned with establishing the neural processes involved in global and local processing. Over the past twenty years, neuropsychological and neurophysiological studies using hierarchical letter stimuli (Figure 17.5) have found evidence of a right hemisphere bias for global processing (perception of the whole) and a left hemisphere bias for local processing (perception of the focal aspects) using reaction times in both normals and patients (Hellige 1993). Previous studies, however, did not indicate where this differential hemispheric activation took place.

In the first experiment (directed attention), subjects were asked to attend to and name either the global or the local aspect of the figures in separate blocks of trials (Figure 17.5a). As psychophysical differences in global and local processing may be confounded by stimulus size, size effects were controlled by presenting both large and small hierarchical figures in a factorial experimental design employing non-congruent stimuli. When subjects attended to the global aspect of figures, significant increases in relative rCBF were observed in the *right* lingual gyrus (between V2/V3). When subjects attended to the local attribute, there was a significant relative rCBF increase in the *left* inferior occipital cortex (between V1/V2 and V2/V3). Thus, although the findings of the experiment were in keeping with previous studies, i.e. globally directed attention involved the right hemisphere and locally directed attention the left hemisphere, the striking feature of this study was the demonstration that early visual areas in the prestriate cortex were differentially involved.

The absence of differential rCBF increases in the expected lateral temporal-parietal areas, during the local or global tasks, was explained by the fact that subjects were not explicitly required to switch their attention between the two perceptual levels. A second PET experiment, however, tested this hypothesis directly by measuring the rCBF changes that correlated with the number of attentional target switches between perceptual levels. In the second experiment (Figure 17.5b), a pre-selected target letter appeared at either the global or the local level and subjects were required to indicate at which of the two levels the target had appeared. In this divided attention task, the number of target switches from local to global and vice versa covaried with temporal-parietal activation and suggests that temporal-parietal areas can exert attentional control over the perceptual processes taking place in prestriate cortex. The finding of the second

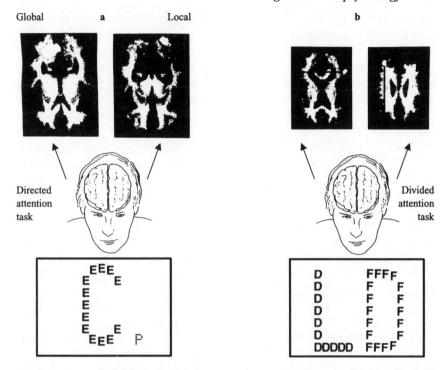

Figure 17.5 Schematic illustration of Fink *et al.* (1996) PET experiment. Example of figures used as stimuli during the *directed attention task* (left) and the *divided attention task* (right). The C, P, L and D letters represent the global level and the E, H, D and F the local level.

(a): During the *directed attention* task, subjects were required to attend to either the global or the local level and to name the appropriate letter (in this case 'E' and 'H' during the local processing task and 'C' and 'P' during the global processing task). *Global* processing was found more in the right hemisphere, *local* processing in the left hemisphere.

(b): During the *divided attention task*, a preselected target letter appeared at either the global or the local level (in this case a 'D'); subjects were required to name the level at which the target appeared. During this task, activation involved temporo-parietal areas in both left and right hemisphere.

experiment also confirmed previous reports which showed a 'top-down' modulation of early visual areas (Dupont *et al.* 1993; Motter 1993).

Some limitations of functional imaging

Despite its potential, PET suffers from a number of methodological concerns, all of which need to be considered when evaluating its contribution to cognitive neuropsychology (Chertkow and Bub 1994; Kosslyn 1996; Nadeau and Crosson

1995; Sergent 1994). First, there is the issue of the relatively poor signal to noise ratio for cognitive functions, which can be in the region of only 5 per cent by comparison with 25 per cent blood flow changes in the primary motor or sensory cortex. Second, it is important to consider the effect of factors intrinsic to the experimental design, such as rate of stimulation, extent of attentional demands, practice effects, task difficulty and the order, number of repetitions and duration of exposure of stimuli (Frackowiak 1994). Perhaps the most problematic limitation is the relatively poor spatial localization (currently between 2–5 mm) and temporal resolution of about 40 sec (Corbetta 1993). Another weakness of functional imaging methods remains the ambiguity of the null result (Sergent *et al.* 1992). There is no guarantee that all potential areas involved in performing a particular task will necessarily show differential activations. Certain cognitive processes may fail to register; for example, most PET studies using visual stimuli fail to demonstrate explicit activation of the lateral geniculate nucleus. Consequently it is still important to derive evidence from converging sources of information (Farah 1994b).

TOWARDS A COGNITIVE NEUROPSYCHIATRY

The current syndrome classification of the functional psychoses (e.g. DSM-IV) has been the subject of much criticism within psychiatry (Bental *et al.* 1990; Crow 1986; David 1993; Liddle 1987). The main criticisms relate to its lack of explanatory power, its diagnostic imprecision and, more recently, the general lack of a theoretically motivated psychological account. For many, psychiatry is 'a medical discipline long on disorders and short on explanation' (McHugh 1995). In a recent review, Charlton (1995) criticizes psychiatry for failing to contribute significantly to the understanding of the functional psychoses and suggests that the conventional classification should be 'abandoned in favour of developing a cognitive nosology . . . based upon a modern understanding of human psychological architecture and classifying patients in terms of lesions to informational processing systems'.

Since cognitive neuropsychology evolved out of investigations involving brain-damaged patients, it is not surprising that the revival of neuropsychiatry in recent years has recently begun to look to cognitive neuropsychology for an understanding of common psychopathologies (David 1993; Keefe 1995). Despite the fact that many psychiatric conditions remain as yet 'functional', it is none the less possible to explain some common psychopathologies in terms of impairments to selective psychological modules or processes. Furthermore, the absence of a structural correlate is not of itself a reason for choosing to ignore a *neuro*-psychological account. It is well established that many physical symptoms in neurological practice have no adequate physiological explanation (Ron 1994). The extent to which discrete psychopathologies can be mapped on to physiological processes currently remains a question for future investigation; however, recent developments with functional brain imaging have already made considerable inroads by investigating the abnormal physiological brain activations found in several mainstream psychiatric conditions. Examples employing functional imaging include depression (Bench *et al.* 1992; Drevets *et al.* 1992), auditory hallucinations (McGuire *et al.* 1993), post-traumatic stress disorder (Raunch *et al.* 1996), schizophrenia (Frith 1995; Liddle *et al.* 1992; Silbersweig *et al.* 1995) and obsessive-compulsive disorder (McGuire *et al.* 1994).

There is growing evidence that psychiatry may be invigorated by the contribution of a cognitive neuropsychological emphasis (O'Carroll 1992). Since studies began looking at schizophrenia and brain dysfunction, evidence of neuropsychological impairments has led to assertions that schizophrenia may be associated with subcortical dysfunctions (Patterson 1987), a left hemisphere deficit (Gur 1977), impaired transcallosal integration (Craft *et al.* 1987) and frontal dysfunction (Levin 1984). The cognitive approach to schizophrenia has already produced some interesting insights regarding possible deficits such as impairments of memory (McKenna *et al.* 1990), initiation and decision making (Shallice *et al.* 1991).

The cognitive neuropsychological emphasis has also led to the reconsideration of the content of delusions together with a renewed interest in the disrupted belief systems thought to be involved at the psychological core of the mental illness. Examples where this type of approach has been explicitly used to explain psychiatric conditions include the elucidation of disorders of reasoning (Garety and Hemsley 1994), alien control (Frith and Done 1989), reality monitoring (Johnson 1991), delusional memories (Kopelman *et al.* 1995), thought disorder (David and Cutting 1994; Frith 1992), autistic behaviour (Baron-Cohen *et al.* 1993; Happé 1994), hallucinations (Halligan *et al.* 1994), supernumerary phantom limbs (Halligan *et al.* 1993), reduplication (Marshall *et al.* 1995), psychogenic amnesia (Kopelman *et al.* 1994), somatoparaphrenia (Halligan *et al.* 1995) and paranoid disorders (Bentall 1990; Chadwick 1992). Using normal informational processing systems as the domain by which psychiatric disorders should be explained, there is now considerable research in the literature, some of which is summarized in a recent book of case studies (Halligan and Marshall 1996).

The prior lack of systematic investigation into the nature of delusions has been due, in part, to an overemphasis on form rather than content (Winters and Neale 1983). Much of the ground-breaking research in this new field however has focused on detailed investigations of a relatively circumscribed and bizarre set of delusions collectively known as disorders of misidentification. The main disorders of misidentification include *Capgras* – where the patient believes that a relative has been replaced by impostors (Ellis and Young 1990; Young *et al.* 1993); *Fregoli* – where the patient believes that a certain person has assumed different physical appearances (Ellis and Young 1990; Edelstyn *et al.* 1996), and *Cotard* – where the patients think they are dead (Young *et al.* 1994; Young and Leafhead 1996).

The cognitive neuropsychology approach seeks an explanation for each type of delusion in terms of a breakdown of normal mechanisms responsible for the interaction of emotion and cognition aspects. Furthermore, it is important to consider the specific content of the delusional belief in these cases, since it may represent the patient's attempt to make sense of perceptual anomalies related to facial identity. Attempts to explain these different forms of delusional misidentification make use of previous neuropsychological evidence from normal face processing. The current account which attempts to explain Capgras suggests that information about the facial identity of a subject is conveyed by a route in the brain that has been disconnected from relevant affective information regarding the full identity of the owner of the face. This putative impairment of face processing thus provides the necessary (but not the sufficient) basis for the formation of the delusion when the patient attempts to reconcile the subject's identity without the relevant affective information (Young and Leafhead 1996).

Although it is unlikely that a unified theory of all delusions will be forthcoming in the near future, theories of normal belief formation will eventually cast light on both the content of delusions and on the processes whereby beliefs are formed. Whether this cognitive exercise will be capable of extension to the major impairments in the affective psychoses still remains unanswered. The effects of the new approach have however already given rise to the new, exciting, multidisciplinary field of 'cognitive neuropsychiatry' (David 1993; Ellis and De Pauw 1994) which seeks to emphasize the cognitive dimension when attempting to deconstruct traditional syndromes of clinical psychiatry. Evidence of interest in this field can be seen from the growing numbers of recent books (David and Cutting 1994; Frith 1992; Halligan and Marshall 1996), together with the launch in 1996 of the new quarterly journal *Cognitive Neuropsychiatry.*

CODA

Advances in cognitive neuropsychology are not limited to the selective areas covered in this chapter; similar developments have taken place in other cognitive disorders such as memory, reading, writing, motor control, problem solving, object recognition, imagery, calculation and emotion. The main contribution of the cognitive neuropsychological approach lies in the theoretical framework it offers for informing the understanding of breakdown in cognitive functioning. By adopting a modular view, where relatively discrete processing units operate to service complex cognitive operations, it has been possible to understand some of the many puzzling dissociations found after brain damage. The cognitive approach has in turn facilitated the development of new theoretical models concerning normal cognitive processes and revitalized the need to evaluate and revise previous ones. After the fractionation of the cognitive architecture, an outstanding question for future research is to understand how such relatively independent processes interact or bind so as to enable normal perception to take place so apparently effortlessly (Friedman-Hill *et al.* 1995).

The challenge for cognitive neuropsychology is whether it is capable of harnessing the new potential offered by functional imaging to move beyond the identification of peripheral modules and to establish the neural connectivity involved in many apparently simple cognitive functions. Future developments will no doubt also have to consider the status of the transparency assumption. A further challenge will be to see whether the current approach is best suited to investigating the functional organization of central cognitive processes (such as planning, problem solving and belief formation) which, according to Fodor (1983), are unlikely to be modular. Whatever the responses to these challenges, the future study of cognitive neuropsychology should produce a rich harvest of new and exciting findings.

From its modest beginnings in the nineteenth century, cognitive neuropsychology has over the last twenty-five years become an established discipline and a dominant theoretical influence within mainstream psychology. Today, as the 'Decade of the Brain' draws to a close, cognitive neuropsychology can justifiably claim several influential undergraduate and postgraduate texts, an established and reputable journal, over thirty university psychology professors in the UK alone, together with the emergence of several postgraduate degree courses.

REFERENCES

Baron-Cohen, S., Tager-Flusberg, H. and Cohen, D.J. (1993) *Understanding Other Minds: Perspectives from Autism*, Oxford: Oxford University Press.

Bauer, R.M. (1984) 'Autonomic recognition of names and faces in prosopagnosia: a neuropsychological application of the guilty knowledge test', *Neuropsychologia* 22: 457–469.

Bench, C.J., Frith, C.D., Grasby, P.M., Friston, K.J., Paulesu, E., Frackowiak, R.S.J. and Dolan, R.J. (1992) 'Investigations of the functional anatomy of attention using the Stroop test', *Neuropsychologia* 31: 907–922.

Bentall, R.P. (1990) *Reconstructing Schizophrenia*, London: Routledge.

Berti, A. and Rizzolatti, G. (1992) 'Visual processing without awareness: evidence from unilateral neglect', *Journal of Cognitive Neuroscience* 4: 345–351.

Bradshaw, J. and Mattingley, J. (1995) *Clinical Neuropsychology: Behaviour and Brain Science*, New York: Academic Press.

Broca, P. (1861) 'Remarques sur le siège de la faculté du langage articulé, suivies d'une observation d'aphemi', *Bulletins de la Société Anatomique de Paris* 2: 330–357.

Caramazza, A. (1986) 'On drawing inferences about the structure of normal cognitive systems from the analysis of patterns of impaired performance: the case for single-patient studies', *Brain and Cognition* 5: 41–66.

—— (1992) 'Is cognitive neuropsychology possible?', *Journal of Cognitive Neuroscience* 4: 80–95.

Caramazza, A. and Badecker, W. (1991) 'Clinical syndromes are not God's gift to cognitive neuropsychology: a reply to a rebuttal to an answer to a response to the case against syndrome-based research', *Brain and Cognition* 16: 211–227.

—— (1989) 'Patient classification in neuropsychological research', *Brain and Cognition* 10: 256–295.

Cermak, L. (1982) *Human Memory and Amnesia*, Hillsdale, NJ: Lawrence Erlbaum.

Chadwick, P.K. (1992) *Borderline: A Psychological Study of Paranoia and Delusional Thinking*, London: Routledge.

Charlton, B. (1995) 'Cognitive neuropsychiatry and the future of diagnosis: a "PC" model of the mind', *British Journal of Psychiatry* 167: 149–158.

Chertkow, H. and Bub, D. (1994) 'Functional activation and cognition: the ^{15}O PET subtraction method', in *Localisation and Neuroimaging in Neuropsychology*, New York: Academic Press.

Corbetta, M. (1993) 'Positron emission tomography as a tool to study human vision and attention', *Proceedings of the National Academy of Science* 90: 10901–10903.

Corbetta, M., Miezin, F.M., Shulman, G.L. and Petersen, S.E. (1993) 'A PET study of visuospatial attention', *Journal of Neuroscience* 13: 1202–1226.

Coslett, H.B. and Saffran, E.M. (1994) 'Mechanisms of implicit reading in alexia', in M.J. Farah and G. Ratcliff (eds) *The Neuropsychology of High Level Vision: Collected Tutorial Essays*, Hillsdale, NJ: Lawrence Erlbaum.

Cosmides, L. and Tooby, J. (1995) 'From function to structure: the role of evolutionary biology and computational theories of cognitive neuroscience', in M.S. Gazzaniga (ed.) *The Cognitive Neurosciences*, Boston, MA: MIT Press.

Craft, S., Willerman, L. and Bigler, E. (1987) 'Callosal dysfunction in schizophrenia and schizo-affective disorder', *Journal of Abnormal Psychology* 96: 205–213.

Crow, T.J. (1986) 'The continuum of psychosis and its implications for the study of the gene', *British Journal of Psychiatry* 149: 419–429.

Damasio, A.R. (1990) 'Category-related recognition defects as a clue to the neural substrates of knowledge', *TINS* 13: 95–98.

Damasio, H., Grabowski, T.J., Tranel, D., Hichwa, R.D. and Damasio, A.R. (1996) 'A neural basis for lexical retrieval', *Nature* 380: 499–505.

David, A.S. (1993) 'Cognitive neuropsychiatry?', *Psychological Medicine* 23: 1–5.

David, A.S. and Cutting, J.C. (eds) (1994) *The Neuropsychology of Schizophrenia*, Hove, Sussex: Lawrence Erlbaum.

Drevets, W.C., Videen, T.O., MacLeod, A.K., Haller, J.W. and Raichle, M.E. (1992) 'PET images of blood flow changes during anxiety: correction', *Science* 256: 1696.

Dunn, J.C. and Kirsner, K. (1988) 'Discovering functionally independent mental processes: the principle of reversed association', *Psychological Review* 95: 91–101.

Dupont, P., Orban, G.A., Vogels, R., Bormans, G., Nuyts, J., Schiepers, C., De Roo, M. and Mortelmans, L. (1993) 'Different perceptual tasks performed with the same visual stimulus attribute activate different regions of the human brain: a position emission tomography study', *Proceedings of the National Academy of Science* 90: 10927–10931.

Edelstyn, N.M.J., Riddoch, M.J., Oyebode, F., Humphreys, G.W. and Forde, E. (1996) 'Visual processing in patients with Fregoli Syndrome', *Cognitive Neuropsychiatry* 1, 2: 103–124.

Ellis, A.W. (1987) 'Intimations of modularity, or, the modularity of the mind', in M. Coltheart, G. Sartori and R. Job (eds) *The Cognitive Neuropsychology of Language*, London: Lawrence Erlbaum Associates.

Ellis, H.D. and De Pauw, K.W. (1994) 'The cognitive neuropsychiatric origins of the Capgras delusion', in A.S. David and J.C. Cutting (eds) *The Neuropsychology of Schizophrenia*, Hove, Sussex: Lawrence Erlbaum.

Ellis, H.D. and Young, A.W. (1990) 'Accounting for delusional misidentifications', *British Journal of Psychiatry* 157: 239–248.

—— (1996) *Human Cognitive Neuropsychology: A Textbook with Readings*, Hove, Sussex: Lawrence Erlbaum.

Ellis, A.W., Young, A.W. and Flude, B.M. (1987) '"Afferent dysgraphia" in a patient and in normal subjects', *Cognitive Neuropsychology* 4: 465–486.

Farah, M. (1994a) 'Neuropsychological inference with an interactive brain: a critique of the "locality" assumption', *Brain and Behavioural Sciences* 17: 43–104.

—— (1994b) 'Beyond "pet" methodologies to converging evidence', *TINS* 17: 514–515.

Fink, G.R., Halligan, P.W., Marshall, J.C., Frith, C.D., Frackowiak, R.S.J. and Dolan, R. (1996) 'Where does visual attention select the forest and the trees?', *Nature* 382: 626–628.

Fodor, J.A. (1983) *The Modularity of Mind*, Cambridge, MA: MIT Press.

Frackowiak, R.S.J. (1994) 'Functional mapping of verbal memory and language', *TINS* 17: 109–115.

Friedman-Hill, S.R., Robertson, L.C. and Treisman, A. (1995) 'Parietal contributions to visual feature binding: evidence from a patient with bilateral lesions', *Science* 269: 853–855.

Frith, C.D. (1992) *The Cognitive Neuropsychology of Schizophrenia*, Hove, Sussex: Lawrence Erlbaum.

—— (1995) 'Functional imaging and cognitive abnormalities', *Lancet* 346: 615–620.

Frith, C.D. and Done, J.D. (1989) 'Experiences of alien control in schizophrenics reflect a disorder in the central monitoring action', *Psychological Medicine* 19: 359–363.

Garety, P.A. and Hemsley, D.R. (1994) *Delusions: Investigations into the Psychology of Delusional Reasoning*, Oxford: Oxford University Press.

Graves, R.J. (1851) 'Singular defect and impotence of memory after paralysis', *Dublin Quarterly Journal of Medical Science* 11: 1–4.

Gur, R.E. (1977) 'Motoric laterality imbalance in schizophrenia. A possible concomitant of left hemisphere dysfunction', *Archives of General Psychiatry* 34: 33–37.

Halligan, P.W. (1995) 'Drawing attention to neglect; the contribution of line bisection', *The Psychologist* 8: 257–264.

Halligan, P.W. and Marshall, J.C. (1988) 'How long is a piece of string? A study of line bisection in a case of visual neglect', *Cortex* 24: 321–328.

—— (1992) 'Left visuo-spatial neglect – a meaningless entity?', *Cortex* 28: 525–535.

—— (1993) 'The history and clinical presentation of visual neglect', in I. Robertson and J.C. Marshall (eds) *Unilateral Neglect: Clinical and Experimental Studies*, London: Lawrence Erlbaum.

—— (1994) *Spatial Neglect. Position Papers on Theory and Practice*, Hove, Sussex: Lawrence Erlbaum.

—— (eds) (1996) *Method in Madness: Case Studies in Cognitive Neuropsychiatry*, Hove, Sussex: Psychology Press.

Halligan, P.W. and Robertson, I.H. (1992) 'The assessment of unilateral neglect', in J. Crawford, D. Parker and W. McKinlay (eds) *A Handbook of Neuropsychological Assessment*, London: Lawrence Erlbaum.

Halligan, P.W., Marshall, J.C. and Ramachandren, V.S. (1994) 'Ghosts in the machine; a case description of visual and haptic hallucinations after right hemisphere stroke', *Cognitive Neuropsychology* 11: 459–477.

Halligan, P.W., Marshall, J.C. and Wade, D.T. (1989) 'Visuospatial neglect: underlying factors and test sensitivity', *Lancet* 2 (October): 908–911.

—— (1993) 'Three arms: a case study of supernumerary phantom limb after right hemisphere stroke', *Journal of Neurology, Neurosurgery and Psychiatry* 56: 159–166.

—— (1995) 'Unilateral somatoparaphrenia after right hemisphere stroke; a case description', *Cortex* 31: 173–182.

Happé, F. (1994) *Autism: An Introduction to Psychological Theory*, London: UCL Press.

Heilman, K.M. and Valenstein, E. (1993) *Clinical Neuropsychology*, New York: Oxford University Press.

Hellige, J.B. (1993) *Hemispheric Asymmetry: What's Right and What's Left*, Cambridge, MA: Harvard University Press.

Howard, D. and Patterson, K. (1989) 'Models for therapy', in X. Seron and G. Deloche (eds) *Cognitive Approaches in Neuropsychological Rehabilitation*, Hillsdale, NJ: Lawrence Erlbaum.

Humphreys, G.W. and Bruce, V. (1989) *Visual Cognition: Computational, Experimental and Neuropsychological Perspectives*, Hove, Sussex: Lawrence Erlbaum.

Humphreys, G.W. and Riddoch, M.J. (1987) 'On telling your fruit from your vegetables: a consideration of category-specific deficits after brain damage', *TINS* 10: 145–148.

Johnson, M.K. (1991) 'Reality monitoring: evidence from confabulation in organic brain disease patients', in G.P. Prigatano and D.L. Schacter (eds) *Awareness of Deficit after Brain Injury*, New York: Oxford University Press.

Jones, G.V. (1983) 'On double dissociation of function', *Neuropsychologia* 21: 397–400.

Keefe, R.S.E. (1995) 'The contribution of neuropsychology to psychiatry', *American Journal of Psychiatry* 152: 6–15.

Kopelman, M.D., Guinan, F.M. and Lewis, P.D.R. (1995) 'Delusional memory confabulation and frontal lobe dysfunction: a case study of De Clérambault's syndrome', *Neurocase* 1: 71–77.

Kopelman, M.D., Christensen, H., Puffett, A. and Stanhope, N. (1994) 'The Great Escape: a neurophysiological study of psychogenic amnesia', *Neuropsychologica* 32: 675–691.

Kosslyn, S.M. (1996) 'Neural systems and psychiatric disorders', *Cognitive Neuropsychiatry* 1: 89–93.

Kosslyn, S.M. and Intriligator, J.M. (1992) 'Is cognitive neuropsychology plausible? The perils of sitting on a one-legged stool', *Journal of Cognitive Neuroscience* 4: 96–106.

Ladavas, E., Paladini, R. and Cubelli, R. (1993) 'Implicit associative priming in a patient with left visual neglect', *Neuropsychologia* 31: 1307–1320.

Lahav, R. (1993) 'What neuropsychology tells us about consciousness', *Philosophy of Science* 60: 67–85.

Levin, S. (1984) 'Frontal lobe dysfunctions in schizophrenia II. Impairments of psychological and brain functions', *Journal of Psychiatric Research* 18: 57–72.

Lezak, M.D. (1995) *Neuropsychological Assessment (3rd edn)*, New York: Oxford University Press.

Liddle, P.F. (1987) 'The symptoms of chronic schizophrenia: a re-examination of the positive-negative dichotomy', *British Journal of Psychiatry* 151: 145–151.

Liddle, P.F., Friston, K.H., Frith, C.D., Hirsch, S.R., Jones, T. and Frackowiak, R.S. (1992) 'Patterns of cerebral blood flow in schizophrenia', *British Journal of Psychiatry* 160: 179–186.

McCarthy, R.A. and Warrington, E.K. (1990) *Cognitive Neuropsychology. A Clinical Introduction*, San Diego: Academic Press.

McClosky, M. (1993) 'Theory and evidence in cognitive neuropsychology: a "radical" response to Robertson, Knight, Rafal and Shimamura (1993)', *Journal of Experimental Psychology: Learning, Memory and Cognition* 19: 718–734.

McGlinchey-Berroth, R., Milberg, W.P., Verfaellie, M., Grande, L., D'Esposito, M. and Alexander, M. (1996) 'Semantic processing and orthographic specificity in hemispatial neglect', *Journal of Cognitive Neuroscience* 8: 291–304.

McGuire, P.K., Shah, P. and Murray, R.M. (1993) 'Increased blood flow in Broca's area during auditory hallucinations in schizophrenia', *Lancet* 342: 703–706.

McGuire, P.K., Bench, C.J., Frith, C.D., Marks, I.M., Frackowiak, R.S.J. and Dolan, R.J. (1994) 'Functional anatomy of obsessive-compulsive phenomena', *British Journal of Psychiatry* 164: 459–468.

McHugh, P.R. (1995). 'Witches, multiple personalities, and other psychiatric artefacts', *Nature Medicine* 1: 110–114.

McKenna, P.J., Tamlyn, D., Lund, C.E., Mortimer, A.M., Hammond, S. and Baddeley, A.D. (1990) 'Amnesic syndrome in schizophrenia', *Psychology of Medicine* 20: 967–972.

Manning, L. and Kartsounis, L.D. (1993) 'Confabulations related to tacit awareness in visual neglect', *Behavioural Neurology* 6: 211–213.

Margolin, D.I. (1991) 'Resolving enigmas about Wernicke's aphasia and other higher cortical disorders', *Archives of Neurology* 48: 751–65.

Marshall, J.C. and Halligan, P.W. (1988) 'Blindsight and insight in visuospatial neglect', *Nature* 336: 776–777.

—— (1989) 'When right goes left: an investigation of line bisection in a case of visual neglect', *Cortex* 25: 503–515.

—— (1995) 'Seeing the forest but only half the trees?', *Nature* 373: 521–523.

Marshall, J.C., Halligan, P.W. and Wade, D.T. (1995) 'Reduplication of an event after head injury? A cautionary case report', *Cortex* 31: 183–190.

Michel, F. and Peronnet, F. (1980) 'A case of cortical deafness: clinical and electrophysiological data', *Brain and Language* 10: 367–377.

Mijovic-Prelac, D., Shin, L.M., Chabris, C.F. and Kosslyn, S.M. (1994) 'When does "No" really mean "yes"? A case study in unilateral visual neglect', *Neuropsychologia* 32: 151–158.

Miller, E. (1993) 'Dissociating single cases in neuropsychology', *British Journal of Clinical Psychology* 32: 155–167.

—— (1996) 'Phrenology, neuropsychology and rehabilitation', *Neuropsychological Rehabilitation* 6: 245–255.

Milner, A.D. and Rugg, M.D. (1992) *The Neuropsychology of Consciousness*, London: Academic Press.

Moscovitch, M. and Umilta, C. (1991) 'Conscious and nonconscious aspects of memory: a neuropsychological framework of modules and central systems', in R.G. Lister and H.J. Weingartner (eds) *Perspectives on Cognitive Neuroscience*, Oxford: Oxford University Press.

Moscovitch, M., Wincour, G. and McLachlan, D. (1986) 'Memory as assessed by recognition and reading time in normal and memory impaired people with Alzheimer's disease and other neurological disorders', *Journal of Experimental Psychology* 115: 331–347.

Motter, B.C. (1993) 'Focal attention produces spatially selective processing in visual cortical areas V1, V2 and V4 in the presence of competing stimuli', *Journal of Neurophysiology* 70: 909–919.

Nadeau, S.E. and Crosson, B. (1995) 'A guide to the functional imaging of cognitive processes', *Neuropsychiatry, Neuropsychology and Behavioural Neurology* 8: 143–162.

Neisser, U. (1967) *Cognitive Psychology*, New York: Appleton-Century-Crofts.

O'Carroll, R. (1992) 'Neuropsychology of psychosis', *Current Opinion in Psychiatry* 5: 38–44.

Osborne, J. (1833) 'On the loss of the faculty of speech depending upon forgetfulness of the art of using the vocal organs', *Dublin Journal of Medical and Chemical Science* 4: 157–170.

Paillard, J., Michael, F. and Stelmach, G. (1983) 'Localisation without content: a tactile analogue of "blindsight"', *Archives of Neurology* 40: 548–551.

Pardo, J.V., Fox, P.T. and Raichle, M.E. (1991) 'Localisation of a human system for sustained attention by positron emission tomography', *Nature* 349: 61–63.

Parkin, A.J. (1996) *Explorations in Cognitive Neuropsychology*, Oxford: Blackwell.

Patterson, T. (1987) 'Studies toward the subcortical pathogenesis of schizophrenia', *Schizophrenia Bulletin* 13: 555–576.

Perenin, M.T. and Rossetti, Y. (1996) 'Grasping without form discrimination in a hemianopic field', *NeuroReport* 7: 793–797.

Posner, M.I. and Petersen, S.E. (1990) 'The attention system of the human brain', *Annual Review of Neuroscience* 13: 25–42.

Rafal, R., Smith, W., Krantz, J., Cohen, A. and Brennan, C. (1990) 'Extrageniculate vision in hemianopic humans: saccade inhibition by signals in the blind field', *Science* 250: 118–121.

Raunch, S.L., van der Kolk, B.A., Fisler, R.E., Alpert, N.M., Orr, S.P., Savage, C.R., Fischman, A.J., Jenike, M.A. and Pitman, R.K. (1996) 'A symptom provocation study of post-traumatic stress disorder using positron emission tomography and script-driven imagery', *Archives of General Psychiatry* 53: 380–387.

Renault, B., Signoret, J.L., Debruille, B., Breton, F. and Bolgert, F. (1989) 'Brain potentials reveal covert facial recognition in prosopagnosia', *Neuropsychologia* 27: 905–912.

Riddoch, M.J. and Humphreys. G.W. (1994) *Cognitive Neuropsychology and Cognitive Rehabilitation*, Hove, Sussex: Lawrence Erlbaum.

Ro, T. and Rafal, R.D. (1996) 'Perception of geometric illusions in hemispatial neglect', *Neuropsychologia* 34: 973–978.

Robertson, I. (1994) 'Methodology in neuropsychological rehabilitation research', *Neuropsychological Rehabilitation* 4: 1–6.

Robertson, I. and Marshall, J.C. (1993) *Unilateral Neglect: Clinical and Experimental Studies*, London: Lawrence Erlbaum.

Robertson, L.C., Knight, R.T., Rafal, R. and Shimamura, A.P. (1993) 'Cognitive neuropsychology is more than single case studies', *Journal of Experimental Psychology: Learning, Memory and Cognition* 19: 710–717.

Ron, M.A. (1994) 'Somatisation in neurological practice', *Journal of Neurology, Neurosurgery and Psychiatry* 57: 1161–1164.

Rossetti, Y., Rode, G. and Boisson, D. (1995) 'Implicit processing of somaesthetic information: a dissociation between where and how?', *NeuroReport* 6: 506–510.

Schacter, D.L., McAndrews, M.P. and Moscovitch, M. (1988) 'Access to consciousness: dissociations between implicit and explicit knowledge of neuropsychological syndromes', in L. Weiskrantz (ed.) *Thought Without Language*, Oxford: Clarendon Press.

Sergent, J. (1994) 'Brain-imaging studies of cogntive functions', *TINS* 17: 22.

Sergent, J., Zuck, E., Terriah, S. and MacDonald, B. (1992) 'Distributed neural network underlying musical sight reading and keyboard', *Science* 257: 61–63.

Shallice, T. (1988) *From Neuropsychology to Mental Structure*, Cambridge: Cambridge University Press.

Shallice, T., Burgess, P.W. and Frith, C.D. (1991) 'Can the neuropsychological case-study approach be applied to schizophrenia?', *Psychological Medicine* 21: 661–673.

Shallice, T., Fletcher, P., Frith, C.D., Grasby, P., Frackowiak, R.S.J. and Dolan, R. (1994) 'Brain regions associated with acquisition and retrieval of verbal episodic memory', *Nature* 368: 633–635.

Silbersweig, D.A., Stern, E., Frith, C.D., Cahill, C., Holmes, A., Grootoonk, S., Seaward, J., McKenna, P., Chua, S.E., Schnorr, L., Jones, T. and Frackowiak, R.S.J. (1995) 'A functional neuroanatomy of hallucinations in schizophrenia', *Nature* 378: 176–179.

Sokol, S.M., McCloskey, M., Cohen, N.J. and Aliminosa, D. (1991) 'Cognitive representations and processes in arithmetic: inferences from the performance of brain-damaged subjects', *Journal of Experimental Psychology: Learning, Memory and Cognition* 17: 355–376.

Stoerig, P. (1996) 'Varieties of vision: from blind responses to conscious recognition', *TINS* 19: 401–406.

Thaiss, L. and De Bleser, R. (1992) 'Visual agnosia: a case of reduced attentional 'spotlight'?', *Cortex* 28: 601–621.

Tranel, D. and Damasio, A.R. (1985) 'Knowledge without awareness: an autonomic index of facial recognition by prosopagnosics', *Science* 228: 1453–1545.

Tyler, L.K. (1992) 'The distinction between implicit and explicit language function: evidence from aphasia', in A.D. Milner and M.D. Rugg (eds) *The Neuropsychology of Consciousness*, London: Academic Press.

Vandernberghe, R., Price, C., Wise, R., Josephs, O. and Frackowiak, R.S.J. (1996) 'Functional anatomy of a common semantic system for words and pictures', *Nature* 383: 254–217.

Warrington, E.K. and McCarthy, R. (1987) 'Categories of knowledge: further fractionations and an attempted integration', *Brain* 110: 1273–1296.

Warrington, E.K. and Shallice, T. (1984) 'Category specific semantic impairments', *Brain* 107: 829–854.

Weiskrantz, L. (1986) *Blindsight. A Case Study and Implications*, Oxford: Oxford University Press.

—— (1989) 'Remembering dissociations', in H.L. Roediger and F.I.M. Craik (eds) *Varieties of Memory and Consciousness – Essays in Honour of Endel Tulving*, Hillsdale, NJ: Lawrence Erlbaum.

—— (1990) 'Outlooks for blindsight: explicit methodologies for implicit processes', *Proceedings of the Royal Society London* 239: 247–278.

—— (1991) 'Disconnected awareness for detecting, processing, and remembering in neurological patients', *Journal of the Royal Society of Medicine* 84: 466–470.

Weiskrantz, L., Warrington, E.K., Sanders, M.D. and Marshall, J.C. (1974) 'Visual capacity in the hemianopic field following a restricted occipital ablation', *Brain* 97: 709–728.

Wernicke, C. (1874) *Der aphasische Symptomen Complex*, Breslau: Cohn und Weigart (trans in G.H. Eggert, *Wernicke's Works on Aphasia*, The Hague: Mouton, 1977).

Winters, K.C. and Neale, J.M. (1993) 'Delusions and delusional thinking in psychotics: a review of the literature', *Clinical Psychology Review* 3: 227–253.

Young, A.W. (1994) 'Covert recognition', in M.J. Farah and G. Ratcliff (eds) *The Neuropsychology of High Level Vision: Collected Tutorial Essays*, Hillsdale, NJ: Lawrence Erlbaum.

—— (1996) 'Dissociable aspects of consciousness', in M.Velmans (ed.) *The Science of Consciousness: Psychological, Neuropsychological and Clinical Reviews*, London: Routledge.

Young, A.W. and Leafhead, K.M. (1996) 'Betwixt life and death: case studies of the Cotard delusion', in P.W. Halligan and J.C. Marshall (eds) *Method in Madness: Case Studies in Cognitive Neuropsychiatry*, Hove, Sussex: The Psychology Press.

Young, A.W., Leafhead, K.M. and Szulecka, T.K. (1994) 'The Capgras and Cotard delusion', *Psychopathology* 27: 226–231.

Young, A.W., Reid, I., Wright, S. and Hellawell, D.J. (1993) 'Face-processing impairments and the Capgras delusion', *British Journal of Psychiatry* 162: 695–698.

Zeki, S. (1993) *A Vision of the Brain*, Oxford: Blackwell.

Zihl, J., Tretter, F. and Singer, W. (1980) 'Phasic electrodermal responses in patients with central blindness', *Behavioural Brain Research* 1: 197–203.

Zurif, E., Swinney, D. and Fodor, J.A. (1991) 'An evaluation of assumptions underlying the single-patient-only position in neuropsychological research: a reply', *Brain and Cognition* 16: 198–210.

18 A theory of emotion and its brain mechanisms

Edmund T. Rolls[*]

An aim of this chapter is to illustrate how physiological psychology has developed in the last hundred years by taking a nineteenth-century theory of emotion, and showing how it is now becoming possible to delineate the actual information processing that takes place in the brain to implement emotion, thus helping to provide a firm foundation for a theory of emotion. This chapter also points to some issues that should be solved in the first part of the twenty-first century, and to another, the problem of consciousness, that may still be debated for a long time, but to which cognitive neuroscience is bringing much new insight.

First, problems with peripheral theories of emotion such as the James-Lange theory of emotion, and some of its recent descendants are considered. A modern theory of emotion is then presented, and it is shown how at least some of its processes can be seen to be implemented in the information processing performed by certain brain regions. Rooting a theory of emotion in brain processes in this way is helpful not only because it helps to provide a firm foundation for the theory, but also because it leads towards an understanding of the emotional and related changes that follow damage to certain parts of the brain. It will also enable drugs for the treatment of anxiety and depression to be developed that are targeted at brain areas specifically known to be involved in emotion. Finally, some searching unsolved questions for the future are briefly highlighted, such as how behaviour is selected based on the emotional and cognitive state, and the available rewards and punishments; and why emotional feelings should feel like anything, which is part of the much larger problem of consciousness.

[*] The author has worked on some of the experiments described here with G.C. Baylis, M.J. Burton, M.E. Hasselmo, C.M. Leonard, F. Mora, D.I. Perrett, M.K. Sanghera, T.R. Scott, S.J. Thorpe and F.A.W. Wilson. Their collaboration, and helpful discussions with or communications from M. Davies, C.C.W. Taylor (Corpus Christi College, Oxford) and M.S. Dawkins are sincerely acknowledged. Some of the research described was supported by the Medical Research Council.

THE JAMES–LANGE THEORY OF EMOTION, AND SOME OF ITS DESCENDANTS

The James–Lange theory postulates that certain stimuli produce bodily responses, including somatic and autonomic responses, and that it is the sensing of these bodily changes that gives rise to the feeling of emotion (James 1884, 1890; Lange 1885). This theory is encapsulated by the statement 'I feel frightened because I am running away.' This theory has gradually been weakened by evidence that there is no detailed pattern of autonomic responses that corresponds to each emotion; that disconnection from the periphery (for example, after spinal cord damage or damage to the sympathetic and vagus autonomic nerves) does not abolish behavioural signs of emotion or emotional feelings (see Cannon 1927; Grossman 1967; Hohmann 1966; Oatley and Jenkins 1996); that emotional intensity can be modulated by peripheral injections of, for example, adrenaline (epinephrine) that produce autonomic effects, but that it is the cognitive state as induced by environmental stimuli, and not the autonomic state, that produces an emotion, and determines what the emotion is (Schachter and Singer 1962); and that peripheral autonomic blockade with pharmacological agents does not prevent emotions from being felt (Reisenzein 1983). The James–Lange theory, and theories which are closely related to it, suppose that feedback from parts of the periphery, such as the face (see Adelmann and Zajonc 1989), or body as in Damasio's somatic marker hypothesis (Damasio 1994), leads to emotional feelings. However, such theories have a major weakness in that they do not give an adequate account of which stimuli produce the peripheral change that is postulated to lead eventually to emotion. In other words, these theories do not provide an account of the rules by which only some environmental stimuli produce emotions, or how neurally only such stimuli produce emotions.

We turn in the remainder of this chapter to the foundations of a theory which attempts to overcome these difficulties and to the neural implementation of the processes involved. But first note that another problem with bodily mediation theories is that introducing bodily responses, and then sensing of these body responses, into the chain by which stimuli come to elicit emotions, is that this must introduce noise into the system. Once the brain has decided that some stimuli should elicit emotional responses, it would be much more direct, and less noisy, to interface this signal to the emotional system in the brain, rather than inserting a peripheral loop into the circuit. Damasio (1994) may partially circumvent this last problem in his theory by allowing central representations of somatic markers to become conditioned to bodily somatic markers, so that after the appropriate learning, a peripheral somatic change may not be needed. However, this scheme still suffers from noise inherent in producing bodily responses, in sensing them, and in conditioning central representations of the somatic markers to the bodily states. The prediction would apparently be that if an emotional response were produced to a visual stimulus, then this would necessarily involve activity in the somatosensory cortex or other brain region in which the 'somatic marker' would be represented. This prediction could be tested (for example, in patients with somatosensory cortex damage), but it seems most unlikely that an emotion produced by a visual reinforcer would require activity in the somatosensory cortex. As noted, this class of theory does not in any case provide an account of which stimuli cause emotions, and the mechanisms by which these stimuli lead to a brain representation in the first place which leads to emotion.

A THEORY OF EMOTION

Emotions can usefully be defined as states produced by instrumental reinforcing stimuli (for a more full account, see Rolls 1990, 1992b, 1995a, 1986a, 1986b, and earlier work by Millenson 1967; Weiskrantz 1968; Gray 1975, 1987). Instrumental reinforcers are stimuli which if their occurrence, termination or omission is made contingent upon the making of a response, alter the probability of the future emission of that response. Some stimuli are unlearned reinforcers (for example, the taste of food if the animal is hungry, or pain); while others may become reinforcing because of their association with such primary reinforcers, thereby becoming 'secondary reinforcers'. This type of learning may thus be called 'stimulus-reinforcement association', and probably occurs via the process of classical conditioning. If a reinforcer increases the probability of emission of a response on which it is contingent, it is said to be a 'positive reinforcer' or 'reward'; if it decreases the probability of such a response it is a 'negative reinforcer' or 'punishment'. For example, fear is an emotional state which might be produced by a sound (the conditioned stimulus) that has previously been associated with an electrical shock (the primary reinforcer).

The converse reinforcement contingencies produce the opposite effects on behaviour. The omission or termination of a positive reinforcer ('extinction' and 'time out' respectively, sometimes described as 'punishing') decrease the probability of responses. Responses followed by the omission or termination of a negative reinforcer increase in probability, this pair of negative reinforcement operations being termed 'active avoidance' and 'escape' respectively (see also Gray 1975 and Mackintosh 1983).

The different emotions can be described and classified according to whether the reinforcer is positive or negative, and by the reinforcement contingency. An outline of such a classification scheme, elaborated more precisely by Rolls (1990), is shown in Figure 18.1. The mechanisms described here would not be limited in the range of emotions for which they could account. Some of the factors which enable a very wide range of human emotions to be analysed with this foundation are elaborated elsewhere (Rolls 1990), and include the following:

- The reinforcement contingency (see Figure 18.1).
- The intensity of the reinforcer (see Figure 18.1).

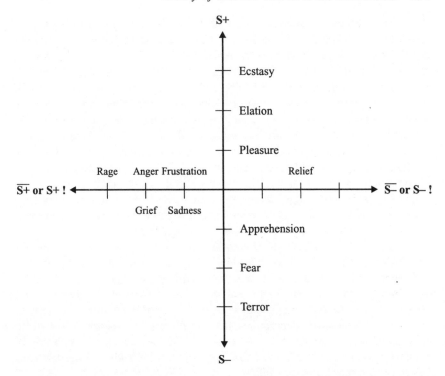

Figure 18.1 Some of the emotions associated with different reinforcement contingencies are indicated. Intensity increases away from the centre of the diagram, on a continuous scale. The classification scheme created by the different reinforcement contingencies consists of (1) the presentation of a positive reinforcer (S+), (2) the presentation of a negative reinforcer (S−), (3) the omission of a positive reinforcer ($\overline{S+}$) or the termination of a positive reinforcer (S+!), and (4) the omission of a negative reinforcer ($\overline{S−}$) or the termination of a negative reinforcer (S−!).

- Any environmental stimulus might have a number of different reinforcement associations. For example, a stimulus might be associated with the presentation both of a reward and of a punishment, allowing states such as conflict and guilt to arise.
- Emotions elicited by stimuli associated with different primary reinforcers will be different.
- Emotions elicited by different secondary reinforcing stimuli will be different from each other (even if the primary reinforcer is similar).
- The emotion elicited can depend on whether an active or passive behavioural response is possible. For example, if an active behavioural response can occur to the omission of an S+, then anger might be produced, but if only passive behaviour is possible, then sadness, depression or grief might occur.

By combining these six factors, it is possible to account for a very wide range of emotions (for elaboration, see Rolls 1990). It is also worth noting that emotions can be produced just as much by the recall of reinforcing events as by external reinforcing stimuli; that cognitive processing (whether conscious or not) is important in many emotions, for very complex cognitive processing may be required to determine whether environmental events are reinforcing or not; that emotions normally consist of cognitive processing which determines the reinforcing valence of the stimulus, and elicited mood change if the valence is positive or negative; and that stability of mood implies that absolute levels of reinforcement must be represented over moderately long time spans by the firing of mood-related neurons, a difficult operation which may contribute to 'spontaneous' mood swings, depression which occurs without a clear external cause, and the multiplicity of hormonal and transmitter systems which seem to be involved in the control of mood (see also Rolls 1990).

In terms of the neural bases of emotion, the most important point from this introduction is that in order to understand the neural bases of emotion, we need to consider brain mechanisms involved in reward and punishment, and involved in learning about which environmental stimuli are associated, or are no longer associated, with rewards and punishments. Before considering this, it is useful to summarize the functions of emotions, because these functions are important for understanding the output systems to which brain mechanisms involved in emotion must interface. The *functions*, described more fully elsewhere (Rolls 1990), can be summarized as follows:

- *The elicitation of autonomic responses* (e.g. a change in heart rate) and endocrine responses (e.g. the release of adrenaline). These prepare the body for action. There are output pathways from the amygdala and orbitofrontal cortex directly, and via the hypothalamus, to the brainstem autonomic nuclei.
- Flexibility of behavioural responses to reinforcing stimuli. Emotional (and motivational) states allow a simple interface between sensory inputs and motor outputs, because only the valence of the stimulus to which attention is being paid needs to be passed to the motor system, rather than a full representation of the sensory world. In addition, when a stimulus in the environment elicits an emotional state (because it is a primary reinforcer or because of classical conditioning), we can flexibly choose any appropriate instrumental response to obtain the reward, or avoid the punishment. This is more flexible than simply learning a fixed behavioural response to a stimulus, i.e. response habit or stimulus-response learning (see Gray 1975; Rolls 1990). Pathways from the amygdala and orbitofrontal cortex to the striatum are implicated in these functions.

This function is based on the crucial role which rewards and punishments have on behaviour. Animals are equipped with neural systems that enable them to evaluate which environmental stimuli, whether learned or not, are rewarding and punishing; that is, will be worked for or avoided. A crucial part of this system is that with many competing rewards, goals, and priorities, there must be a selection system for enabling the most important of these goals to become the object of behaviour at any one time. This selection process must be capable of responding to many different types of reward decoded in different brain systems that have evolved at different times, even including the use in humans of a language system to enable long-term plans to be made (see Rolls 1997a). These many different brain systems, some involving implicit evaluation of rewards, and others explicit, verbal, conscious evaluation of rewards and planned long-term goals, must all enter into the selector of behaviour. This selector, although itself poorly understood, might include a process of competition between all the competing calls on output, and might involve the basal ganglia (see Rolls and Johnstone 1992; Rolls 1994a; Rolls and Treves 1997, Chapter 9).

- *Emotion is motivating.* For example, fear learned by stimulus-reinforcement association formation provides the motivation for actions performed to avoid noxious stimuli.
- *Communication.* For example, monkeys may communicate their emotional state to others, by making an open-mouth threat to indicate the extent to which they are willing to compete for resources, and this may influence the behaviour of other animals. This aspect of emotion was emphasized by Darwin (1872). There are neural systems in the amygdala and overlying temporal cortical visual areas which are specialized for the face-related aspects of this processing.
- *Social bonding.* Examples of this are the emotions associated with the attachment of parents to their young, and the attachment of the young to their parents (see Dawkins 1989).
- The current mood state can affect the *cognitive evaluation of events or memories* (see Blaney 1986; Oatley and Jenkins 1996), and this may have the function of facilitating continuity in the interpretation of the reinforcing value of events in the environment. A hypothesis on the neural pathways which implement this is presented in the section 'Effects of emotions on cognitive processing'.
- Emotion may facilitate the *storage of memories.*

One way in which this occurs is that episodic memory (i.e. one's memory of particular episodes) is facilitated by emotional states. This may be advantageous, in that storing many details of the prevailing situation when a strong reinforcer is delivered may be useful in generating appropriate behaviour in situations with some similarities in the future. This function may be implemented by the relatively non-specific projecting systems to the cerebral cortex and hippocampus, including the cholinergic pathways in the basal forebrain and medial septum, and the ascending noradrenergic pathways (see Wilson and Rolls

1990a, 1990b; Treves and Rolls 1994; Rolls and Treves 1997). A second way in which emotion may affect the storage of memories is that the current emotional state may be stored with episodic memories, providing a mechanism for the current emotional state to affect which memories are recalled. A third way in which emotion may affect the storage of memories is by guiding the cerebral cortex in the representations of the world which are set up. For example, in the visual system, it may be useful to build perceptual representations or analysers which are different from each other if they are associated with different reinforcers, and to be less likely to build them if they have no association with reinforcement. Ways in which back projections from parts of the brain important in emotion (such as the amygdala) to parts of the cerebral cortex could perform this function are discussed by Rolls (1989a, 1990, 1992b, and Rolls and Treves 1997).

Another function of emotion is that by enduring for minutes or longer after a reinforcing stimulus has occurred, it may help to produce *persistent and continuing motivation and direction of behaviour* to help achieve a goal or goals. Emotion may trigger the *recall of memories* stored in neocortical representations. Amygdala back projections to the cortex could perform this for emotion in a way analogous to that in which the hippocampus could implement the retrieval in the neocortex of recent (episodic) memories (Treves and Rolls 1994).

THE NEURAL BASES OF EMOTION

Some of the main brain regions implicated in emotion will now be considered, in the light of the theory just given on the nature and functions of emotion. The description here is abbreviated, focusing on the main conceptual points. More detailed accounts of the evidence, and references to the original literature, are provided by Rolls (1990, 1992b, 1995a, 1996). The brain regions discussed include the amygdala and orbitofrontal cortex. Some of these brain regions are indicated in Figures 18.2 and 18.3. Particular attention is paid to the functions of these regions in primates, for in primates the neocortex undergoes great development and provides major inputs to these regions, in some cases to parts of these structures thought not to be present in non-primates. An example of this is the projection from the primate neocortex in the anterior part of the temporal lobe to the basal accessory nucleus of the amygdala (see below).

The amygdala

Connections of the amygdala

The amygdala receives massive projections in the primate from the overlying temporal lobe cortex (see Amaral *et al.* 1992). These come in the monkey to overlapping but partly separate regions of the lateral and basal amygdala from the inferior temporal visual cortex, the superior temporal auditory cortex, the

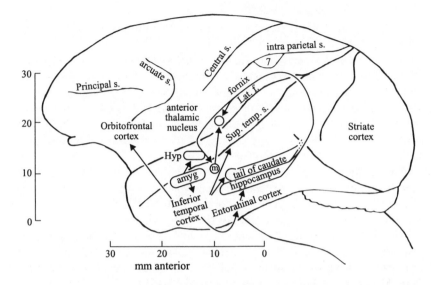

Figure 18.2 Some of the pathways described in the text are shown on this lateral view of the rhesus monkey brain: amyg = amygdala; Central s. = central sulcus; Hyp = hypothalamus/substantia innominata/basal forebrain; Lat. f. = lateral (or Sylvian) fissure; m = mammillary body; Sup. temp. s. = superior temporal sulcus; 7 = posterior parietal cortex, area 7

cortex of the temporal pole, and the cortex in the superior temporal sulcus. These inputs thus come from the higher stages of sensory processing in the visual and auditory modalities, and not from early cortical processing areas. The amygdala also receives from the part of the insula that receives projections from the somatosensory cortical areas (Mesulam and Mufson 1982). It also receives projections from the posterior orbitofrontal cortex (see Figure 18.2). Subcortical inputs to the amygdala include projections from the hypothalamus and substantia innominata, and from olfactory structures.

Although there are some inputs from early on in some sensory pathways, for example, auditory inputs from the medial geniculate nucleus (LeDoux 1987, 1992, 1994), this route is unlikely to be involved in most emotions, for which cortical analysis of the stimulus is likely to be required. Emotions are usually elicited to environmental stimuli analysed to the object level (including other organisms), and not to retinal arrays of spots or pure tones. Consistent with this view, neurons in the inferior temporal visual cortex do not have responses related to the association with reinforcement of visual stimuli (Rolls *et al.* 1977); whereas such neurons are found in the amygdala and orbitofrontal cortex (see below; cf Figures 18.2 and 18.3). Similarly, processing in the taste system of primates up to and including the primary taste cortex reflects the identity of the tastant, whereas its hedonic value, as influenced by hunger, is reflected in the responses of neurons in the secondary taste cortex (Rolls 1989b, 1994b; and see Figure 18.3).

The outputs of the amygdala (Amaral *et al.* 1992) include the well-known projections to the hypothalamus and also directly to the autonomic centres in the medulla oblongata, providing a route for cortically processed signals to reach the brainstem. A further interesting output of the amygdala is to the ventral striatum (Heimer *et al.* 1982) including the nucleus accumbens, for via this route information processed in the amygdala could gain access to the basal ganglia and thus influence motor output. (The output of the amygdala also reaches more dorsal parts of the striatum.) The amygdala also projects to the medial part of the mediodorsal nucleus of the thalamus, which projects to the orbitofrontal cortex and provides the amygdala with another output. In addition, the amygdala has direct projections back to many areas of the temporal, orbitofrontal and insular cortices from which it receives inputs (Amaral *et al.* 1992). It is suggested elsewhere (Rolls 1989a, 1989c) that the functions of these back projections include the guidance of information representation and storage in the neocortex, and recall (when this is related to reinforcing stimuli).

These anatomical connections of the amygdala indicate that it is placed to receive highly processed information from the cortex and to influence motor systems, autonomic systems, some of the cortical areas from which it receives inputs, and other limbic areas. The functions mediated through these connections will now be considered, using information available from the effects of damage to the amygdala and from the activity of neurons in the amygdala.

Effects of amygdala lesions

Bilateral removal of the amygdala in monkeys produces tameness, a lack of emotional responsiveness, excessive examination of objects, often with the mouth, and consumption of previously rejected items such as meat (Weiskrantz 1956; cf. Kluver and Bucy 1939). In analyses of the bases of these behavioural changes, it has been observed that there are deficits in learning to associate stimuli with primary reinforcement, including both punishments (Weiskrantz 1956) and rewards (Jones and Mishkin 1972; Gaffan 1992; Aggleton 1993). The association learning deficit is present when the associations must be learned from a previously neutral stimulus (for example, the sight of an object) to a primary reinforcing stimulus (such as the taste of food). The impairment is not found when the association learning is between a visual stimulus and an auditory stimulus which is already a secondary reinforcer (because of prior pairing with food). Thus the amygdala is involved in learning associations between neutral stimuli and primary (but not secondary) reinforcers (see Gaffan 1992). Further evidence linking the amygdala to reinforcement mechanisms is that monkeys will work in order to obtain electrical stimulation of the amygdala, and that

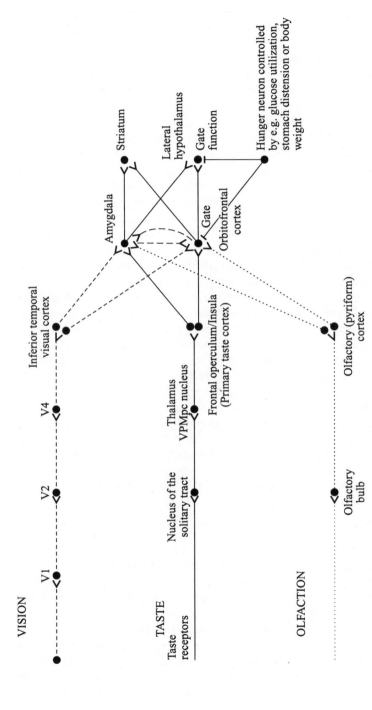

Figure 18.3 Diagrammatic representation of some of the connections described in the text. V1 – striate visual cortex. V2 and V4 – cortical visual areas. In primates, sensory analysis proceeds in the visual system as far as the inferior temporal cortex and the primary gustatory cortex; beyond these areas, in, for example, the amygdala and orbitofrontal cortex, the hedonic value of the stimuli, and whether they are reinforcing or are associated with reinforcement, is represented.

single neurons in the amygdala are activated by brain-stimulation reward of a number of different sites (Rolls 1975; Rolls *et al.* 1980).

The symptoms of the Kluver-Bucy syndrome, including the emotional changes, could be a result of this type of deficit in learning stimulus-reinforcement associations (Jones and Mishkin 1972; Aggleton and Passingham 1981; Mishkin and Aggleton 1981; Rolls 1986a, 1986b, 1990, 1992b). For example, the tameness, the hypoemotionality, the increased orality and the altered responses to food would arise because of damage to the normal mechanism by which stimuli become associated with reward or punishment.

The amygdala is well placed anatomically for learning associations between objects and primary reinforcers, for it receives inputs from the higher parts of the visual system, and from systems processing primary reinforcers such as taste, smell and touch (see Figure 18.3). The association learning in the amygdala may be implemented by Hebb-modifiable synapses from visual and auditory neurons on to neurons receiving inputs from taste, olfactory or somatosensory primary reinforcers (cf. Taira and Rolls 1996). Consistent with this, Davis (1992) has found that at least one type of associative learning in the amygdala can be blocked by local application to the amygdala of a NMDA receptor blocker. Further, Cador *et al.* (1989) obtained evidence consistent with the hypothesis that the learned incentive (conditioned reinforcing) effects of previously neutral stimuli paired with rewards are mediated by the amygdala acting through the ventral striatum, in that amphetamine injections into the ventral striatum enhanced the effects of a conditioned reinforcing stimulus only if the amygdala was intact (see also Everitt and Robbins 1992).

There is thus much evidence to show that the amygdala is involved in responses made to stimuli associated by learning with primary reinforcement. There is evidence that it may also be involved in whether novel stimuli are approached, for monkeys with amygdala lesions place novel foods and non-food objects in their mouths, and rats with amygdala lesions have decreased neophobia, in that they more quickly accept new foods (Rolls and Rolls 1973; see also Dunn and Everitt 1988; Rolls 1992b; Wilson and Rolls 1993, 1997).

Neuronal activity in the primate amygdala to reinforcing stimuli

Recordings from single neurons in the amygdala of the monkey have shown that some neurons do respond to visual stimuli, consistent with the inputs from the temporal lobe visual cortex (Sanghera *et al.* 1979). Other neurons responded to auditory, gustatory, olfactory or somatosensory stimuli, or in relation to movements. In tests of whether the neurons responded on the basis of the association of stimuli with reinforcement, it was found that approximately 20 per cent of the neurons with visual responses had responses which occurred primarily to stimuli associated with reinforcement, for example, to food and to a range of stimuli which the monkey had learned signified food in a visual discrimination task (Sanghera *et al.* 1979; Rolls 1981; Wilson and Rolls 1993,

1997). However, none of these neurons (in contrast to some neurons in the hypothalamus and orbitofrontal cortex described below) responded exclusively to rewarded stimuli, in that all responded at least partly to one or more neutral, novel or aversive stimuli. Neurons with responses which are probably similar to these have also been described by Ono *et al.* (1980), and by Nishijo *et al.* (1988) (and see Ono and Nishijo, 1992).

The degree to which the responses of these amygdala neurons are associated with reinforcement has been assessed in learning tasks. When the association between a visual stimulus and reinforcement was altered by reversal (so that the visual stimulus formerly associated with juice reward became associated with aversive saline and vice versa), it was found that ten out of eleven neurons did not reverse their responses, and for the other neuron the evidence was not clear (Sanghera *et al.* 1979; Wilson and Rolls 1993, 1997; see also Rolls 1992b). In contrast, neurons in the orbitofrontal cortex do show very rapid reversal of their responses in visual discrimination reversal and it therefore seems likely that the orbitofrontal cortex is especially involved when repeated relearning and reassessment of stimulus-reinforcement associations is required, as described below, rather than initial learning, in which the amygdala may be involved.

The crucial site of the stimulus-reinforcement association learning, which underlies the responses of amygdala neurons to learned reinforcing stimuli, is probably within the amygdala itself, and not at earlier stages of processing. Evidence for this is that neurons in the inferior temporal cortical visual areas do not reflect the reward associations of visual stimuli, but respond to visual stimuli based on their physical characteristics (Rolls *et al.* 1977; Wallis and Rolls 1997). Neurons from these areas project into the amygdala, where neurons which reflect the reinforcement association are found. Another line of evidence on this is that the inferior temporal cortical areas are mainly unimodal visual and there are no inputs from the taste and somatosensory systems which could introduce the primary reinforcers needed for the stimulus-reinforcement association learning. In contrast, such primary reinforcers are represented in the amygdala, which is a multimodal brain region. Although Le Doux's (1994) model of emotional learning does show that for very simple auditory stimuli (pure tones), some effect of pairing with aversive somatosensory stimuli is evident in the rat before the auditory information has reached the amygdala (in subcortical areas such as a part of the medial geniculate nucleus), this almost certainly does not reflect what normally occurs in primates. Normally, a visual stimulus will need to be analysed to the object level (for example, to the level of face identity, and this requires cortical processing) before the representation is appropriate for input to a stimulus-reinforcement evaluation system such as the amygdala or orbitofrontal cortex. The point here is that we do not normally have emotions to stimuli which require as little processing as pure tones. Instead, emotions are normally produced by complex visual stimuli (such as faces) or complex auditory stimuli (such as a particular person's voice). Thus cortical processing to the object level is required in most normal emotional situations, and these cortical object representations are projected to reach multimodal areas such as the amygdala and orbitofrontal cortex before the reinforcement label is attached.

Responses of these amygdala neurons to novel stimuli which are reinforcing

As described above, some of the amygdala neurons that responded to rewarding visual stimuli also responded to some other stimuli that were not associated with reward. Wilson and Rolls (1993, 1997) discovered a possible reason for this. They showed that these neurons with reward-related responses also responded to relatively novel visual stimuli, in, for example, visual recognition memory tasks. When monkeys are given such relatively novel stimuli outside the task, they will reach out for and explore the objects, and in this respect the novel stimuli are reinforcing. Repeated presentation of the stimuli results in habituation of the neuronal response and of behavioural approach, if the stimuli are not associated with primary reinforcement. It is· thus suggested that the amygdala neurons described operate as filters which provide an output if a stimulus is associated with a positive reinforcer, or is positively reinforcing because of relative novelty. The functions of this output may be to influence the interest shown in a stimulus, whether it is approached or avoided, whether an affective response occurs to it, and whether a representation of the stimulus is made or maintained via an action mediated through either the basal forebrain nucleus of Meynert or the back projections to the cerebral cortex (Rolls 1987, 1989a, 1990, 1992b, 1995c, 1997a).

It is an important adaptation to the environment to explore relatively novel objects or situations, for in this way advantage due to gene inheritance can become expressed and selected for. This function appears to be implemented in the amygdala in this way. Lesions of the amygdala impair the operation of this mechanism, in that objects are approached and explored indiscriminately, relatively independently of whether they are associated with positive or negative reinforcement, or are novel or familiar.

Neuronal responses in the primate amygdala to faces

Another interesting group of neurons in the amygdala responds primarily to faces (Rolls 1981; Leonard *et al.* 1985). Each of these neurons responds to some but not all of a set of faces, and thus across an ensemble could convey information about the identity of the face. These neurons are found especially in the basal accessory nucleus of the amygdala (Leonard *et al.* 1985), a part of the amygdala that develops markedly in primates (Amaral *et al.* 1992).

This is probably part of a system which has evolved for the rapid and reliable identification of individuals from their faces, and of facial expressions, because of the importance of this in primate social behaviour (Rolls 1981, 1984, 1990, 1992a, 1992b, 1992c; Perrett and Rolls 1982; Leonard *et al.* 1985).

Cortical cells found in certain of the temporal lobe regions (e.g. Tea, Tem and

TPO: Baylis *et al.* 1987) which project into the amygdala have properties which would enable them to provide useful inputs to such an associative mechanism in the amygdala (see Rolls 1989a, 1990, 1992a, 1992b, 1992c, 1994a, 1994b, 1997a; Rolls and Treves 1997; Wallis and Rolls 1996). Some of these cells are tuned to face identity, and others to face expression (Hasselmo *et al.* 1989). These cortical neurons in many cases use ensemble encoding with sparse distributed representations (Baylis *et al.* 1985; Rolls and Treves 1990). This type of tuning is appropriate for input to an associative memory such as that believed to be implemented in the amygdala, for it allows many memories to be stored, and also allows generalization and graceful degradation (Rolls 1987, 1989a; Rolls and Treves 1990, 1997).

One output from the amygdala for this information is probably via the ventral striatum, for a small population of neurons has been found in the ventral striatum with responses selective for faces (Rolls and Williams 1987; Williams *et al.* 1993).

The evidence described above implicates the amygdala in the learning of associations between stimuli and reinforcement. This means that it must be important in learned emotional responses, and at least part of the importance of the amygdala in emotion appears to be that it is involved in this type of emotional learning.

The orbitofrontal cortex

The orbitofrontal cortex (see Figures 18.2 and 18.3) receives inputs via the mediodorsal nucleus of the thalamus, pars magnocellularis, which itself receives afferents from temporal lobe structures such as the prepyriform (olfactory) cortex, amygdala and inferior temporal cortex. Another set of inputs reaches the orbitofrontal cortex directly from the inferior temporal cortex, the cortex in the superior temporal sulcus, the temporal pole, and the amygdala; a third set reaches it from the primary taste cortex in the insula and frontal operculum and the primary olfactory (pyriform) cortex (see Figure 18.3), and a fourth set comprises the at least partly dopaminergic projection from the ventral tegmental area. The orbitofrontal cortex projects back to temporal lobe areas such as the inferior temporal cortex, and, in addition, to the entorhinal cortex and cingulate cortex. The orbitofrontal cortex also projects to the preoptic region and lateral hypothalamus, to the ventral tegmental area, and to the head of the caudate nucleus (see Rolls 1996).

Damage to the caudal orbitofrontal cortex in the monkey produces emotional changes. These include decreased aggression to humans and to stimuli such as a snake and a doll, and a reduced tendency to reject foods such as meat (Butter *et al.* 1969, 1970; Butter and Snyder 1972). In the human, euphoria, irresponsibility and lack of affect can follow frontal lobe damage (see Kolb and Whishaw 1990).

These changes which follow frontal lobe damage may be related to a failure to react normally to and learn from non-reward in a number of different situations. This failure is evident as a tendency to respond when responses are inappropriate, for example, no longer rewarded. For example, monkeys with orbitofrontal damage are impaired on go/no go task performance, in that they go on the no go trials (Iversen and Mishkin 1970), in an object reversal task in that they respond to the object which was formerly rewarded with food, and in extinction in that they continue to respond to an object which is no longer rewarded (Butter 1969; Jones and Mishkin 1972; see also Rolls 1990). The visual discrimination learning deficit shown by monkeys with orbitofrontal cortex damage (Jones and Mishkin 1972; Baylis and Gaffan 1991), may be due to the tendency of these monkeys not to withhold responses to non-rewarded stimuli (Jones and Mishkin 1972).

The hypothesis that the orbitofrontal cortex is involved in correcting responses made to stimuli previously associated with reinforcement has been investigated by making recordings from single neurons in the orbitofrontal cortex while monkeys performed these tasks known to be impaired by damage to the orbitofrontal cortex (Thorpe *et al.* 1983). It has been found that one class of neurons in the orbitofrontal cortex of the monkey responds in certain non-reward situations (Thorpe *et al.* 1983). For example, some neurons responded in extinction, immediately after a lick had been made to a visual stimulus which had previously been associated with fruit juice reward, and other neurons responded in a reversal task, immediately after the monkey had responded to the previously rewarded visual stimulus, but had obtained punishment rather than reward. Another class of orbitofrontal neuron responded to particular visual stimuli only if they were associated with reward, and these neurons showed one trial stimulus-reinforcement association reversal. Another class of neuron conveyed information about whether a reward had been given, for example, responding to the taste of sucrose, or for other neurons of saline (Thorpe *et al.* 1983).

A number of recent discoveries have provided a firm basis for understanding how the orbitofrontal cortex receives information about primary rewards, and is involved in learning stimulus-reward associations using these reward representations (see Rolls 1996). The orbitofrontal neurons with gustatory responses have now been analysed further (Rolls 1989b, 1994b). They have been shown to form the secondary taste cortex (defined by receiving inputs from the primary taste cortex, just behind the caudal orbitofrontal cortex), and the tertiary taste cortex (defined as cortical areas that receive anatomically from the secondary taste cortex) (Baylis *et al.* 1994; see also Rolls 1996, 1997b). The activity of neurons in these secondary and tertiary taste cortical areas is related to reward, in that those which respond to the taste of food do so only if the monkey is hungry (Rolls *et al.* 1989). Moreover, in part of this orbitofrontal region, some neurons combine taste and olfactory inputs, in that they are bimodal (Rolls 1989b, 1995b; Rolls and Baylis 1994), and are affected by olfactory-to-taste association learning in 40 per cent of cases (Critchley and Rolls 1996a; Rolls *et al.* 1996) and by feeding the monkey to satiety, which reduces the reward value (Critchley and Rolls 1996b; see also Rolls 1997b). Further evidence for very rapid visual-taste association learning reflected in the responses of orbitofrontal cortex neurons has been found (Rolls *et al.* 1996), and it has been shown that these visual responses reflect reward, in that feeding the monkey to satiety reduces the responses of these neurons to zero (Critchley and Rolls 1996b).

It is suggested that these types of information are represented in the responses of orbitofrontal neurons because they are part of a mechanism which evaluates whether a reward is expected, and generates a mismatch (evident as a firing of the non-reward neurons) if reward is not obtained when it is expected (Thorpe *et al.* 1983; Rolls 1990, 1996). These neuronal responses provide further evidence that the orbitofrontal cortex is involved in emotional responses, particularly when these involve correcting previously learned reinforcement contingencies, in situations which include those usually described as involving frustration.

The role of the orbitofrontal cortex in human behaviour

It is of interest and potential clinical importance that a number of the symptoms of frontal lobe damage in humans appear to be related to this type of function of altering behaviour when stimulus-reinforcement associations alter, as described next. Thus, humans with frontal lobe damage can show impairments in a number of tasks in which an alteration of behavioural strategy is required in response to a change in environmental reinforcement contingencies (see Goodglass and Kaplan 1979; Jouandet and Gazzaniga 1979; Milner 1963, 1982; Kolb and Whishaw 1990). Some of the personality changes that can follow frontal lobe damage may be related to a similar type of dysfunction. For example, the euphoria, irresponsibility, lack of affect and lack of concern for the present or future which can follow frontal lobe damage (see Hecaen and Albert 1978) may also be related to a dysfunction in altering behaviour appropriately in response to a change in reinforcement contingencies. Indeed, insofar as the orbitofrontal cortex is involved in the disconnection of stimulus-reinforcement associations, and such associations are important in learned emotional responses (see above), then it follows that the orbitofrontal cortex is involved in emotional responses by correcting stimulus-reinforcement associations when they become inappropriate.

These hypotheses, and the role in particular of the orbitofrontal cortex in human behaviour, have been investigated in recent studies in humans with damage to the ventral parts of the frontal lobe. (The description 'ventral' is given to indicate that there was pathology in the orbitofrontal or related parts of the frontal lobe, and not in the more dorso-lateral parts of the frontal lobe.) A task which was directed at assessing the rapid alteration of stimulus-reinforcement associations was used. In the visual discrimination reversal task, patients could learn to obtain points by touching one stimulus when it appeared on a video monitor, but had to withhold a response when a different visual stimulus appeared, otherwise a point was lost. After the subjects had acquired the visual discrimination, the reinforcement contingencies unexpectedly reversed.

The patients with ventral frontal lesions made more errors in the reversal (or in a similar extinction) task, and completed fewer reversals than control patients with damage elsewhere in the frontal lobes or in other brain regions (Rolls *et al.* 1994). The impairment correlated highly with the socially inappropriate or disinhibited behaviour of the patients, and also with their subjective evaluation of the changes in their emotional state since the brain damage. The patients were not impaired at other types of memory task, such as paired associate learning. The findings are being extended in current research (see Rolls 1996), in which visual discrimination acquisition and reversal are also found to be impaired in a visual discrimination task in which two stimuli are always present on the video monitor, and the patient obtains points by touching the correct stimulus, and loses points by touching the incorrect stimulus. It is of interest that the patients can often verbalize the correct response, yet commit the incorrect action. This is consistent with the hypothesis that the orbitofrontal cortex is normally involved in executing behaviour when the behaviour is performed by evaluating the reinforcement associations of environmental stimuli (see below). The orbitofrontal cortex appears to be involved in this in both humans and non-human primates, when the learning must be performed rapidly, for example, in acquisition, and during reversal.

To investigate the possible significance of face-related inputs to orbitofrontal visual neurons described above, we also tested the responses of these patients to faces. We included tests of face (and also voice) expression decoding, because these are ways in which the reinforcing quality of individuals is often indicated. Impairments in the identification of facial and vocal emotional expression were demonstrated in a group of patients with ventral frontal lobe damage who had socially inappropriate behaviour (Hornak *et al.* 1996). The expression identification impairments could occur independently of perceptual impairments in facial recognition, voice discrimination or environmental sound recognition. The face and voice expression problems did not necessarily occur together in the same patients, providing an indication of separate processing. Poor performance on both expression tests was correlated with the degree of alteration of emotional experience reported by the patients. There was also a strong positive correlation between the degree of altered emotional experience and the severity of the behavioural problems (such as disinhibition) found in these patients. A comparison group of patients with brain damage outside the ventral frontal lobe region, without these behavioural problems, was unimpaired on the face expression identification test, was significantly less impaired at vocal expression identification, and reported little subjective emotional change (Hornak *et al.* 1996). In current studies, these findings are being extended, and it is being found that patients with face expression decoding problems do not necessarily have impairments at visual discrimination reversal and vice versa. This is consistent with some topography in the orbitofrontal cortex (see e.g. Rolls and Baylis 1994).

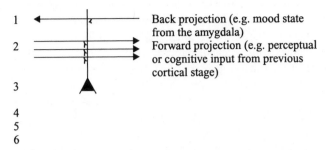

Back projection (e.g. mood state from the amygdala)

Forward projection (e.g. perceptual or cognitive input from previous cortical stage)

Figure 18.4 Pyramidal cells in, for example, layers 2 and 3 of the temporal lobe association cortex receive forward inputs from preceding cortical stages of processing, and also back projections from the amygdala. It is suggested that the back projections from the amygdala make modifiable synapses on the apical dendrites of cortical pyramidal cells during learning when amygdala neurons are active in relation to a mood state; and that the back projections from the amygdala via these modified synapses allow mood state to influence later cognitive processing, for example, by facilitating some perceptual representations.

Effects of emotion on cognitive processing

Emotional states may affect whether or how strongly memories are stored using the basal forebrain memory strobe (see above); may be stored as part of many memories using, for example, amygdala-entorhinal inputs to the hippocampus; and may influence both the recall of such memories, and the operation of cognitive processing, by amygdalo-cortical back projections (Figure 18.4; see also Rolls 1990, 1992b; Treves and Rolls 1994).

CONSCIOUSNESS AND EMOTION

It may be noted that it might be possible to build a computer which would perform the above functions of emotions, and yet we might not want to ascribe to it emotional feelings. This particular point raises the general issue of consciousness and its functions. The topic of emotional feelings is of considerable interest, and one view on consciousness, influenced by contemporary cognitive neuroscience, is elaborated elsewhere (Rolls 1997a). According to that view, consciousness is related to the operation of a higher-order thought system, which enables one to think about one's own thoughts, and thus to correct long chains of reasoning that are involved in planning. This is suggested to be the adaptive value of consciousness.

In this context, it is of interest to comment on how the evolution of a system for flexible planning might affect emotions. Consider grief which may occur when a reward is terminated and no immediate action is possible, in the passive condition discussed above. It may be adaptive by leading to a cessation of the formerly rewarded behaviour, and thus facilitating the possible identification of other positive reinforcers in the environment. In human beings, grief may be particularly potent because it becomes represented in a system which can plan ahead and understand the enduring implications of the loss.

However, it must be emphasized that this view of emotion (Rolls 1997a) is only preliminary, and theories of consciousness are likely to develop considerably, so that current theories of consciousness should not be taken to have practical implications. Particular issues not solved are how emotional and other processing streams lead to the selection of particular behavioural responses, and why emotional and other feelings should feel like anything at all.

REFERENCES

Adelmann, P.K. and Zajonc, R.B. (1989) 'Facial efference and the experience of emotion', *Annual Review of Psychology* 40: 240–280.

Aggleton, J.P. (1993) 'The contribution of the amygdala to normal and abnormal emotional states', *Trends in Neuroscience* 16: 328–333.

Aggleton, J.P. and Passingham, R.E. (1981) 'Syndrome produced by lesions of the amygdala in monkeys (Macaca mulatta)', *Journal of Comparative Physiology* 95: 961–977.

Amaral, D.G., Price, J.L., Pitkanen, A. and Carmichael, S.T. (1992) 'Anatomical organization of the primate amygdaloid complex', in J.P. Aggleton (ed.) *The Amygdala* (pp. 1–66), New York: John Wiley & Sons.

Baylis, G.C., Rolls, E.T. and Leonard, C.M. (1985) 'Selectivity between faces in the responses of a population of neurons in the cortex in the superior temporal sulcus of the monkey', *Brain Research* 342: 91–102.

—— (1987) 'Functional subdivisions of temporal lobe neocortex', *Journal of Neuroscience* 7: 330–342.

Baylis, L.L. and Gaffan, D. (1991) 'Amygdalectomy and ventromedial prefrontal ablation produce similar deficits in food choice and in simple object discrimination learning for an unseen reward', *Experimental Brain Research* 86: 617–622.

Baylis, L.L., Rolls, E.T. and Baylis, G.C. (1994) 'Afferent connections of the caudolateral orbitofrontal cortex taste area of the primate', *Neuroscience* 64: 801–812.

Blaney, P.H. (1986) 'Affect and memory: a review', *Psychology Bulletin* 99: 229–246.

Butter, C.M. (1969) 'Perseveration in extinction and in discrimination reversal tasks following selective prefrontal ablations in Macaca mulatta', *Physiology and Behavior* 4: 163–171.

Butter, C.M. and Snyder, D.R. (1972) 'Alterations in aversive and aggressive behaviors following orbitofrontal lesions in rhesus monkeys', *Acta Neurobiologiae Experimentalis* 32: 525–565.

Butter, C.M., McDonald, J.A. and Snyder, D.R. (1969) 'Orality, preference behavior, and reinforcement value of non-food objects in monkeys with orbital frontal lesions', *Science* 164: 1306–1307.

Butter, C.M., Snyder, D.R. and McDonald, J.A. (1970) 'Effects of orbitofrontal lesions on aversive and aggressive behaviors in rhesus monkeys', *Journal of Comparative and Physiological Psychology* 72: 132–144.

Cador, M., Robbins, T.W. and Everitt, B.J. (1989) 'Involvement of the amygdala in stimulus-reward associations: interaction with the ventral striatum', *Neuroscience* 30: 77–86.

Cannon, W.B. (1927) 'The James-Lange theory of emotion. A critical reexamination and an alternative theory', *American Journal of Psychology* 39: 106–124.

Critchley, H.D. and Rolls, E.T. (1996a) 'Olfactory neuronal responses in the primate orbitofrontal cortex: analysis in an olfactory discrimination task', *Journal of Neurophysiology* 75: 1659–1672.

—— (1996b) 'Hunger and satiety modify the responses of olfactory and visual neurons in the primate orbitofrontal cortex', *Journal of Neurophysiology* 75: 1673–1686.

Damasio, A.R. (1994) *Descartes' Error*, New York: Putnam.

Davis, M. (1992) 'The role of the amygdala in conditioned fear', in J.P. Aggleton (ed.) *The Amygdala* (pp. 255–305), New York: John Wiley & Sons.

Dawkins, R. (1989) *The Selfish Gene* (2nd edn), Oxford: Oxford University Press.

Dunn, L.T. and Everitt, B.J. (1988) 'Double dissociations of the effects of amygdala and insular cortex lesions on conditioned taste aversion, passive avoidance, and neophobia in the rat using the excitotoxin ibotenic acid', *Behavioral Neuroscience* 102: 3–23.

Everitt, B.J. and Robbins, T.W. (1992) 'Amygdala-ventral striatal interactions and reward-related processes', in J.P. Aggleton (ed.) *The Amygdala* (pp. 401–430), New York: John Wiley & Sons.

Gaffan, D. (1992) 'Amygdala and the memory of reward', in J.P. Aggleton (ed.) *The Amygdala* (pp. 471–483), New York: John Wiley & Sons.

Goodglass, H. and Kaplan, E. (1979) 'Assessment of cognitive deficit in brain-injured patient', in M.S. Gazzaniga (ed.) *Handbook of Behavioral Neurobiology, Vol. 2 Neuropsychology* (pp. 3–22), New York: Plenum.

Gray, J.A. (1975) *Elements of a Two-Process Theory of Learning*, London: Academic Press.

—— (1987) *The Psychology of Fear and Stress (2nd edn)*, Cambridge: Cambridge University Press.

Grossman, S.P. (1967) *A Textbook of Physiological Psychology*, New York: John Wiley & Sons.

Hasselmo, M.E., Rolls, E.T. and Baylis, G.C. (1989) 'The role of expression and identity in the face-selective responses of neurons in the temporal visual cortex of the monkey', *Behavioural Brain Research* 32: 203–218.

Hecaen, H. and Albert, M.L. (1978) *Human Neuropsychology*, New York: John Wiley & Sons.

Heimer, L., Switzer, R.E. and Van Hoesen, G.W. (1982) 'Ventral striatum and ventral pallidum. Components of the motor system?', *Trends in Neurosciences* 5: 83–87.

Hohmann, G.W. (1966) 'Some effects of spinal cord lesions on experienced emotional feelings', *Psychophysiology* 3: 143–156.

Hornak, J., Rolls, E.T. and Wade, D. (1996) 'Face and voice expression identification in patients with emotional and behavioural changes following ventral frontal lobe damage', *Neuropsychologia* 34: 247–261.

Iversen, S.D. and Mishkin, M. (1970) 'Perseverative interference in monkey following selective lesions of the inferior prefrontal convexity', *Experimental Brain Research* 11: 376–386.

James, W. (1884) 'What is an emotion?', *Mind* 9: 188–205.

—— (1890) *The Principles of Psychology*, New York: Dover.

Jones, B. and Mishkin, M. (1972) 'Limbic lesions and the problem of stimulus-reinforcement associations', *Experimental Neurology* 36: 362–377.

Jouandet, M. and Gazzaniga, M.S. (1979) 'The frontal lobes', in M.S. Gazzaniga (ed.) *Handbook of Behavioral Neurobiology, Vol. 2, Neuropsychology* (pp. 25–59), New York: Plenum.

Kluver, H. and Bucy, P.C. (1939) 'Preliminary analysis of functions of the temporal lobes in monkeys', *Archives of Neurology and Psychiatry* 42: 979–1000.

Kolb, B. and Whishaw, I.Q. (1990) *Fundamentals of Human Neuropsychology* (3rd edn), New York: Freeman.

Lange, C. (1885) 'The emotions', in E. Dunlap (ed.) *The Emotions*, Baltimore, MD: Williams & Wilkins.

LeDoux, J.E. (1987) 'Emotion', in F. Plum and V.B. Mountcastle (eds) *Handbook of Physiology The Nervous System V. Higher Function* (pp. 419–459), Washington, DC: American Physiological Society.

—— (1992) 'Emotion and the amygdala', in J.P. Aggleton (ed.) *The Amygdala* (pp. 339–351), New York: John Wiley & Sons.

—— (1994) 'Emotion, memory and the brain', *Scientific American* 220 (June): 50–57.

Leonard, C.M., Rolls, E.T., Wilson, F.A.W. and Baylis, G.C. (1985) 'Neurons in the amygdala of the monkey with responses selective for faces', *Behavioural Brain Research* 15: 159–176.

Mackintosh, N.J. (1983) *Conditioning and Associative Learning*, Oxford: Oxford University Press.

Mesulam, M-M. and Mufson, E.J. (1982) 'Insula of the old world monkey. III. Efferent cortical output and comments on function', *Journal of Comparative Neurology* 212: 38–52.

Millenson, J.R. (1967) *Principles of Behavioral Analysis*, New York: Macmillan.

Milner, B. (1963) 'Effects of different brain lesions on card sorting', *Archives of Neurology* 9: 90–100.

—— (1982) 'Some cognitive effects of frontal-lobe lesions in man', *Philosophical Transactions of the Royal Society* B298: 211–226.

Mishkin, M. and Aggleton, J. (1981) 'Multiple functional contributions of the amygdala in the monkey', in Y. Ben-Ari (ed.) *The Amygdaloid Complex* (pp. 409–420), Amsterdam: Elsevier.

Nishijo, H., Ono, T. and Nishino, H. (1988) 'Single neuron responses in amygdala of alert monkey during complex sensory stimulation with affective significance', *Journal of Neuroscience* 8, 35: 70–83.

Oatley, K. and Jenkins, J.M. (1996) *Understanding Emotions*, Oxford: Blackwell.

Ono, T. and Nishijo, H. (1992) 'Neurophysiological basis of the Kluver-Bucy syndrome: responses of monkey amygdaloid neurons to biologically significant objects', in J.P. Aggleton (ed.) *The Amygdala* (pp. 167–190), New York: John Wiley & Sons.

Ono, T., Nishino, H., Sasaki, K., Fukuda, M. and Muramoto, K. (1980) 'Role of the lateral hypothalamus and amygdala in feeding behavior', *Brain Research Bulletin Supplement* 4, 5: 143–149.

Perrett, D.I. and Rolls, E.T. (1982) 'Neural mechanisms underlying the visual analysis of faces', in J.P. Ewert, R.R. Capranica and D.J. Ingle *Advances in Vertebrate Neuroethology*, New York: Plenum Press.

Reisenzein, S. (1983) 'The Schachter theory of emotion: two decades later, *Psychological Bulletin* 94: 239–264.

Rolls, E.T. (1975) *The Brain and Reward*, Oxford: Pergamon Press.

—— (1981) 'Responses of amygdaloid neurons in the primate', in Y. Ben-Ari (ed.) *The Amygdaloid Complex* (pp. 383–393), Amsterdam: Elsevier.

—— (1984) 'Neurons in the cortex of the temporal lobe and in the amygdala of the monkey with responses selective for faces', *Human Neurobiology* 3: 209–222.

—— (1986a) 'A theory of emotion, and its application to understanding the neural basis of emotion', in Y. Oomura (ed.) *Emotions: Neural and Chemical Control* (pp. 325–344), Tokyo: Japan Scientific Societies Press, and Karger: Basel.

—— (1986b) 'Neural systems involved in emotion in primates', in R. Plutchik and H. Kellerman (eds) *Emotion: Theory, Research, and Experience. Volume 3: Biological Foundations of Emotion* (pp. 125–143), New York: Academic Press.

—— (1987) 'Information representation, processing and storage in the brain: analysis at the single neuron level', in J.P. Changeux and M. Konishi (eds) *The Neural and Molecular Bases of Learning* (pp. 503–540), Chichester, Sussex: John Wiley & Sons.

—— (1989a) 'Functions of neuronal networks in the hippocampus and neocortex in memory', in J.H. Byrne and W.O. Berry, *Neural Models of Plasticity: Experimental and Theoretical Approaches* (pp. 240–265), San Diego: Academic Press.

—— (1989b) 'Information processing in the taste system of primates', *Journal of Experimental Biology* 146: 141–164.

—— (1989c) 'The representation and storage of information in neuronal networks in the primate cerebral cortex and hippocampus', in R. Durbin, C. Miall and G. Mitchison (eds) *The Computing Neuron* (pp. 125–159), Wokingham, Berkshire: Addison-Wesley.

—— (1990) 'A theory of emotion, and its application to understanding the neural basis of emotion', *Cognition and Emotion* 4: 161–190.

—— (1992a) 'Neurophysiological mechanisms underlying face processing within and beyond the temporal cortical visual areas', *Philosophical Transactions of the Royal Society* 335: 11–21.

—— (1992b) 'Neurophysiology and functions of the primate amygdala', in J.P. Aggleton (ed.) *The Amygdala* (pp. 143–165), New York: John Wiley & Sons.

—— (1992c) 'The processing of face information in the primate temporal lobe', in V. Bruce and M. Burton (eds) *Processing Images of Faces* (pp. 41–68), Norwood, NJ: Ablex.

—— (1994a) 'Neurophysiology and cognitive functions of the striatum', *Revue Neurologique* (Paris) 150: 648–660.

—— (1994b) 'Neural processing related to feeding in primates', in C.R. Legg and D.A. Booth (eds) *Appetite: Neural and Behavioural Bases* (pp. 11–53), Oxford: Oxford University Press.

—— (1994c) 'Brain mechanisms for invariant visual recognition and learning', *Behavioural Processes* 33: 113–138.

—— (1995a) 'A theory of emotion and consciousness, and its application to understanding the neural basis of emotion', in M.S. Gazzaniga (ed.) *The Cognitive Neurosciences* (pp. 1091–1106), Cambridge, MA: MIT Press.

—— (1995b) 'Central taste anatomy and neurophysiology', in R.L. Doty (ed.) *Handbook of Olfaction and Gustation* (pp. 549–573), New York: Dekker.

—— (1995c) 'Learning mechanisms in the temporal lobe visual cortex', *Behavioural Brain Research* 66: 177–185.

—— (1996) 'The orbitofrontal cortex', *Philosophical Transactions of the Royal Society* B 351: 1433–1444.

—— (1997a) 'Brain mechanisms of vision, memory, and consciousness', in M. Ito, Y. Miyashita and E.T. Rolls (eds) *Cognition, Computation, and Consciousness*, Oxford: Oxford University Press.

—— (1997b) 'Taste and olfactory processing in the brain', in R.W.A. Linden (ed.) *Frontiers of Oral Biology: The Scientific Basis of Eating*, Karger: Basel.

Rolls, E.T. and Baylis, L.L. (1994) 'Gustatory, olfactory and visual convergence within the primate orbitofrontal cortex', *Journal of Neuroscience* 14: 5437–5452.

Rolls, E.T. and Johnstone, S. (1992) 'Neurophysiological analysis of striatal function', in G. Vallar, S.F. Cappa and C.W. Wallesch (eds) *Neuropsychological Disorders Associated with Subcortical Lesions* (pp. 61–97), Oxford: Oxford University Press.

Rolls, E.T. and Rolls, B.J. (1973) 'Altered food preferences after lesions in the basolateral region of the amygdala in the rat', *Journal of Comparative and Physiological Psychology* 83: 248–259.

Rolls, E.T. and Treves, A. (1990) 'The relative advantages of sparse versus distributed encoding for associative neuronal networks in the brain', *Network* 1: 407–421.

—— (1997) *Neuronal Networks and Brain Function*, Oxford: Oxford University Press.

Rolls, E.T. and Williams, G.V. (1987) 'Sensory and movement-related neuronal activity in different regions of the primate striatum', in J.S. Schneider and T.I. Lidsky (eds) *Basal*

Ganglia and Behavior: Sensory Aspects and Motor Functioning (pp. 37–59), Bern: Hans Huber.

Rolls, E.T., Burton, M.J. and Mora, F. (1980) 'Neurophysiological analysis of brain-stimulation reward in the monkey', *Brain Research* 194: 339–357.

Rolls, E.T., Judge, S.J. and Sanghera, M. (1977) 'Activity of neurones in the inferotemporal cortex of the alert monkey', *Brain Research* 130: 229–238.

Rolls, E.T., Sienkiewicz, Z.J. and Yaxley, S. (1989) 'Hunger modulates the responses to gustatory stimuli of single neurons in the caudolateral orbitofrontal cortex of the macaque monkey', *European Journal of Neuroscience* 1: 53–60.

Rolls, E.T., Critchley, H., Mason, R. and Wakeman, E.A. (1996) 'Orbitofrontal cortex neurons: role in olfactory and visual association learning', *Journal of Neurophysiology* 75: 1970–1981.

Rolls, E.T., Hornak, J., Wade, D. and McGrath, J. (1994) 'Emotion-related learning in patients with social and emotional changes associated with frontal lobe damage', *Journal of Neurology, Neurosurgery and Psychiatry* 57: 1518–1524.

Sanghera, M.K., Rolls, E.T. and Roper-Hall, A. (1979) 'Visual responses of neurons in the dorsolateral amygdala of the alert monkey', *Experimental Neurology* 63: 610–626.

Schachter, S. and Singer, J. (1962) 'Cognitive, social and physiological determinants of emotional state', *Psychological Review* 69: 378–399.

Taira, K. and Rolls, E.T. (1996) 'Receiving grooming as a reinforcer for the monkey', *Physiology and Behavior* 59: 1189–1192.

Thorpe, S.J., Rolls, E.T. and Maddison, S. (1983) 'Neuronal activity in the orbitofrontal cortex of the behaving monkey', *Experimental Brain Research* 49: 93–115.

Treves, A. and Rolls, E.T. (1994) 'A computational analysis of the role of the hippocampus in memory', *Hippocampus* 4: 374–391.

Wallis, G. and Rolls, E.T. (1997) 'Invariant face and object recognition in the visual system', *Progress in Neurobiology*, 51: 167–194.

Weiskrantz, L. (1956) 'Behavioral changes associated with ablation of the amygdaloid complex in monkeys', *Journal of Comparative and Physiological Psychology* 49: 381–391.

—— (1968) 'Emotion', in L. Weiskrantz (ed.) *Analysis of Behavioral Change* (pp. 50–90), New York and London: Harper & Row.

Williams, G.V., Rolls, E.T., Leonard, C.M. and Stern, C. (1993) 'Neuronal responses in the ventral striatum of the behaving monkey', *Behavioural Brain Research* 55: 243–252.

Wilson, F.A.W. and Rolls, E.T. (1990a) 'Neuronal responses related to reinforcement in the primate basal forebrain', *Brain Research* 502: 213–231.

—— (1990b) 'Neuronal responses related to the novelty and familiarity of visual stimuli in the substantia innominata, diagonal band of Broca and periventricular region of the primate', *Experimental Brain Research* 80: 104–120.

—— (1993) 'The effects of stimulus novelty and familiarity on neuronal activity in the amygdala of monkeys performing recognition memory tasks', *Experimental Brain Research* 93: 367–382.

—— (1997) 'The primate amygdala and reinforcement: a dissociation between rule-based and associatively-mediated memory revealed in amygdala neuronal activity', in preparation.

Name index

Subject index

ability, cognitive 7, 273
abnormal psychology 94–5, 97, 312; *see
also* behavioural deviation *and* clinical
psychology *and* mental illness
absolutism 176–8
achievement goals 229
action: control 234; orientation 234;
phases, model of 230–2; research 141,
271; sets 254–5; tendencies, competing
233–4
active: behaviour 299; development
43–4
acupuncture 171, 174, 185
adaptability 201; social 74; *see also*
change
adaptive behaviour 74
aesthetic relativism 178; *see also*
relativism
affect theory of attention 254–63; *see also*
emotion
affordances, behavioural 11–12
alternative medicine 171–91; and
postmodernism 175–6; and relativism
176–81; sociological perspective 181–2
American Association of Applied
Psychology 92
American Association of Clinical
Psychologists 89
American Group Psychotherapy
Association 118
American Psychological Association 88,
92, 97, 101, 128, 145, 147, 148
amnesia *see* memory
amygdala 302–9; connections 302–4;
lesions 304–8; *see also* brain damage
anger, and attention 258–60
animal: psychophysics 56; research 60, 61,
66; threat 262–7

anxiety 99, 252–70, 296; and attention
256, 257, 261, 263; and facial threat
261, 262; *see also* fear
aphasia 272, 279; *see also* language
appearance, physical 18
applied psychology 131–4, 196
approach: and emotion 255; goals 236
aptitude testing *see* testing
artificial intelligence 242, 271
assertiveness 19, 31
assessment *see* testing
association: free 109, 110; stimulus-
reinforcement 309
attention 252, 253; affect theory of
254–63; and anger 258–60; and anxiety
256, 257, 261, 263; automatic 257,
264–7; and consciousness 252–70;
control 234; and fear 256–66; focusing
282, 283; modulation 283; pre- 264–6,
273; selective 253, 263, 282, 283;
spotlight metaphor 253–4, 266, 267;
standard social science model 253;
systems 284
attractiveness *see* appearance
autism 287
automatic: attention capturing 257, 264–7;
goal behaviour 236
autonomy goals 228
avoidance: active 298; goals 236; and
emotion 255, 257
awareness: impairments 279; selective 17

backward masking 264–7
behaviour: abnormal 94, 97, 312; active
299; adaptive 74; affordances 11, 12;
challenging 77, 78; constraints 11, 12;
contradictions 31; cultural context 26;
developmental 5; disturbed 48; goal